The Digital Economy and International Trade

The Digital Economy and International Trade

Transnational Data Flows Regulation

Robert Walters

Wolters Kluwer

Published by:
Kluwer Law International B.V.
PO Box 316
2400 AH Alphen aan den Rijn
The Netherlands
E-mail: lrs-sales@wolterskluwer.com
Website: www.wolterskluwer.com/en/solutions/kluwerlawinternational

Sold and distributed by:
Wolters Kluwer Legal & Regulatory U.S.
7201 McKinney Circle
Frederick, MD 21704
United States of America
E-mail: customer.service@wolterskluwer.com

ISBN 978-94-035-3725-2

e-Book: ISBN 978-94-035-3745-0
web-PDF: ISBN 978-94-035-3770-2

About the Author

Dr Robert Walters is a Senior Lecturer at Victoria University, Melbourne, Australia. Dr Walters is an Adjunct Professor of Law at the European Faculty of Law, Slovenia, Europe, an Adjunct Senior Research Fellow at the University Western Australia, and admitted to practice law in Australia. Dr Walters is a qualified International Arbitrator. In 2021 and 2022, he undertook a full Professorship at the European Faculty of Law. He is a member of the ASEAN Law Association – Singapore, Asia Pacific Scholar (Privacy/Data Protection) Network. His work on cross-border data flows in the new digital economy has been recognised globally, and in 2021 and 2022, he was engaged by national governments to undertake a legal project for data flows, data adequacy, data protection, cyber security and artificial intelligence (AI) across Commonwealth countries. This work was commissioned to strengthen economic outcomes for a number of Commonwealth countries in the digital economy and international trade. Dr Walters specialises in transnational commercial and private law (data flows, data protection, cyber security, AI, cross-border insolvency/restructuring, netting arrangements, contracts, arbitration).

Table of Contents

Foreword

This book is timely in calling for greater uniformity in the regulation of transnational data flows. While highlighting the economic benefits that data flows will bring to the global digital economy and trade, it also illustrates that the purpose underlying the national laws governing data flows are generally consistent, notably in seeking to protect personal data from abuse.

However, those laws often diverge with regard to both their underlying concepts and the way they function in order to achieve their specific purposes. As demonstrated in this book, not only does this lead to uncertainty in the application of national law to data flows within an increasingly globalised data economy but also undermines the operability of those laws in a world order in which harmonisation exists and is a prerequisite.

The author ably addresses these issues, commencing with the legal concept as to whether data is a good or service as defined in national law and in bilateral, regional, and multilateral treaties. The author's examination of the tension between free data flows and the protection of data covers several legal states including the United Kingdom, the United States, Japan, Singapore, Canada, New Zealand and Australia, as well as regional entities such as the EU. Its central focus throughout is on identifying how evolving law and policies, principles and standards have impacted the tension between the free use of data and the protection of data from misuse.

In seeking a balance between the free and the regulated use of data, the book demonstrates a growing recognition of the virtue of reconciling 'data free flow with trust' (DFFT), as highlighted in 2019 by the G20 Ministers of Trade and the Digital Economy. It is a debate that is still early in its inception. Still, the book demonstrates that it constitutes an important directional shift away from an all-or-nothing free market in data and efforts to prohibit trade in personal data within an interconnected digital economy.

Essentially, the book aims to define data. Is it a good or a service, or can it be both? In addressing this question, it is argued that data can be either, depending on the law that is being used to facilitate data trade, data transfers or data protection. Apart from examining the national laws and the laws of the EU, the author compares several bilateral and multilateral free trade agreements, addressing the shortcomings of these instruments and providing a pathway forward. He argues that more work can be undertaken to strengthen trade agreements to facilitate data flows while ensuring a high level of data protection. Moreover, the author briefly addresses the issues in selected standards rules and private law that have emerged as important tools that assist the private sector to facilitate data flows across jurisdictions.

Importantly, too, the book proposes an efficient balance between the harmonised regulation of data flows and trust in those regulations. The author recognises that such influences reflect ideological dissension over the boundaries of free markets that existed in pre-digital regional and multilateral markets. That recognition is embodied in a pervasive question. Does mass private harm arising from the use of personal data in our 'new' digital economy pose sufficient public harm to justify harmonised constraints on freedom in, and from, that 'free' market? In raising this question, the book invites debate that will undoubtedly extend well into the future.

Professor Dr Leon Trakman
Barrister & Arbitrator
Former Dean, Law
University New South Wales

Preface

Transnational flows of personal data, while nothing new, have become an integral component of the new digital economy. It is a growing area of regulation and the law. Personal data has begun to pervade every sector of the economy as the world continues to experience increases in digital connectivity. This book examines the economic benefits of data in the digital economy and international trade. The new digital economy has been expressed as the Fourth Industrial Revolution (IR4) that will result in the integration of both public and private technological systems and infrastructures. This integration will see personal data become not only an economic activity: it will be used to inform social, human health and environmental outcomes.

Cross-border data flows have evolved and changed since they emerged in the 1970s. What began as a principle-based framework established by the Organisation for Economic Development and Cooperation (OECD), has driven the development of national laws significantly since the 1980s. The principles established by the OECD are important and will continue to play a major role in the future regulation of data (whether for its flow across international borders or its protection). Yet, the question this book poses is: does the principle-based approach strike the right balance for data in the new digital economy? That is, will it meet the countries' requirements for the delivery of IR4? This book does not attempt to eschew principles; instead, it suggests that they be internalised by means of an international treaty, convention or model law. By scaling up the national approach to the international arena, greater legal harmonisation can be achieved. For many decades, international laws have been highly successful in providing legal certainty for investment in the trade of goods and services. It is time for the same approach to be adopted for data in the digital economy.

This book is timely as it calls directly for the internationalisation of the law regulating transnational data flows. Significantly, it also calls for the internationalisation of broader data flow/protection law. In this book, it will posit that interoperability, while serving technology systems and infrastructure well, has not achieved the same in terms of the law. In other words, interoperability has been used to make the case that national data laws have similar concepts, principles and protections. In practice, there are similarities in these areas, although there is also significant divergence. It is this divergence that is creating legal uncertainty and hampering the expansion of the digital economy. In this book, it will be argued that interoperability is the first step to legal harmonisation and the internationalisation of the law. To this end, the book examines the states of Australia, Indonesia, India, Canada, Japan, Singapore, New Zealand, United Kingdom, United States and the supranational polity of the European Union.

Drawing upon Simon Chesterman's[1] work on AI, there is a strong case for an international organisation to be established to govern data flows. This is because, similar to AI, data has been regulated today according to three factors: the rights of individuals and entities whether it supports the consumer or business, and sovereignty. Regulation based on the first two factors seeks to protect the business or consumer, while regulation based on sovereignty is determined by the state.

Here, it is also suggested that data flows being sent to locations outside the country of origin must be reported to the national regulator. This gives greater transparency to organisations that are profiting from this data and will increase their accountability. It is no different from having to report an annual tax return. This book is timely and makes an important and valuable contribution to the current developments of law and policy designed to encourage and protect data flows in the digital economy, which will in turn enhance the economic and social wellbeing of all.

Dr Robert Walters
Senior Lecturer, Victoria University, Australia

1. Simon Chesterman, *Beyond Asimov's Three Laws: The Case for an International AI Agency*, 2021, https://eandt.theiet.org/content/articles/2021/08/beyond-asimov-s-three-laws-the-case-for-an-international-ai-agency.

Acknowledgements

I acknowledge the work undertaken by Professor Simon Chesterman, Dean of Law, Singapore National University, and Professor Graham Greenleaf, University New South Wales. This book draws extensively on the work undertaken by Professor Greenleaf, and by Professor Colin Bennett, University Victoria, Canada.

I also acknowledge Professor Dr Sinta Dewi, Faculty of Law, University of Padjadjaran, Bandung, Indonesia, with whom we are collaborating on a similar book focusing on Indonesia data laws.

I thank my personal friends, Emeritus Professor Dr Leon Trakman, former Dean of Law, University New South Wales and Professor Dr Bruno Zeller, University Western Australia.

PART I Cross-Border Data Flows

CHAPTER 1

Problem Definition

This chapter begins by outlining a central problem: defining and understanding the regulation of cross-border data flows. Chapter 1 demonstrates how the transnational regulation of cross-border data flows has evolved and changed since its beginnings in the 1970s, and will also show that there has been a divergent progress made in this area. Although the principle-based framework, established by the Organisation for Economic Development and Cooperation (OECD), has served the international community well, the question remains as to whether this model needs to be enhanced. This book calls for a shift from a principle-based model that has seen the rise of data interoperability and data adequacy, to one suited to legal convergence and harmonisation. It will be argued that this shift will provide greater certainty for data in the new digital economy and will help to foster economic growth and create jobs and business opportunities.

There is no call for the OECD Principles to be disposed of; rather, they should be aggregated and embedded into an international legal mechanism such as a convention, treaty, model law or other principles that have been implemented successfully by UNCITRAL and UNIDROIT.[2] *As they currently stand, compliance with the OECD Principles is voluntary. By including them in international law, legal convergence and harmonisation could be achieved. For instance, the OECD Principles would not be diluted in any way where there was an agreed international definition of personal data/information. Furthermore, they would not be weakened by having an agreed position of consent amongst other provisions of the law, such as the appointment of*

2. For example, International Institute for the Unification of Private Law. UNIDROIT Governing Council adopted the Principles on the Operation of Close-out Netting Provisions prepared by an UNIDROIT Committee of Governmental Experts and submitted to the Council, https://www.unidroit.org/unidroit-principles-on-the-operation-of-close-out-netting-provisions-adopted-by-the-governing-council/. United Nations Commission on International Trade Law, https://uncitral.un.org.

controllers, processors, data officers, and what and how transnational data transfers should be undertaken. If these Principles are coupled with specific provisions within international law, a greater level of legal certainty would be provided which, in turn, would encourage investment in the new digital economy. This will also help to manage the potentially greater vulnerabilities of data resulting from Fourth Industrial Revolution (IR4). IR4 is being embraced by many countries around the world, and it is asserted that further law reform is needed for the full economic benefits to be realised. Interoperability has served the technology sector well. It has enabled technologies developed by different entities to communicate and interact. The concept of interoperability has been extended to the law. In this book, this current direction is challenged. Here, it is argued that the harmonisation of data laws will provide significantly better economic and social outcomes than interoperability alone can achieve.

Another major issue for governments and regulators today is the necessity to balance the trade in data within the new and emerging digital economy, with the need to ensure a high level of protection for individuals whose data is being traded. Moreover, another consideration is the outbreak of COVID-19 that resulted in a global pandemic being declared and the national borders of most countries being closed during 2020, with limited entries and exits permitted by national governments. What followed was a rapid transition into online activities and communications by businesses, government, education, health, trade and the general public. This proved to be a godsend for those individuals and entities transferring and trading in personal data. Some nation states took the initiative to establish a level of agreement for the transborder flow of personal data, particularly health data, as was seen between Australia and Singapore.

Rather than examining the extent of security breaches related to data flows, two case studies are presented of high-profile judicial and regulatory decisions demonstrating the challenges of data flows and their governance. The cases highlight the lack of certainty in relation to the number of data points that can identify an individual's activity over the Internet. Several key economies will be examined: Australia, Canada, Indonesia, India, Japan, Singapore, New Zealand, the United Kingdom (UK), the United States (US) and the supranational polity of the European Union (EU), to determine the regulatory mechanisms that have been established to facilitate transnational trade and the flow of data. Because the UK is no longer a member of the EU, it will be examined as an independent nation state. A selection of bilateral and multilateral trade and digital/economic agreements will be examined to highlight another area of fragmentation that has emerged with regard to the general governing of data and data flows. It is acknowledged that some would disagree that the regulation of data flows should be included in trade agreements. However, nation states have only recently begun to develop this as an area of regulation. That is, apart from those nation states and jurisdictions that have mature regulatory data frameworks, for many nation states, this is a new area of law.

Moreover, something that is not often considered in law is that the programmes undertaken by governments around the world that are intended to: (1) achieve legal harmonisation, and (2) strengthen their country-to-country relationships. Thus, this book concludes by highlighting the burgeoning area of data-digital diplomacy and the need for it to be embedded in national and supranational policy frameworks. The benefits of doing so extend far beyond traditional economic and social outcomes. It will assist like-minded countries that have a rule of law and rules-based order, to expand on the already well-founded data principles. In a period of increasing geopolitical, economic and social tension, this is an additional programme that can be pursued effectively to ensure the ongoing rules and law for data flows in the digital economy are strengthened and well-grounded over the longer term.

Bilateral and multilateral trade and digital agreements are international legal instruments that have been introduced to provide some governance regarding data protection and privacy. In this book, it is argued that it is time for these instruments to be strengthened, and any forthcoming agreements developed should include data flows and promote legal harmonisation. Due to the significant law compared throughout this book, the EU General Data Protection Regulation (GDPR) is adopted as the benchmark. However, it is not argued that data flow regulation should take a rights-based policy perspective. Rather, a balance should be struck between data access in the digital economy and the high level of protection that it requires. This is going to be difficult to achieve and may never be settled. However, a starting point can be the internationalisation of data flow law and the strengthening of bilateral and multilateral trade arrangements.

§1.01 INTRODUCTION

The regulation and application of cross-border data transfers are becoming increasingly important to the world economy. Beginning in the 1970s in Europe, transborder data flow regulation has gradually spread around the world.[3] A number of instruments regulating transborder data flows have been enacted on an international scale, some legally binding, and others not. The variety of instruments, the diversity of international organisations that have enacted them, and the failure to agree on a global standard for data protection have meant that there is a lack of overall global harmonisation.[4] Christopher Kuner raised this issue in 2013 and, a decade later, little has changed. This book will examine the current-day regulation of cross-border data

3. Christopher Kuner, *Transborder Data Flows and Privacy Law*, Oxford University Press (2013), p. 25.
4. *Ibid.*, p. 26.

transfers. It will highlight how nation states, including the EU, have by and large approached this issue independently, leading to very little legal harmonisation. To examine this issue, Australia, Indonesia, India, Canada, Japan, Singapore, New Zealand, the UK, the US and the supranational polity of the EU are chosen for comparison.

Richard Baldwin posits that data flows today are transforming international trade in a number of ways. He notes that, increasingly, businesses use the Internet to export goods.[5] Services are being consumed and purchased at growing rates per annum, and the data collected from transactions is enabling entities to undertake a number of activities not only for market research but also to ascertain individual consumers' requirements, preferences and spending patterns. Today, more than ever, data flows are becoming essential to global value chains (GVCs), which in turn create new opportunities for participation.[6]

The growth of the digital services industry has dramatically transformed online economic activity. For instance, the World Bank has estimated that the share of digital services exports increased by 33.23% from 2010 to 2017.[7] Consistent with the World Bank, the World Economic Forum (WEF) estimated that in 2020 alone there were 40 zettabytes of data in the digital space, amounting to forty times more bytes than there are stars in the universe.[8] They go on to say that massive volumes of bytes move across borders daily. In another study, it was estimated that '64.2 zettabytes (or 64.2 trillion gigabytes) of data were created or replicated globally in 2020 alone, and this amount will grow at a compound annual growth rate of 23 per cent'.[9] Furthermore, it was noted that most of this data is personal data, meaning it relates to or can be used to identify individual persons, otherwise known as data subjects.[10] However, this has been difficult to quantify due to the volumes and technologies involved in facilitating the activity of data transfers. Nonetheless, data flows are necessary not just for the efficient and smooth functioning of business but also for consumer-to-consumer interactions. These flows are the backbone of today's diversified value and supply chains. Interconnected infrastructure and services mean that international data flows occur even for

5. Richard Baldwin, *The Great Convergence: Information Technology and the New Globalization*. Cambridge, Mass: Harvard University Press (2016), p. 6. Refers to knowledge flows that uses data.
6. *Ibid.*
7. World Bank, 'ICT Service Exports', https://data.worldbank.org/indicator/BX.GSR.CCIS.ZS?end=2017&start=2010&view=chart.
8. World Economic Forum, Data Free Flow with Trust (DFFT): Paths Towards Free and Trusted Data Flows, Platform for Shaping the Future of Trade and Global Economic Interdependence (2020), p. 3.
9. *Data Creation and Replication Will Grow at a Faster Rate Than Installed Storage Capacity, According to the IDC Global DataSphere and StorageSphere Forecasts, Business Wire*, 24 March 2021, www.businesswire.com/news/home/20210324005175/en/Data- Creation-and-Replication-Will-Grow-at-a-Faster-Rate-Than-Installed-Storage-Capacity- According-to-the-IDC-Global-DataSphere-and-StorageSphere-Forecasts. In Seharish Gillani, Ahmed Dermish and Jeremiah Grossman of the UNCDF Policy Accelerator, *The Role of Data Protection in the Digital Economy*, Macmillan Keck 2021, https://static1.squarespace.com/static/5f2d7a54b7f75718fa4d2eef/t/61c39ac52e86d360a8301fd6/1640210452857/EN-UNCDF-Brief-Data-Protection-2021.pdf.
10. *Ibid.*

local business operations or consumer communications.[11] Put another way, data flows can be domestic and transnational. For instance, an entity located in Melbourne Australia can transfer data to an entity located in Sydney, Australia. Likewise, the entity in Melbourne, Australia can transfer the data to an entity in London, UK.

More recently, in 2021, it was estimated that 60% of the world's Gross Domestic Product (GDP) was digitised.[12] For instance, US exports of digitally enabled services to the EU reached more than USD 167 billion in 2019. On the other hand, the EU exported USD 130 billion to the US. Although this is a small fraction of what is being traded globally, as it involves only two jurisdictions, it indicates the extent and economic importance of the digital economy and its potential growth.

Even before the global pandemic, cross-border data transfers have benefitted consumers by giving them access to a wider range of goods and services at a lower cost.[13] This type of online activity increased substantially during the height of the pandemic and continues today. At the time of writing (2022), the United Nations Conference on Trade and Development released digital trade data for 2019 and 2020. They note that the COVID-19 pandemic has given businesses and individuals a sudden and strong impetus to adopt or increase their use of digital tools to continue economic activity.[14] By accelerating digitalisation and strengthening the reliance on digital technologies, COVID-19 has heightened the importance of international information and communications technology (ICT) related to global trade in goods and services. Subsequently, the share of ICT goods in merchandise imports surged from around 13% in 2019 to nearly 16% in 2020 – the greatest annual increase since records began in 2000.[15]

Furthermore, ICT services accounted for almost 14% of total services exports worldwide in 2020, while digitally deliverable services increased to nearly 64% of total services exports – having contracted relatively little despite an unprecedented 20% decline in total services trade.[16] However, at the same time as this growth was increasing internationally, countries differed significantly in regard to the demand for ICT goods, and the use of ICTs to continue trade in services by means of digital delivery. ICT goods trade declined sharply in the least developed countries (LDCs) and Africa between 2019 and 2020, and while all regions increased ICT and digitally deliverable products' share in total services trade, LDC exports of ICT services declined

11. World Economic Forum, Data Free Flow with Trust (DFFT): Paths Towards Free and Trusted Data Flows, Platform for Shaping the Future of Trade and Global Economic Interdependence (2020), p. 3.
12. Tanguy Van Overstraeten, Cross-Border Data Flows: A Necessary Part of Global Trade, 2021, http://www.amchameu.eu/blog/cross-border-data-flows-necessary-part-global-trade, also *see* Danial Hamilton and Joseph Quinlan., *The Transatlantic Economy 2021: Annual Survey of Jobs, Trade and Investment between the United States and Europe*, Washington, DC: Foreign Policy Institute, Johns Hopkins University SAIS/Woodrow Wilson Center, 2021.
13. *Ibid.*
14. United Nations Conference on Trade and Development, Impacts of the COVID-19 Pandemic on Trade in the Digital Economy, UNCTAD Technical notes on OCT for Development No. 19, https://unctad.org/system/files/official-document/tn_unctad_ict4d19_en.pdf.
15. *Ibid.*
16. *Ibid.*

by 22%, accounting for a 9% fall in digitally deliverable exports generally.[17] The question is whether there will be a similar or increased level of global digital activity post-pandemic. According to Statista, as of January 2021, there were 4.66 billion active Internet users worldwide: 59.5% of the global population.[18] Of these, 92.6% (4.32 billion) accessed the Internet via mobile devices, although this is a relatively small proportion of the population actively connected to the Internet. They note that Northern Europe ranked first with a 95% Internet penetration rate.[19] Further, Statista makes the point that the countries with the highest level of Internet penetration include the United Arab Emirates, Denmark, and South Korea. While, at the opposite end of the spectrum, North Korea has the lowest level of penetration and access. As of 2019, the Asia region had the largest number of online users, with more than 2.3 billion at the latest count.[20] Europe was ranked second with almost 728 million Internet users,[21] and this number is likely to continue to grow as the digital economy expands to all regions and countries of the world.

This ubiquitous use of the Internet has meant that in today's digitalised and globally interconnected world, data has become the lifeblood of economic and social interactions.[22] The proliferation of devices and sensors, the exponential growth in computing power, the plummeting costs of data storage and the growing ability to deliver more data at greater speed, have altered how we conduct our lives and how businesses operate.[23] Undoubtedly, data has transformed how people interact; altered the configuration of GVCs; given rise to new information industries (e.g., cloud computing, 3D printing or the Internet of Things); changed how services are produced and delivered; and, even affected how we grow and trade food.[24]

However, a general response by governments and regulators globally has been to restrict rather than enable the trade and transfer of data across international borders. For instance, data flow restrictions manifest as forced joint ventures (through foreign equity caps); transfer, and thereby disclosure, of underlying technology, source code, or a requirement to obtain licences for establishing data centres, undertaking data collection or providing cloud and e-commerce services.[25] More recently, there have been proposals to restrict the use of algorithms and data applications developed abroad. There are various reasons for taking this position, not the least of which is that such restrictions will enable a nation state to control the flow of its citizens' data transnationally. However, it has been proposed that market access negotiations should

17. *Ibid.*
18. Statista, Global Digital Population as at January 2021, https://www.statista.com/statistics/617136/digital-population-worldwide/.
19. *Ibid.*
20. *Ibid.*
21. *Ibid.*
22. Organisation for Economic Co-operation and Development, Mapping Approaches to Data and Data Flows, Report for the G20 Digital Economy Task Force (2020), p. 4.
23. *Ibid.*
24. *Ibid.*
25. World Economic Forum, Data Free Flow with Trust (DFFT): Paths Towards Free and Trusted Data Flows, Platform for Shaping the Future of Trade and Global Economic Interdependence (2020), p. 6.

address any disproportionate restrictions.[26] There is ample evidence that this process has begun. This book will demonstrate how there has been a level of convergence and harmonisation of cross-border legal mechanisms being applied to data. It will further highlight that while remaining a highly fragmented area of the law, the legal and policy mechanisms that have begun to support the transnational flow of data are well underway.

Pertinent to the overall theme of this book, the OECD reinforces the argument that the legal landscape for transnational data flows is incoherent, complex, cumbersome and lacking in continuity. The OECD argues that there is no one, single mechanism that facilitates what has come to be called 'data flows with trust'.[27] The concept of trust is not new in any legal framework. However, it has arguably taken on a greater level of importance as the digital economy evolves, changes and expands. In part, this is because people do not know or understand what is taking place behind the computer screen. Once data has been input into the computer and transferred to the Internet, there are relatively few people in the world who actually understand what and how that data is being used and for what purpose. According to the OECD, national governments are continually pursuing different, or even multiple and complementary, approaches to regulating cross-border data flows. These include but are not limited to:

> *Plurilateral arrangements:* these are intended to achieve consensus regarding privacy and personal data protection, including in relation to international transfers, have also been widely adopted by 96 economies.[28]
>
> *Trade agreements:* since 2008, 72 economies have included provisions on data flows. Not all provisions have the same depth – 45% of agreements include binding commitments on data flows (for all types of data).[29]
>
> *Standards and technology-driven initiatives:* these include ISO standards and privacy-enhancing technologies (PETs) including cryptography and sandboxes,

26. *Ibid.*
27. Organisation for Economic Cooperation and Development, Mapping Commonalities in Regulatory Approaches to Cross-Border Data Transfers, 2021, p. 3, https://www.oecd.org/officialdocuments/publicdisplaydocumentpdf/?cote=TAD/TC/WP(2020)15/FINAL&docLanguage=En. A range of *unilateral mechanisms* for safeguarding cross-border transfers exists. These vary according to whether safeguards require public sector approval before transfer (pre-authorised safeguards), or whether they leave discretion as to how to safeguard transfers to the private sector (open safeguards). The analysis reveals that pre-authorised safeguards, such as public adequacy decisions (AD) and *ex ante* legal safeguards, are more common (65%). However, open safeguards which include accountability principles, private sector adequacy evaluations and contracts, are also widely used (54%). Most countries incorporate some form of safeguard into their data transfers, but they go about it in different ways.
28. *Ibid.* As both a consequence, and a driver, of these arrangements, 68% of the elements covered in existing domestic privacy and data protection regulation across a sample of OECD and emerging economies overlap. This suggests that there is a high degree of commonality in existing frameworks and therefore some common ground to build on to enable data transfers.
29. *Ibid.* Of those with binding provisions, almost all include exceptions allowing parties to restrict data flows to meet 'legitimate public policy objectives' and all couple data flow provisions with provisions on privacy or consumer protection frameworks (including through references to plurilateral arrangements).

and are being used increasingly by organisations to protect and control access to data.[30]

These will all be explored further throughout this book. Importantly, the OECD reaffirms the need for a more constant approach to be taken in this growing and economically important activity. The mechanisms above and other tools will be examined to demonstrate the gaps and divergence in approaches taken by nation states.

§1.02 WHAT IS DATA?

The concept of data is nothing new and it has a long history. It has been present in many different forms for centuries. According to Bernard Marr, 'data whether personal, scientific or commercial can be traced back to C 18,000 BCE'.[31] Marr makes the point that tally sticks are the earliest examples of humans storing and analysing data. He cites the 'Ishango Bone (that) was discovered in 1960 in what is now Uganda and is thought to be one of the earliest pieces of evidence of prehistoric data storage. Palaeolithic tribespeople would mark notches into sticks or bones, to keep track of trading activity or supplies'.[32] Further, in 'C 2400 BCE, Marr in his research notes that the abacus was the first dedicated device constructed specifically for performing calculations in Babylon. The first libraries also appeared around this time, representing our first attempts at mass data storage'.[33] Between '300 BC and 48 AD, Marr highlights that the Library of Alexandria had one of the largest collections of data in the ancient world. It stored an estimated half a million scrolls. Unfortunately, in 48AD it is thought to have been destroyed by the invading Romans'.[34] Furthermore, from 'C 100 to 200 AD, the Antikythera Mechanism was thought to be the first mechanical computer by Greek scientists'.[35]

Moving forward to the twenty-first century, in 1928, Germany's Frits Pfleumer invented a method of storing information magnetically on tape. Nearly twenty years later in 1944, Fremont Rider a librarian at Wesleyan University, Connecticut, US, published a paper titled: *The Scholar and the Future of the Research Library*, which documented the earliest attempts to quantify the amount of information being produced as a means of storing academic works.[36] Subsequently, libraries around the world have adopted systems and infrastructures to store large quantities of books, journals and reports of academic scholarship, government and industry. From the

30. *Ibid.*
31. Bernard Marr, *A Brief History of Big Data Everyone Should Read,* World Economic Forum, https://www.weforum.org/agenda/2015/02/a-brief-history-of-big-data-everyone-should-read/.
32. *Ibid.*
33. *Ibid.*
34. *Ibid.*
35. *Ibid.*
36. *Ibid.*

1960s through to 2022, the amount of data (personal, commercial, scientific, government, etc.) formerly collected and stored on paper and in personal, government and business files, has grown considerably and is now, by and large, all online.

In the contemporary world of 2022, data flows are part of everyday life. Individuals and entities that are connected in some way to the Internet are transmitting and transferring data both locally and internationally. Today, most of us at some stage use a computer, laptop or smartphone to undertake consumer activities online. This activity is done through an electronic commerce platform, which comprises domestic and international data flows. The data travels to or is transmitted between servers located in different nation states around the world. Therefore, data flows are both the provision of the digital service itself and the data generated when using a service, such as business, personal and other kinds of user-generated data.[37]

While it is outside the scope of this book to examine the technical aspects of data transfer over the Internet, Oracle points out that: server data transfer (SDT) is a server-side delivery method for transferring user data from the Oracle Data Cloud platform into your system.[38] After an ID swap has been performed on a user, the platform can deliver data on that user to the server-side profile store without firing a pixel. By means of an ID, the system identifies categories and campaigns (numerically and enables apps) on a mobile to be identified. It is data subjects' unique identifier online, accessed via computers, laptops and tablets, amongst others. Alternatively, the user data can be saved in hourly or daily batch files that can be downloaded via secure file transfer protocol or an Amazon S3 bucket.[39] Hence, unique user IDs can be exchanged between an entity's site and the Oracle Data Cloud platform when a user performs an action such as visiting a web page.[40] What occurs next is that the platform synchronises your UUIDs (universally unique identifiers) to the network of user profiles that are linked together in the Oracle ID Graph, which is used to manage IDs and user attributes for all customers.[41] This synchronisation enables you to receive data via SDT as explained below:

> Desktop sites, depending on your environment, you make calls to an Oracle Data Cloud core tag or image pixel. The Oracle Data Cloud core tag HTML code and built-in JavaScript functions for sending UUIDs and user attributes and it can be deployed directly on your site or in a tag management system. The image pixel is typically used in environments that require pixels for making tag calls, such as display media. Mobile sites and mobile hybrid apps Deploy an Oracle Data Cloud core tag for mobile sites. Mobile apps implement the Oracle Data Cloud Android and IOS SDKs in your apps.[42]

37. Kommerskollegium, *No Transfer, No Trade* (2014), https://www.kommers.se/Documents/dokumentarkiv/publikationer/2014/No_Transfer_No_Trade_webb. Pdf, 6.
38. Oracle Data Management Platform, Server Data Transfer, https://docs.oracle.com/en/cloud/saas/data-cloud/data-cloud-help-center/IntegratingBlueKaiPlatform/DataDelivery/intro_to_sdt.html.
39. *Ibid.*
40. *Ibid.*
41. *Ibid.*
42. *Ibid.*

Further to the above, the use of real-time SDT endpoint enables users' data to be collected via an HTTP POST or GET request. In this situation, the transmission of data occurs when the user data is transferred directly to a server after a qualifying user is ID-synced on the network used by the individual, or the Oracle Cloud network.[43] Therefore, by default, the data subject's data is sent without authentication and sent to an endpoint in a specific JSON (JavaScript Object Notation) format that includes a common UUID.[44] This brief explanation shows how data is applied within the Cloud. What this does not confirm is the location of Cloud servers. For example, Tencent, an Internet-based platform, operates across seventy zones and twenty-six regions that span Asia, the US, the EU and Central Asia.[45] Equinix, a company specialising in Internet connection and data centres, operates in six countries in the Asia Pacific region alone, with up to thirteen locations in Australia, China, Singapore, Hong Kong, India, Japan and Korea.[46] Thus, data could be transferred from Australia to Singapore and travel through all the other aforementioned countries before landing in Singapore. Is it this point that is unclear to data subjects? It further highlights another area of a lack of transparency. The additional question that arises is the security of this data as it travels through Cloud. What systems are in place to ensure that it is not syphoned off or tampered with as it passes through a third or fourth data server before reaching its destination? As it passes through additional servers, can it be stored? Responses to these questions are not readily available to businesses or the general community.

Equinix is just one organisation amongst many that provide the technology and systems to facilitate cross-border data flows. As a solution, some scholars compartmentalise data into different categories and suggest that different types of data should be treated differently. Tim Cooper and Ryan LaSalle argue that personal data is a component of data pertaining to users who use the Internet for business and accounted for 75% of the global digital data in 2016.[47] This amount of data was generated by large companies and does not take into consideration small- and medium-sized businesses generating data today.[48] Personal data can also generate business value, given that it is traded extensively via various digital services and is an important driver of the digital economy. Nivedita Sen classifies personal data as the data related to individuals,[49] while company data is the data flowing between corporations. Further, business data can also include digitised content such as software and audiovisual content; and social data referring to behavioural patterns data, public data, confidential business data, machine-to-machine data and metadata, determined using personal data.

43. *Ibid.*
44. *Ibid.*
45. Tencent, Cloud Global Infrastructure, 2022, https://intl.cloud.tencent.com/?lang=en&pg=&gclid=EAIaIQobChMIuvCltJmk9wIVLpFmAh18uAHfEAAYAiAAEgLnIPD_BwE&gclsrc=aw.ds.
46. EQUINIX, Asia Pacific Data Centers, 2022, https://equinix.sg.
47. Tim Cooper and Ryan LaSalle, '*Guarding and Growing Personal Data Value*' (2016) Accenture pp. 9-11.
48. *Ibid.*
49. Nivedita Sen, 'Understanding the Role of the WTO in International Data Flows: Taking the Liberalization or the Regulatory Autonomy Path?' (2018) Journal of International Economic Law 324.

Aaronson and Leblond[50] categorise personal data as:

> public data, confidential business data, machine-to-machine data and metadata, determined using personal data. The authors further categorise data into personal although they do not specifically define each of these terms protect personal and confidential business data more strongly than other types of anonymised and day-to-day business data.[51]

Ira Rubinstein takes a wider view and categorises personal data and other types of data (non-personal data) arguing that the 'data cannot always be neatly distinguished in practice'. For Rubinstein, big data technologies can generate large quantities of data that include but are not limited to 'public data, confidential business data, machine-to-machine data and metadata, determined using personal data'.[52] Nevertheless, what is common to all these types of data is that all of them are captured by modern technology. While Rubenstein focuses on the data being collected by large entities, more work needs to be undertaken to better understand the extent to which personal data is being collected and used by small- and medium-sized businesses. Significantly too, more work is needed to comprehend the extent to which data is being collected and used by industrial and professional (primary production, food processing, consumer sales, environmental management, health services, legal and financial) sectors. Arguably, this might not be feasible because as technology evolves and changes, the extent to which data is collected and used will also change. Ultimately, is data a good or a service? Furthermore, is it a tradeable good or service that offers economic benefits and other positive outcomes to those involved in cross-border data flows?

Data: A Good or a Service?

Is data a good or a service? Is it a tradeable good or a tradeable service? These questions alone are probably the most complex to answer with absolute clarity, as acknowledged by leading scholars and practitioners in this field. This is because it is far from settled whether our personal data is either a good or a service, or both. What has emerged is the way that data collected on platforms has been monetised. Put another way, is it the consumer (data subject) who has become the product today, given that his/her data is being used? For instance, there are companies that 'collect the personal data of their users in order to monetize them to third parties, generally for advertising purposes. Similarly, companies benefit from offering services at no cost, because the more consumers use its services, the more information they collect about them'.[53]

50. Susan Ariel Aaronson and Patrick Leblond, 'Another Digital Divide: The Rise of Data Realms and Its Implications for the WTO' (2018) 21(2) Journal of International Economic Law 245, 250.
51. *Ibid.*
52. Ira Rubinstein, 'Big Data: The End of Privacy or a New Beginning?' (2013) 74 International Data Privacy Law 78.
53. Guillaume Desjardins, Your Personal Data Is the Currency of the Digital Age, The Conversation, 2020, Associate Professor, Industrial Relations, Université du Québec en Outaouais.

More recently, the OECD categorised data as an increasingly critical resource that generates many benefits across society,[54] thereby making data a public good. This, in part, certainly applies to data that is used in science-related domains such as environmental and health services.[55] The prevailing view which has been endorsed by the 'United Nations Secretary-General's Roadmap for Digital Cooperation', the Digital Public Goods Alliance, defines digital public goods as:

> open-source software, open data, open artificial intelligence models, open standards and open content that adhere to privacy and other applicable laws and best practices, do no harm, and help attain the Sustainable Development Goals.[56]

Based on the above, what has emerged is that data has been tied to models of digital services and goods. Open data as a concept has emerged as a policy position or model that some nation states have begun to implement. Svetlana Yakovleva and Kristina Irion posit that the 'global economy, digital trade is closely linked to cross-border data flows'.[57] The models espoused by these authors are aligned with the fact that, currently, data is being defined in a way that protects and controls its use. The models regulate the user of the data. The '2016 report of McKinsey Global Institute estimates that cross-border data flows now exert a larger impact on the global gross domestic product than trading goods'.[58] This is the flow of the data that is attached to the goods or services underpinning this transition in GDP [gross domestic product].

Therefore, the notion of data as a good or service, at this stage, is unlikely to be definitive. At best, what has emerged is a level of consensus that the data falls within different categories which, by and large, constitute one of three models (*see* Table 1.1).

54. Organisation for Economic Development and Cooperation, Mapping Approaches to Data and Data Flows, Report for the G20 Digital Economy Task Force, Saudi Arabia (2020), p. 7.
55. Health Data Governance Summit, Health Data as a Global Public Good, 2021, https://cdn.who.int/media/docs/default-source/world-health-data-platform/events/health-data-governance-summit/preread-2-who-data-governance-summit_health-data-as-a-public-good.pdf?sfvrsn=2d1e3ad8_8.
56. *Ibid.*, p. 5. *See also*, Linnet Taylor, *The Ethics of Big Data as a Public Good: Which Public? Whose good?* The Royal Society, 2016, p. 1.
57. Svetlana Yakovleva and Kristina Irion, 'Pitching Trade Against Privacy: Reconciling EU Governance of Personal Data Flows with External Trade' (August 2020) 10(3) International Data Privacy Law pp. 201-221, https://doi.org/10.1093/idpl/ipaa003.
58. *Ibid.*, also *see* McKinsey Global Institute, 'Digital Globalization: The New Era of Global Flow' (2016), https://www.mckinsey.com/~/media/McKinsey/Business%20Functions/McKinsey%20Digital/Our%20Insights/Digital%20globalization%20The%20new%20era%20of%20global%20flows/MGI-Digital-globalization-Full-report.ashx, accessed 5 March 2020.

Table 1.1 Main Features of Data Models Used for the Categorisation of Countries[59]

	Cross-Border Data Transfers	*Domestic Data Processing*
Open Transfers and Processing Model	Self-certification, self-assessment schemes; *ex post* accountability; trade agreements and plurilateral/bilateral arrangements as the only means to regulate data transfers.	Lack of comprehensive data protection framework; lack of informed consent; limited sectoral regulations; privacy as a consumer right.
Conditional Transfers and Processing Model	Conditions to be fulfilled *ex ante*, including adequacy of the recipient country, binding corporate rules (BCR), standard contractual clauses (SCC), data subject consent, codes of conduct.	Broad data subject rights, data subject consent, right to access, modify and delete personal data, establishment of data protection authorities (DPAs) or agencies; privacy as a fundamental human right.
Limited Transfers and Processing Model	Strict conditions, including bans to transfer data cross-border; local processing requirements: ad hoc government authorisation for data transfers; infrastructure requirements; *ex ante* security assessments.	Extensive exceptions for government access to personal data; privacy versus security and social order.

Ferracane and van der Marel make the case that Open Data 'is distinguished by the absence of restrictions to cross-border movements of personal data, and countries applying this model tend to see privacy as a consumer right. Data transfers are either unregulated or rely on voluntary private sector standards and ex-post accountability'.[60] They assert that under the 'conditional model, data transfers and processing are based on regulatory safeguards. Countries adopting this model take a comprehensive and fundamental rights approach to data protection with preventative regulation'.[61] Their

59. Martina F. Ferracane and Erik van der Marel, *Regulating Personal Data: Linking Different Models to Digital Services Trade*, VoxEU, 2021, https://voxeu.org/article/regulating-personal-data-linking-different-models-digital-services-trade, For a more comprehensive discussion on Open Data espoused by the World Economic Forum.
60. *Ibid.*
61. *Ibid.* For personal data transfers, certain conditions need to be fulfilled *ex ante*. These include, amongst others, adequacy findings of the recipient country, the adoption of mandatory data protection protocols, such as binding corporate rules, standard contract clauses, data subject consent requirements and codes of conduct. For data processing, this model is marked by a comprehensive regime for personal data protection with extensive data subject rights.

analysis confirms this book's position and the works of other scholars and legal practitioners in this area of the law: that is, the current legal framework for cross-border data flows is abed on national, not international, law. As will be demonstrated in this book, even the emerging agreements and rules that have been established are far from coherent and consistent. Problematic too is how, apart from a level of regional convergence, at the international level, this is far from the case. Arguably, this can be seen in the EU and the UK framework, and to a lesser extent, in Australia, the US, and Singapore. The control model has emerged in countries where the 'concept of the right to privacy is fairly recent. This model features strict conditions including bans to transfer data cross-border, strong local processing requirements, and ad hoc government authorisation for data transfers'.[62]

That said, the McKinsey Institute argues that personal data when coupled with data analytics is a service based on data, stating that:

> Data have several characteristics that make them unique as an asset. The first is their non-rivalrous nature – that is, the same piece of data can be used by more than one party simultaneously. This makes data similar to other intangible assets such as knowledge and intellectual property. But few organizations list data or information assets on their balance sheets. Most data are monetised indirectly (through selling analytics as a service based on data) rather than through direct sale, which makes its value difficult to disaggregate from other elements in an offering. In some cases, data can be used for barter, which also makes the underlying price tricky to calculate. For example, when a customer signs up for a loyalty card to get discounts or when an individual uses a social media or internet search platform for free, the customer, wittingly or not, trades personal data for services.[63]

Viewed this way, the personal data itself that is being traded is not a service; rather, it is the analytics derived from the data which becomes the service(s). Therefore, it could be categorised as an indirect or additional service. Logically, without the personal data generated by consumer activity, data analytics cannot be produced. Therefore, no service whatsoever is provided. What this does is rule out in part the notion that personal data is a good. However, daily, countless people worldwide engage in online transactions when ordering goods, such as household items (e.g., appliances), revealing their personal data whenever they make a purchase. Again, this is an indirect attachment of data to the purchase and, arguably, cannot be a good. The nature of the data collection process, and the use of that data, makes it likely that at some time in the future, the data could become a good. Hence, it is argued that whether data is a good or a service is far from being established, even though current evidence suggests that it is closer to a service.

62. *Ibid.* For domestic processing, this model comes with an extensive and systematic control over personal data to protect national security and public order, including indiscriminate government access to data.
63. Nicolaus Henke et al., *The Age of Analytics: Competing in a Data-Driven World*, McKinsey Global Institute (2016), p. 44.

However, Trakman, Walters and Zeller[64] argue that data could constitute a good when applied according to the Convention on the Sales of Goods 1980 (CISG). In other words, the authors take the contractual approach based on the doctrinal rationale that freedom of contract grants a pervasive right giving persons with rights to data the freedom to sell or otherwise transfer that data to others. When personal data is not being protected by database rights, freedom to contract protects that data.[65] Most noteworthy, the authors take the position that:

> the law of contract can help to facilitate trade in personal data, while also in providing a level of privacy protection. This protection is achieved through contractual terms, providing that the owner of personal property and the commercial user are continuously and directly connected contractually. Insofar as these connections are lacking, copyright law(s) can help to fill the gap by ensuring the protection and facilitation of trade in that personal data.[66]

Moreover, this begs the question: how can the CISG be applied? Trakman, Walters and Zeller argue that in order for the CISG to respond affirmatively, it has to be able to facilitate the transfer, trade and protection of data collectively, not separately. This position has also been supported by Morgan Corley who argues that the CISG must satisfy three criteria: (1) simplicity, (2) practicality, and (3) clarity.[67] By applying these criteria, Trakman, Walters and Zeller go further to argue that the CISG:

> can help to redress domestic laws that regulate the sale of personal data inconsistently and sometimes ineffectively. It can regulate the sale, transfer, dissemination, and to a lesser extent the protection of personal data across signatory states, while also affirming the choice of law rules of those states. Specifically, the CISG automatically applies to contracts of sale that satisfy its requirements, so long as state signatories have not excluded the CISG from applying to contracts concluded domestically, as permitted by Article 6 of the CISG.[68]

The authors conclude that:

> the CISG applies to contracts for the sale of personal data as 'goods' that are owned, particularly through copyright as property. This appeal to the CISG is also compelling, given divergence across jurisdictions over propertied rights in personal data, and the CISG's applicability to trade in intangible goods that encompass personal data.[69]

Therefore, when data is subject to international trade and is afforded some copyright, the CISG would have to categorise the data as a good in order for it to be applied, as it is well understood that the CISG applies only to goods, according to

---

64. Leon Trakman, Robert Walters and Bruno Zeller, *Trade in Personal Data: Extending International Legal Mechanisms to Facilitate Transnational Trade in Personal Data?* (2020) European Data Protection Law Review pp. 1-3.
65. *Ibid.*, p. 8.
66. *Ibid.*
67. *Ibid.* Morgan Corley, '*The Need for an International Convention on Data Privacy: Taking a Cue from the CISG*' (2016) 41 Brooklyn Journal of International Law, 721.
68. *Ibid.*, p. 16.
69. *Ibid.*

Article 3.[70] The narrow view taken by this proposition is a first step to categorising data as a good in the affirmative. However, it does not extend to include data that has a copyright as one of its properties. Hence, it is argued that under the CISG, data is not unequivocally regarded as a good outside of the transnational contract laws.

Importantly, the OECD makes the point that the use and the re-use of data across the economy emphasise the importance of data as a new form of capital for twenty-first-century knowledge economies.[71] Personal data is 'contextual and emerges through processing and analysis. Techniques including software, artificial intelligence (AI) and visualisation tools are needed to extract insights, convert data into information and ultimately generate knowledge to support decision-making. Analysis of data can reveal information that firms can use to modify and improve their business practices and produce new goods and services'.[72] Further, its value 'depends on the timeliness of its use. This implies that while data cannot be depleted, it can depreciate, in particular when it becomes less relevant for the particular purpose of its intended use'.[73] Economically and socially, data undergoes two stages: first, analysis transforms it into knowledge and, second, this knowledge is used for decision making (taking action), 'a phase which is most important for businesses'.[74] In a 2013 study undertaken in the US, data was being used to provide a 'digital record of an individual's behaviour by accurately prediction personal attributes such as sexual orientation, ethnicity, religious and political views, personality traits, intelligence, happiness, use of addictive substances, parental separation, age, and gender'.[75] The results of the analysis were:

> based on a dataset of over 58,000 volunteers who provided their likes, detailed demographic profiles, and the results of several psychometric tests.[76] The model correctly discriminated between sexes, men in 88% of cases, African Americans and Caucasian Americans in 95% of cases, and between Democrats and Republicans in 85% of cases. For the personality trait 'Openness', prediction accuracy is close to the test–retest accuracy of a standard personality test.[77]

This small study demonstrated how data can be used to identify people and their personal preferences, and how data categories have evolved to become sophisticated datasets for everyone who has created a social media presence. Essential for the new digital economy is the ability of data not only to flow freely but also to be traded amongst states and private entities transnationally. This has been reinforced by the OECD since large and small firms, goods and services traders, businesses across all

70. *Ibid.*, p. 11. Convention on the Sale of Goods 1980, Article 3.
71. Organisation for Economic Development and Cooperation, Mapping Approaches to Data and Data Flows, Report for the G20 Digital Economy Task Force, Saudi Arabia (2020), p. 7.
72. *Ibid.*, p. 7.
73. *Ibid.*
74. *Ibid.*
75. Michal Kosinski, David Stillwell and Thore Graepel, *Private Traits and Attributes Are Predictable from Digital Records of Human Behaviour, Free School Lane,* The Psychometrics Centre, University of Cambridge, Cambridge CB2 3RQ United Kingdom; and Microsoft Research, Cambridge CB1 2FB, United Kingdom (2013).
76. *Ibid.*
77. *Ibid.*

industries, and GVCs are increasingly reliant on data transfers for their operations.[78] Therefore, data increasingly underpins international trade transactions, reducing trade costs which support growing trade in goods, and enabling trade in services that were previously considered non-tradable. Most notable is how the OECD has highlighted the importance of cross-border data flows, further emphasising the relevance of this book. The OECD asserts that 'cross-border data flows are especially important for micro, small and medium-sized enterprises, enabling a new breed of "micro multinationals" which is "born global" and is constantly connected. Data flows allow businesses to access IT services, such as cloud computing, reducing the need for costly upfront investment in digital infrastructure'.[79] To date, personal data has not been defined as either a good or a service. It may never be defined as one of these; rather, it might be structured under distinct models. This is due to the tension between the protection of data as a privacy right, and the need for economic activity that is generated by data transfers. Furthermore, data transfer and the digital infrastructure that supports it is a rapidly evolving area of the economy because, as technology develops and changes, data itself may be used differently. Therefore, in some circumstances, it may be a good rather than a service, and vice versa. Alternatively, data could merely support a good or a service and, therefore, an unequivocal definition might never be established.

Data Defined by the Law – should there be a gap between these subheadings throughout?

Data in the modern technological era has taken on its own meaning. It has been defined by the law as any information that helps to identify a person by their online activity. Therefore, most if not all legal frameworks created for data protection view data more specifically as 'personal data'. Data Protection law(s) are now viewed as a tool for privacy.[80] Essentially, the concept of personal data as defined by the law goes beyond the traditional notion of what can identify a person, such as his/her name, date of birth and place of residence. In addition to this basic information, today, data can include all the identifying features derived from biometrics, DNA, and more or less any information that can lead to identifying a person online. To elaborate, the EU, GDPR 2016/679, Article 4 states:

> 'personal data' means any information relating to an identified or identifiable natural person ('data subject'); an identifiable natural person is one who can be identified, directly or indirectly, in particular by reference to an identifier such as a name, an identification number, location data, an online identifier or to one or more factors specific to the physical, physiological, genetic, mental, economic, cultural or social identity of that natural person.[81]

78. *Ibid.*, p. 10. Data has also allowed new bundles that have blurred distinctions between goods and services.
79. *Ibid.*
80. Robert Walters, Leon Trakman and Bruno Zeller, *Data Protection A Comparative Analysis of Asia-Pacific and European Approaches*, Springer (2019), p. 14.
81. General Data Protection Regulation (EU) 2016/679 of the European Parliament and of the Council of 27 April 2016, on the protection of natural persons with regard to the processing of personal data and on the free movement of such data, and repealing Directive 95/46/EC, Official Journal of the European Union L 119/1.

This approach highlights how regulators and governments have attempted to be all things to everyone by offering a broad definition intended to capture all and anything that can identify a person who is connected to the Internet. The modern-day definition is consistent with the OECD Guidelines on the Protection of Privacy and Transborder Flows of Personal Data[82] and its principles of collection, quality, security and openness. Significantly, the definition of personal data can vary from country to country.

Further to the above, Walters, Trakman and Zeller in referring to Paul De Hert and Serg Gutwirth, characterise data protection as a tool of transparency.[83] These tools have been derived from the protection of personal freedoms embodied in the constitutions and laws of democratic societies. De Hert and Gutwirth go on to say that:

> The development of the democratic constitutional state has led to the invention and elaboration of two complementary sorts of legal tools which both aim at the same end, namely the control and limitation of power. We make a distinction between on the one hand tools that tend to guarantee non-interference in individual matters or the opacity of the individual, and on the other, tools that tend to guarantee the transparency/accountability of the powerful.[84]

The tools of opacity are quite different from the tools of transparency. Opacity tools embody normative choices about the limits of power; transparency tools come into play after these normative choices have been made in order to channel the normatively accepted exercise of power.[85] While the latter are directed towards the control and channelling of legitimate uses of power, the former are protecting the citizens against illegitimate and excessive uses of power. Many scholars argue that data protection and privacy have converged primarily as a legal framework to protect people's personal data and are defined by the law and as rights.[86] Walters, Trakman and Zeller go further, stating:

> This convergence also includes finding a balance between economic development and innovation in the digital economy. Even though privacy and data protection is an evolving area of law and economic development, it has not matured as a measure of redressing economic and personal harm comparably to the protection of intellectual property, copyright, criminal procedure and international trade law.[87]

---

82. Organisation for Economic Cooperation and Development Guidelines on the Protection of Privacy and Transborder Flows of Personal Data, https://www.oecd.org/sti/ieconomy/oecdguidelinesontheprotectionofprivacyandtransborderflowsofpersonaldata.htm.
83. De Hert P, Gutwirth S, *Privacy, Data Protection and Law Enforcement. Opacity of the Individual and Transparency of Power*. In: Erik Claes, A. Duff & Serg Gutwirth (eds), *Privacy and the Criminal Law*, Intersentia (2009), pp. 61-104. In Robert Walters, Leon Trakman and Bruno Zeller, *Data Protection: A Comparative Analysis of Asia-Pacific and European Approaches*, Springer (2019), p. 14.
84. *Ibid.*, De Hert and Gutwirth.
85. Robert Walters, Leon Trakman and Bruno Zeller, *Data Protection: A Comparative Analysis of Asia-Pacific and European Approaches*, Springer (2019), p. 14.
86. *Ibid.*
87. *Ibid.*

An understanding of the reach of personal data and how it has been defined demonstrates how its application involves a complex and fine balance between commercial activity in international trade in the digital economy and ensuring it is afforded a high level of protection. Nonetheless, the question arises as to whether the current international trade policy and framework facilitate cross-border data flows. The next section examines the importance, to international data trading, of the General Agreement on Trade in Services (GATS) and the World Trade Organisation.

§1.03 TRANSNATIONAL TRADE

The GATS, a multilateral agreement covering global trade in services, defines trade in services.[88] In principle, the GATS applies to all service sectors, with two exceptions. In accordance with Article I:2, the GATS covers services supplied: (a) from the territory of one Member into the territory of any other Member (Mode 1 – Cross-border trade); (b) in the territory of one Member to the service consumer of any other Member (Mode 2 – Consumption abroad); (c) by a service supplier of one Member, through commercial presence, in the territory of any other Member (Mode 3 – Commercial presence); and (d) by a service supplier of one Member, through the presence of natural persons of a Member in the territory of any other Member (Mode 4 – Presence of natural persons).[89]

However, Article I(3) of the GATS excludes 'services supplied in the exercise of governmental authority'. These are services that are supplied neither on a commercial basis nor in competition with other suppliers. Cases in point are social security schemes and any other public services such as health or education, that are provided under non-market conditions. Furthermore, Air Transport Services are exempted from coverage measures affecting air traffic rights and services directly related to the exercise of such rights.

The GATS' treatment of data can best be described from four perspectives. First, during cross-border activity, users in one state receive services from a third country, through a telecommunications or postal network. These services include, but are not limited to, consultancy or market research reports, telemedical advice, distance training, or architectural drawings.[90] Second is the consumption of data abroad, in cases where nationals of Slovenia (a Member State of the EU), such as tourists, students, or patients, have moved abroad to Australia to consume the respective services. Third, there is a commercial presence, whereby a service is provided in the UK, with an office or subsidiary in Singapore, Australia, the US, India or another country. These services are usually provided by banks, financial institutions, legal firms, hotel groups, and construction companies, amongst others. Fourth, a foreign

88. World trade Organisation, Trade Services Division, The General Agreement on Trade in Services, 2013, https://www.wto.org/english/tratop_e/serv_e/gsintr_e.pdf, Article I.1. Also *see*, General Agreement on Trade in Services, Article I.1, https://www.wto.org/english/docs_e/legal_e/26-gats_01_e.htm.
89. *Ibid.*, Definition of Services Trade and Modes of Supply, Article I.2.
90. *Ibid.*, p. 3.

national of Indonesia provides a service from his/her home state to an organisation based in another state such as Japan.[91]

The above is further supported by the classification of services under twelve areas established by members of the World Trade Organisation (WTO):[92]

(1) Business services (including professional services and computer services).
(2) Communication services.
(3) Construction and related engineering services.
(4) Distribution services.
(5) Educational services.
(6) Environmental services.
(7) Financial services (including insurance and banking).
(8) Health-related and social services.
(9) Tourism and travel-related services.
(10) Recreational, cultural and sporting services.
(11) Transport services.
(12) Other services not included elsewhere.[93]

However, nowadays, data is being collected from areas beyond those listed above. It is collected and used in legal and other professions, and mobile devices add another dimension to communication services. Data is used in construction and engineering and can be found in modern cities around the world in their railroads and other transport infrastructures. The influx of overseas students seeking an education in a foreign country has produced large volumes of data. Environmental services have been another sector that has moved quickly to embrace the use of data for waste management, as an example. Financial services such as banks and insurance companies have been collecting data for decades in one form or another. The concept of digital trade is broadly perceived as encompassing international trade enabled by digital technologies. The WTO defines 'electronic commerce' as 'the production, distribution, marketing, sale or delivery of goods and services by electronic means'.[94]

Today, the online collection of data in the commerce sector alone is vast, varied, complex and large, along with the health sector. In addition to the above, tourism and recreation (sport) have been collecting data for many years, primarily to predict and manage events and promote sports or tourism. Other sectors that have emerged as significant users of data are primary production, food processing and other consumer-related activities such as online purchasing. These emerging areas are growing at such a rate that it has been very difficult to determine the amount of data that is being used.

91. *Ibid.*
92. World Trade Organisation, as of 2016, there were 164 members.
93. World Trade Organisation, Trade Services Division, The General Agreement on Trade in Services, 2013, https://www.wto.org/english/tratop_e/serv_e/gsintr_e.pdf, Article I.1., p. 4, document, MTN.GNS/W/120. *See also* Robert Walters, Cross Border Data Flows – An Evolving Multilayered Regulatory Approach Required! *Global Privacy Law Review, Wolters Kluwer, 2022.*
94. WTO, (1998), Work Program on Electronic Commerce, WT/L/247.

Article III[95] of the WTO promotes the concept of transparency amongst Member States. That is, the general understanding was that the obligations imposed by Article III in regard to transparency apply to all laws and regulations affecting the supply of a service through electronic means.[96] Furthermore, Article III.3, requires that each member shall promptly and at least annually inform the Council for Trade in Services of the introduction of any new, or any changes to existing, laws, regulations or administrative guidelines which significantly affect trade in services covered by its specific commitments under this Agreement. This has not been fully realised in the area of cross-border data flows, although most countries have established or are in the process of developing laws for data protection. Problematic though, is that, while it is beyond the scope of this book to analyse every country, most countries' data protection or privacy laws are limited to providing extensive cross-border data flow provisions (*see* jurisdictional chapters, on analysis of countries examined in this book). Members of the WTO have the right to request information from other members in relation to the general application or international agreements, such as Free Trade Agreements (FTA) and their implementation of specific provisions. That is, Article III.4, allows a member country to respond to a request from another member country for specific information in relation to an FTA.[97] For instance, it would not be unreasonable for Australia to request the UK to provide information regarding their most recent FTA on the provisions related to cross-border data flows, if they exist. Therefore, this book will analyse the most recent FTAs that have been established since 2010, to confirm or otherwise the extent to which cross-border data flows are considered. However, the question arises as to the way that confidential information can be managed under the concept of transparency. Article III *bis* provides for disclosure of confidential information, whereby a member country is not obliged to provide another member country with confidential information, particularly if that information is contrary to the public interest. In other words, it enables governments to protect sensitive policy and commercial information. Yet, in 2015, the European Council confirmed that the Commission could not negotiate away privacy rights in trade agreements:

> The Council stresses the need to create a global level playing field in the area of digital trade and strongly supports the Commission's intention to pursue this goal in full international data privacy agreements after the GDPR and Schrems 6 compliance with and without prejudice to the EU's data protection and data privacy rules, which are not negotiated in or affected by trade agreements.[98]

95. WTO, Analytical Index, GATS - Article III (Practice) https://www.wto.org/english/res_e/publications_e/ai17_e/gats_art3_oth.pdf.
96. World Trade Organisation, Trade in Services, S/L/74, 27 July 1999 (99-3194), Work Programme on Electronic Commerce, Progress Report to the General Council, Adopted by the Council for Trade in Services on 19 July 1999.
97. *Ibid.*, also *see* Article III.5, 5. Any Member may notify to the Council for Trade in Services any measure, taken by any other Member, which it considers affects the operation of this Agreement.
98. Graham Greenleaf, International data privacy agreements after the GDPR and *Schrems Privacy Laws & Business International Report* (2016) 139, pp. 5-6.

It has been well established that the EU, since the establishment of Directive 95/46/EC,[99] adopted a rights-based approach towards the governance of data, including data flows. Twenty-seven years on, and a question arises, will there be a need for the EU to compromise on the rights-based approach in order to open up data access in the digital economy? Moreover, how can the current rights-based approach be retained when implementing Open Data? This is a question that needs to be addressed by the EU and its Member States. However, it is argued that, in part, some rights should be strengthened (*see* final chapter, disclosure, access and deletion), yet another area that should be reviewed. In addition, outside the technology sector, little is known about the storage of all this data and its security, particularly in the cloud. What and how this is done warrants a comprehensive examination.

Notwithstanding the above, Article IV encourages the participation of developing countries. Under the current structure and formation of cross-border data laws and data protection laws more generally, it is widely understood that developing countries such as India and Indonesia, while yet to implement specific data protection laws, were beginning to develop them as of January 2022.[100] These nation states are just two that have looked to developed countries such as Australia, the US, the UK and the EU for guidance in developing their own legal framework. Article V goes further by promoting the concept of economic integration. Arguably, in the new digital economy, to date, this has been difficult to achieve as countries are at different stages of economic development. For instance, jurisdictions such as Australia, the UK, the US and the EU have had well-established data protection laws in place for more than two decades. Therefore, there is a higher level of economic and legal integration, although data protection laws are still highly fragmented.[101] To date, there has been little to no international consensus on data protection laws, let alone cross-border data flows and the laws that facilitate this activity. Thus, as can be seen across the world, the current regulation of cross-border data flows lies in domestic legislation. Article VI requires that each member ensures that all measures of general application affecting trade in services be administered in a reasonable, objective and impartial manner.[102]

In the remaining applicable articles, members have the ability to recognise the education or experience obtained, requirements met, or licenses or certifications granted in a particular country.[103] Importantly, Article VIII requires that member countries minimise the opportunity for monopolies to be established. However, under the current national, regional and international legal frameworks, this is unavoidable. Monopolies have formed and have been successful in retaining a high level of control over the current trade-in data. While problematic, this practice is inevitable as new

99. Directive 95/46/EC of the European Parliament and of the Council of 24 October 1995 on the protection of individuals with regard to the processing of personal data and on the free movement of such data OJ L 281.
100. Robert Walters, Leon Trakman and Bruno Zeller, *Data Protection Law: A Comparative Analysis of Asia-Pacific and European Approaches*, Springer (2019), Chapters 6 & 7.
101. *Ibid.*, Chapter 17.
102. World Trade Organisation, Analytical Index, GATS – Article VI, Domestic Regulation, https://www.wto.org/english/res_e/publications_e/ai17_e/gats_art3_oth.pdf.
103. *Ibid.*, Article VII, Recognition.

products and services come onto the market. Data is no different. It has been found that, over time, the market becomes more accessible and allows other entities to participate. In the world of data flows, this will be a gradual process. Nonetheless, market access be affected by a key driver enabling nation states to enter new markets for products and services. Article XVI ensures there is a high level of balanced market access so that one party is not favoured over another. The remaining GATS Articles are outside the scope of this section.

Nowadays, personal data constitutes a substantial proportion of trade in transnational services. GATS can facilitate the coming together of nation states for the purpose of developing a consistent and coherent framework for cross-border data flows. As this book will demonstrate, to date, the current cross-border data regime lacks consistency and coherence. The GATS established in 2001 at the Doha Ministerial Conference[104] have provided a successful multilateral legal framework for trade-in services. As highlighted in this section, because data pervades every sector of the economy, the GATS will play an increasingly important role as their provisions continue to find their way into FTAs (*see* individual jurisdiction chapters). Increasingly, data itself is being considered in complex trade negotiations. The data itself is generating large quantities of statistics which, over time, will need to be understood by policymakers and legal practitioners (trade agreement negotiators), to effect strong market access in the trade-in data as a service as this activity continues to be globalised.

World Trade Organisation

In May 1998, WTO members undertook a comprehensive Work Programme on Electronic Commerce to examine trade-related issues associated with global e-commerce. Recently, discussions have included an examination of the COVID-19 pandemic's impact on e-commerce, including the implications for cross-border trade.[105] An important conclusion arrived at by the WTO is that e-commerce is an 'important tool/solution for consumers in times of crisis, and that it is also an economic driver, including for small businesses'.[106] Thus, further work by the WTO may give a better understanding of the impact of COVID-19 on the world digital economy and, in turn, of data.

Bilateral and Multilateral Agreements

Bilateral and multilateral trade agreements are nothing new as the means of strengthening cooperation between countries so as to deepen relationships, expand trade and encourage economic development. Such agreements are underpinned by the rules of the WTO and GATS. Multilateral trade agreements, otherwise referred to by the WTO

104. World Trade Organisation, Services Negotiations, https://www.wto.org/english/tratop_e/serv_e/s_negs_e.htm.
105. World Trade Organisation, Report Looks at Role of e-Commerce During the COVID-19 Pandemic, 2020, https://www.wto.org/english//tratop_e/covid19_e/ecommerce_report_e.pdf. Also, Work Programme on e-Commerce, https://www.wto.org/english/tratop_e/ecom_e/ecom_work_programme_e.htm.
106. *Ibid.*, p. 7.

as Regional Trade Agreements (RTAs),[107] 'have risen in number and reach over the years, including a notable increase in large plurilateral agreements'.[108] The WTO RTAs are 'reciprocal preferential trade agreements between two or more partners, constitute one of the derogations and subject to a set of rules'.[109] One of the major challenges that has arisen, according to the WTO, is the more RTAs are developed, the more they add to the 'spaghetti bowl' of existing agreements.[110] In other words, RTAs while on the rise, have not superseded existing agreements; thus, there is no formal expiry of older and probably outdated agreements. This being the case, it does not support the digital economy and data flows. Those that have little to no relevance, will remain that way. However, the unknown is there could be rules or particular provisions in the older agreements that influence and could impact more recent agreements. Given these preliminary observations, however, Antonella Nocco, Gianmarco Ottaviano, and Matteo Salto believe that 'multilateralism in trade is currently under attack'.[111] The authors go on to say that, 'countries that used to be its most fervent supporters seem dissatisfied with its outcomes and think that they would be better off breaking multilateral agreements. At the same time, faced with the exorbitant market power of giant corporations, governments are increasingly active in unilateral protectionist policies'.[112] In their view, RTAs are efficient in regard to free trade. They account for geography, market size and technology of the trade partners, and can increase global welfare with respect to the free trade outcome. The EU has been developing RTAs since the 1950s. The treaty establishing the European Coal and Steel Community in 1951[113] was followed in subsequent years by a number of treaties up until the Lisbon Treaty in 2007. Additionally, these treaties achieve a level of harmonisation of the values, rules and standards governing transnational trade, provided that each participating country follows the RTAs as agreed. Any deviation from treaty agreements only erodes their effectiveness.

More generally, whether RTAs or bilateral agreements, they have been viewed as a 'precedent for a potential integration of countries as trade liberalisation not only aims to strengthen relations but can also offer significant gains for the parties that intervene in the process by eliminating tariff and non-tariff barriers within the general framework of trade agreements'.[114] They also facilitate the 'reallocation of productive factors in each country as well as encouraging changes in production, consumption, exports,

107. World Trade Organisation, Regional Trade Agreements, https://rtais.wto.org/UI/PublicMaintainRTAHome.aspx.
108. *Ibid.*, https://www.wto.org/english/tratop_e/region_e/region_e.htm.
109. *Ibid.*
110. *Ibid.*
111. Antonella Nocco, Gianmarco Ottaviano and Matteo Salto, *Why Multilateral Trade Policies Are the Most Efficient Way to Economic Growth, BAFFI CAREFIN Centre Research Paper No. 2019-109*. VoxEU, https://voxeu.org/article/geography-competition-and-optimal-multilateral-trade-policy.
112. *Ibid.*
113. Heribert Dieter, 'The Multilateral Trading System and Preferential Trade Agreements: Can the Negative Effects Be Minimized?' (2009) 15(3) Global Governance 393.
114. Kabir Hassan, 'Is SAARC a Viable Economic Block? Evidence from Gravity Model' (2001) Journal of Asian Economics 3. In Jose J. Baena-Rojas and Susana Herrero-Olarte, 'From

imports, and even influencing the price of all factors and goods of the parties involved'.[115] However, problems arise when trade agreements are developed for reasons other than economic outcomes. Michael Sampson argues that some states develop such agreements on 'political rather than economic considerations'.[116] When politics are involved in such agreements, the pursuit of a different objective, no matter who is involved, dilutes the current regulations based on the rule of law. Thus, if Sampson is correct in his assertion, such a challenge adds complexity to the digital economy and the establishment of a harmonised set of international laws for data flows, which is urgently needed.

Significantly, Julian Maluck, Nicole Glaneman and Reik Donner make the point that there has been an increase in the development of bilateral trade agreements (BTAs).[117] Maluck et al. argue that BTAs 'affect global trade, since the reorganization of flows of goods and services has prominent impacts on the contracting countries' economies, but also on other parties that are (directly or indirectly) engaged in trade with these countries'.[118] BTAs have become important to countries such as Australia, India and the US. Maluck et al. point out that in these states, the relative importance of the 'export linkages to their partners has increased more strongly than the relative importance of the import linkages from their partners'.[119] Conversely, in other countries, such as Singapore which imports many goods, particularly food and commodities, BTAs have become essential for their economic development. The use of BTAs has 'increased considerably in number and economic relevance, over the last decade'.[120] Julian Maluck, Nicole Glanemann, and Reik Donner argue that such agreements substantially affect global trade since the reorganisation of flows of goods and services has significant impacts on the contracting countries' economies, as well as on other parties that are (directly or indirectly) engaged in trade with these countries. Despite

---

Preferential Trade Arrangements to Free Trade Agreements: One of the Downturns of Cooperation in International Relations?' (2020) 9(8) Social Sciences 139, https://doi.org/10.3390/socsci9080139.

115. Alberto Trejos, *Instrumentos para la Evaluación del Impacto de Acuerdos Comerciales*. Ciudad de México: CEPAL (2009). In Jose J. Baena-Rojas and Susana Herrero-Olarte, 'From Preferential Trade Arrangements to Free Trade Agreements: One of the Downturns of Cooperation in International Relations?' (2020) 9(8) Social Sciences 139, https://doi.org/10.3390/socsci9080139.
116. Michael Sampson, 'The Evolution of China's Regional Trade Agreements: Power Dynamics and the Future of the Asia-Pacific' (2021) 32 The Pacific Review 259-261, https://doi.org/10.1080/09512748.2019.1660397.
117. Julian Maluck, Nicole Glaneman and Reik Donner, 'Bilateral Trade Agreements and the Interconnectedness of Global Trade' (2018) 6 Interdisciplinary Physics 1, https://doi.org/10.3389/fphy.2018.00134.
118. *Ibid.*, p. 1.
119. *Ibid.*
120. Julian Maluck, Nicole Glanemann and Reik Donner, 'Bilateral Trade Agreements and the Interconnectedness of Global Trade' (2018), https://doi.org/10.3389/fphy.2018.00134. Also *see*, Prema-chandra Athukorala, 'Free Trade Agreements in the World Trade System: Substance and Semantics', https://doi.org/10.1177/0015732519886771. Dani Rodrik, 'What Do Trade Agreements Really Do?' (2018) 32(2) Journal of Economic Perspectives 73-90. Martinez-Zarzoso, Santiago Chelala, 'Trade Agreements and International Technology Transfer' (Springer 2021) 157 Review of World Economics (2021) 631-665.

their growth, they have provided important input-output linkages between the contractual parties' national economic sectors by defining a new measure of Trade Interconnectedness (TI), indicating the relative importance of direct and indirect production linkages between the two countries in the international trade network.[121] It is this TI that has been transformed by the Internet so that trade is now being conducted in ways that were unimaginable only a decade ago.

Against this backdrop, and while not specifically a trade agreement, what has emerged recently has been Digital Economic Partnership Agreements (DEPA).[122] These are a new form of agreement. Being the first of its kind, New Zealand is the depository[123] for these agreements. The report by the New Zealand government titled the *International Treaty Examination of the Digital Economy Partnership Agreement: New Zealand Chile* states:

> Conclusion of the Digital Economy Partnership Agreement (DEPA or the Agreement) comes at a time of considerable disruption to international trade and supply chains due to COVID-19. New Zealand's immediate goal has been to bring the pandemic under control within our borders and to mitigate as far as possible its negative impacts on our people, health systems and the economy. Work is also under way on New Zealand's trade recovery, to help ensure that New Zealand is in the best possible position to emerge from the COVID-19 pandemic as quickly as possible ... Digital trade (digitally-enabled transactions of goods and services, whether digitally or physically delivered) has grown rapidly, racing ahead of existing global trade rules and norms. In the context of the COVID-19 pandemic, this takes on even greater significance as these rules will be more important than ever in assisting with the global economic recovery. The DEPA is a first step towards establishing those rules and best practice for the digital era. It contains a series of modules covering topics relevant to the digital economy and digital trade.[124]

Even more pertinent, this new form of agreement is arguably going to serve the digital economy well and is a recognition that trade is diversifying. It is timely and reinforces the rules-based system while providing a level of flexibility to manage and govern data in the new digital economy. Further, it provides a baseline for nation states to come together and develop future rules for data in a period of constant innovation and technological change. To that end, Michael Peters notes that with the continued 'race for leadership in technological developments, as the leader may gain an economic as well as a strategic advantage, by controlling the data and related technologies, particularly with regard to AI' which may well lead to the fragmentation of the digital

121. *Ibid.*
122. Singapore Government, The Digital Economy Partnership Agreement (DEPA) between Singapore, Chile and New Zealand is the first DEA concluded by Singapore, https://www.mti.gov.sg/Improving-Trade/Digital-Economy-Agreements/The-Digital-Economy-Partnership-Agreement.
123. International treaty examination of the Digital Economy Partnership Agreement: New Zealand Chile, together with Relationship to other Agreements Side Letter: New Zealand Singapore, Relationship to other Agreements Side Letter: New Zealand Chile, Report of the Economic Development, Science and Innovation Committee, July 2020, https://www.parliament.nz/resource/en-NZ/SCR_99654/9521a3186a49ccc666b1dc4f545dbac1874be78b.
124. *Ibid.*, p. 4.

realm and the development of dual or multiple internet ecologies'.[125] This fragmentation exists across the international and national framework for data. The question is whether the DEPA and its equivalents will add another complex layer to trade agreements that, in practice, become inconsistent and incoherent. However, it will be demonstrated that, apart from utilising DEPAs, more work can be undertaken to improve and strengthen trade agreements. This will strengthen the governance and regulation of data transfers, which is a specific area of emerging law. Hence, this book is timely as it demonstrates that there is a significant gap in the development of trade agreements with respect to data flows, data adequacy and data protection. While it is acknowledged that trade agreements made before 2015 are unlikely to have taken into account any of the transnational developments in data flows and the digital economy, even post-2015, they have been inconsistent, ad hoc and significantly fragmented. The year 2015 has been chosen because many states around the world had only just implemented data laws, from 2010-2012 onwards. The notable exceptions were Australia, the EU, the UK and the US which had established some data protection laws between the 1980s and 2000, other nation states such as Singapore did so only after 2010. India and Indonesia are yet to establish specific data laws. Hence, this book will demonstrate how trade agreements can form the basis for the establishment of specific rules for cross-border data flows.

Fourth Industrial Revolution

Notwithstanding the above, the proliferation of data that is now a substantial part of the digital economy will greatly increase due to the IR4[126] which integrates IT systems with physical systems to achieve a cyber-physical system that represents the real world as a virtual reality.[127] There are also several opposing opinions.

Arguably, one of the most complex challenges will be the scale of data flow that is likely to affect and expose the potential vulnerabilities of personal data protection (PDP) over the Internet. The IR4 has been described as the next wave of globalisation. Importantly, 'digitally enabled trade, otherwise referred to as e-commerce, has become the major global trade growth story. As the digital age takes hold, services are growing in importance in international trade, both in their own right and as a support to trade in goods'.[128] As stated in this chapter, data has already become, and will continue to be, an integral part of this economic growth. Regarding the IR4, the most salient fact is that:

---

125. Michael Peters, 'Digital Trade, Digital Economy and the Digital Economy Partnership Agreement' (2022) Educational Philosophy and Theory, DOI: 10.1080/00131857.2022.2041413.
126. Jane Drake-Brockman et al., *Impact of Digital Technologies and the Fourth Industrial Revolution on Trade in Services*, Task Force 1, Trade, Investment and Growth, T20, 2020, pp. 2-3, https://www.g20-insights.org/wp-content/uploads/2020/11/T20_TF1_PB4.pdf. Also *see* Klaus Schaub, *The Fourth Industrial Revolution: What It Means, How to Respond*, 2021, https://jmss.vic.edu.au/wp-content/uploads/2021/06/The_Fourth_Industrial_Revolution.pdf.
127. Antonella Petrillo, Fabio De Felice, Raffaele Cioffi and Federico Zomparelli, Fourth Industrial Revolution: Current Practices, Challenges, and Opportunities (2018), DOI: 10.5772/intechopen.72304, https://www.intechopen.com/chapters/58010.
128. Jane Drake-Brockman et al., *Impact of Digital Technologies and the Fourth Industrial Revolution on Trade in Services*, Task Force 1, Trade, Investment and Growth, T20, 2020, pp. 2-3.

> International trade involving consumers cannot occur without collecting and sending personal data, such as names, addresses, and billing information, across borders. For services suppliers, complex data privacy regimes reduce flexibility, increase compliance costs, and inhibit managing operations efficiently. The increasing burden of diverse local privacy rules also impacts the price of consumer goods and services. This is an emerging problem as companies collect and analyse personal data to better understand customers' preferences and willingness to pay and adapt offerings accordingly.[129]

The reality is that personal data is now a part of the new economy. As consumers continue to rely on and use technology to purchase everyday items such as household goods, clothing, consumables, and food amongst other things, the growth in personal data generated by these trading activities appears to be nowhere near reaching its peak in 2022. A number of nation states, including the jurisdictions examined in this book, have embraced the policy initiative of the IR4, whether formally or informally. Australia,[130] Singapore, India and the UK, along with the other jurisdictions, are in the process of adopting the IR4, and acquiring a better understanding of the economic and social benefits it will bring. On the one side, the extent to which each jurisdiction implements IR4 will vary, depending on the state of their respective economies. However, regardless of a country's location in the world, there is little doubt that the IR4 will overtake everyone, requiring a response from governments and regulators. The IR4 has been described as consisting of high-end and modern technology, such as AI,[131] Blockchain,[132] and the Internet of Things.[133] Blockchain is software technology that companies are using to establish smart contracts and ensure the efficiency and security of transactions conducted via the Internet in order to respond in real-time to

129. *Ibid.*
130. Australian Government, Industry Testlabs in Australian, https://www.industry.gov.au/data-and-publications/industry-40-testlabs-in-australia. Singapore, GovTech, https://www.tech.gov.sg/media/technews/its-the-fourth-industrial-revolution-do-you-know-where-your-jobs-are-at. Government of India, https://pib.gov.in/Pressreleaseshare.aspx?PRID = 1549516. United Kingdom, https://www.gov.uk/government/publications/regulation-for-the-fourth-industrial-revolution/regulation-for-the-fourth-industrial-revolution.
131. CRS In Focus IF10608, Overview of Artificial Intelligence, by Laurie A. Harris; CRS In Focus IF10810, Blockchain and International Trade, by Rachel F. Fefer; CRS In Focus IF11239, The Internet of Things (IoT): An Overview, by Patricia Moloney Figliola, John Karr, et. al.; and COVID-19, 4IR, and the Future of Work, APEC Policy Brief No. 34, June 2020. In Congressional Research Services, *Data Flows, Online Privacy, and Trade Policy* (2020), p. 1, https://sgp.fas.org/crs/misc/R45584.pdf. Artificial Intelligence can generally be thought of as computerised systems that work and react in ways commonly thought to require intelligence, such as solving complex problems in real-world situations.
132. *Ibid.* Blockchain is a distributed record-keeping system (each user can keep a copy of the records) that provides for auditable transactions and secures those transactions with encryption. Using blockchain, each transaction is traceable to a user, each set of transactions is verifiable, and the data in the blockchain cannot be edited without each user's knowledge. Compared to traditional technologies, blockchain allows two or more parties without a trusted relationship to engage in reliable transactions without relying on intermediaries or central authority (e.g., a bank or government).
133. *Ibid.* Internet of Things is a system of interrelated devices connected to a network and/or to one another, exchanging data without necessarily requiring human-to-machine interaction. In other words, IoT is a collection of electronic devices that can share information amongst themselves.

customers' claims or requirements, provide transparency, and reduce supply chain costs, all of which depend on open data flows of digital trade.[134] For example, 'Walmart and IBM built a blockchain platform to increase transparency of global supply chains and improve traceability for certain imported food products.'[135] Such programmes and platforms are providing extensive economic, social and human health benefits in this sector alone. For the first time, consumers can track and trace the origin of their food. The indirect benefit is that consumers are able to better understand the primary production process and the supply chain that takes the produce from the farm gate to the plate. The breadth and depth of knowledge and data that consumers now have at their disposal will change consumer demands and habits in this, and other, sectors. However, this could place data at risk of privacy breaches, loss, theft and misuse.

Arguably, this technology is not fully understood by mainstream sectors of business and government. Businesses need expert IT personnel who can understand their complex requirements and operations. It is further argued that these technologies are going to generate, analyse and use large quantities of personal data. Hence, the vulnerabilities of data in transnational transfers are far from being addressed, and therefore there are likely to be significant data breaches. As briefly mentioned, the current rights-based laws are not aligned with IR4 technology which does not allow a data subject to access and delete personal data. This needs to be reconciled, raising an urgent need to conduct research on legal frameworks, policy and various aspects of the new technologies. Therefore, a starting point has to be the internationalisation of this area of the law. This must begin at the highest possible level and, because it deals with international trade, the United Nations Commission on International Trade Law (UNCITRAL) has the expertise and skills to achieve this, together with support from the International Institute for the Unification of Private Law.

Nonetheless, a major challenge for the IR4 is balancing the needs of cross-border data flows with that of data privacy and protection over the Internet. Jane Drake-Brockman et al. call for 'the recognition of the idea that solutions may lie in the interoperability of data privacy approaches'.[136] To achieve this, the authors argue that:

> it begins with domestic policymakers ensuring that their legal frameworks clarify that firms with a legal nexus in their jurisdiction are responsible for managing data in a certain manner, wherever the data are transferred and stored. A country's data-protection rules thus travel with the data. Potential models of how to proceed include the OECD Privacy Principles and the APEC Cross-Border Privacy Regime.[137]

134. *Ibid.*, p. 7.
135. *Ibid.*
136. Jane Drake-Brockman et al., *Impact of Digital Technologies and the Fourth Industrial Revolution on Trade in Services*, Task Force 1, Trade, Investment and Growth, T20, 2020, pp. 2-3, https://www.g20-insights.org/wp-content/uploads/2020/11/T20_TF1_PB4.pdf.
137. *Ibid.*

They explain that 'facilitating e-commerce, including cross-border data flows, can enable businesses to realise economies of scale and scope'[138] and that interoperability is a far better option than seeking legal harmonisation. Arguably, this is a form of legal convergence although it does not achieve full harmonisation. For instance, the authors cite the 'Swiss-US Privacy Shield, and the APEC Cross-Border Privacy Rules (CBPR) are examples of formal mechanisms to build interoperability.'[139] Interoperability is a tool that can be used to overcome the lack of legal harmonisation. A pertinent question is whether it has outlived its application and operation for the regulation required for data in the digital economy. Furthermore, can it assist, in part, to address data in the digital economy within FTAs, Digital or other Agreements prepared between and by multiple states? Also, what is meant by legal interoperability? These questions will be answered throughout this book. The next section discusses transnational data flows and the evolving fragmentation of their governance (in terms of both policy and the law) regionally and internationally.

§1.04 TRANSNATIONAL DATA FLOWS: A HIGHLY FRAGMENTED APPROACH

This section demonstrates that there are significant divergent approaches or policy aims that international and regional institutions are individually trying to achieve in regard to data in the new digital economy. While the current divergence is understandable, it has created an environment of complex, disconnected and competing aims. This section begins with the WEF.

World Economic Forum

The current international policy and legal framework that enables and facilitates transnational data flows are highly fragmented. Notably, one of the key policy drivers of the new digital economy has come from the WEF, and the concept of Open Data. The WEF makes the point that 'data will only get us so far, and we need for it to be open'.[140] Stephen Walker, referring to Professor Klaus Schwab, has made a number of observations about the increasing importance of data and connectivity in realising the IR4. He singled out one of the key issues facing the government in this next wave of industrialisation: increased public demand for transparency. Professor Schwab stated that:

> If [governments] prove capable of embracing a world of disruptive change, subjecting their structures to the levels of transparency and efficiency that will

138. *Ibid.*
139. *Ibid.*
140. Stephen Walker, *Data Will Only Get Us So Far. We Need It To Be Open*, World Economic Forum, 2016, https://www.weforum.org/agenda/2016/01/data-will-only-get-us-so-far-we-need-it-to-be-open/.

> enable them to maintain their competitive edge, they will endure. If they cannot evolve, they will face increasing trouble.[141]

Transparency, while not a new concept, is increasingly being challenged as nation states continue to look inwards. Nonetheless, the very notion of transparency in relation to transnational flows of data directly imposes on governments the responsibility to ensure that the legal environment is as open as possible. However, this is difficult to achieve as some governments are embracing the idea of developing a framework where data is open and can move around the world as freely as possible. Centrally, it is a framework that limits the extent to which governments and regulators restrict the flow of data transnationally. On the one hand, this flow of data requires essential safeguards and controls to ensure that all personal data is protected. On the other hand, some governments do not wholly favour transparency, and therefore open data flow is far from being realised. In regard to policy on open data, over time, will the current controls and safeguards protecting personal data be diluted or eroded? At the time of writing (2022), there appeared to be little to no inclination on the part of any governments or regulators to dilute any of the controls or safeguards for personal data being transferred internationally. Moreover, there is nothing to suggest that this may occur during the next decade as more governments and regulators embrace the concept of open data.

The formal and functional requirements underpinning the concept of open data are the Open Data Charter and the Open Charter Barometer. The Open Data Charter[142] (the Charter) reinforces the concept and direction of this book by stating that:

> The world is witnessing a significant global transformation, facilitated by technology and digital media, and fuelled by data and information. This transformation has enormous potential to foster more transparent, accountable, efficient, responsive, and effective governments and civil society and private sector organizations, and to support the design, delivery, and assessment of sustainable development goals on a global scale.[143]

Importantly, the Charter developed six core principles for the unlocking of data in the digital economy. These principles include:

(1) Open By default.[144]

141. *Ibid.* The World Economic Forum was established in 1971 and is independent, impartial and not tied to special interests. It provides a platform to discuss and resolve international policy issues such as cross-border data flows, cybersecurity and artificial intelligence.
142. Open Data Charter, 2015, https://opendatacharter.net/principles/. The Open Data Charter is a collaboration between over 150 governments and organisations working to open up data based on a shared set of principles.
143. *Ibid.*
144. *Ibid.* This represents a real shift in how government operates and how it interacts with citizens. At the moment we often have to ask officials for the specific information we want. Open by default turns this on its head and says that there should be a presumption of publication for all. Governments need to justify data that's kept closed, for example for security or data protection reasons. To make this work, citizens must also feel confident that open data will not compromise their right to privacy.

(2) Timely and Comprehensive.[145]
(3) Accessible and Useable.[146]
(4) Comparable and Interoperable.[147]
(5) For Improved Governance and Citizen Engagement.[148]
(6) For Inclusion Development and Innovation.[149]

Most noteworthy, these principles allow users to compare, combine, and follow the connections amongst different datasets, tracing data across a number of programmes and sectors. They can guide governments, citizens, and public and private sector organisations to work towards better outcomes for public services in areas such as health, education, public safety, environmental protection, human rights, and natural disasters.[150] This reaffirms that open data will not only unlock the entire economy, but it will also enable data to pervade every sector of the economy, unlike anything that has been seen throughout history. Furthermore, the Charter states that it will contribute to the generation of inclusive economic growth by supporting the creation and strengthening of new markets, enterprises, and jobs,[151] all of which are just beginning to emerge. For instance, over the past five years, there has been a significant growth in employment in areas such as data privacy, data analytics, data science and cyber security, and it is anticipated that this trend will continue.

Arguably and as the Charter asserts, open data will unlock the flow of information around the world, increase transparency and accountability, provide innovative, evidence-based policy solutions and deliver economic benefits and social development to all members of society.[152] Undoubtedly, based on the above, the emerging digital

145. *Ibid.* Open data is only valuable if it's still relevant. Getting information published quickly and in a comprehensive way is central to its potential for success. As much as possible governments should provide data in its original, unmodified form.
146. *Ibid.* Ensuring that data is machine readable and easy to find will make data go further. Portals are one way of achieving this. But it's also important to think about the user experience of those accessing data, including the file formats that information is provided. Data should be free of charge, under an open license, for example, those developed by Creative Commons.
147. *Ibid.* Data has a multiplier effect. The more quality datasets you have access to, and the easier it is for them to talk to each other, the more potential value you can get from them. Commonly agreed data standards play a crucial role in making this happen.
148. *Ibid.* Open data has the capacity to let citizens (and others in government) have a better idea of what officials and politicians are doing. This transparency can improve public services and help hold governments to account.
149. *Ibid.* Open data can help spur inclusive economic development. For example, greater access to data can make farming more efficient, or it can be used to tackle climate change. Finally, we often think of open data as just about improving government performance, but there's a whole universe out there of entrepreneurs making money off the back of open data.
150. *Ibid.*
151. *Ibid.* Enabling cross-sector collaboration: Supporting collaboration amongst governments, citizens, and civil society and private sector organisations on the design of policies and the delivery of better public services; Following the money: Showing how and where public money is spent, which incentivises governments to demonstrate that they are using public money effectively; Improving governance of natural resources: Increasing awareness about how countries' natural resources are used, how extractives revenues are spent, and how land is transacted and managed.
152. *Ibid.* Monitoring impact: Supporting assessments of the impact of public programmes, which in turn allows governments and civil society and private sector organisations to respond more

economy and the use of data are only beginning to be realised. However, a difficulty may arise as to which governments will fully embrace this new policy direction and which will not. To measure the take-up of the open data concept, the Open Data Barometer has been included in the overall framework. The most recent Open Data Barometer was established in 2018.[153] It measures national governments' responses to the open data concept and how each country is going about implementing the concept. Countries were categorised into three groups: the champions, the contenders, and the stragglers. Of the thirty countries examined, the most progressive have been democratic states: Canada, the UK, the US, Australia, France, South Korea, Japan and New Zealand.[154] The contenders consisted of Germany, Uruguay, Colombia, Russia, Brazil, Italy, India, Argentina, Ukraine and the Philippines.[155] Notably, this group were made up of both democratic and socialist countries, with Germany and Italy being members of the EU. The third group, and the one requiring the most work, comprised Chile, Indonesia, South Africa, Paraguay, China, Costa Rica, Turkey, Panama, Guatemala, Saudi Arabia and Sierra Leone. A mix of socialist and democratic countries constituted this third group. Most noteworthy is the low level of maturity this group had (in 2018) in terms of data protection law and privacy law in general. As of 2018, South Africa had not implemented national data protection laws. Indonesia was still developing and debating its proposed law. China had implemented cybersecurity laws but was only beginning to develop specific data protection laws. In addition, countries' notions of privacy vary significantly. Constituted in this manner, there is a sound argument for more countries to be included in this analysis. It is asserted that, in order to fully understand the reach and application of the Charter, further research is needed.

---

effectively to the particular needs of local communities. Promoting equitable growth: Supporting sustainable and inclusive growth through the creation and strengthening of markets, enterprises, and jobs; Geolocating data: Providing geospatial and earth observation references, which support comparability and interoperability and effective analysis by allowing data to be layered geographically; Improved decision making: Enabling citizens to make better informed choices about the services they receive and the service standards they should expect.

153. Open Data Barometer, World Wide Web Foundation, https://opendatabarometer.org/doc/leadersEdition/ODB-leadersEdition-Report.pdf.

154. *Ibid.*

155. *Ibid.*

Figure 1.1 World Map of Data Models for Cross-Border Data Flows, 2019[156]

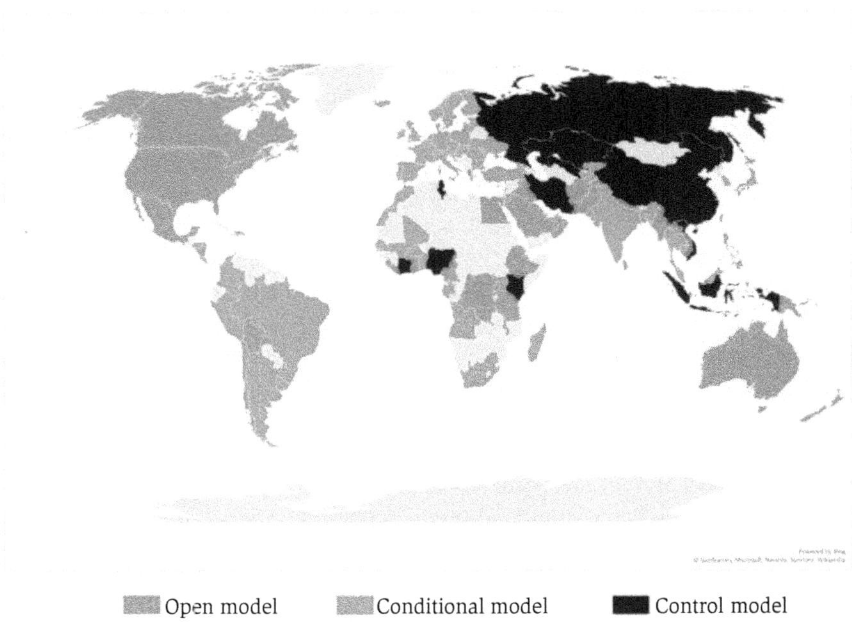

The importance of Figure 1.1 cannot be understated as it shows that very few nation states are currently implementing the open data concept. Not doing so will significantly restrict the full potential of the digital economy and the flow of data, and the economic, social, human health and environmental benefits this will bring.

Many nation states outside the West do not embrace, or have struggled with, the concept of open data and privacy over the Internet, resulting in the current fragmentation of policy and the law. Moreover, the stage at which each country is at in its development and implementation of data laws will invariably influence the way that nation states will view, adopt and apply the open data concept, if at all. Evidently, a significant amount of work needs to be undertaken by the international community to implement the open data concept. This is an area that requires ongoing research and monitoring over the coming decade, as it will impact cross-border data flows, and the laws and policies facilitating transnational data transfers.

Nevertheless, there are a number of international and regional institutions, organisations and polities that have for some time been developing policies and laws to enable cross-border data flows. According to the World Bank, cross-border data flows are becoming the defining hallmark of international trade in the twenty-first century.

156. Martina Ferracane and Erik van der Marel, *Regulating Personal Data: Linking Different Models to Digital Services Trade*, VoxEU, 2021, https://voxeu.org/article/regulating-personal-data-linking-different-models-digital-services-trade.

While the trade in goods has slowed in the last decade, cross-border flows of data have surged dramatically, multiplying an estimated hundred times between 2005 and 2021.[157] Significantly though, courts from developing countries have also faced similar challenges in retrieving data from foreign jurisdictions, resorting at times to heavy-handed measures to overcome them.[158] Countries are adopting diverse regulatory responses to the increasing volumes of cross-border data.[159] Amongst them, bans on transferring data abroad or the obligations to store data in servers physically located in the country (data localisation) have attracted particular attention (*see* Chapter 12). Some studies have focused on the costs that such measures impact the economy – predicting alarming declines in GDP, foreign investments, international trade and productivity, and concluding that 'any gains stemming from data localization are too small to outweigh losses in terms of welfare and output in the general economy'.[160] The World Bank proposed a number of solutions to these dichotomies, one of which was that more work be undertaken when preparing trade agreements, which is explored later in this book. Significantly, this book expands on the position taken by the World Bank and argues strongly that in order for data flows to be fully integrated into the digital economy, the only way to achieve this is through internationalisation of the law and legal harmonisation. Anything short of that leaves the international community with the status quo, and nation states that do not believe in, or, want to reshape, or, even disband the current rules-based principle(s) and rules of law framework.

World Bank

The World Bank argues that the transfer and trade in data internationally can be improved through regulation. In support of this stance, this book examines other areas where reform is required to strengthen the adoption of the open data concept. The World Bank maintains that the durable nature of market power in data-driven markets and the challenges of designing antitrust remedies, ensuring that markets do not slip into entrenched market power in the first place, may be even more important than enforcing antitrust rules *ex post*.[161] In countries without a developed antitrust regime, including many low-income countries, this is the only line of policy response that encourages competitive data-driven markets.

157. Martín Molinuevo and Simon Gaillard, World Bank Group, Macroeconomics, Trade & Investment, Trade, Cross-Border Data, and the Next Regulatory Frontier: Law Enforcement and Data Localization requirements, MTI Practice Notes, 2018, https://documents1.worldbank.org/curated/en/903261543589829872/pdf/132606-BRI-PUBLIC-add-series-MTI-Practice-Note-3.pdf.
158. *Ibid.*, also *see*, Matthias Bauer, Hosuk Lee Makiyama and Erik van der Marel, 'The Costs of Data Localisation' (2014) ECIPE. Kommerskollegium, 'No Transfer, No Trade: The Importance of Cross-Border Data Transfers for Companies Based in Sweden', (2014) National Board of Trade of Sweden. Erik van der Marel, Hosuk Lee Makiyama, Matthia Bauer and Bert Verschelde, 'A Methodology to Estimate the Costs of Data Regulation', (2016) 146(2) International Economics 12-39, Anupam Chander and Uyen P. Le, 'Data Nationalism' (2015) 64(3) Emory Law Journal.
159. *Ibid.*
160. *Ibid.*
161. World Bank Group, Creating Value in the Data Economy: The Role of Competition, Trade, and Tax Policy, Chapter 7, 2021, 233, https://openknowledge.worldbank.org/bitstream/handle/10986/35218/9781464816000_Ch07.pdf.

The World Bank also emphasises the need to adopt mandatory and voluntary schemes to improve access to data. Governments need to do more work and provide regulatory options to facilitate access to data in digital ecosystems.[162] This requires governments to establish minimum standards and then provide the platform for the industry to develop sector-specific schemes. This is not a new structure; it has been used effectively in many well-developed industries such as primary production, agricultural and veterinary chemicals, airline industry (aircraft), food hygiene and processing, and the medical sector. The final chapter suggests a pathway forward and additional key factors that can help to improve the regulation of cross-border data flows.

Organisation for Economic Cooperation and Development [OECD]

The OECD notes that while there have been increasing attempts by some nation states to restrict cross-border data flows and the storage of that data, t the international community has made some progress towards developing international and regional legal frameworks.[163] In 1980, the OECD established the Guidelines on the Protection of Privacy and Transborder Flows of Personal Data (updated in 2013), followed five years later by the Declaration on Transborder Data Flows 1985. Both the Guidelines and the Declaration have been instrumental in establishing the policy platform for nation states to develop their respective data protection laws that, in part, provide for cross-border data flows.

In 2016, in the OECD Ministerial Declaration on the Digital Economy, ministers and high-level representatives from forty-one countries and the EU declared that they would support the free flow of information, through policies that reinforce the Internet's openness, while respecting applicable frameworks for privacy and data protection, and strengthening digital security.[164] They are of the view that specifically, given a particular level of data protection, international data agreements aim to increase the interoperability between (or even harmonise) different frameworks across national jurisdictions.[165] Relative to a situation with similar levels of data protection but incompatible regulatory approaches, this can reduce regulatory burdens and foster cross-border data flows for participating countries. The preamble of the original OECD (1980) Privacy Guidelines explicitly argues that disparities in national laws threaten to hamper the free flow of personal data across frontiers, causing potentially serious disruptions to important sectors of the economy. The preamble also states that this potential risk has been the reason why 'OECD member countries considered it necessary to develop Guidelines which would help to harmonise national privacy legislation and, while upholding such human rights [data privacy], would at the same time prevent interruptions in international flows of data'.[166]

162. *Ibid.*
163. Vincenzo Spiezia and Jan Tscheke, *International Agreements on Cross-Border Data Flows and International Trade: A Statistical Analysis*, Organisation for Economic Cooperation and Development, OECD Science, Technology and Industry Working Papers 2020/09, p. 16.
164. *Ibid.*, p. 6.
165. *Ibid.*
166. *Ibid.*

Most importantly, Part II of the 2013 Guidelines on the Protection of Privacy and Transborder Flows of Personal Data (the Guidelines) established what arguably are the most important set of principles concerning data flows. The principles have directed governments and regulators in their development of data laws. The principles are:

- *Collection Limitation* – There should be limits to the collection of personal data and any such data should be obtained by lawful and fair means and, where appropriate, with the knowledge or consent of the data subject.[167]
- *Data Quality* – Personal data should be relevant to the purposes for which they are to be used, and, to the extent necessary for those purposes, should be accurate, complete and kept up-to-date.[168]
- *Purpose Specification* – The purposes for which personal data are collected should be specified not later than at the time of data collection and the subsequent use limited to the fulfilment of those purposes or such others as are not incompatible with those purposes and as are specified on each occasion of change of purpose.[169]
- *Use Limitation* – Personal data should not be disclosed, made available or otherwise used for purposes other than those specified, with the consent of the data subject, by the authority of law.[170]
- *Security Safeguards* – Personal data should be protected by reasonable security safeguards against such risks as loss or unauthorised access, destruction, use, modification or disclosure of data.[171]
- *Openness* – There should be a general policy of openness about developments, practices and policies with respect to personal data. Means should be readily available of establishing the existence and nature of personal data, the main purposes of their use, as well as the identity and usual residence of the data controller.[172]
- *Individual Participation* – An individual should have the right (a) to obtain from a data controller, or otherwise, confirmation of whether or not the data

167. OECD Guidelines on the Protection of Privacy and Transborder Flows of Personal Data, 2013, https://www.oecd.org/sti/ieconomy/oecdguidelinesontheprotectionofprivacyandtransborderflowsofpersonaldata.htm. The OECD's thirty-eight member include: Austria, Australia, Belgium, Canada, Chile, Colombia, Costa Rica, Czech Republic, Denmark, Estonia, Finland, France, Germany, Greece, Hungary, Iceland, Ireland, Israel, Italy, Japan, Korea, Latvia, Lithuania, Luxembourg, Mexico, the Netherlands, New Zealand, Norway, Poland, Portugal, Slovak, Slovenia, Spain, Sweden, Switzerland, Turkey, the United Kingdom and the United States.
168. *Ibid*. *See also*, Professor Graham Greenleaf Asia-Pacific Developments in Information Privacy Law and Its Interpretation, 2006, pp. 3-11, https://www.google.com/search?q=Greenleaf+oecd+pRINSIPLES, Graham Greenleaf, 'APEC Privacy Principles Version 2: Not Quite so Lite, and NZ Wants OECD Full strength' 2003 10(3) Privacy Law and Policy Reporter 45. Graham Greenleaf, 'It's Nearly 2020, so What Fate Awaits the 1980 OECD Privacy Guidelines?' (A Background Paper for the 2019 OECD Privacy Guidelines Review) (2019) 159 Privacy Laws & Business International Report 18-21, pp. 3-6.
169. *Ibid.*, pp. 3-11.
170. *Ibid.*
171. *Ibid.*
172. *Ibid.*

controller has data relating to him; (b) to have communicated to him, data relating to him within a reasonable time; at a charge, if any, that is not excessive;in a reasonable manner; and in a form that is readily intelligible to him; (c) to be given reasons if a request made under subparagraphs(a) and (b) is denied, and to be able to challenge such denial; and (d) to challenge data relating to him and, if the challenge is successful to have the data erased, rectified, completed or amended.[173]

- *Accountability* – A data controller should be accountable for complying with measures which give effect to the principles stated above.[174]

These principles can be found in all of the jurisdictions examined in this book, to varying degrees. Some jurisdictions such as the EU, the UK and Australia have fully embraced these principles within their respective data protection laws. On the other hand, Indonesia and India[175] have yet to establish specific data protection laws indicating full adoption of the aforementioned principles. Since the 2013 review of the Guidelines, the OECD has acknowledged that personal data has come to play an even more important role in all economies, societies and everyday lives. That is close-to-real-time collection and analysis of large volumes of data, generated from a myriad of devices, transactions, production and communication processes coupled with the increasing use of AI, are accelerating knowledge and value creation across society. These trends in data collection, analysis and use are transforming business models and organisational practice across all sectors of our economies.[176]

In 2021, the OECD undertook a review of the Guidelines,[177] which confirmed the importance of privacy as an international reference on minimum standards for privacy and PDP that adherents implement in practice through legislation, enforcement and policy measures. Significant though is how, against the backdrop of technological developments which continue to evolve, this issue creates tensions with established legal norms.[178] Graham Greenleaf makes an important point: 'changed international environment for privacy post-GDPR 2016/679[179] leaves the OECD with a choice. The choice depends to a significant extent on what approach the US decides to take'.[180] He believes that:

173. *Ibid.*
174. *Ibid.*
175. Robert Walters, Leon Trakman and Bruno Zeller, *Data Protection Law: A Comparative Analysis of Asia-Pacific and European Approaches*, Springer (2019), Chapters 6 and 7.
176. *Ibid.*
177. OECD, Report on the Implementation of the Recommendation of the Council Concerning Guidelines Governing the Protection of Privacy and Transborder Flows of Personal Data, JT03473010, (2021), pp. 4-6.
178. *Ibid.*, p. 6.
179. Regulation (EU) 2016/679 of the European Parliament and of the Council of 27 April 2016 on the protection of natural persons with regard to the processing of personal data and on the free movement of such data, and repealing Directive 95/46/EC (General Data Protection Regulation)
180. Graham Greenleaf, 'It's Nearly 2020, so What Fate Awaits the 1980 OECD Privacy Guidelines?' (A Background Paper for the 2019 OECD Privacy Guidelines Review) (2019) 159 Privacy Laws & Business International Report 18-2, UNSW Law Research Paper No. 19-42, Graham Greenleaf

> one option is to leave the OECD Guidelines as they are, ignoring almost all of the stronger rights for data subjects, and stronger obligations on controllers and processors, becoming common in many of the data privacy laws already enacted in 134 countries. This might be coupled, as in 2013, with adding a few stronger implementation features, and some more restrictions on data export limitations or data localisation.[181]

The second option according to Greenleaf, and retaining Part Two of the 2013 version:

> is to add a considerable range of new rights and obligations reflecting some of the content of the GDPR and Convention 108 + , thus positioning the OECD Guidelines as a more credible contender to be a moderate minimum standard of data privacy protections, and as a candidate for what convergence (or even 'interoperability') initiatives could aim to implement.[182]

In Greenleaf's reference to the US, it is not understood whether it would agree to such a proposal. To date, the US has not been willing to establish a federal law for data protection, let alone a comprehensive single legal framework for data flows. Is the reference to convergence a step towards harmonisation? Arguably, it could be conceived as such, although in my view it maintains the status quo.

The position taken by the OECD will be reinforced throughout this book. On the one hand, there is tension between the future digital economy and the need for governments to create a legal framework to open up the flow of data. On the other, there is an expectation from citizens in most communities that their respective governments retain or even strengthen the controls established to protect their personal data, particularly if it is being transferred internationally. A further more pressing issue is that while these OECD Guidelines provide a benchmark, they are not enforceable, and no state is required to integrate them into its national data laws. The non-binding nature of the OECD Principles and Guidelines only accentuates the fragmentation of the legal and policy landscape. However, they can indirectly become enforceable when provided for by national laws, and the provisions that support the OECD Principles themselves. The Guidelines themselves only recommend that member countries adhere to the Principles in order to achieve a minimum standard; reduce the differences between national laws; protect personal data, and eliminate restrictions on transborder flows of data.[183] Despite the continued development and application of this approach, the OECD itself has acknowledged that there have been a number of

AM, Professor of Law & Information Systems, UNSW, Australia, and a member of the OECD's Privacy Guidelines Expert Group (PGEG).

181. *Ibid.*

182. *Ibid.* Whether this option will appeal to the US probably depends on whether it moves to adopt a federal data privacy law, and therefore becomes interested in negotiating a future position for US interests, rather than defending a now-untenable position of the past. Part Two of the OECD Guidelines 2013, deal with Cross-Border Privacy Law enforcement Co-operation.

183. OECD Guidelines on the Protection of Privacy and Transborder Flows of Personal Data, https://www.oecd.org/sti/ieconomy/oecdguidelinesontheprotectionofprivacyandtransborder flowsofpersonaldata.htm.

member countries who have recommended the establishment of an international binding convention.[184]

Nonetheless, and while the 2021 review was important, it retained the principles-based approach that has emerged as the baseline for data flows and their regulation. There is no doubt that these principles have been pivotal in securing data flows, albeit, in an ad hoc and incoherent way by nation states. On this basis, it is argued that it could be time for the current principle-based approach to be reconsidered. It has provided the foundation for the development and implementation of concepts such as interoperability and data adequacy, albeit not by all jurisdictions. An essential question arises: can the principles-based approach be revised? Furthermore: is there an appetite for change and what might that change look like? In this book, it is argued that interoperability, data adequacy and the principle-based model could be the first step to legal harmonisation. The second step is to progress to the internationalisation of data laws, particularly in the area of data flows. However, it is argued that by internationalising the data framework to obtain a deeper level of legal harmonisation, this will provide greater legal certainty for data and the digital economy. Some member countries of the OECD see the advantages of undertaking such a process and have called for a binding international convention.[185] Additionally, member countries reaffirm the above and are of the view that the current OECD Guidelines are a good starting point for the internationalisation of this area of the law through an international convention.[186] Here it is argued that the current approach is significantly fragmented, and by continuing down this path, this only increases the cost to business and hampers doing business in the digital economy. The problem with the current model is that it requires an organisation to expend a significant amount of cost and effort to understand both its own national data laws and those of other jurisdictions to which personal data is being transferred. Thus, if governments are serious about opening up the digital economy to small- and medium-sized businesses, legal harmonisation will reduce transaction costs and make it easier for entities to enter and exit the market.

Madrid Resolution International Standards on the Protection of Personal Data and Privacy

The 2009 Madrid Resolution came about as a 'result of joint work by data protection authorities in fifty countries under the leadership of the Spanish Data Protection Agency'.[187] It provides a model incorporating universal standards of data protection, thus covering data protection values and principles that are safeguarded on five continents. It was developed to provide proactive 'measures such as procedures to detect and prevent security breaches, the appointment of a data protection officer,

184. *Ibid.*, at 30.
185. *Ibid.*
186. *Ibid.*
187. Mrs Andreja Rither, *Protection of Privacy and Personal Data on the Internet and Online Media*, 2011, paragraphs 27, 50, 51. European Council, http://assembly.coe.int/CommitteeDocs/2011/RihtervieprivееE.pdf, also *see* Madrid Resolution, *International Standards on the Protection of Personal Data and Privacy*, 2009, https://edps.europa.eu/sites/edp/files/publication/09-11-05_madrid_int_standards_en.pdf.

privacy impact assessments, and the accountability principle which calls for internal arrangements that can be used to demonstrate that the controller is complying with data protection rules'[188]

The Madrid Resolution (MR) was intended to expand upon the OECD Principles, and improve the facilitation of the international flows of personal data while maintaining a high level of protection for that data. It reinforces the OECD Principles and addresses the following:

- Principle of lawfulness.
- Purpose specification.
- Lawfulness and fairness.
- Proportionality.
- Data quality.
- Openness.
- Accountability.
- Legitimacy.
- Sensitive data.
- Provision of processing services.[189]

Hence, the MRs promote the digital economy and the open data concept. Moreover, it adds to the already-important principles of accountability, purpose specification, and data quality, by focusing also on legitimacy and sensitive data along with processing services. Under the principle of legitimacy, the MR restricts the processing of data to situations where consent has been provided by the data subject.[190] However, this is problematic because the variables applying to the giving of consent vary from nation to nation. For instance, the EU has a high threshold for what constitutes consent. At the other end of the spectrum, consent in New Zealand has limited effect. The MR further requires that the rights and freedoms of the data subject prevail[191] when personal data is being processed.

The MR defines personal data as 'any information relating to an identified natural person or a person who may be identified by means reasonably likely to be used'.[192] This indicates the MR's strong focus on the rights-based approach, at least according to the principle of legitimacy.

188. *Ibid.*, p. 13.
189. Madrid Resolution, *International Standards on the Protection of Personal Data and Privacy*, 2009, sections 4-12, https://edps.europa.eu/sites/edp/files/publication/09-11-05_madrid_int_standards_en.pdf. Working Group comprises Data Authorities from (Austria), (Belgium), (Burkina-Fasso), (Canada), (Czech Republic), (France), (Germany), (Hong Kong), (Ireland), (Netherlands), (Portugal), (Slovenia), (Spain), (Switzerland), (United Kingdom). Note, some states such as Spain have representatives from provinces within such as Catalonia.
190. *Ibid.*, at 12, After obtaining the free, unambiguous and informed consent of the data subject.
191. *Ibid.*, at 12.
192. *Ibid.* Where the processing is necessary for the maintenance or the performance of a legal relationship between the responsible person and the data subject; or where the processing is necessary for complying with an obligation imposed on the responsible person by the applicable national legislation, or is carried out by a public authority where necessary for the legitimate exercise of its powers.

The issue of sensitive data has taken on greater significance. In some nation states, data subjects have more protection and control of sensitive data. The states examined in this book, and others worldwide, have different notions of what constitutes personal data. Some states do not separate general personal data from sensitive data. The MR defines sensitive data as that which affects the 'data subject's most intimate sphere, gives rise to discrimination and can pose a serious risk to the data subject'.[193] In addition to this, the MR provides a level of detail that can be seen in some nation states' definition of personal data, which may include information about race, ethnic origin, political opinions, religious or philosophical beliefs, health status, and gender orientation. For some jurisdictions, this data constitutes the most intimate and personal information pertaining to an individual. Such data can be polarising and can signify whether a person belongs to the mainstream or to a minority group. Therefore, it is argued that individual rights are prioritised by the MR.

Another indication that the MR takes the rights-based approach, is that it places some responsibility on the individual processing the data. In part, it extends the rights-based approach to ensure a level of adequacy by requiring that 'the responsible person ensures that the processing service provider guarantees, at least, the level of protection contained in this document and in the applicable national legislation'.[194] Adequacy decisions (ADs) by the EU have become increasingly important to the flow of data as the same level of protection should be afforded to both the sender and the receiver of data. The prevailing view is that, while many national states other than the EU do not have an AD programme, they do require a level of protection that is similar to that of the country of origin.

Therefore, the international transfers of data according to Principle 15, 'can be undertaken when the state to which such data are transmitted affords, as a minimum, the level of protection provided for in this document'.[195] Significant though is how international transfers can be made to a nation state that does not have the equivalent level of protection afforded by the MR, and whether the recipient will guarantee the same level of protection. While not diluting the overall aim of the MR, to ensure there is equal protection of both parties in international transfers, it also provides a baseline for multinational organisations to operate. Put another way, if an organisation has offices in Paris, Madrid, London, Canada and Hong Kong, international transfers of data can proceed although the respective national laws differ in terms of the level of protection afforded to data subjects. Provided that the office in Hong Kong can guarantee that the data received in Canada will be afforded the same level of protection as in Hong Kong, the transfer can take place. A similar level of transfer can also be undertaken under contractual arrangements between the parties. However, the contract itself would need to stipulate that a level of protection has been afforded to the data being transferred. This also applies in some jurisdictions where organisations are required to obtain the regulator's approval for the transfer of data. While discussion of

193. *Ibid.*, at 13.
194. *Ibid.*
195. *Ibid.*, at 15.

this issue is beyond the scope of this book, some nation states require that international data transfers can proceed only after the relevant authority has given approval.

Notwithstanding the above, it can be asserted that the MR follows the EU model in that, regarding any data transfers, the data subjects have certain rights that give them some control of their data. Furthermore, data subjects have the right to access their personal data. They can also request that their data be rectified or deleted. Rectification can be undertaken where the personal data is incomplete, inaccurate, unnecessary or excessive.[196] When there is a legitimate reason for doing so, a data subject may object to the processing of personal data.[197] The remainder of the MR principles promotes the security of the data, coordination and cooperation amongst states. In effect, it is argued that the MR replicate many elements of the rights-based model of the EU. In one of the major attempts to establish a baseline of internationally agreed standards for data transfers since the 1980s OECD Principles and Convention 108, the MR achieves a level of success. Problematic though is the lack of nation states participating in the MR, which is no more than twenty as of 2022. Another important issue is that while they briefly depart from the rights-based model, the MR principles more or less reinforce today's legal framework for ensuring that data is afforded as high a level of equivalent protection by the recipient states as possible. The MR does not mention the development of international laws or the need for legal harmonisation. Therefore, the MR needs to be revisited and amended to include new principles for international law and harmonisation of cross-border laws.

United National Commission for Trade and Development

The United National Commission for Trade and Development (UNTCAD) is another international organisation that has for some time been working in the area of transnational data flows. In 2021, UNTCAD released a Digital Economy report: *Cross-border data flows and development: For* whom the data flow.[198] Specifically, the report notes that the outbreak of the COVID-19 'pandemic has accelerated the process of digital transformation and added urgency for Governments to respond. A key challenge is how to govern and harness the surge in digital data for the global good. It has been estimated that global Internet traffic in 2022 will exceed all the Internet traffic up to 2016'.[199] As well as not being a regulator, UNTCAD has no responsibility for developing international or regional legal instruments to facilitate data flows, although it conducts comprehensive research to provide governments and private sectors with

196. *Ibid.*, at 16-17. Deletion of personal data is not justified where personal data must be retained for the performance of an obligation imposed on the responsible person by the applicable national legislation, or possibly by the contractual relationship between the responsible person and the data subject.
197. *Ibid.*, at 17.
198. United National Commission for Trade and Development [UNCTAD], Digital 2021 Economy Report: Cross-Border Data Flows and Development: For Whom the Data Flow. Within the UNCTAD Division on Technology and Logistics, the ICT Policy Section carries out policy-oriented analytical work on the development implications of information and communications technologies (ICTs) and e-commerce. There are 195 members of UNCTAD.
199. *Ibid.*, p. v.

information on 'trade, investment, finance and technology'.[200] Apart from providing training in the Digital Trade, UNTCAD's research reveals how complex the regulation of data and data flows has become in the contemporary world, asserting that 'the complexities involved in governing data and data flows across borders in ways that can bring sustainable development benefits'. It also stresses that the state of the international debate on how to regulate cross-border data flows is at an impasse, and positions tend to be polarised. The current regulatory landscape is 'patchy, reflecting starkly different approaches adopted by different countries, with strong influences from the major economic powers'.[201] The position taken by UNCTAD reaffirms that this book is timely. This book emphasises the need for a global policy that can mitigate or eliminate the legal impediments and problems facing governments and regulators who are attempting to open up the digital economy and expand the trade in data. In doing so, this work will make a significant contribution to the policy and legal debate in and across this area of the economy.

The UNCTAD also makes the point that any attempt to 'understand data and their flows requires a number of steps'.[202] This is without having to understand the legal framework. Yet, they are interconnected because data has been defined by national law. To date, no single international definition of personal data has been offered. The UNCTAD argues that:

> there has always been data and information associated with commercial transactions – such as billing data, banking data, names and delivery addresses – which are mainly volunteered and rarely create policy-related issues, as long as new digital economy players work by the same rules as the conventional economy ... raw data gathered from individual activities, products, events and behaviours have no value in themselves, but can generate value once aggregated, processed and monetized, or used for social purposes ... the raw data is converted into digital intelligence in the form of statistics, databases and insights, and information such as the results for data products, may be considered as services in trade statistics when sold across borders.[203]

Most importantly, according to UNCTAD, data flows do not constitute the trade in data. Therefore, the regulatory landscape of UNCTAD should be different from that of the traditional trade in goods and services. This approach creates a tension in the current attempt to harmonise cross-border data flows and the law that underpins this activity. In part, this argument is in direct conflict with the long-standing rules and guidelines that have been established to facilitate data flows in order to boost economic activity. It also reveals the various and often opposing positions taken by organisations that are closely examining this new economy. However, UNCTAD is arguing that data flows are not trade-in data although they may constitute services and, therefore, data flows should not be regulated in the same way as other services or goods.

200. UNCTAD, Publications, 2022, https://unctad.org/publications.
201. UNCTAD, Digital 2021 Economy Report: Cross-Border Data Flows and Development: For Whom the Data Flow, p. vi.
202. *Ibid.*, p. 4.
203. *Ibid.*

An important issue that has arisen is how international trade governance is informed by statistics that rely on the types, values and locations of trade (including source and destination).[204] UNCTAD notes that such an approach is challenging, if not impossible, when tracking cross-border data flows. They note that, currently, no official statistics exist.[205] While this is the case at present (2022), given the rate at which technologies are developing, it is possible that in future we will have the infrastructure and systems required to track and collate international data flows and the amount or cost of the data involved in the transaction. The UNCTAD also makes the point that although well-established approaches are being applied to international trade across different territories (e.g., rules of origin), they cannot be easily applied to data, given their nature.[206] For them, the flows of raw data that are not linked to a specific exchange of a good or service are not included in the concept of digital trade. Yet, as highlighted earlier when combined with data analytics, the data itself can be considered part of a service.

Furthermore, UNCTAD states:

> data suggest that they need to be treated differently from conventional goods and services, including in their international transfers. In the new context of the data-driven digital economy, concepts such as ownership and sovereignty are being challenged. Rather than trying to determine who 'owns' the data, what matters is who has the right to access, control and use the data.[207]

Therefore, what has emerged are competing views on the trade or flow of data. This may never be reconciled unless governments and regulators tax the transaction, or regulate it in the same way as is done for general goods and other services.

Asia Pacific Economic Cooperation [APEC] CBPR

First, the CBPR 2015, in part, 'provide a regional system of data certification'.[208] The framework is a government-backed data privacy certification that companies can obtain to signify their willingness to comply with internationally recognised data privacy protections. Significantly, however, the CBPR is recognised only in a small number of 'trade agreements among Canada, Mexico and the US. Japan has recognized the CBPR System to enable cross-border data transfers in compliance with domestic law'.[209] Thus, there is more work to be done by member countries. The current membership of APEC is made up of the major economies of the world such as the US, China, Japan, Canada and Russia. As of January 2022, APEC had only twenty-three

204. *Ibid.*, p. 5.
205. *Ibid.*
206. *Ibid.*
207. *Ibid.*, pp. 4-5.
208. Asia Pacific Economic Cooperation Cross-Border Privacy Rules, 2022, https://www.apec.org/about-us/about-apec/fact-sheets/what-is-the-cross-border-privacy-rules-system. Members as at January 2022, Australia; Brunei Darussalam; Canada; Chile; People's Republic of China; Hong Kong, China; Indonesia; Japan; Republic of Korea; Malaysia; Mexico; New Zealand; Papua New Guinea; Peru; the Philippines; the Russian Federation; Singapore; Chinese Taipei; Thailand; the United States of America; Vietnam.
209. *Ibid.*

members. The notable absentees that are examined in this book are Indonesia, India and the UK. Nevertheless, it could be an appropriate time for them to consider joining this multilateral organisation, in order to strengthen the level of international cooperation and development of rules and standards for cross-border data flows. Now that the UK is no longer a member of the EU, it is free to join this group.

Most notably, the CBPR require member countries to provide a level of PDP that includes:

- Enforceable standards.[210]
- Accountability.[211]
- Risk-based protections.[212]
- Consumer-friendly complaint handling.[213]
- Consumer empowerment.[214]
- Consistent protections.[215]
- Cross-border enforcement cooperation.[216]

The framework above constitutes a set of principles that provide Member States with a basis on which to establish guidelines in addition to their national laws on privacy and data protection. The APEC framework does not replace the national laws of Member States; rather, it adds another set of control mechanisms. Although it is a non-binding instrument, the national laws of Member States should ensure that there 'are appropriate binding mechanisms and principles that can be enforced. Graham Greenleaf notes that the result of some Asia–Pacific countries acceding to Convention 108 and the Optional Protocol would be a multi-tiered system of international data protection in the Asia–Pacific'.[217] Greenleaf argues that for the first-tier countries:

210. *Ibid.* To join, participating economies must demonstrate that CBPR programme requirements will be legally enforceable against certified companies.
211. *Ibid.* To become certified, a company must demonstrate to an Accountability Agent – an independent CBPR System-recognised public or private sector entity – that they meet the CBPR programme requirements, and the company is subject to ongoing monitoring and enforcement.
212. *Ibid.* Certified companies must implement security safeguards for personal data that are proportional to the probability and severity of the harm threatened, the confidential nature or sensitivity of the information, and the context in which it is held.
213. *Ibid.* Accountability Agents receive and investigate complaints and resolve disputes between consumers and certified companies in relation to non-compliance with its programme requirements.
214. *Ibid.* Certified companies must provide consumers with the opportunity to access and correct their personal data. Further, by publicly certifying to the CBPR System's requirements, consumers gain insight into the privacy practices on business with which they choose to do business.
215. *Ibid.* While governments may impose additional requirements with which certified companies must still comply, all participants must agree to abide by the fifty CBPR programme requirements, facilitating the implementation of the same baseline protections across different legal regimes.
216. *Ibid.* The CBPR System provides a mechanism for regulatory authorities to cooperate on the enforcement of programme requirements.
217. Graham Greenleaf, 'Five years of the APEC Privacy Framework: Failure or promise?' (2009) 25(1) Computer Law & Security Review 42.

> membership of the Council of Europe Convention and Additional Protocol would guarantee free flow of personal information both between their Asia-Pacific peers who are also members, and with European countries. On the second tier, other regional countries with existing privacy laws would be likely to have those laws regarded as 'adequate' by other countries in the region for data export purposes.[218]

He also makes the point that:

> for the remaining countries ('economies'), APEC's Privacy Framework would provide a relatively low level of privacy protection to which economies with little or no existing protection could adopt by whatever means they chose, and a CBPR procedure which might give them some assistance in relation to data exports with similar economies or (with more difficulty), the countries that are also in the second or first tier. It would be an initiative which would allow all Asia-Pacific countries to move forward.[219]

Professor Greenleaf offered these insights in 2009, and while they still have a level of application, it is time to expand on the concept of adequacy over the longer term. In my view it may not serve or provide the necessary framework for the digital economy to thrive particularly given the onset of the IR4. However, a note of caution is required, even under an adequacy framework or full harmonisation, there might be an increased risk of data falling into the wrong hands. While some nation states are pushing forward with the implementation of the open data concept, unless this is undertaken in a way that encourages all nations to buy into the project, it will be highly problematic with some nations accessing and using data for purposes and practices that could undermine the social and economic fabric of societies.

Today, this is no more evident than under Australia's privacy model, where the Privacy Act (PA) 1988 is underpinned by the Australian Privacy Principles. Both the Act and APPs provide a pathway for the regulatory enforcement of privacy for cross-border data flows (*see* Chapter 2). It further promotes the idea that the private sector of member countries can also be party to the rules, which makes them accountable to the regulator. Importantly, they are another layer of controls that set a minimum standard for member countries to protect the privacy of data subjects in cross-border data flows. Additionally, it attempts to balance the policy objectives of nation states by minimising the possibility of establishing unnecessary barriers that will restrict data and information flows. Essentially, the framework goes some way to ensuring that data flows are not impeded; instead, they are improved and strengthened and complement the transnational trade and economic development of APEC members.

The CBPR is very similar to the OECD Principles. However, they do diverge on some points. The enforceable standards under the CBPR can be aligned with accountability under the OECD Principles. The notable difference is that under the CBPR, the focus is on the data subject as a consumer. Hence, it is more concerned with consumer empowerment and the handling of complaints. It could be argued that this aligns with

218. *Ibid.*
219. *Ibid.*

individual participation. Both the CBPR and the OECD provide for the data subjects to exert their right of control over their data. Another notable similarity is the cross-border enforcement cooperation since both encourage this activity at a nation state level. Yet, in practice, this might not occur as readily as is required.

Association of Southeast Asian Nations

The Association of Southeast Asian Nations (ASEAN)[220] has released a number of strategic documents that guide the development of cross-border data flows throughout South East Asia. The most recent is the ASEAN Master Digital Plan 2021 (Digital Plan),[221] best described as a high-level policy initiative that facilitates three desirable outcomes: (1) to extend current efforts and ensure connectivity to the Internet throughout ASEAN; (2) to ensure that any connectivity is safe and relevant to the needs of end-users; and (3) to provide the platform for existing barriers to be removed to ensure business and consumers can operate in a coherent and efficient environment. These three outcomes, while aspirational within a five-year period, are underpinned by a number of desirable actions. Notably, the achievement of these desired outcomes will deliver a 'trusted digital service and prevent consumer harm. A key part of this is ensuring that cybersecurity and digital data governance best practices are adopted as widely as possible, both to mitigate the direct impact of a breach on business and consumers and to build'.[222] As detailed below, a core element of the development and implementation of data policy and law within the digital economy is the assurance that there will be a high level of trust. Establishing this level of trust will support system certainty, infrastructure, and frameworks. One of the main enabling actions of DO3 is to 'identify improvements in legal and regulatory measures on the management of protection of data and other data-related activities that could be harmful'.[223]

Further to the above, DO4 provides that there is a sustainable competitive market for the supply of digital services. To achieve this, ASEAN is going to continue to identify opportunities to 'harmonise digital regulation to facilitate cross-border data flows'.[224]

220. Association of South East Asian Nations [ASEAN], a Regional Bloc that is made of member countries including, Brunei, Cambodia, Indonesia, Laos, Malaysia, Myanmar, the Philippines, Singapore, Thailand, and Vietnam, https://asean.org/about-asean/member-states/.
221. ASEAN Master Digital Plan 2021-2025, https://asean.org/book/asean-digital-masterplan-2025/ A DO is an action or an aim that directs the future governance of digital regulation.
222. *Ibid.*, p. 6.
223. *Ibid.*, p. 16.
224. *Ibid.*, p. 17. At p. 22, the Digital Plan makes the point that the AMS should build on the ASEAN Framework on Personal Data Protection (2016) and ASEAN Framework on Digital Data Governance to build harmonised principles-based data protection and privacy regulations and frameworks, including on data management and cross-border data flows. This will facilitate cross- border digital trade by encouraging user trust in sharing their personal data. ASEAN should build on the Implementing Guidelines for the ASEAN Cross Border Data Flows Mechanism (2021) to develop, recognise and implement a suite of data transfer mechanisms to facilitate cross-border data flows. This would improve the region's ability to ensure the eventual interoperability of standards with APEC CBPR, the European Union's GDPR amongst others. ASEAN could develop a framework for common policies for extremely large collections of data and the use of machine learning and AI on those collections.

Regarding cross-border data flows, the Digital Plan expands on the open data concept by encouraging ASEAN Member States to build upon existing work by commissioning a research project to map the remaining barriers to cross-border digital data flows within ASEAN. Once the barriers are mapped and prioritised, ASEAN could identify opportunities to either align regulation (respect of data localisation requirements) or develop mutual recognition of data protection regimes. In the meantime, regulatory sandboxes could be explored as an option to facilitate cross-border data flows.[225] However, ASEAN is facing challenges similar to those of the rest of the world, in that Member States will need to balance the need to open up cross-border data flows with that of protecting citizens' personal data. This will not be easy to achieve in the short to medium term because each Member State has vastly different laws, and some states such as Indonesia have been developing and debating specific data protection laws for more than five years. In addition, the ASEAN Telecommunications and Information Technology Ministers Meeting – Framework on Digital Governance[226] 'sets out the strategic priorities, principles and initiatives to guide the ASEAN Member States in their policy and regulatory approaches towards digital data governance in the digital economy'.[227]

Figure 1.2 shows the four priority areas of the Framework on Digital Governance.[228]

225. *Ibid.*, p. 23.
226. ASEAN Telecommunications and Information Technology Ministers Meeting – Framework on Digital Governance, 2012, https://asean.org/wp-content/uploads/2012/05/6B-ASEAN-Framework-on-Digital-Data-Governance_Endorsedv1.pdf.
227. *Ibid.*, p. 2.
228. *Ibid.*

Figure 1.2 ASEAN Framework for Digital Governance 2012[229]

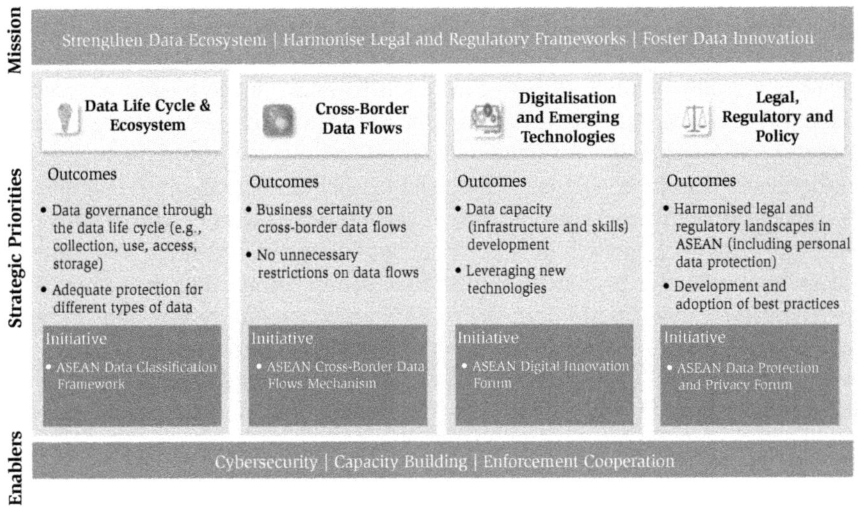

Centrally, the priority areas of data life cycle, cross-border data flows, digitisation and emerging technologies and legal, regulatory and policy will be fundamental to the delivery of the Digital Plan and achieving a balance between data flows of data and the protection of citizens (consumers). One of the most important directions in the framework is that Member States develop pathways to harmonise legal and regulatory frameworks. It is calling for greater legal harmonisation and convergence within and across the ASEAN Member States, which should be strengthened to take this to the international level. However, ASEAN should consider promoting this framework globally so as to assist the international community to develop a single and agreed framework for data flows and data protection. This strategic direction should be underpinned by the following seven principles:

(1) Data Integrity and Trustworthiness.
(2) Data Use and Access Control.
(3) Data Security.
(4) Cross-Border Data Flows.
(5) Capacity Development.
(6) PDP and Privacy Regulation.

229. ASEAN Telecommunications and Information Technology Ministers Meeting – Framework on Digital Governance, 2012, https://asean.org/wp-content/uploads/2012/05/6B-ASEAN-Framework-on-Digital-Data-Governance_Endorsedv1.pdf.

(7) Development and Adoption of Best Practices.[230]

Arguably, these principles reflect the OECD Principles under the Guidelines on the Protection of Privacy and Transborder Flows of Personal Data, as detailed earlier in this chapter. The ensuing issue for ASEAN collectively is the fragmented approach taken by Member States under their current data protection laws.[231] A key theme emerging in ASEAN strategic policy documents is the necessity to build a high level of trust over time. This cannot be achieved without the right legal and policy settings. ASEAN is on the right track, although the challenge will be not only to harmonise the laws of the respective Member States but also to encourage harmonisation of those member countries that have not established specific laws in this area. One significant problem is that Member States have social, religious and cultural differences which means that they have different views of Internet-related privacy and cross-border data flows. Also, the citizens of some Member States have different levels of understanding of data flows and Internet privacy. For instance, Singapore and Indonesia, although they are neighbours, have different views on Internet-related privacy. The late Lee Kwan Yew, in his speech to the National Day Rally in 1986, quoted in the Straits Times on 20 April 1987, stated:

> I am often accused of interfering in the private lives of citizens. Yes, if I did not, had I not done that, we wouldn't be here today. And I say without the slightest remorse, that we wouldn't be here, we would not have made economic progress, if we had not intervened on very personal matters – who your neighbour is, how you live, the noise you make, how you spit, or what language you use. We decide what is right.[232]

Singapore has chartered its own course in many areas of policy and the law, underpinned by the fact that this country follows British common law. It has become one of the most successful nations in the world in regard to alleviating poverty, transitioning from being a third- to a first-world country in less than fifty years.[233] This is despite the fact that this country has no natural resources and relies on many imports. On the other hand, the Indonesian legal system is based on civil law that is also a mix of customary and religious law. Of the ASEAN Member States, Indonesia is the largest economy and has the largest population. There are three kinds of laws (are) enacted to regulate citizens in Indonesia. First, customary law, for example, the citizens of Indonesia still use this in their daily lives. Second, civil law, which is

---

230. *Ibid.*, pp. 3-8. The principle on personal data protection and privacy regulation establishes the need for harmonisation of personal data protection regulations within ASEAN. ASEAN Member States should endeavour to work towards establishing personal data protection regulations in their respective countries. The principle on cross-border data flows is intended to maximise the free flow of data within ASEAN to foster a vibrant data ecosystem while at the same time ensuring that the data transferred is given the necessary protection.
231. Robert Walters, Leon Trakman and Bruno Zeller, *Data Protection Law: A Comparative Analysis of Asia-Pacific and European Approaches*, Springer (2019), Chapter 17.
232. In Quotes: Lee Kwan Yew, *British Broadcasting Commission*, 2015, https://www.bbc.com/news/world-asia-31582842.
233. Jon Quah, *Why Singapore Works: Five Secrets of Singapore's Success*, Emerald Publishing Limited, (2018), p. 5.

influenced by Dutch colonisation, and third, Islamic law. Interestingly, dating back to Dutch colonisation, inhabitants of the Indonesian archipelago have been divided for legal purposes into various 'population groups' (*golongan rakyat, bevolkingsgroupen*), based primarily on racial origin.[234]

Unlike Singapore and other neighbours such as Australia, Indonesian courts have considered what privacy means to the state and its citizens. In 2003, the court affirmed the growing importance of privacy. In *006/PUU-I/2003, KPKPN v. KPK*, the Court stated that 'privacy rights are derogable rights therefore the State can impose restrictions to prevent the abuse of authority through wiretapping and recording, laws and regulations on wiretapping and recording procedures are needed'.[235] This case concerned the application and use of powers by law enforcement agencies using technology and the impact on privacy and demonstrates that privacy was becoming more important as a wider societal issue within the Indonesian community.[236] Three years later, in 2006, the Indonesian Constitutional Court in *Judgment No. 012, 016/PUU-IV/2006*, affirmed the importance of privacy as a fundamental right within the state. The Court stated:

> According to Article 28F of the Indonesian Constitution, there is a guarantee regarding privacy rights that cannot be breached by whatever means since it has been considered a human right. The right to privacy is a fundamental human right and recognized under Article 17 International Covenant on Civil and Political Rights (ICCPR) which has been ratified by Indonesia since 2005 (Law no. 12 of 2005). Personal information of the Applicant has been intercepted and recorded according to Article 12 (1) letter without permission whereas, according to the Law, all applicant's communication both privately or publicly shall be protected.[237]

These different approaches taken by two Member States of ASEAN, without considering the other Member States, are significant. It has since been found that Singapore has encroached on the private lives of its citizens. Apart from the difference in the legal families adopted by Singapore and Indonesia, at the time of writing, both countries were planning to implement specific data protection laws. However, Member States of Indonesia's understanding of privacy generally is relatively young, as highlighted by the ratification of key international law in 2005 and the judiciary affirming this in 2006. Arguably, in order to implement the ASEAN strategic direction successfully, there is a significant amount of work to do to ensure that the citizens of

234. Ahmad, A *Law and Development in Changing Indonesia*, IDE Asian Law Series No. 8 Law and Development in Asian Countries, Institute of Developing Economies (IDE), JETRO, (2001). In Robert Walters, Leon Trakman and Bruno Zeller, *Data Protection Law: A Comparative Analysis of Asia-Pacific and European Approaches*, Springer (2019), p. 170.
235. Sinta Dewi, *Balancing Privacy Rights and Legal Enforcement: Indonesia Practices*, Presented at the 2011 IAITL Legal Conference Series, Lecturer at Faculty of Law, Department of Law and Technology, University of Padjadjaran Bandung, Indonesia. In Robert Walters, Leon Trakman and Bruno Zeller, *Data Protection Law: A Comparative Analysis of Asia-Pacific and European Approaches*, Springer (2019), p. 170.
236. *Ibid.*, 170.
237. Judgment No. 012, *016/PUU-IV/2006*. In Robert Walters, Leon Trakman and Bruno Zeller, *Data Protection Law: A Comparative Analysis of Asia-Pacific and European Approaches*, Springer (2019), p. 170.

each state have some knowledge of cross-border data flows and the protections afforded to that data.

Model Contractual Clauses (MCCs), otherwise known as SCC, are being used as a legal tool for data transfers.[238] Of the documents analysed under ASEAN, the MCCs are the only legal mechanisms that have been developed. They are 'contractual terms and conditions that may be included in the binding legal agreements between parties transferring personal data to each other across borders'.[239] To date, they have been considered standards and are not mandatory. More generally, privacy and data protection across the ASEAN Member States vary considerably. Furthermore, ASEAN is adopting a broad and flexible approach to the regulatory standards for data flows. That is, they recognise that other mechanisms, tools and standards can be used to provide the same level of data protection. These recognise 'codes of conduct, binding corporate rules, certifications, such as ISO series relating to security and privacy techniques, APEC Cross Border Privacy Rules and Privacy Recognition for Processors Systems, or other legally enforceable mechanisms'.[240] The clauses have been developed specifically to operate between a controller and processor, or controller and controller. Similar to general legislation, the MCCs provide an overall framework for contractual relations between parties transferring data across international borders.

Council of Europe Convention 108

Convention 108, established in 1981, was intended to 'secure in the territory of each Party for every individual, whatever his nationality or residence, respect for his rights and fundamental freedoms, and in particular his right to privacy, with regard to automatic processing of personal data relating to him'.[241] Specifically, Article 14 provides for the transborder flows of personal data. It facilitates the transfer across national borders, by whatever medium, of personal data undergoing automatic processing or collected with a view to their being automatically processed. Article 14.2 provides that when the recipient is subject to the jurisdiction of a state or international organisation which is not party to this Convention, the transfer of personal data may take place only where an appropriate level of protection based on the provisions of this Convention is secured. Article 14.3 seeks to ensure an appropriate level of protection for the data involved in the international transfer. It requires that the law of that state or international organisation, including the applicable international treaties or agreements, or ad hoc or approved standardised safeguards provided by legally binding and

238. ASEAN, Model Contractual Clauses for Cross Border Data Flows, https://asean.org/wp-content/uploads/3-ASEAN-Model-Contractual-Clauses-for-Cross-Border-Data-Flows_Final.pdf. Final Copy Endorsed by the 2nd ASEAN Digital Senior Officials' Meeting (ADGSOM), January 2021.
239. *Ibid.*, p. 4.
240. *Ibid.*
241. Council of Europe, Convention for the Protection of Individuals with Regard to Automatic Processing of Personal Data, Strasbourg, 28.I.1981, Article 14, https://www.europarl.europa.eu/meetdocs/2014_2019/plmrep/COMMITTEES/LIBE/DV/2018/09-10/Convention_108_EN.pdf. There are fifty-five nation states that are Party to the Convention.

enforceable instruments, are adopted and implemented by the persons involved in the transfer and further processing.

Article 14.4 also requires that each Party provide that the transfer of personal data may take place if the data subject has given explicit, specific and free consent after being informed of risks posed by the absence of appropriate safeguards; or the specific interests of the data subject require it in the particular case; or legitimate interests prevail. It also extends to include instances involving an important public interest provided for by law, where such transfer constitutes a necessary and proportionate measure in a democratic society, or it constitutes a necessary and proportionate measure in a democratic society that values freedom of expression. Thus, this would apply to situations where data needs to be transferred on the grounds of national security or law enforcement. Moreover, Article 14.5 provides that each party must ensure that there is a supervisory authority in place. Today, most nation states have either established or are in the process of establishing a dedicated regulatory/supervising authority to oversee the governance of personal data. As part of this process, the provisions of domestic laws should ensure that the parties involved in data transfers are able to provide the regulator with information about the data being transferred, upon request.[242]

Most noteworthy is that Article 14 'applies only to the outflow of data, not to its inflow, since the latter are covered by the data protection regime of the recipient Party'.[243] Significant too is that data 'processed within the jurisdiction of a Party always remains protected by the relevant data protection principles of the Convention. While there may be a wide variety of systems of protection, protection afforded has to be of such quality as to ensure that human rights are not affected by globalisation and transborder data flows'.[244]

Arguably, Convention 108, has been significant in establishing the baseline of legal provisions for governing data transfers. Having been in place since 1981, the Convention demonstrates how the importance of providing a layer of protection to personal data transfers has been a long-time concern of regulators, particularly across Europe. It was one of the first legal instruments to set the rules and underscore the principles of the OECD Guidelines on data transfers. It has also provided the basis for the promotion of fundamental values to protect personal data when transferred across international borders, and privacy over the Internet. In 2013, Graham Greenleaf published a paper titled *'Modernising' Data Protection Convention 108: A Safe Basis for a Global Privacy Treaty?*[245] As the title suggests, the paper examines whether Convention 108 could become an international convention. Greenleaf notes that, in order for Convention 108 to become truly international, more nations would have to accede to and indirectly embrace the rights-based approach to data protection. This has not occurred and is unlikely to do so in the short to medium future. Put another way, it

242. *Ibid.*, Article 14.6.
243. *Ibid.*, p. 27.
244. *Ibid.*, pp. 27-28.
245. Graham Greenleaf, 'Modernising' Data Protection Convention 108: A Safe Basis for a Global Privacy Treaty' (2013) Computer Law & Security Review 2013 435-436.

would require nation states to embrace the European standards and norms, although many countries around the world have already adopted much of the EU framework.

Colin Bennett and Charles Raab believe that international agreements on data protection have had several overlapping functions. These instruments include:

(i) instruments of harmonisation;
(ii) templates for states to fashion their own data protection regimes;
(iii) exemplars, producing a progressive and inexorable desire to be within the community of nations that has adopted data protection legislation; and
(iv) penetrative force (instruments of coercion).[246]

This is the first point raised by Bennett and Raab that is pertinent to the issues discussed in this book. Despite being repetitive, in this book, a strong argument is made for legal reform that will achieve a high level of legal harmonisation that goes beyond interoperability. The current international bilateral and multilateral agreements provide a starting point. Therefore, it is argued that FTAs and Digital Agreements are important to the evolving governance framework for data flows and the digital economy. Moreover, these agreements provide a basis for the new digital economy, in the same way that they have done for the traditional trade in goods and services. Yet, Bygraves believes that the first three agreements listed by Bennett and Raab can be met by Convention 108.[247] However, an ensuring question is whether harmonisation can be achieved by Convention 108, because of its limited accession by nation states. It will never be fully accepted and adopted on an international scale/level. Additionally, it is by and large based on a level of adequacy and interoperability. This is something beyond the reach of a higher level of legal harmonisation. Hence, there has to be a starting point, and it is argued that FTAs-Digital Agreements can provide for and facilitate this level of law reform. Another option is to develop either a convention or a model law.

In addressing the highly fragmented legal landscape of data flows and data protection, Morgan Corley[248] also questions whether there is a need to internationalise data laws. Corley states:

> trying to formulate a solution to this global problem, it is useful to look at another area of international law created at a moment when international cooperation was crucial in order to allow the global market and economy to operate fluidly. International sales of goods once faced a similar need for cooperation between nations, which resulted in the creation of a private international law that has been

246. Colin Bennett, Charles Raab, *The Governance of Privacy: Policy Instruments in Global Perspective*, MIT Press (2006), p. 113. In Lee Bygrave, 'The "Strasbourg Effect" on Data Protection in Light of the "Brussels Effect": Logic, Mechanics and Prospects' (2021) Computer Law & Security Review, https://doi.org/10.1016/j.clsr.2020.105460.
247. Lee Bygrave, 'The "Strasbourg Effect" on Data Protection in Light of the "Brussels Effect": Logic, Mechanics and Prospects' (2021) Computer Law & Security Review 2-4, https://doi.org/10.1016/j.clsr.2020.105460.
248. Morgan Corley, 'The Need for an International Convention on Data Privacy: Taking a Cue from the CISG' (2016) 41 Brooklyn Journal International Law.

> hailed as 'by far the most thorough example of diplomatic drafting in multi-jurisdictional private law ever'. This law is the United Nations Convention on Contracts for the International Sale of Goods.[249]

Corley further argues that it is time for an international convention for data. Importantly, since the rise of data transfers over the Internet, there have been calls for the internationalisation of data law, even though those calls have been made by individuals. Leading international legal scholars such as Greenleaf have posited that Convention 108 could provide the basis for internalisation. However, scholars such as Corley call for a broader perspective and seek to replicate existing trade law that has been highly successful. Corley posits:

> In order to alleviate the problems that currently plague the data industry, an international convention on the collection, transfer, and processing of personal data is needed. To both facilitate and ensure its success, drafters should employ the CISG as an example for modelling this new convention. By doing so, drafters can build upon the strengths and the weaknesses of the CISG, which has generated years of research and analysis.[250]

In view of this proposition, it is argued that an analysis of existing regional and international legal frameworks, while these are not new, will provide the basis for a well-considered international law for data flows and data protection. Corley, Greenleaf and, to a lesser extent, Bennett and Rabb underpin the overall argument presented in this book: it is time for the current legal landscape associated with data flows and data protection to evolve and accommodate the international context. For a further discussion of the CISG 1980, and its possible influence on data flows and the law, *see* section §1.02.

It is also worth noting that although countries have adopted elements of the EU model, they diverge significantly in terms of the standards being applied in practice. This is because, in some countries, the protection and privacy of data conveyed via the Internet are all but non-existent. Additionally, because countries seek to meet their own sovereign needs, they view data protection and privacy very differently due to their cultural, religious, ethnic and linguistic characteristics. Today, Convention 108 still serves as an important tool. Could it be improved? In short - yes. Could it be elevated to an international convention that all nation states will agree to ratify and implement? In 2002, this would be impossible. Is it likely that more states will accede to Convention 108? This is the unknown, and it is up to individual states to make the decision. It will largely depend on whether there is political pressure and the will to change. On the other side, it could provide the basis for the development of a single international convention not only for data flows but also for data protection, to ensure an adequate balance between the two concepts.

---

249. *Ibid.*, p. 724.
250. *Ibid.* United Nations Convention on Contracts for the International Sale of Goods, opened for signature 11 April 1980, S. Treaty DOC. No. 98-9 (1983), 1489 U.N.T.S. 3, entered into force 1 January 1988.

Commonwealth Model Laws on Protection of Personal Information and Privacy

The Commonwealth Secretariate established the Model Bill on the Protection of Personal Information in 2017 (MBPPI).[251] It is outside the scope of this book to analyse the Commonwealth countries examined in this book (Australia, Canada, India, New Zealand, Singapore and the UK), regarding the extent to which they express or reflect the sections and provisions of their respective data-privacy laws. Nonetheless, the MBPPI has gone some way to provide some standard of governance for cross-border data flows. Rather than using the standard terminology related to cross-border data flows or cross-border data transfers, the MBPPI refers to 'use of personal information outside the country'.[252]

The MBPPI has what can best be described as a principled, flexible and security-oriented approach. It defines 'use' to mean the actions of an 'organisation that has custody or control of personal information or data, means to handle or deal with the information or data, including the transfer of the information or data to an agent of the organisation, but does not include the disclosure of the information or data'.[253] In addressing one of the core principles, section 18 of the MBPPI requires a level of security for personal information/data when it has been transferred to a third party for processing, including a third party outside the data's country of origin. For instance, under the MBPPI, personal information being transferred from Australia to New Zealand would need to be secure in the receiving country.

Section 15 goes further by requiring that personal information from outside of the country of origin can be used only if this is permitted in that country, and only if it remains secure and confidential. It requires that the individual data subject's privacy be protected. Finally, section 16 provides for personal information to be disclosed outside the country of origin. Under this section, personal data cannot be disclosed unless the organisation receiving the data ensures that the processes it applies to the data are comparable to those of the originating country. Moreover, the receiving organisation is required to maintain confidentiality and ensure the highest possible protection of data privacy.

The Model Privacy Bill (MPB) recognises that personal information/data is a significant component of trade and business in today's data-driven economy.[254] The MPB sought to give effect to the OECD Guidelines on the Protection of Privacy and Transborder Flows of Personal Data, first prepared for consideration by Senior Officials of Commonwealth Law Ministries in 2001.[255] Above all, it promotes the idea that 'adequate laws and policies for data protection, and in particular, cross-border flow of personal data are critical to participation in global value chains'.[256] However, it is

251. Commonwealth Secretariat, Model Bill on the Protection of Personal Information, 2017, https://thecommonwealth.org/sites/default/files/key_reform_pdfs/P15370_6_ROL_Model_Bill_Protection_Personal_Information_2.pdf.
252. *Ibid.*, sections 15 and 16.
253. *Ibid.*, section 4.
254. Commonwealth Secretariate, Model Privacy Bill, https://thecommonwealth.org/sites/default/files/key_reform_pdfs/P15370_9_ROL_Model_Privacy_Bill_0.pdf.
255. *Ibid.*
256. *Ibid.*, p. 1.

limited regarding the extent to which cross-border data flows and their governance are to proceed. Notably, it deals only with information privacy which is the most common aspect of privacy regulated by statute, and which involves the establishment of rules governing the collection and handling of personal information such as those relating to the status of credit or medical records.[257] Essentially, it provides the platform for a consistent set of principles to be adopted by member countries to ensure that a high level of privacy is afforded by national laws. It is limited in its scope and deals with the collection, use, storage, security, disclosure and retention of personal information by public authorities. It encourages member countries to establish a regulator, such as a privacy commissioner office that hears complaints and is accountable to Parliament.

In drawing any salutary conclusion, the MBPPI and MPB, while expressed as Model Bills (indirectly laws), encourage member countries, particularly those developing their national data laws, to consider these Bills as a possible regulatory framework. While the Commonwealth Secretariat has provided a valuable tool for member countries to follow, when compared to the long-standing national laws that have been in place, these Bills lack detail. The provisions pertaining to cross-border data flows do nothing more than ensure an adequate level of protection is provided by the receiving country for both the data and the privacy of the data subject. For these Model Bills to be fully operational, more work is needed to internationalise them. For example, there needs to be a collaboration with the institution responsible for Convention 108, amongst others. Problematic though, is that there are only 54 Commonwealth member countries,[258] accounting for a little more than one-quarter of the world's 195 nations.[259] Thus, at best, the Model Bills need to be revised to align them with current national laws. They are non-binding on member countries and are by and large there to assist those developing countries that do not have a history of data protection law and are beginning to establish such laws for the first time.

Thus far, the book has demonstrated the fragmented approach that has been taken by international and regional institutions towards the development of policy for transnational flow of data. While each institution/organisation has its own responsibilities and charter, there appears to be little to no collaboration. Most, if not all organisations' strategic documents, strategies and reports, except for the binding contractual clauses, have adopted the OECD Principles as a default, although these are now more than 40 years old. Arguably, they have served the international community very well, and without them, the world would be in a very challenging place regarding data protection law and cross-border data flows. Therefore, these Principles must be retained at all costs, and there appears to be no country wishing to remove them. Nonetheless, these Principles go only so far. The most pressing problem that has arisen concerns the lack of international and regional law for cross-border data flows. It is argued that the EU appears to be the most advanced in this regard, although there is still much work to be done. The prevailing view is that while the EU has a solid legal

257. *Ibid.*
258. The Commonwealth, https://thecommonwealth.org/member-countries.
259. Worldometer, 2022, https://www.worldometers.info/geography/how-many-countries-are-there-in-the-world/.

framework, which is predominantly rights-based, to date, it has focused on achieving data adequacy by means of interoperability. This alone will not achieve the significant level of legal or policy harmonisation required to address the barriers to opening up the digital economy so that data can flow internationally as freely as possible.

One of the first signs of stronger international cooperation in relation to data flows emerged at the Group of 7 (G7) meeting in September 2021. It called for a number of considerations that include 'Government Access and Data Flow at International Level: What Role for Regulatory Cooperation in Ensuring Real Trust?'.[260] The G7 Group went further, calling for the need to develop 'a Framework for Cross-Border Transfer of Personal Data and Cooperation between G7 Data Protection Authorities'.[261] In encouraging strong international cooperation, the G7 Group, while stopping short of recommending the development of an international legal framework, understand the need to strengthen the current legal frameworks at a national level. The G7 should consider taking this a step further and recommending an international legal instrument and the establishment of an international organisation for data governance.

On this basis, the cross-border flow of data has resulted in some jurisdictions adopting additional rules and laws that provide for a level of data adequacy. The book identifies areas for improvement that can be added to policy makers' considerations in order to obtain incremental adjustments that, over time, will result in more efficiencies and opening up the digital economy. It argues that the notion of interoperability needs to be expanded. Further, it argues that bilateral and multilateral agreements will be an effective mechanism for achieving legal harmonisation and internationalisation of data law.

The next section briefly discusses data adequacy, which is an emerging legal and policy concept. It calls for a single international legal instrument that takes interoperability one step further and ensures there is a high level of legal harmonisation. This will enable data in the digital economy to develop and achieve optimal economic and social benefits worldwide, not just for a single nation state or a group of states.

§1.05 DATA ADEQUACY

Data adequacy has emerged as another new area of policy and law in transnational data flows. It is not new. Yet, it complements cross-border data flow law and policy because it enables a country to assess and decide whether their data laws meet a relevant and equivalent criterion. It further complements and supports the concept of legal interoperability and harmonisation. On the other hand, data adequacy is not a new concept, having been operational since the former Directive 95/46,[262] and further

260. Office of the Privacy Commissioner Canada, Data free Flow with Trust, September 2021, https://www.priv.gc.ca/en/opc-news/speeches/2021/communique-g7_210907/#fn1.
261. *Ibid.*
262. European Commission, Directive 95/46/EC of the European Parliament and the Court of the Council of October 1995, on the protection of individuals with regard to the processing of personal data and on the free movement of such data, Official Journal of the European Communities No. L 281/31. Note that this Directive has been replaced with the General Data

developed by the Court of Justice of the European Union (CJEU).[263] Directive 95/46 has now been replaced by the GDPR 2016/679.[264] The GDPR is, arguably the most advanced when it comes to adequacy provisions under Article 45.

In using the EU's adequacy framework as the benchmark, they have sought to take the approach to data protection that consists of assessing the adequacy of the data protection offered by the laws of a particular jurisdiction against a set of principles that includes purpose limitation, transparency, quality, proportionality, security, access, and rectification.[265] The principles are based on the OECD Guidelines on the Protection of Privacy and Transborder Flows of Personal Data, as highlighted earlier in this chapter. Section 19 of the Guidelines states that:

> implementing domestically the principles set forth in Parts Two and Three, Member countries should establish legal, administrative or other procedures or institutions for the protection of privacy and individual liberties in respect of personal data. Member countries should in particular endeavour to provide for adequate sanctions and remedies in case of failures to comply with measures which implement the principles set forth in Parts Two and Three.[266]

In 1997, The European Commission released the report on First Orientations on Transfers of Personal Data to Third Countries - Possible Ways Forward in Assessing Adequacy by the Working Party on the Protection of Individuals with regard to the Processing of Personal Data.[267] Even though the report was released to support the former Directive 95/46, it arguably remains a good reference for understanding the operation of adequacy. Thus, the treatment of privacy and data flows under the Working Party report stipulated various types of transfers that should be considered when assessing adequacy. At the time, these were:

Protection Regulation (EU) 2016/679 of the European Parliament and of the Council of 27 April 2016, on the protection of natural persons with regard to the processing of personal data and on the free movement of such data, and repealing Directive 95/46/EC, Official Journal of the European Union L 119/1.

263. Case C-311/18 *Schrems and Facebook Ireland v. Data Protection Commissioner* (Schrems II) (2020) and Case C-362/14 *Schrems v. Data Protection Commissioner* (Schrems I) (2015). These are the two most high-profile cases in the European Union, concerning the role of adequacy in transnational data flows.
264. General Data Protection Regulation (EU) 2016/679 of the European Parliament and of the Council of 27 April 2016, on the protection of natural persons with regard to the processing of personal data and on the free movement of such data, and repealing Directive 95/46/EC, Official Journal of the European Union L 119/1.
265. Jennifer Stoddart, Benny Chian, Yann Joly, 'Adequacy Decisions in European Law Related to International Data Transfers and Control Mechanisms Applied by the Member States' (2016) 44 The Journal of Law, Medicine & Ethics 143-155.
266. OECD Guidelines on the Protection of Privacy and Transborder Flows of Personal Data, section 19, 2013, https://www.oecd.org/sti/ieconomy/oecdguidelinesontheprotectionofprivacyand transborderflowsofpersonaldata.htm. Also *see* Graham Greenleaf, 'Do Not Dismiss "Adequacy": European Data Privacy Standards Are Entrenched' (2011) 114 Privacy Laws & Business International Report 16-17.
267. European Commission, *Working Party on the Protection of Individuals with Regard to the Processing of Personal Data, First Orientations on Transfers of Personal Data to Third Countries – Possible Ways Forward in Assessing Adequacy*, Discussion Document adopted by the Working Party on 26 June 1997, https://ec.europa.eu/justice/article-29/documentation/opinion-recommendation/files/1997/wp4_en.pdf.

- those transfers involving certain sensitive categories of data as defined by Article 8 of the directive;
- transfers which carry the risk of financial loss (credit card payments over the Internet);
- transfers carrying a risk to personal safety;
- transfers made for the purposes of making a decision which significantly affects the individual (recruitment or promotion decisions, the granting of credit);
- transfers which carry a risk of serious embarrassment or tarnishing of an individual's reputation;
- transfers which may result in specific actions which constitute a significant intrusion into an individual's private life, such as unsolicited telephone calls;
- repetitive transfers involving massive volumes of data (transactional data processed over telecommunications networks, the Internet); and
- transfers involving the collection of data in a particularly covert or clandestine manner (Internet cookies).[268]

Centrally too, the report makes the important point that the 'purpose of data protection is to afford protection to the individual about whom data are processed'.[269] It reinforces this with:

> The obligations and rights set down in directive 95/46/EC are based on those set down in Council of Europe Convention N°108 (1981), which in turn are not dissimilar from those included in the OECD guidelines (1980). It would therefore appear that there is a degree of consensus as to the content of data protection rules which stretches well beyond the fifteen states of the Community.[270]

Viewed this way, it is clear that any meaningful analysis of adequate protection must comprise two basic elements: the content of the rules applicable, and the means for ensuring their effective application.[271] This has now been revised under the GDPR (*see* Chapter 3).

Christopher Kuner makes the important point that even past adequacy assessment undertaken by the European Commission, 'does not always require that third countries found adequate themselves prohibit the transfer of personal data to non-adequate countries. For example, the Canadian Personal Information Protection and Electronic Documents Act (PIPED Act (PIPEDA)) has been found adequate, even though the Act itself contains no such prohibition'.[272] Kuner is of the view that the rationale behind the adequacy concept is the desire to maintain a high level of data protection throughout the EU by preventing the circumvention of EU rules through the transfer of processing to third countries with a lower standard of data protection. While

268. Section 2.
269. *Ibid.*
270. *Ibid.*
271. *Ibid.*
272. Christopher Kuner, Developing an Adequate Legal Framework for International Data Transfers. In: Gutwirth (eds), *Reinventing Data Protection*, Springer (2009), pp. 263-273.

Kuner's point is legitimate, nowadays, it can be argued that data adequacy has gone beyond the above. It now transcends the international community so that the digital economy can grow and expand. Without such a system or framework, the flow of data would be severely restricted. As the adequacy assessments, framework and decisions have expanded over the past two decades, this accords with Professor Graham Greenleaf's position that the '3rd Generation of evolving global data privacy standards will be decided by which of [the EU GDPR's] new content principles and enforcement requirements are likely to become standard elements of data privacy laws outside the EU'.[273] This could explain that since Directive 95/46 and GDPR 2016/769, relatively few ADs have been made by the EU. For instance, as of January 2022, there had only been a total of fifteen ADs pertaining to Andorra, Argentina, Canada (commercial organisations), Faroe Islands, Guernsey, Israel, Isle of Man, Japan, Jersey, New Zealand, Republic of Korea, Switzerland, UK and Uruguay.[274]

Japan provides a good example of the influence of the EU's ADs. It changed its national laws to ensure it received adequacy, making two concessions in the Supplementary Rules to satisfy the EU's adequacy requirements. First, Japan agreed to begin classifying sexual orientation and trade union membership status as sensitive to ensure that the rights of data subjects will apply to all personal data – contrary to prior practice. Second, the Supplementary Rules ensure that data subjects' rights will apply to all personal data transferred from the EU, irrespective of their retention period, even though Japanese law does not provide such protections.[275] Some scholars have suggested that this appears to be a 'prehistory to the adequacy requirement, which reveals it to be a compromise solution'.[276] Nothing could be further from the truth. It is a level of compromise enabling regulators to speed up the process of legal recognition in order to remove barriers to the economic and social development achieved by the analysis of data. As stated above, adequacy is the first step to legal harmonisation. It is not a silver bullet that will achieve long-term economic and social benefits that data in the digital economy will provide when the sector is fully opened and unimpeded by unnecessary regulation. In putting forward this argument, government and regulators should not stop at adequacy arrangements or assessments. There needs to be international collaboration by national governments to achieve this.

Christopher Wolf noted that:

> the United States and the European Union clearly share a commitment to promoting the rights of individuals to have their personal data protected and to facilitating interoperability of our commercial data privacy regimes. The European Union and

273. Graham Greenleaf, *International Data Privacy Agreements After the GDPR and* Schrems, Univ. of N.S.W. Law Research Series, Paper No. 29, (2016). Also *see* Graham Greenleaf, 'Japan and Korea: Different Paths to EU Adequacy' (2018) 156 Privacy Laws & Business International Report 9, 11.
274. European Commission, Adequacy decisions, https://ec.europa.eu/info/law/law-topic/data-protection/international-dimension-data-protection/adequacy-decisions_en.
275. Flora Y. Wang, 'Cooperative Data Privacy: The Japanese Model of Data Privacy and the EU-Japan GDPR Adequacy Agreement' (2020) 33 Harvard Journal of Law & Technology 672.
276. Paul Schwartz, *Global Data Privacy: The EU Way*, Jefferson E. Peyser Professor of Law at UC Berkeley School of Law; Director, Berkeley Center for Law & Technology, (2019), p. 10.

> the United States are global leaders in protecting individual freedoms, including privacy, while at the same time fostering innovation and trade that are so critical to the world economy, notably in the present times. Stronger transatlantic cooperation in the field of data protection will enhance consumer trust and promote the continued growth of the global Internet economy.[277]

Under the former Directive 95/46, Wolf notes that the major difference between the 'US and EU privacy regimes is the way in which each regulates cross-border data flows. In the US, enforcement of privacy protections across borders has – relied on holding those who transfer data accountable for its safe-keeping, and self-regulatory codes of conduct to protect the privacy of personal information that flows across borders.'[278] Wolf further explains that the EU, 'has a more formal approach. Article 25 of the Directive generally prohibits transfers of personal data to a third country unless that third country ensures an adequate level of protection'.[279] Problematic though, which does not appear to have been resolved, is how Wolf points out those countries that have acceded to Convention 108, have assumed a level of what he calls 'de facto adequacy'. In acceding to both Convention 108 and the Additional Protocol, the requirements of Directive 95/46 are met. Therefore, there appeared to be no incentive for countries that acceded to Convention 108 to apply for a formal AD. This only further reinforces the incoherent approach that has been taken to provide for a level of international harmonisation. Another important point is that adequacy when coupled with interoperability has a good level of effectiveness, providing a layer of certainty for the market. However, taking this one step further to legal harmonisation will allow the international community to overcome the legal, policy, practical, economic, social and environmental barriers to reaping the potential benefits of data flows in the digital economy.

§1.06 LEGAL INTEROPERABILITY: LEGAL HARMONISATION

Legal interoperability is not the same as legal harmonisation. This section will argue that legal interoperability is and must be the first step to legal harmonisation so that cross-border data flows can play their intended role in the digital economy and deliver the economic and social benefits that will be derived from this activity. The concept of interoperability has been a by-product of the current international response to data flows, largely driven by the technology sector.

According to Wolfgang Kerber and Heike Schweitzer, 'interoperability has become a buzzword in European policy debates on the future of the digital economy'.[280] They note that in the 'Digital Agenda, the EU Commission has identified a lack of interoperability as one out of seven "most significant obstacles" to the

277. Christopher Wolf, 'Delusions of Adequacy? Examining the Case for Finding the United States Adequate for Cross-Border EU-U.S. Data Transfers' (2013) 43 Washington University Journal of Law & Policy 228.
278. *Ibid.*, p. 232.
279. *Ibid.*
280. Wolfgang Kerber, Heike Schweitzer, 'Interoperability in the Digital Economy' (2017) Journal of Intellectual Property, Information Technology and E-Commerce Law 39.

"virtuous cycle" of digitalization'.[281] The authors go on to say that one of the difficulties of the interoperability 'discussion is the absence of a clear definition of interoperability'.[282] According to Kerber and Schweitzer, 'interoperability denotes the ability of a system, product or service to communicate and function with other (technically different) systems, products or services'.[283] Significantly, they note that 'interoperability issues in the digital economy will typically relate to information exchange and data'.[284]

The above authors, refer to John Palfrey and Urs Gasser not that the latter 'define interoperability as the ability to transfer and render useful data and other information across technology systems, applications or components'.[285] Palfrey and Grasser point to data flows as being the sequence in which data transfer, use and transformation are performed during the execution of a computer program'.[286] The authors go on to say that 'interoperability is the ability of two or more systems or components to exchange information and to use the information that has been exchanged'.[287] However, this definition was given in 1990 when the technology was in its infancy, and data protection laws around the world had hardly been conceived by the majority of nation states. Moreover, this definition applies to the technology that uses data; today, it has been expanded beyond technology to include the law.

Kerber and Schweitzer also refer to the EU Software Copyright Directive[288] and the EU Directive on Digital Goods and Services[289] to highlight similar approaches to interoperability. Directive 2009/24/EC asserts that 'the functional interconnection and interaction is generally known as "interoperability"; such interoperability can be defined as the ability to exchange information and mutually use the information which has been exchanged'.[290] Importantly, Article 6 stipulates that the right holder shall not be required where reproduction of the code and translation of its form within the meaning of points (a) and (b) of Article 4(1) are indispensable to obtain the information necessary to achieve the interoperability of an independently created computer program with other programs, provided that the following conditions are met the

281. *Ibid.*, p. 39.
282. *Ibid.*, p. 40.
283. *Ibid.*
284. *Ibid.*
285. *Ibid.* Also *see* John Palfrey and, Ur Grasser, *Standard Glossary of Software Engineering Terminology*, 1990, http://www.mit.jyu.fi/ope/kurssit/TIES462/Materiaalit/IEEE_Software EngGlossary.pdf.
286. John Palfrey and Ur Grasser, *Standard Glossary of Software Engineering Terminology*, 1990, p. 24, http://www.mit.jyu.fi/ope/kurssit/TIES462/Materiaalit/IEEE_SoftwareEngGlossary.pdf.
287. *Ibid.*, p. 42.
288. Wolfgang Kerber and Heike Schweitzer, 'Interoperability in the Digital Economy' (2017) Journal of Intellectual Property, Information Technology and E-Commerce Law 40. Also *see*, Directive 2009/24/EC of the European Parliament and of the Council of 23 April 2009 on the legal protection of computer programs (Codified version) (Text with EEA relevance) OJ L 111.
289. *Ibid.*, Directive (EU) 2019/770 of the European Parliament and of the Council of 20 May 2019 on certain aspects concerning contracts for the supply of digital content and digital services, PE/26/2019/REV/1, OJ L 136.
290. Directive 2009/24/EC of the European Parliament and of the Council of 23 April 2009 on the legal protection of computer programs (Codified version) (Text with EEA relevance) OJ L 111, Preamble 10.

information necessary to achieve interoperability has not previously been readily available to the persons referred to in point.[291] Additionally, under Directive (EU) 2019/770, the notion of interoperability relates to whether and to what extent digital content or digital service is able to function with hardware or software that is different from those with which digital content or digital services of the same type are normally used. Successful functioning could include, for instance, the ability of the digital content or digital service to exchange information with such other software or hardware and to use the information exchanged.[292]

Further, according to Article 2, 'interoperability constitutes the ability of the digital content or digital service to function with hardware or software different from those with which digital content or digital services of the same type are normally used'.[293]

The Directive also states that 'interoperability can be relevant on different layers; for example, syntactic/technical interoperability refers to the possibility that systems can physically connect to each other and can exchange data, whereas semantic interoperability refers to the ability of systems to understand the meaning of the information exchanged'.[294] Kerber and Schweitzer support the view of Palfrey and Gasser: that interoperability is aligned to the systems, infrastructure and technology that supports these, that provide for and facilitate data transfers. Given this backdrop, uniform standards allow for more mass production and a lower number of product variants. The resulting economies of scale and scope as well as network externalities can bring large cost advantages. Interoperability may also allow for a modularisation of components of products, which can be used for different (often customised) products. It can reduce the costs for consumers (and increase their benefits).[295] On the other side, 'interoperability and the use of uniform standards may also increase costs and risks both for firms and consumers. Significant too, interoperability can lead to a greater degree of homogeneity and limit the scope for innovation and therefore the extent to

291. *Ibid.*, Article 6. 2. The provisions of paragraph 1 shall not permit the information obtained through its application (a) to be used for goals other than to achieve the interoperability of the independently created computer program (b) to be given to others, except when necessary for the interoperability of the independently created computer program; or (c) to be used for the development, production or marketing of a computer program substantially similar in its expression, or for any other act which infringes copyright.
292. Directive (EU) 2019/770 of the European Parliament and of the Council of 20 May 2019 on certain aspects concerning contracts for the supply of digital content and digital services, PE/26/2019/REV/1, OJ L 136, Preamble, 43.
293. *Ibid.*, Article 2.12.
294. Wolfgang Kerber and Heike Schweitzer, 'Interoperability in the Digital Economy' (2017) Journal of Intellectual Property, Information Technology and E-Commerce Law 40-41. The extent and specific design of the interoperability of products, services, and platforms of a firm is influenced by both technological decisions and legal constructs. Namely, it depends not only on (1) technological decisions of the firm but also on (2) its decisions (a) to allow interoperability through contractual arrangements with customers and suppliers, (b) its willingness to disclose the necessary interface information and (c) its toleration of the unilateral development of adapters and converters by other firms. The different forms and degrees of interoperability indicate the complexity of the interoperability issue.
295. *Ibid.*

which specific consumer preferences can be fulfilled by way of product differentiation'.[296] Furthermore, it must be noted that within the EU context, 'interoperability does not mean "compatibility", as recital 68 clarifies'.[297]

Paul De Hert et al., in relation to the interoperability of systems, cite recital 68 of the GDPR which states that data controllers should be encouraged to develop interoperable formats that enable data portability. However, although data controllers should strive to achieve full interoperability of digital systems, they should be encouraged, not obliged, to develop these interoperable formats.[298] This confirms the timeliness of this book as it reaffirms the need for another approach to minimise the barriers and challenges to interoperability. Scholars note that interoperability is systems-based rather than law-based, and that interoperability 'between devices and systems is of utmost importance'.[299] However, in the context of ADs, it is emerging as a more complex concept applied to create a level of regulatory certainty for data in the digital economy. Arguably, interoperability is still a grey area, indicating the need for clarification of standards. On the one hand, policymakers may view this approach as one that is agile and flexible. On the other hand, it introduces some ambiguity, which could translate into a lack of legal certainty. This further highlights the need for law reform across the entire framework for cross-border data flows and data adequacy.

Notwithstanding the above, legal interoperability has been described as a concept of and in transnational law[300] and achieves a level of harmonisation. However, it does not establish a high level of legal harmonisation, which in turn increases transaction costs and the costs of doing business. Eliezer Sanchez Lasaballett argues that 'differences between legal systems are problematic since they give rise to transaction costs, in particular, when two parties to a legal transaction are subject to different legal systems or jurisdictions'.[301] In citing an example of contract law which is applied to the international trade of goods and services, Lasaballett argues that

---

296. *Ibid.*
297. Paul De Hert, Vagelis Papakonstant, Gianclaudio Malgieri, Laurent Beslay and Ignacio Sanchez, 'The Right to Data Portability in the GDPR: Towards User-Centric Interoperability of Digital Services' (2018) 34(2) Computer Law & Security. Review 193, 197. Also *see*, Recital 68, GDPR: 'the data subject's right to transmit or receive personal data concerning him or her should not create an obligation from the controller to adopt or maintain processing systems which are technically compatible'. Also *see*: Björn Lundqvist, 'Standardization for the Digital Economy: The Issue of Interoperability and Access Under Competition Law' (December 2017) The Antitrust Bulletin 15-16.
298. *Ibid.* Also *see*: Michel Girard, *Standards for the Digital Economy: Creating and Architecture for Data Collection, Access and Analytics*, Centre for International Governance Innovation (2022), p. 6. Central to interoperability is the choice of an appropriate Application Programming Interface (API) to allow for data transmission, use and tracking.
299. *Ibid.* At p. 18, Horizontal interoperability denotes the interoperability of competing products, services or platforms. One example is the interconnection between communication networks. Vertical interoperability refers to the interoperability of a product, service or platform with complementary products and services.
300. Amedeo Santosuosso and Alessandra Malerba, 'Legal Interoperability as a Comprehensive Concept in Transnational Law' (2014) 6(1) Law, Innovation and Technology 51-73. Also *see*, Rolf H Weber, *Legal Interoperability as a Tool for Combatting Fragmentation*, Paper series: No. 4, Global Commission on Internet Governance, (2014).
301. Eliezer Sanchez Lasaballett, 'Conceptualizing Harmonization: The Case for Contract Law' (2019) 24(1) Uniform Law Review 73-74, https://doi.org/10.1093/ulr/unz007.

'parties may agree on choosing the contract law from one of their jurisdictions to regulate the transaction; alternatively, they may choose the contract law of a third jurisdiction. It could also be that parties are not free to choose a particular law since a mandatory rule of conflict of laws imposes one party's jurisdiction to regulate the transaction'.[302] However, under the law for data protection and data flows, this choice is not often provided. According to Lasaballett, under contract law, at least one of the parties will incur costs associated with becoming familiar with the nature and scope of their rights and duties under an unfamiliar legal system. Yet, this might not be the case under data laws. It has not been fully determined whether one party or both parties to the data transfers have higher transaction costs. This is another complex area requiring further research.

Lasaballett also notes that a lack of harmonisation in substantive law hinders the effective enforcement of the rights and obligations of legal and natural persons in any jurisdiction.[303] This is definitely the case in terms of compliance with data laws around the world. She makes the case that harmonisation reduces transaction costs, facilitates access to courts and justice, and makes available a broader range of remedies appropriate to the modern demands of society. This holds true in different fields of the law including corporate, trade, criminal, and environmental law,[304] all of which will be utilising data and participating in data flows. According to Lasaballett, in contract law, harmonisation becomes an effective instrument for removing barriers to the cross-border exchange of goods and services by reducing the transaction costs borne by firms and individuals, thereby improving economic welfare.[305] The trade in services alone has seen, and will continue to see, a significant rise in the transfer of data across international borders.

In this context, interoperability 'addresses the process of making legal rules cooperate across jurisdictions, on different subsidiary levels within a single state or between two or more states'.[306] There are two types of interoperability:

(1) syntactic interoperability, which is the ability of diverse systems to communicate with each other and exchange data; and
(2) semantic interoperability, which is the ability to interpret and use those data and pieces of information in a significant way, is useful to the end-user.[307]

The authors note that with the:

302. *Ibid.*, pp. 73-74.
303. *Ibid.* Also *see* Mads Andenas and Camilla Baasch Andersen, 'Towards a Theory of Harmonisation' (2011) Theory and Practice of Harmonisation 572-574.
304. *Ibid.*
305. *Ibid.*
306. Amedeo Santosuosso and Alessandra Malerba, 'Legal Interoperability as a Comprehensive Concept in Transnational Law' (2014) 6(1) Law, Innovation and Technology 51-73. Also *see*, Rolf H Weber, *Legal Interoperability as a Tool for Combatting Fragmentation*, Paper series: No. 4, Global Commission on Internet Governance, (2014).
307. *Ibid.*, p. 52.

> increasing fragmentation of the legal environment in cyberspace, efforts must be undertaken to achieve higher levels of legal and policy interoperability in order to facilitate global communication, to reduce costs in cross-border business, and to drive innovation and economic growth. Interoperable legal rules can also create a level playing field for the next generation of technologies and cultural exchange.[308]

Derived from the technology sector, where systems and infrastructure not only can talk to each but also allow different systems to recognise each other, the notion of interoperability has been extended to law and policy.

Today, from the perspective of systems and infrastructure, interoperability plays an important role in financial transactions, mobile communication, web services, e-commerce, e-health and smart energy,[309] amongst others. Gasser and Palfrey argue that 'public policy makers have an important role to play by creating a legal and regulatory ecosystem that incentivises the private sector to work towards higher levels of interoperability'.[310] They also make the point that legal interoperability enables the flow of goods, services, and information across legal systems. According to Gasser and Palfrey, interoperability is a mechanism that reduces the costs associated with cross-jurisdictional business transactions. Additionally, it suggests that legal interoperability, at least in the ICT space with its unique characteristics, drives innovation, competition, trade, and economic growth. Furthermore, it supposedly increases levels of best practice-oriented legal interoperability and may also foster fundamental values and rights, such as information privacy and freedom of expression.[311] Gasser and Palfrey also state that:

> legal interoperability is not a binary concept. It maps onto a continuum. On the one hand, the laws 'on the books' might reach different degrees of interoperability, ranging from roughly harmonised norms to identical provisions. On the other hand, even interoperable legal norms might be enforced differently across jurisdictions, resulting in lower levels of interoperability – in action.[312]

Viewed this way, it goes some way to establishing a level of legal harmonisation, although, in some circumstances, it can fall far short of achieving this. Therefore, is interoperability more efficient than legal harmonisation? Furthermore, can legal harmonisation be achieved in the area of cross-border data flows?

Problematic though is that the current models and rules pertaining to cross-border data flows have only recently begun to emerge. Since they are in their infancy, nation states have the opportunity to go beyond the consideration of interoperability, leading to better efficiency and legal certainty. For instance, 'models and sets of rules aimed at facilitating legal interoperability may be elaborated by players on an equal footing, in the context of harmonisation efforts; may be unilaterally imposed, in a top-down fashion, by a player enjoying an asymmetric power relationship with the

308. *Ibid.*
309. Urs Gasser and John Palfrey, *Fostering Innovation and Trade in the Global Information Society: The Different Facets and Roles of Interoperability*, Working Paper No. 2011/39, (2011), pp. 2-3.
310. *Ibid.*, p. 6.
311. *Ibid.*, p. 9.
312. *Ibid.*, p. 10.

other players; or may be fostered through transnational diffusion'.[313] de Filippi and Belli believe that legal harmonisation 'relies on the cooperative effort of a group of – usually governmental – actors to elaborate a suitable solution to a shared and frequently transnational problem'.[314] In their view, legal harmonisation:

> backs legal interoperability via intergovernmental processes taking place within bilateral, plurilateral or multilateral fora. It relies on the formulation of multilateral agreements, such as conventions, and subsequent implementation of policies consistent with such agreements by the entities that participated in the formulation process.[315]

Achieving legal harmonisation is often complex, cumbersome and undertaken over a longer period of time, due to the multiple actors involved. On the other hand, legal interoperability can be undertaken between government and government. This is the first step to legal harmonisation.

Graham Greenleaf highlights the challenges faced by interoperability. He believes it 'cannot be an end in itself in data protection negotiations, but only a means of reducing formalities through cross-recognition of fully compatible and equivalent standards and mechanisms. Otherwise "interoperability" is just a mask for capitulation to the demand the stronger party'.[316] For Greenleaf, interoperability is sensible (perhaps even meaningful) only between legal instruments of like pedigree. He draws on the fragmented approach to data regulation more generally, stating:

> Convention 108 is a binding international agreement. The OECD Guidelines are just that, guidelines, they have no legal effect anywhere, even though all OECD countries except Turkey and the USA have enacted comprehensive data privacy laws for their private sectors, based on these guidelines. The APEC Framework is the same, there are no APEC 'rules', its Framework is a non-binding instrument and APEC is not an international organisation in the normal sense or even a treaty.[317]

Greenleaf argues that there cannot be any worthwhile interoperability between legally binding requirements and mere voluntary commitments, a stance taken in this book. Arguably, this is further heightened by other international organisations that have developed high-level policy concepts to direct the future of data governance and the law. Further, he notes that:

> the choice of 'appropriate' protection as a standard to replace 'adequacy' requires particular care to be taken that it does not accommodate 'interoperability' with other supposed data protection standards which will result in abandonment of

313. Primavera de Filippi, Luca Belli, *Net Neutrality Compendium: Human Rights, Free Competition, and the Future of the Internet*, Springer, (2015), p. 285. *See also*, Jörgens, H, *Governance by Diffusion – Implementing Global Norms Through Cross- National Imitation and Learning*, Environmental Policy Research Centre of FFU-report. 07-2003.
314. *Ibid.*, p. 285.
315. *Ibid.*
316. Graham Greenleaf, '"Modernising" Data Protection Convention 108: A Safe Basis for A Global Privacy Treaty' (2013) Computer Law & Security Review 435-436.
317. *Ibid.*, pp. 435-436.

> proper investigation of whether the standard of privacy existing in countries at the other end of the interoperability chain do in fact meet the standards of the Convention. Those who support data protection need to help stiffen European resolve to confront the challenges presented by American pressure to prematurely adopt 'interoperability', and the ideologies that drive it.[318]

The way to overcome these complex challenges is to aggregate the current accepted international principles and concepts and apply them internationally. As a regional bloc, the EU has been the most successful in achieving a high level of legal harmonisation and convergence, which is at the heart of the single economic market. In achieving this, the level of legal convergence, but more importantly, legal harmonisation, has been significantly successful. Across the EU, 'there is a broadening awareness that trade and investment liberalisation should be matched with harmonised minimum standards to avoid a regulatory race to the bottom'.[319] The economic benefits of the EU's legal harmonisation have been significant, particularly in creating an environment of certainty and trust. However, legal harmonisation even on a multilateral basis is significantly challenging when there is little or no strong legal support. In order to be a member of the EU, a state must transpose supranational law into its own national laws. In other settings, this is not the case and, generally, under any bilateral or multilateral arrangements or partnerships, it is largely voluntary. This means that under the current FTA arrangements, there might be a reference to cross-border data transfers, which are binding, although the provisions themselves are usually very broad.

Nonetheless, over time, it has been substantially proven that legal harmonisation 'arises from its ability to reduce transaction and compliance costs for firms operating or selling in multiple jurisdictions as well as providing benefits associated with joint production of regulatory products'.[320] Moreover, where businesses are having to comply with multiple sets of regulations across jurisdictions, this adds significant costs to the conducting of business across international borders. The result is that harmonised standards reduce the need to gather and analyse information about different regulatory standards across jurisdictions.[321] Hence, and while not embarking on an exhaustive discussion of the pros and cons of interoperability versus harmonisation, in this book, interoperability is seen as a positive first step towards nations states working with their counterparts to achieve cross-border data flows. However, interoperability does not address the ongoing facilitation of data flows in international trade. For transnational data transfers to be fully effective in the digital economy, there must be a concerted effort by states to collaborate closely and address the current legal gaps and

318. *Ibid.*
319. Luke Nottage, Justine Malbon, Jeanie Paterson and Caron Beaton-Wells, *ASEAN Consumer Law Harmonisation and Cooperation: Achievements and Challenges*, Cambridge University Press, (2019), p. 419.
320. Neil Quigley, *The Economics of Harmonisation: Implications for Reform of Commercial Law and Regulation in New Zealand*, 2003, p. 3, http://researcharchive.vuw.ac.nz/xmlui/bitstream/handle/10063/3885/Harmonisation_of_laws_200803.pdf?sequence=1.
321. *Ibid.*

tensions. While challenging, this is what will strengthen the overall economic benefits generated by data flows and trade in data.

The current policy and legal approach at both regional and international levels are incoherent, complex and cumbersome, with some rules, concepts and principles applying in some states and not others. This has created an environment where there is a lack of certainty about the regulatory framework. It only partly underpins the economic drivers that are required in the new digital economy. To open up the economic opportunities offered by the digital economy, a new legal framework is required, in the form of international law (convention, model law, principles or some other mechanism) and legal harmonisation. Failure to change this over the longer term will undermine trust, which constitutes one of the most important policy tools being used by governments worldwide to promote cross-border data flows and the digital economy. The next section examines briefly the importance of and for government to develop an international legal framework that will ensure a high level of trust.

§1.07 THE CONCEPT OF TRUST

It has become increasingly clear that the benefits of digital trade for both businesses and consumers depend strongly on the degree of trust (recognising that this can be understood differently) in the digital environment.[322] Individuals will not engage with businesses they do not 'trust' and businesses will struggle to reap the benefits of scale unless they can operate with 'trust' globally.[323] The concept of trust is not new and has been extensively written about by philosophers and legal scholars since time immemorial. Apropos of trust, according to John Locke, people have a supreme authority to remove the legislative power:

> when they find the legislative act contrary to the *trust* reposed in them: for all power given with trust for the attaining an end, being limited by that end, whenever that end is manifestly neglected, or opposed, the trust must necessarily be forfeited, and the power devolve into the hands of those that gave it, who may place it anew where they shall think best for their safety and security.[324]

While it is often difficult to reach an agreement on what the concept of trust means to the law, general policy, and the entire community, in the context of data flows, this concept is now used by governments to change the attitude and, importantly, the behaviour of everyone in regard to the regulation of data flows. Today, it is common to see trust as an element of the communications and policy position of some governments around the world. In 2019, the concept of DFFT, championed by Japan

---

322. General Data Protection Regulation (EU) 2016/679 of the European Parliament and of the Council of 27 April 2016, on the protection of natural persons with regard to the processing of personal data and on the free movement of such data, and repealing Directive 95/46/EC, Official Journal of the European Union L 119/1.
323. *Ibid.*
324. John Locke, *Second Treatise of Government*, Cambridge: Hackett Publishing, (1980), p. 73. According to him, power 'ought to be exercised by established and promulgated laws; that the people may know their duty, and be safe and secure within the limits of the law'.

under the G20 'Osaka Track', encapsulates the policy impetus to find a balanced solution to the challenges posed by data flows.[325]

According to Graham Greenleaf data free flow with trust (DFFT) may be a new label, but it is not a new concept when applied to data privacy or cybersecurity. The idea that the free flow of personal data could only be guaranteed by trust between countries has been around since at least 1980. In the original OECD Privacy Guidelines and Council of Europe data protection Convention, trust is induced by adherence to minimum standards of data protection.[326] Agreement on what constitutes the 'minimum standards' has been the problem. It is not clear why shifting discussions back to a WTO forum will have any effect on data privacy, although it might have an impact on IP and cybersecurity. Greenleaf further highlights that the fragmentation of the global regulation of transnational data flows continues. Countries continue to have different views concerning the framework that should be applied. The Joint Statement by the leaders of the BRICS [Brazil, Russia, India, China, South Africa][327] countries (both those that did not sign on to the Osaka Track) stressed the centrality of the WTO to a rules-based multilateral trading system; however, no explicit 'BRICS solidarity' was evident. India's Piyush Goyal said that data was a 'new form of wealth', important for development and raising the need to take into account the requirements of developing countries within WTO discussions rather than outside them.[328] It further reinforces the argument that more needs to be done at regional and international levels to establish to build an agreed legal framework such as that which has been effective in the trade in goods for a number of decades.

The ensuing challenges concern the way that the DFFT vision can be implemented beyond a bilateral context, across multiple institutions, regions and stakeholders.[329] Researchers have determined the link between openness and trust, but this

325. Graham Greenleaf, 'G20 Makes Declaration of Data Free Flow with Trust: Support and Dissent' (2019) (160) Privacy Laws & Business International Report, UNSW LRS (2020) 37, p. 1.
326. *Ibid.* Also *see*, Convention 108, Article 10 – Additional obligations. In order to ensure that the right to the protection of personal data is effective, additional obligations are imposed on the controller as well as, where applicable, the processor(s). According to *paragraph 1*, the obligation on the controller to ensure adequate data protection is linked to the responsibility to verify and be in a position to demonstrate that data processing is in compliance with the applicable law. The data protection principles set out in the Convention, which are to be applied at all stages of processing, including the design phase, aim at protecting data subjects and are also a mechanism for enhancing their trust. P. 25, https://rm.coe.int/convention-108-convention-for-the-protection-of-individuals-with-regar/16808b36f1, OECD, Guidelines governing the protection of privacy and transborder flows of personal data. A loss of trust or confidence can have serious consequences for organisations. As a result, the security of personal data has become an issue of great concern to governments, businesses and individuals, p. 26, https://www.oecd.org/sti/ieconomy/2013-oecd-privacy-guidelines.pdf.
327. *Ibid.* Also *see*, *Joint Statement on BRICS Leaders' Informal Meeting on the margins of G20 Summit*, 28 June 2019 http://pib.nic.in/PressReleseDetail.aspx?PRID = 1576270 Signed by the leaders of Brazil, Russia, India, China and South Africa.
328. *Ibid.* Also *see*, 'G20 summit: India does not sign Osaka declaration on cross-border data flow' https://scroll.in/latest/928811/g20- summit-india-does-not-sign-osaka-declaration-on-cross-border-data-flow.
329. Susan Aaronson, Fukunari Kimura, Hosuk Lee-Makiyama and Sheery Stephenson, 'Actions to Make "Data Free Flow with Trust" Operational in Practice' (2021) Taskforce 4 Digital Transformation 3-4.

depends on each relationship, which raises the question: what is the lowest common denominator of trust for the G20? In addition, trade disciplines are not the primary means of building trust. Trade agreements only guarantee an openness that is appropriate to the pre-existing level of trust.[330] Therefore, the question arises where does the distrust lie? Is it with the community or consumer, or is it a much broader and complex issue that needs to be resolved?

In 2021, Susan Aaronson et al. stated that many individuals distrust corporations and governments as they worry that personal data may be collected and exploited without their explicit consent. Many oppose the international transfer of their personal information to jurisdictions where data protection is weaker, not properly enforced, or where they may lack judicial rights to redress.[331] A December 2020 poll conducted by the Oxford Internet Institute found that 71% of Internet users are worried about how their personal data may be collected, analysed and monetised.[332] Aaronson argues that governments respond by attempting to either 'territorialise' data by demanding that personal information (or other sensitive data) stays within their jurisdiction by applying their privacy, fiscal and security laws in an extraterritorial manner or by banning cross-border flows of certain personal (or other types of) data. Aaronson maintains that this generates a lack of trust and creates conflicts between governments.

Without establishing systems and processes that can help to engender trust, the number of restrictions on data flows will continue to grow. However, distrust can be caused by many factors, as there is no single policy or legal issue that creates distrust in government and the system of governance itself. In this regard, COVID-19 provides a good example. During the pandemic, citizens in various countries have reacted very differently to the control measures their governments have imposed. In some countries, there have been violent protests, whereas, in other countries, citizens have fully complied with government directions. On the one hand, it must be noted though that this is due in part to the governance of the state and the level of trust in the government. On the other hand, globally, there is an increasing distrust of the vaccines being administered to control and contain COVID-19.

Aaronson asserts that there is no singular path to building trust for all relationships, and therefore this process is much more complex than setting out minimum regulatory standards or agreeing to commitments for trade openness in trade agreements. While rules on data flows are important for ensuring transparency, predictability and stability of the multilateral system, trust in the context of data flows can primarily and indirectly be achieved by making progress in two areas.[333]

Pertinent to the above, there are a number of governments such as the UK, Singapore, US, New Zealand, Canada and Australia which have placed the concept of trust at the front and centre of the policy debate and development of cross-border flow(s) regulation. To achieve this, these states, as well as other jurisdictions, are either developing or implementing a level of regulation for the transnational flow of data. This

330. *Ibid.*, pp. 3-4.
331. *Ibid.*
332. *Ibid.*
333. *Ibid.*

is gradually beginning to provide a level of legal certainty for individuals and entities, which will encourage them to engage in the digital economy via data flows. What the business community have at the current time is a state of legal uncertainty, which discourages potential new entrants to the market. It also makes it difficult for well-established entities to navigate the complex legal environment.

§1.08 THE ECONOMY AND GLOBAL TRADE

It is difficult to measure the economic benefits derived from transnational data flows, particularly since there are insufficient data and information available. There is a need to determine the amount of data used in trade, and the amount used in services. In addition, the emerging FinTech sector is using personal data, although there is relatively little information on this sector. These three areas, together with a regulatory framework, need to be addressed.

In this period of extended de-globalisation, the digital economy and the growth of data transfers are becoming increasingly globalised. This has produced a fragmented approach to the legal and policy framework that does not provide a conducive environment for data in the digital economy. According to Aaronson et al., there are 'no agreed multilateral rules governing regulatory aspects to cross-border data flows, and governments have taken very different approaches towards them. The global economy is experiencing a rapid fragmentation of jurisdictions over data governance with numerous regimes that have carved up the world economy into – digital silos'.[334] The only agreed measures that most nation states apply are the OECD Principles. Although in some nation states, these Principles are reflected within national laws, they are underpinned by more specific provisions that enable them to be enforced. Therefore, what is the current state of the global digital economy? More importantly, what is data value in the global economy?

Notwithstanding the above, it is difficult to measure data traffic, and no matter which approach is used, the trend is steeply upwards.[335] UNCTAD suggests that global Internet Protocol (IP) traffic in 2022 – domestic and international – will exceed all Internet traffic prior to 2016.[336] They also note that the COVID-19 pandemic has had a dramatic impact on Internet traffic as, increasingly, most activities took place online. During the peak of COVID-19 in 2020-2021, global Internet bandwidth rose by 35%, the largest annual increase since 2013.[337] It has been estimated that about 80% of all Internet traffic relates to videos, social networking and gaming. Monthly global data traffic is expected to surge from 230 exabytes in 2020 to 780 exabytes by 2026.[338]

334. Susan Aaronson, Fukunari, Hosek Lee-Makiyama and Sherry Stephenson, *Actions to Make 'Data Free Flow with Trust' Operational in Practice*, 2021, G20 Insights, https://www.g20-insights.org/policy_briefs/actions-to-make-data-free-flow-with-trust-operational-in-practice/.
335. United Nations Conference on Trade and Development, *Digital Economy Report 2021*, p. 1, https://unctad.org/system/files/official-document/der2021_overview_en_0.pdf.
336. *Ibid.*, p. 1.
337. *Ibid.*
338. *Ibid.*

Another significant question arises: what does this mean for the global economy, in real economic terms?

The task of measuring the economic impact of data on the digital economy and the economy in general is complex. There is little information available. However, nearly a decade ago in 2014, the free flow of data was estimated to have contributed USD 2.8 trillion to the global economy,[339] a figure that could reach USD 11 trillion by 2025.[340] It has been estimated that approximately 12% of international trade in goods occurs through global e-commerce platforms such as Alibaba and Amazon.[341] In the US, digital trade has augmented GDP by 3.4%-4.8% by increasing productivity and lowering the costs of trade; it has also increased wages and is likely to create as many as 2.4 million new jobs.[342] However, GVCs are being reshaped by cross-border data flows and new technologies, including digital platforms, the Internet of Things, and automation and AI.[343]

The most recent analysis in 2021, highlights that 'global data flows are a necessary component of international trade'.[344] That is, digital services and the data they generate are becoming an increasingly important feature of the global economy. In 2022 alone, '60% of the world's gross domestic product is projected to be digitised'.[345] As the trend towards digitalisation of the global economy continues to increase, so does the importance of trade in digital services. Nowhere is this more evident than in the transatlantic trade relationship, whereby the 'US exports of digitally-enabled services to the EU reached more than USD 167 billion in 2019. Conversely, it was estimated that the EU exported $130 billion to the US.'[346] Based on these figures alone of trade across the Atlantic Ocean, data in the digital economy is likely to far exceed the traditional trade in traditional goods and services. The author also mentions that data transfers are increasingly underpinning the importance of the digital economy. Given that this is the case, it has been recognised that cross-border data 'transfers have been beneficial to consumer welfare, by giving access to a wider range of goods and services at a lower cost'.[347] Hence, data flows transnationally have become 'good for businesses'.[348] This promotes the growth of the small- and medium-sized business sector of the economy. Governments around the world have emphasised that this sector of the economy needs to be opened up, not only in traditional areas of the economy but also in the data and

339. Susan Lund et al, *Globalisation in Transition: The Future of Trade and Value Chains*, McKinsey Global Institute, 2019.
340. Joshua Meltzer and, Peter Lovelock, *Regulating for a Digital Economy, Understanding the Importance of cross-Border Data Flows in Asia*, Brookings Institute, 2018, https://www.brookings.edu/wp-content/uploads/2018/03/digital-economy_meltzer_lovelock_web.pdf.
341. *Ibid.*
342. *Ibid.*
343. *Ibid.*
344. Tanguy Van Overstraaten, EU/US: Cross-Border Data Flows – A Necessary Part of Global Trade, 2021, https://www.linklaters.com/en/insights/blogs/digilinks/2021/june/eu---cross-border-data-flows---a-necessary-part-of-global-trade.
345. The Transatlantic Digital Economy, 2021, https://www.thrivingtogether.eu/analysis/148-the-transatlantic-digital-economy.
346. *Ibid.*
347. *Ibid.*
348. *Ibid.*

digital economy. It is estimated that, by lifting restrictions on data transfers, service imports could increase by an average of 5% across all countries.[349] This supports the position taken in this book: that between the EU and the US alone, the number of 'data policies restricting data uses domestically as well as its flow across borders has increased significantly (source)'.[350] It does not account for the regulatory impediments or restrictions.[351] Thus, this book takes this argument one step further and challenges the well-understood position that data protection laws are significantly fragmented. It further argues that at the international level, there is a lack of coordination and there is an urgent need not only for a high level of legal harmonisation but also for international law to open up this sector of the economy.

Nonetheless, as noted by Frontier economics, cross-border data flows will be a core 'driver of international trade'.[352] While the study focuses on the benefits to Europe, it provides a snapshot of what can be expected of other nation states. Centrally, the study shows how cross-border data flows will allow trade in the data value chain: data collection, aggregation, analysis, and use can be imported or exported.[353] Going a step further, it will allow for coordinating operations across GVCs, facilitate the flow of inputs of goods and services, and arguably significantly reduce transaction costs.[354] This last point about reducing transaction costs alone will be integral to the expansion of the economy, as individuals and entities realise the benefits. It is believed that data will reduce the costs of 'contracts and specifications order, packaging and delivery. For services sectors, in particular, cross-border data flows can increase the scope for supplying services remotely, limiting the need to avoid the fixed costs associated with establishing a physical presence':[355]

Case Study – One Airbus

The collection, aggregation, analysis and use of data have become fundamental to the airline industry – the latest Airbus A350 has 50,000 sensors on board. Airbus believes that the *'aviation industry is now entering into its next revolution: connected, fully-digital aviation'*. For example, in June 2017, Airbus launched Skywise, an open data platform that aggregates and processes large volumes of data from aircraft sensors, as well as operational data and maintenance data recorded by pilots, flight attendants, engineers, maintenance technicians and airport representatives. Skywise hosts data from Airbus, suppliers and more than one hundred airlines including EasyJet, Emirates and AirAsia. The data – and the cross-border data flows that unpin the collection, aggregation and processing of the data – enable services that provide real-time and longer-term benefits for Airbus, airlines, suppliers and consumers. Real-time remote access to in-flight data

349. *Ibid.*
350. *Ibid.*
351. *Ibid.*
352. Frontier Economics, *The Value of Cross-Border Data Flows to Europe: Risks and Opportunities*, 2021, pp. 12-13. Frontier Economics finds that cross-border data flows make a significant contribution to the EU economy.
353. *Ibid.*, p. 12. Data can be exported: sold or licensed to customers abroad; exports and imports of data-enabled products and services (connected cars, online platforms) typically require cross-border data flows.
354. *Ibid.*
355. *Ibid.*

helps in identifying problems early on and enables maintenance crews on the ground to be prepared for when the plane lands, it has around 180 locations globally and 12,000 suppliers. Each year Airbus' aircraft enable millions of passengers to travel across cities, countries, and continents. collecting 2.5 terabytes of data every day, reducing turn-around times, delays and cancellations. In the long term, Skywise data helps Airbus to understand how their aircraft behave in reality (across different geographies and business models) and improve the design of new aircraft models, and increase reliability, fuel efficiency and safety.

Source: Frontier Economics, 2021.[356]

Given the above, Wendy Li, Makoto Nirei and Kazufumi Yamana[357] highlight how everyday consumers provide their personal data in exchange for a good or service, particularly when purchasing online. In their study, they note that separating the value of data under the above areas, when combined with licensing commission access, has generated more than USD 32.79 billion, and the value-based data-driven business model generated more than USD 204.9 billion[358] in 2019. The authors make the point that the conceptual difficulties include the need to 'understand how online platforms create values from data and monetise that data'.[359] However, getting that 'data and information from online platform firms is difficult'.[360] Even though these estimates provide an outline of the current and potential future worth of the data-driven economy, the ability to accurately assess the value of the data is complex. It is arguably a closed shop, which very few individuals or organisations can access to accurately confirm its overall economic value.[361] Yet in another estimate, 'the flow of digital data increased globally [GDP] by USD 3,691 billion throughout 2020'.[362] The monetary

356. *Ibid.*, p. 18. Other sectors that are set to rely on data flows include but are not limited to Sea transport; Air transport; Other modes of transport; Postal and courier services; Construction; Insurance and pension services; Financial services; Telecommunications services; Computer services; Legal services; Accounting, auditing, bookkeeping, and tax consulting services; Architectural services; Engineering services; and Audiovisual and related services.
357. Wendy C.Y. Li, Makoto Nirei and, Kazufumi Yamana, *Value of Data: There's No Such Thing as a Free Lunch in the Digital Economy*, 2019, https://voxeu.org/article/no-such-thing-free-lunch-digital-economy, or, https://www.rieti.go.jp/jp/publications/dp/19e022.pdf. *See also*: Wendy C. Y. Li, Makoto Nirei, and Kazufumi Yamana, *Value of Data: There's No Such Thing as a Free Lunch in the Digital Economy*, Sixth IMF Statistical Forum, Washington, DC, 19-20 November 2018. In, Robert Walters, 'Cross Border Data Flows: An Evolving Multilayered Regulatory Approach Required!' (2022) Global Privacy Review 29-33.
358. *Ibid.*, however note that these estimates were not able to quantify the amount of data generated from LinkedIn, eBay, Waze, Google. The calculation of the actual amount of data is very difficult to confirm. This is partly because there is a lack of understanding of how the data itself generates a value, the systems used, and the regulatory framework not supporting the need to report on such. The above has not compared this with tax returns from these relevant businesses. The above analysis does not account for the data traded as part of Mergers or Acquisitions.
359. *Ibid.*
360. *Ibid.*
361. Robert Walters, 'Cross Border Data Flows: An Evolving Multilayered Regulatory Approach Required!' (2022) Global Privacy Review.
362. Gary Clyde Hufbauer and Zhiyao (Lucy) Lu, 'Can Digital Flows Compensate for Lethargic Trade and Investment?' (2018) Peterson Institute of Economics. In Congressional Research Services, *Data Flows, Online Privacy, and Trade Policy* (2020), p. 1, https://sgp.fas.org/crs/misc/R45584.pdf.

significance cannot be underestimated. Additionally, international data flows have also been described as being beneficial to consumer welfare, 'by giving access to a wider range of goods and services at a lower cost'.[363] Tanguy Van Overstraeten believes that data flows enable businesses to 'scale up IT capacities and allow SMEs (small- and medium-sized business) to compete more readily with bigger companies'.[364] This is an important sector that policymakers are continuing to grapple with and provide opportunities for SMEs. Van Overstraeten further makes the point that for multinationals, meanwhile, data flows are nothing less than essential for day-to-day business. He believes that efficient supply chain management relies on the smooth flow of goods, services, capital and data. Therefore, the lifting of restrictions on 'data transfers/flows could increase services imports by an average of 5% across all countries'.[365] This in and of itself is highly important. Most people in the community would not be aware of the extent data is being used, as in the Airbus example. As the world economy recovers from the pandemic, it is vital the governments provide a framework for this to occur. In part, what Van Overstraeten argues about can be achieved by providing legal clarity through legal harmonisation.

However, this is another area that needs to be reconciled. With any future law reform whether nationally or internationally, improved reporting is required of data sets, quantity of data collected, the use and processing of that data, and where that data is transferred. To get the balance right between economic growth, trade and privacy, a reporting process similar to tax reporting would be established. While out of the scope of this book, tax reporting has served nation states very well for decades. In part, this has already been proposed. However, the proposal could be extended to reporting data flows. That is, the World Bank, OECD, and G20: have proposed a global Digital Data Tax and a Global Internet Tax Agency to provide legal certainty on cross-border digital tax issues.[366] Nevertheless, the US believes that 'cross-border data flows are central to trade and trade negotiations as organizations'.[367] This will be explored later in this book, whereby an examination of current trade agreements will be undertaken to confirm, or otherwise, the existence, or lack thereof, of cross-border data flows provisions.

A further and more accentuating issue that has emerged is the financial sector, particularly FinTech. FinTech is a new economic activity, and consumers are exploring ways to use this sector as another for personal efficiency and economic activity and gain. According to the OECD, there is evidence that 'consumers are also willing to share

363. Tanguy Van Overstraeten, Cross-Border Data Flows: A Necessary Part of Global Trade, Digital Economy, Trade and External Affairs, Amcham-EU, 2021, http://www.amchameu.eu/blog/cross-border-data-flows-necessary-part-global-trade.
364. *Ibid.*
365. *Ibid.*
366. International Economic, Strategic Analysis for Growth & Development, Trade, Privacy and Cross Border Data flows, https://www.tradeeconomics.com/trade-privacy-and-cross-border-data-flows/.
367. Congressional Research Services, *Data Flows, Online Privacy, and Trade Policy* (2020), p. 1, https://sgp.fas.org/crs/misc/R45584.pdf.

additional personal data with financial providers if this results in perceived benefits'.[368] In referring to two global surveys conducted over the past decade, the OECD note that 'more than a quarter (27%) of Internet users across seventeen countries strongly agree that they are willing to share their personal data in exchange for benefits or rewards, such as lower costs or personalised services. The percentage of users who are firmly unwilling to share their data is around 19%. The survey also indicates that Internet users aged 30-40 are most likely to share data for rewards'.[369] Second, another survey that focused on the financial services sector estimated:

> 60% of the consumers surveyed globally indicate that they would share more data with banks, insurers, or investment advisory firms if this translated into priority services, pricing benefits, more personalised products or non-regulated financial advice. This percentage increases among categories of consumers that are younger and more digitally keen. These consumers are open to begin making financial transactions through the range of websites that allow the purchase of goods and services. Significantly, the OECD note that for these consumers, and for the generations born after the 1990s in particular, GAFAs are also attractive alternatives to traditional financial providers, with 40% of them that would consider banking with a number of online platforms. This is even higher in markets such as the United States, where 50% would be willing to make this switch.[370]

As explained by the OECD, blockchain technologies capture large quantities of personal data during financial transactions. The OECD states: 'blockchain is a technology with huge potential across a wide range of applications. It utilises distributed ledger technology to store information verified by cryptography, which is agreed through a pre-defined network protocol, often without the control of a central authority. The technology can be used to secure the transfer and traceability of value as well as the transfer of data. Its distributed nature of nodes makes it attractive for cyber-security and privacy'.[371] Most significant in this example is when 'personal information that is stored on the blockchain cannot be deleted because of its decentralised character with immutable blocks'.[372] As the FinTech sector continues to rely on this technology, an ensuing question is: how does the current regulatory framework provide consumers with the right to deletion, access, disclosure, amongst others? This is highly problematic. Apart from urgent further research needed in this area, a solution is to regulate that this technology must allow for a data subject to be able to access and delete their personal data. It needs to come from a regulator, or a group of regulators, for the technology sector to act. Taking this position is based on the current regulatory framework enabling citizens in most countries afforded the ability to practice their

368. Organisation for Economic Cooperation and Development, Personal Data Use in Financial Services and the Role of Financial Education: A Consumer-Centric Analysis, 2020, p. 5, https://www.oecd.org/finance/Personal-Data-Use-in-Financial-Services-and-the-Role-of-Financial-Education.pdf.
369. *Ibid.*, p. 20.
370. *Ibid.* Also *see*, Accenture (2019), Accenture Global Financial Services Consumer Study, https://www.accenture.com/_acnmedia/PDF-95/Accenture-2019-Global-Financial-Services-Consumer-Study.pdf.
371. *Ibid.*, p. 12.
372. *Ibid.* pp. 25-26, the OECD calls for further work to be undertaken in this area.

rights. However, it is a call for nation states that have not, to provide a level of regulatory clarity. Without regulatory clarity, consumers are operating in a vacuum not knowing what and how their data is being used. Providing regulatory clarity will also enable the FinTech sector to grow and establish a higher level of economic activity that will be beneficial to the national and global economy. The OECD, while providing a pathway forward, which is needed, by and large, focuses on further research and understanding of this sector. In my view, this is the first step that needs to be shaped in a way that ensures it can provide evidence for any further regulatory reform. A further accentuating issue is that there is no call for an international approach to developing regulations that strike a balance between data rights and FinTech expansion.

Thus, under the new digital economy, achieving an optimal regulatory balance between privacy, data protection and FinTech, and other trade and service sectors will be highly technical. Stacy-Ann Elvy[373] makes the point that in support of many online trades, financial and investment platforms, entities have developed sophisticated tools to assist consumers. Elvy highlights two approaches to addressing the challenges faced in balancing privacy, data protection and economic activity. First is 'the discount pay-for-privacy (PFP) approach. It requires consumers to pay higher fees to avoid data collection and targeted advertisements while offering discounts to consumers who consent to these practices – is the latest business scheme to receive widespread attention'.[374] Second is the growing personal data economy (PDE) that has evolved and today challenges the central role of data brokers and other established companies in the consumer data market. The PDE is a – user-centric data – concept that permits individuals to take ownership of their information so they can share it with businesses on their terms. These are just two examples and there is possible other technology on the market that does similar. While PFP and PDE programmes go some way to striking a balance through data portability and providing consumers with more controls, Elvy argues that they both provide significant challenges, as the agreements and legal frameworks supporting them are fragmented, and 'account for new monetisation schemes'.[375] This is a form of data portability, which has been adopted by the EU and a number of nation states.

Centrally, data portability principles that are clear must be set in light of which transfer of the data will be possible, with the aim of achieving a high level of interoperability.[376] Paul De Hert et al. state that 'a free portability of personal data from one controller to another can be a strong tool for data subjects in order to foster competition of digital services and interoperability of platforms and in order to enhance

373. Stacy-Ann Elvy, 'Paying for privacy and the personal data economy' (2017) 117(6) Columbia Law Review 1369-1372.
374. *Ibid.*, pp. 1445-1447.
375. *Ibid.*, p. 1446.
376. Organisation for Economic Co-operation and Development, *Data Portability, Interoperability and Competition: Note by Israel*, June 2021, https://one.oecd.org/document/DAF/COMP/WD(2021)28/en/pdf.

controllership of individuals on their own data'.[377] Data portability is only a recent addition to the data protection legal framework. This again is another area of the law that is highly fragmented and allows individual data subjects to transfer their data between organisations. However, it is out of the scope of this book to examine the extent of data portability laws.

That said, UNCTAD are of the view that three models have emerged internationally. First, 'the approach of the United States focuses on control of the data by the private sector. Second, the Chinese model emphasises control of data by the Government, while the third is how the EU favours control of data by individuals on the basis of fundamental rights and values. Third, the current context is one of tensions among these areas, particularly between the United States and China. Moreover, global digital corporations are seeking to expand their own data ecosystems'. While I agree with UNCTAD, it is argued that other models have also emerged. For example, Singapore, while following elements of the EU and the US legal frameworks, it is my view that their model addresses their high-level policy commitment of the state to be a smart nation,[378] through high levels of connectivity. With this policy direction in mind, it is argued that their data framework is what can be referred to as the business-friendly model.[379] If so agreed, this would add a fourth model to the other three. However, it is the US, in my view, that takes a more consumer lead approach.

While there has been a significant increase in economic activity from data flows over the past five years, UNCTAD reinforces the importance of this book. They highlight that the 'proliferation of national regulations on cross-border data flows creates uncertainty and elevates compliance costs, which can be particularly pernicious for micro and small enterprises, especially in developing countries. The interconnected nature and high degree of global interdependence in the data-driven digital economy mean that national policies in this area have spill-overs on other countries'.[380] Problematic also has that in the 'absence of global governance of digital platforms, self-regulation has led to market structures defined by platforms that predominantly benefit themselves, with various development and policy implications. The increasingly global reach and influence of major platforms make it even more difficult for any single country to address related policy challenges'.[381] On this basis, it is argued that there is no better time for there to be a consideration for the development of an

377. Paul De Hert, Vagelis Papakonstant, Gianclaudio Malgieri, Laurent Beslay and Ignacio Sanchez, 'The Right to Data Portability in the GDPR: Towards User-Centric Interoperability of Digital Services' (2018) 34(2) Computer Law. & Security Review 193, 193.
378. Woo Jun Jie, *Singapore's Smart Nation Initiative: A Policy and Organisational Perspective*, Lee Kuan Yew School of Public Policy (LKY School), National University of Singapore, (2018), https://lkyspp.nus.edu.sg/docs/default-source/case-studies/singapores-smart-nation-initiative-final_112018.pdf?sfvrsn=354e720a_2.
379. Robert Walters and Marko Novak, *Cyber Security, Artificial Intelligence, Data Protection & the Law*, 1st ed. Springer (2021), Chapter 15. Also *see*: Robert Walters, Leon Trakman and Bruno Zeller, *Data Protection Law: A Comparative Analysis of Asia-Pacific and European Approaches*, Springer (2019), Chapter 17.
380. United Nations Conference on Trade and Development, *Digital Economy Report 2021*, p. 8, https://unctad.org/system/files/official-document/der2021_overview_en_0.pdf.
381. *Ibid.*

international legal instrument that can facilitate a level of legal harmonisation. This would be the first step to developing more legal certainty and economic activity in and across the digital economy for data. It would also provide a more important step for nation states to move away from interoperability, towards legal convergence and harmonisation. This book calls on nation states and international organisations and institutions such as UNCTAD, UNCITRAL, OECD, World Bank and national governments to come together and move away from interoperability to harmonisation of legal concepts through an international convention, model law or other instrument(s).

§1.09 METHODOLOGY AND STRUCTURE

The methodology adopted in this book to analyse these legal developments extends beyond law *stricto sensu* to include technological developments. Part I of this book will begin by examining the international and regional laws, policy concepts and principles that have been established to facilitate the transnational flow of data. Part II will examine the current national laws of Australia, Indonesia, India, Canada, Japan, Singapore, New Zealand, the UK, the US and the supranational polity of the EU. It will confirm what, if any, provisions provide for the cross-border flow of data, in the respective data laws. Second, it will examine and confirm what if any FTAs provide specific provisions for transnational data flows and their protection. Third, it will also examine the newly introduced Digital Agreement established by some states. Fourth, the book will demonstrate the additional legal mechanisms, such as BCR, SCC and international standards, that have been established to assist in facilitating data flows. Part III diverges and considers cybersecurity, obstacles to data flows, dispute resolution, international insolvency and the emergence of the FinTech sector. Finally, it will provide a pathway forward and discuss the increasingly important role that Data Diplomacy is having in the international development of data flows.

This book will invoke more questions than what it will resolve, such as:

- Can the current framework for data protection, data flows and data adequacy co-exist?
- Will data flows and the digital economy eventually require regulators to rethink the current legal landscape?
- How can privacy and data protection over the Internet be secured when there is a competing push of Open Data?
- The current notion of the concept of interoperability has been developed for technology to co-exist, and the law has now been used to achieve a level of compatibility – is interoperability relevant for the law?
- Legal harmonisation and convergence have been achieved in regard to trade in goods and services – can this be done for data in the digital economy?
- The concept of trust is a major policy outcome for governments around the world in the area of data flows, can this ever be fully achieved?
- Case law has identified areas of technology and the law – can we ever fully understand the extent to which a data subject can be identified online?

- Data Diplomacy is emerging as an assistant to cyber diplomacy – how can this be transformed into a dedicated diplomacy programme?
- The current storage arrangements of data within the cloud are restricted to servers located in strategic locations around the world – how do law and policy experts need to understand and build their knowledge of this? This knowledge is largely retained by technologists.

This book will attempt to answer some of the above questions (*see* final chapter). There is a significant amount of knowledge that policy and legal experts need to understand. Many areas within the law and policy are far from settled and may never be. This book does not address the right of access, right to disclosure or deletion afforded to data subjects, by some jurisdictions in transnational data flows. Centrally, the comparative analysis examines how the above jurisdictions have accommodated data flows into their respective data laws, and selected trade agreements.

Research Referencing, Terminology and Limitations

Referencing through the book will at times duplicate and be outside convention due to the breadth and depth of law examined and compared. It has been structured in this way to ensure the reader can clearly identify the legal or scholarly source.

Further to the above, terminology and use of terms include data transfers, international data transfers, and transnational data transfers, which all mean the same.

Additionally, the terms state, nation states, countries or jurisdiction mean all the countries examined in this book including the supranational polity of the EU. This is because the EU is not a country.

The terms personal data, personal information, data or information are all interchangeable and mean personal data. This is because the laws of the respective jurisdictions in this book refer to this data as either personal information or personal data.

The book does not examine all the rights afforded to data subjects where their personal data has been transferred to a third country. The book is a small sample of a much larger area of law that needs urgent and more comprehensive research. While the main focus has been to examine trade agreements. The book also examines recent agreements that have emerged such as Digital Agreements. These may not specifically relate directly to trade, although, indirectly it is argued their importance will underpin future data transfers in the digital economy. Therefore, having a direct benefit to future trade. Moreover, while the book by and large focuses on bilateral agreements, there are times when it diverges to discuss multilateral agreements, because of the expansion of the digital economy. An important limitation has been to reconcile the different national laws and their approach to data flows. On this basis, the national law discussion is narrow and only pertains to data transfer, definition of personal data and consent provisions. The divergence in approach has resulted in country chapters being brief, with no comparative analysis. Taking the position to focus on trade agreements has restricted the national law analysis. This book raises more questions than answers. Importantly, it highlights an area of the law (trade agreements) that can be expanded upon, to strengthen the governance of data flows.

Chapters

There are seventeen chapters that have been divided into *three Parts*. *Part 1*, Chapter 1 is lengthy to provide the reader with the extent of policy, scholarly and law that needs to be addressed when discussing and considering a pathway forward in relation to cross-border data flows. Doing so has demonstrated the Problem Definition as being complex, multilayered and incoherent. There are international and regional organisations all pulling in different directions. The resulting effect has seen a highly fragmented approach to developing law and policy for data flows in the new digital economy. It identifies the models of data laws that have emerged and help facilitate data transfers and economic activity.

Part 2 addresses the current-day data flow laws within the jurisdictions compared. This includes Australia, the EU, the UK, Canada, India, Indonesia, Japan, New Zealand, and the US. In addition, the chapters in this Part extend to the current Multilateral FTAs and other mechanisms these jurisdictions are currently operating within. Each chapter only deals with data flow laws, the definition of data and the operation of consent. It does not address the other rights and obligations that a data subject might have in relation to their data being transferred outside of their country of origin. Moreover, this Part also explores the current cross-border standards and rules that industries have adopted to facilitate data flows and their governance.

Part 3 diverged from the country and jurisdictional comparisons to focus more broadly on specific emerging areas of the law that need to be considered in data flows and the digital economy. This Part attempts to address broader issues related to impeding data flows in the digital economy. It examines the obstacles to data flows and the digital economy. It further explores and discusses cyber security and the new under-regulated area of FinTech-TechFin. This Part further discusses data flows and cross-border insolvency, whereby, entities located in different jurisdictions are subject to financial stress and are declared insolvent. Moreover, data flows are likely to be subject to disputes for example those that are subject to contractual obligations. Finally, this Part discusses the emerging area of data diplomacy and its ability to be used by governments to strengthen the legal framework for data flows.

Chapter 1 introduces the book and highlights the fragmented approach to policy development and regulation of transnational data flows. While a lengthy chapter, it attempts to address the question of what is data and has a lot to unpack as to how its regulation has been evolving and being shaped? Can it be categorised as a good or a service? Chapter 1, apart from highlighting the problem definition, also discussed how data has been characterised into models of law based on economic, risk and sovereign needs. It further demonstrates how the international and regional organisations have approached the development of law and policy in an incoherent and uncoordinated manner that has resulted in a highly fractured legal landscape. The overall Problem Definition highlights how the jurisdictions compared have either established laws that facilitated data flows and in some cases lack laws altogether. Most noteworthy are the WTO-GATS rules that can apply to data flows and help pave the way for the digital economy to expand and grow going forward. Viewed this way, this book is timely and underscores the economic benefits of data flows to the international, regional and national economies. It further underscores the transition in international trade. That is, while globalisation of international trade is being wound back in certain areas of goods and services, technology and the digital economy is the fastest area of globalisation. Therefore, to expand this area of the economy, the current legal frameworks that will be compared in this book, particularly bilateral and multilateral trade agreements are increasingly important. It will help shape and influence the concept of Trust in data flows and its legal landscape.

Chapter 2 examines the developments in and the current day digital economy as it pertains to Australia. It examines the current data laws of Australia and selected trade agreements it has established with the other jurisdictions compared in this book. It does not examine current trade agreements under negotiation. The most recent trade agreement negotiated and signed was between Australia and India in early April 2022.

The EU has been arguably a benchmark in the development of data laws for more than two decades. Their laws have played a major role internationally in establishing the legal norms and principles in the development of data law. Chapter 3 examines the current data EU data laws as they pertain to data flows. It also examines the UK as this country while leaving the EU, still retains the Union's legal framework for data flows and data adequacy. It highlights the role of data adequacy and how it is being used to gain a level of interoperability between the EU and third countries. That interoperability provides for a level of adequacy. It is this adequacy that is publicised and recognition of a similar level of protection for that data when transferred, for example, between the UK and the EU today, is granted. This chapter is also important as it discusses the enforcement of data laws by the EU and raises questions on how data subjects are identified online by a series of data points.

Chapter 4 explores how Canada has approached the law of data flows, and what this means to their economy. Canada, another Commonwealth country along with India, Australia, Singapore and New Zealand has had a mature data legal framework for more than two decades. This chapter will also analyse recent trade agreements Canada has established with the other jurisdictions compared in this book, to confirm whether data flows and their security have been adequately addressed.

India, a Commonwealth country located in central Asia is emerging as an economic priority for many countries around the world. They have one of the largest growing technology sectors, and their economy has for some time been heavily dependent on outsourcing, which has resulted in the collection and use of large quantities of personal data. Chapter 5 highlights how India are yet to have established specific data laws. Their current-day laws are under review. The sectorial approach taken by India has resulted in a highly fractious data flow framework that has allowed for data localisation laws to be also scattered amongst a number of different local laws. This has further resulted in a legal landscape that provides a level of uncertainty. Chapter 5 will also examine a selected number of FTAs India has with other states to confirm, or otherwise, the recognition and reflection of data flows and their security.

Indonesia, similar to India has not implemented specific data laws. Indonesia is located in Southeast Asia and is a member of the ASEAN. ASEAN while not a supranational polity whereby nation states have afforded a level of sovereignty in the same way as the Member States of the EU On this basis, Chapter 6 explores the current data flow laws and selected trade agreements.

Chapter 7 has for some time had a well-grounded legal framework in relation to data. Chapter 7 examines how Japan deals with data flows and the protection of personal data when transferred beyond the state. This chapter also examines a selection of trade agreements that Japan has established with the jurisdictions compared.

New Zealand is one of Australia's closest neighbours. Chapter 8 discusses New Zealand's data law and specifically focuses on data transfers with third countries. They have, for some time, had a mature data legal framework that has a lot of similarities with Australia. This chapter also explores the recent agreement between New Zealand and Singapore that addresses data in the new digital economy, along with a selected number of trade agreements.

The US does not have specific data laws at the national level. To date, they have adopted a sectoral approach whereby, data regulation is governed by various laws such as those under the responsibility of the Federal Trade Commission. Chapter 9 takes a narrow approach and only examines elements of the Federal Trade Commission laws, with a specific focus on the recent judicial decisions in relation to the US-EU Safe-Harbor Framework and its forerunner, Privacy Shield. This is particularly important because this programme has been significantly impacted and imposed under considerable pressure on the transfer of data between the EU and the US. It demonstrates how the EU's rights-based approach has not taken kindly to third countries having an approach whereby the relevant safeguards for data are not at an appropriate equivalent level.

Multilateral trade agreements have also become an important part of country-to-country economic activity. Chapter 10 examines the current-day multilateral trade agreements that the jurisdictions examined are a partner to those agreements. It will demonstrate that there is a need for data flows and data protection to be more comprehensively accounted for when future negotiations are undertaken. Against the backdrop of the above chapters, industry standards and other rules such as BCR and SCC are important additions to the law of data flows. They are used to help facilitate data flows and govern data throughout its life cycle. Therefore, Chapter 11 discusses these rules and industry standards such as the International Standards Organisation.

In diverging from trade agreements, there has been a number of obstacles that have emerged to ensure data flows can be undertaken efficiently and as effective as possible. Chapter 12 discusses the impediments now faced by individuals and entities because of data localisation. That is, the book demonstrates how nation states have taken very different approaches to implementing and not implementing this concept. For example, Australia has restricted data localisation to health data, yet, India has taken a sporadic approach. However, other states have no data localisation requirements. While an impediment to data flows, this chapter discusses the possibility of a digital tax. It calls for a global tax for data flows, which could be implemented by the proposed international institution for data. While it is recognised there will be scholars, regulators, government and practitioners who will strongly oppose such a proposal, doing so will provide more benefits than the obstacles created by such a proposal.

The security of data has become one of the most concerning issues to address when data is transferred across international borders. Chapter 13 explores the security risks to data transfers and the complexity of securing the data and balancing this with the WTO-GAT rules. One of the biggest challenges for organisations both public and private is ensuring there is a high level of security of personal data before, during and post an international transfer. This challenge is not isolated to a single country, region or jurisdiction. Security issues pervade the Internet, at every step in the input, transmission and receipt of personal data. By analysing the security risks to data transfers, this chapter examines the balance that is sometimes not being struck between protecting and securing data transfers in accordance with that of WTO-GAT rules.

The growth in the development of FinTech-TechFin as a new economic activity highlights the possibility of another sector where data will be highly vulnerable to intrusions. Chapter 14 discusses how this sector is largely unregulated and governments are grappling with how to approach regulating and developing laws for this financial sector. This chapter highlights how data flows are a consistent feature of financial activity over the Internet. It calls for a deeper level of urgent research to better understand the extent of data flows across in FinTech-TechFin.

Cross-border insolvency has emerged as an important area of transnational commercial law. On the one hand, Chapter 15 briefly examines data flows in cross-border insolvency. On the other hand, Chapter 16 addresses data flows in dispute resolution. Departing from the traditional discussion in relation to face-to-face arbitration, this chapter examines online arbitration, and what practitioners need to be aware of when undertaking this evolving area of dispute resolution.

The final Chapter 17 further diverges from the law of data flows and adds an additional programme component that can be used by governments to strengthen the rules for transnational data transfers. It introduces the concept of data-digital diplomacy as a new and emerging area of diplomacy outside of cyber security. Adopting such an approach will help governments and regulators to engage other countries and further develop this area of the law. It provides an outline of the programmes that can and are being sued by states. This includes country-to-country, government-to-government engagement, through education, awareness and compliance programmes. It calls for the exchange of skills through the establishment of knowledge and skill hubs while encouraging the exchange of similar technologies. Finally, this chapter provides a pathway forward for data flows and the law, calling for further research to be undertaken. It also calls for consideration of an international body to be established that can oversee the development and internationalisation of data flows and the law. This chapter also recommends that further work be undertaken to establish both a national and international reporting framework for all data transfers to be logged with a regulator, in the same way as tax is recorded.

§1.10 CONCLUSION

This chapter has introduced the book to the current-day regulation of transnational data flows. The regulation and application of cross-border data transfers are becoming increasingly important to the world economy, particularly the digital economy. Beginning in the 1970s in Europe, transborder data flow regulation has spread around the world. A number of instruments regulating transborder data flows have been enacted on an international scale, some legally binding and others not. The variety of instruments, the diversity of international organisations that have enacted them, and the failure to agree on a global standard for data protection have meant that there is a lack of overall global harmonisation.

Additionally, at the international and regional levels, the number of institutions and organisations now playing a role in the future direction and policy development of data laws has risen significantly. Yet, they are as highlighted in this chapter, focusing on specific needs, and there appears to be a lack of coordination on the policy concepts being established. Therefore, the fragmentation is at four levels. First, institutional fragmentation where there appears to be a lack of alignment. Second, the policy concepts being established do not necessarily talk to each other. Third, the disconnection between binding and non-binding instruments. Fourth, nation states have by and large gone their own ways in the development of data laws, which has led to a highly complex and fragmented legal landscape.

The OECD Guidelines and Principles have emerged as the benchmark, however, they are non-binding. They date back to the 1980s (with amendments), have served the international community very well, and can be found in most national laws. As a result, the current-day models for data flows have been described as being open, conditional or controlled. It is argued that those jurisdictions that have embraced the open model are beginning to be rewarded with strong economic activity of data in the digital economy. At the other end of the spectrum, those jurisdictions that have adopted the controlled model have significantly limited the extent to which data can be generated through economic activity. However, some nation states have called for an international binding international Convention to regulate what the Guidelines aim to achieve. It has been acknowledged by the OECD that the current guidelines offer an excellent starting point for the internationalisation and harmonisation of data laws. Doing so will enable data flows, rather than states looking inwards and default to establish restrictive legal measures.

Data is nothing new and can be traced back to C18,000 BCE. This chapter has highlighted how the earliest examples of humans storing and analysing data are the tally sticks. Palaeolithic tribespeople would mark sticks or bones with notches to keep track of trading activity or supplies. Data has different characteristics and has been presented in different ways throughout history. In today's digital economy, data has been defined by models that are open, conditional or controlled. Hence, this issue is determined on a case-by-case basis defined by how and where it is used, and whether it is coupled with analytics, or otherwise. Although no consensus has been reached as to whether data is a good or a service, it tends to be more closely associated with a service. Therefore, under current international trade law, it can fall within the GATS.

Therefore, and based on the above, data transfers will form an integral part of the fourth Industrial Revolution (IR4). However, a problem arises in regard to the implementation of IR4 and data in the digital economy: economic activity needs to be balanced with the need to have appropriate controls in place to ensure that people's privacy over the Internet is maintained and at a high level. This will not be easy to achieve. There will be unprecedented amounts of data flowing from continent to continent and between nation states. The security and vulnerabilities are far from being fully understood. There is the possibility that with millions or trillions of terabytes of data moving around the world at any one time, it could make it easier for that data to fall into the wrong hands of state and non-state actors.

When coupled with IR4, and the explosion of the FinTech sector, there is a lack of understanding of the extent of data flows. The FinTech sector is an emerging area of the economy that is largely unregulated. It relies on technology such as blockchain to facilitate transactions. Problematic though is the ability for the consumer to apply current-day data protection law and request that their data on this technology be accessed, deleted or disclosed by and to them, this is another area that needs to be reconciled, and under the current framework of interoperability and data adequacy, it creates additional uncertainty rather than a high level of clarity.

Against the backdrop of the above, there needs to be a move away from the current Principle-based model, which has served data flows and data protection law well over a number of decades. Moreover, as a consequence of this Principle-based model, other concepts such as interoperability and data adequacy have emerged as the only choice to achieve a level of equivalency between nation states and their legal frameworks. Interoperability has proven effective in managing the flow of information between technology systems and infrastructure. It is being viewed as providing an agile and flexible approach to governing data flows. Yet, there are a number of grey zones that heighten the need for clarification of standards.

Nonetheless, some jurisdictions such as the EU take a hands-on governmental approach, while other jurisdictions such as Australia take a hands-off approach and leave it to the private sector. That is, under the EU data adequacy, decision is made essential by the Commission that involves the EU GDPR and a third country. It is a governmental decision. Whereas, in Australia, the private organisation transferring the data to an organisation located in a third country has full responsibility to ensure a level of equivalent protection. To date, most states are heading the way of interoperability as a way of recognising the level of adequacy of the other states' data laws. As this chapter has demonstrated, interoperability is far from efficient and effective, over the longer term. It is what this book argues is a first step to achieving a level of legal harmonisation.

Significant too, states that have acceded to Convention 108, in theory, do not need to obtain data adequacy from the EU under the GDPR. Therefore, this book calls for more work to be done in this area to achieve legal harmonisation, rather than rely on interoperability. Doing so will close the gap in the otherwise high fragmented legal landscape of data flows, data protection and data adequacy. It further calls for international law to be developed for this area of the economy, in the same way as commercial trade in goods has been successful. Thus, it further highlights the level of fragmentation.

This chapter has demonstrated the importance of cross-border data flows to the current and future economy and trade of the world, not just individual nation states. It has further demonstrated that expected growth in economic activity, if the policy and legal setting are right, will open up the small and medium business sectors. These sectors alone are in need of a much-needed policy boost, coming out of COVID-19 and its economic, social and health impacts.

An accentuating issue for governments and regulators to boost the economy through and by data transfers is by enabling this to occur. To date, the debate and position by most governments has been to create a regulatory environment that instils trust and confidence in the market. Trust is a core element of all commercial law. Without it, there would be a significant lack of certainty. However, the next step for governments and regulators to enhance and strengthen the concept of trust is to go international (*see* Chapter 17).

While regulatory reform is urgently required to open up the digital economy and data flows, it should be undertaken in conjunction with other initiatives. For example, there is a lack of understanding of the extent of data flows internationally. While construed as a possible further legal and administrative burden, to fully grasp the enormity of data flows a reporting system should be considered. However, under many states' data laws, today entities are required to report a breach of the law to their respective Regulatory. This reporting should be extended to reporting international data flows – annually. Apart from providing national economies with valuable economic data, it will create a repository, whereby, developed properly could be a valuable resource whereby any consumer can gain access to track their personal data. It will provide certainty and clarity for consumers and enhance economic growth.

In undertaking the proposed reform, while not easy, it will have significant benefits to and for data in the new digital economy. It will provide greater legal certainty. It will assist in providing great investment, trade, jobs, skills and education. Further, it will provide opportunities for new entrants into the digital economy by reducing the regulatory and legal burden faced by the small- and medium-sized business sectors. A formal and functional outcome will reduce transactional costs for business. Failure to do so, will not meet many government policy objectives of Open Data, establishing a higher level of trust and legal certainty, in a highly complex economic and legal environment. Importantly too, it will bring along other nation states that have not implemented laws that deal with data flows, or, albeit minimally.

On a final point, most states have used the EU model as the benchmark for data laws. The question is: has it struck the right balance between its predominantly rights-based approach to providing enough scope for growing the digital economy by allowing data to flow with ease? The corresponding chapters will examine the national laws along with the free trade and investments agreements of Australia, Indonesia, India, Canada, China, Japan, South Korea, Singapore, New Zealand, the UK, the US and the supranational polity of the EU.

Part II Cross-Border Regulatory Tools and National Laws

Chapter 2
Australia

This chapter builds on the earlier chapter by understanding how cross-border data flows have been dealt with by select nation states, including the EU. It will examine the current provisions of the respective national laws as of January 2022 for the jurisdiction of Australia and a selection of FTA that have been established. Doing so will determine how data flows and data protection has or otherwise been considered. It does not examine other bilateral investment or security agreements between the respective jurisdictions. It will identify the gaps in these agreements and the respective national legal frameworks.

This chapter does not deal with how these jurisdictions have dealt with privacy controls and protections of personal data over the Internet. It commences with defining personal data under each jurisdiction's national laws and in the case of the EU, their legal framework. Further, it does not deal with the consent requirements that have been established, however, where necessary it will be briefly discussed. While in a period of economic, health and Internet tension around the world, the Chapter calls for further work to be undertaken to expand on the current and future FTAs developed by Australia and its trading partners.

Yet, any further interoperability should be the first step for legal harmonisation and the development of international law in this area. While challenging, there should not be significant obstacles to achieving this, as this chapter demonstrates how some nation states have made it very clear that they adopt e-commerce legal instruments that have been developed by the UNCITRAL. Therefore, states should work with UNCITRAL to develop a commercial legal instrument for cross-border data flows.

§2.01 INTRODUCTION

Australia, is the planet's sixth-largest country in the world, and at 7,692,024 km, it accounts for just 5% of the world's land area of 149,450,000 km, and although it is the smallest continental land mass, it is the world's largest island.[382] Australia has an estimated population of 25,726,033[383] and has one of the most ethnically diverse societies in the world today. According to the Australian government, 'almost one in four Australian residents were born outside of Australia and many more are first- or second-generation Australians, the children and grandchildren of recently arrived migrants and refugees. This wide variety of backgrounds, together with the culture of Indigenous Australians who have lived on the Australian continent for more than 50,000 years, have helped create a uniquely Australian identity and spirit'.[384] Before the arrival of British colonisers in 1788, Australia was inhabited by the Indigenous peoples – Aborigines and Torres Strait Islanders sometimes referred to as the First Australians.[385] Aboriginal people inhabited the whole of Australia and Torres Strait Islanders lived on the islands between Australia and Papua New Guinea, in what is now called the Torres Strait.[386] Australia has a rich and diverse history that sets it apart from others in the Indo-Pacific region of the world. Yet, one of its closest neighbours New Zealand has a similar history, inheriting the common law and being colonised by the former British Empire.

Later in this book, New Zealand's approach to cross-border data flows is examined. Thus, it is worth discussing the approach to data flows and how it can benefit the Australian economy. In so doing, it will also briefly discuss New Zealand. Throughout the period, 2004 to 2014-2017, 'Australia and New Zealand have experienced a decline in knowledge-intensive flows into and out of the region.'[387] Pralong et al. state: 'globally, knowledge-intensive flows have been growing at 1.3 times the rate of labour-intensive goods and gaining on their share of all flows, as we have noted'. The authors also point out that:

> knowledge-intensive flows in Australia and New Zealand have fallen from 36 percent of all flows in 2002 to 31 percent in 2012. While this trend reflects the comparative strength of primary resources exports in both countries, Australia and New Zealand now lag behind several major economies in their flows of

382. Australian Government, Geosciences, Australian Size Compared, https://www.ga.gov.au/scientific-topics/national-location-information/dimensions/australias-size-compared.
383. Australian Bureau of Statistics, On 29 January 2022 at 12:13:12 AM (Canberra time), the resident population of Australia is projected to be, https://www.abs.gov.au/ausstats/abs%40.nsf/94713ad445ff1425ca25682000192af2/1647509ef7e25faaca2568a900154b63?OpenDocument.
384. Australian Government, https://info.australia.gov.au/about-australia/our-country/our-people.
385. *Ibid.* Also *see, Mabo v. Queensland (No. 2)* [1992] HCA 23; (1992) 175 CLR 1 (3 June 1992).
386. *Ibid.*
387. David Pralong, James Manyika, Sree Ramaswamy, Ben Fletcher and Kate Yang, *Companions Abroad: Australia and New Zealand's Participation in Global Flows*, 2015, https://www.mckinsey.com/~/media/McKinsey/Locations/Pacific/Australia/flows.pdf.

> knowledge-intensive goods, including Brazil, Russia, India, and China; Mexico; and some Southeast Asian countries.[388]

According to the authors, this is a missed opportunity. In my view, Australia, in particular, has relied for far too long on the mining of mineral resources rather than focusing on and developing the innovation sector of the economy. More alarming, 'in 2013, cross-border data flows per capita in Australia and New Zealand were less than half of those of North America and one-seventh of those of Western Europe'.[389] In a region of the world that is increasingly competitive, Australia needs to do more to invest in innovation and develop the digital economy so that it is in a place to set and influence the rules, rather than having to follow the rules of others. This will not only allow Australia to benefit from data flows but also enable the country to influence the cybersecurity and data programmes it undertakes with other countries. New Zealand needs to also do the same.

The cross-border flow of data out of Australia is regulated by the *PA 1988*. While the principal objective is to promote the protection of the privacy of individuals,[390] it does extend to ensuring a level of data transfers internationally. That is, under section 2A(f), a primary objective of the PA is to 'facilitate the free flow of information across national borders while ensuring that the privacy of individuals is respected'.[391] It aims to strike a balance between allowing for the free flow of data internationally while retaining a high level of privacy protection. This section does not discuss the privacy or data laws of any of the Australian states or territories.[392]

Notwithstanding the above, central to the operation of the PA, are the Australian Privacy Principles (APPs), which are a unique, but important feature of Australia's legal framework. The APPs are binding on individuals and entities. Currently, there are thirteen APPs. They are principle-based law(s) and give organisations some flexibility to develop their internal strategies to manage data flows and protect privacy to meet their own internal requirements. They have been described as being technology-neutral[393] and promoting a level of co-regulation. Most noteworthy is Division 2 of the PA, which provides for the APPs. Section 15 requires that an APP entity (defined under section 6 of the Privacy Act to mean an agency or organisation) must comply with

388. *Ibid.*
389. *Ibid.*
390. Privacy Act 1988, section 2A. Note, this chapter will draw on earlier work undertaken by the author, Robert Walters, from the following books: Robert Walters and Marko Novak, *Cyber Security, Artificial Intelligence, Data Protection & the Law*, 1st ed. Springer (2021), Chapter 15. Also *see*: Robert Walters, Leon Trakman and Bruno Zeller, *Data Protection Law: A Comparative Analysis of Asia-Pacific and European Approaches*, Springer (2019), Chapter 17.
391. *Ibid.*, section 2A(f).
392. Australia is a Federated State made up of six states and two territories: New South Wales, Privacy and Personal Information Protection Act 1998 and Health Records and Information Privacy Act 2002; Victoria, the Privacy and Data Protection Act 2014; Queensland, the Information Privacy Act 2009; Tasmania Personal Information and Protection Act 2004; Western Australia, the state public sector does not currently have a statutory privacy regime; Northern Territory, the Information Act 2002.
393. Office of the Australian Information Commissioner, *Australian Privacy Principles*, https://www.oaic.gov.au/privacy/australian-privacy-principles/read-the-australian-privacy-principles.

Australian Privacy Principles. An APP entity has been defined in accordance with section 5B as: 'a) an agency; or b) an organisation; or c) a small business operator'.[394] However, an entity with an annual turnover of less than AUD 3 million is exempted from the PA and APPs.

On the other side, in order for personal data to be transferred internationally, the first step is to identify what constitutes this type of data. Section 6 provides that personal information is any 'information or an opinion about an identified individual, or an individual who is reasonably identifiable: a) whether the information or opinion is true or not; and b) whether the information or opinion is recorded in a material form or not'.[395] Note the subtle but important difference here is that Australia refers to personal information rather than personal data, unlike other jurisdictions examined in this chapter. Moreover, section 6 provides for another layer of personal information that has been defined as sensitive. This is in order to impose greater control over data and its protection. Sensitive information constitutes an individual's racial or ethnic origin, political opinions, membership of a political association; religious beliefs-affiliations, philosophical beliefs, membership of a professional or trade association, or trade union. It also includes the sexual orientation or practices of an individual, criminal record, health, and genetic or biometric information. In addition to knowing the definition of personal information, a data subject would need to provide consent[396] to the organisation for the data/information to be transferred internationally.

The APPs fall within Schedule 1 of the PA. To facilitate cross-border data flows, APP8 and section 16C establish the framework for data flows internationally. It requires that an APP entity is to work with the recipient entity located in, for example, Singapore or India to ensure the receiver handles that information according to the APPs. It is a reverse onus obligation, in part, because it places the responsibility of the entity transferring the personal information to an entity located outside of the country (Australia) to undertake a high level of due diligence. That is, a level of risk management. Put another way, the responsibility rests with the Australian entity to undertake the assessment. Problematic though is that accordance with APP 8.1 requires the APP 'entity to take such steps as are reasonable in the circumstances to ensure that the overseas recipient does not breach the Australian Privacy Principles in relation to the information'.[397]

Nonetheless, there are two forms of transnational transfers that have been identified under the APPs. First is the disclosure of personal information, and second is the disclosure of that information.[398] While these appear one and the same, they are subtly different. In other words, under APP 8 and APP Guidelines, an entity will disclose personal information to an overseas recipient by sharing that information with

394. Privacy Act 1988, section 5B.
395. *Ibid.*, section 6.
396. Australian Privacy Principles, 2 and 3.
397. *Ibid.*, Australian Privacy Principles 8.1.
398. Australian Privacy Principles Guidelines, https://www.oaic.gov.au/privacy/austral-ian-privacy-principles-guidelines/chapter-8-app-8-cross-border-disclosure-of-personal-infor-mation.

an overseas recipient or revealing the personal information at an international conference or meeting. This also applies to where the APP entity sends a hard copy document or email containing an individual's personal information to an overseas client, or publishes the personal information on the Internet, whether intentionally or not, and it is accessible to an overseas recipient.[399]

On the other side, disclosure in the Australian context is distinctive and takes a broader role than that of disclosure. Disclosure falls within APP 11 and deals with unauthorised access to personal information. That said,

An APP entity is not taken to have disclosed personal information where a 'third party intentionally exploits the entity's security measures and gains unauthorised access to the personal information. This includes unauthorised access following a cyberattack or a theft, including where the third party then makes that personal information available to others outside the entity. However, where a third party gains unauthorised access, the APP entity may breach APP 11 if it did not take reasonable steps to protect the personal information from unauthorised access'.[400] Arguably, this is a safety or risk management mechanism for Australian entities that cannot totally control the transfer of data from end to end when they are using technology systems and infrastructure that is provided by an external party. In addition to the above, the APP Guidelines have also defined the term 'use' to mean 'an organisation or agency uses personal information when it handles and manages that information within the organisation or agency's effective control'.[401] On this basis, use is, in part, being confined to personal information being handled and managed under the effective control of the organisation. However, neither managed, handled nor effective control is defined. Therefore, on its reading, it can be applied broadly. It will require careful consideration of what constitutes personal information being handled. Further, what constitutes the information being managed, and how that information would be under the effective control of an organisation. It is out of scope to fully unpack these terms. Although, in Australia, it would be left to either the Regulator or the Judiciary to make that determination.

Consent

The concept of consent applied to cross-border data flows from Australia can be best described as having a level of ambiguity in the law. As highlighted above, in accordance with section 16C of the PA, a company located in a third country has an obligation to comply with the APPs. However, under this section and 8.1 of the APPs, there are exceptions to this obligation. That is, in accordance with APP 8.27, disclosing

---

399. *Ibid.* The APP Guidelines provide guidance on consent under APP 8 whereby an APP entity should provide the individual with a clear written or oral statement explaining the potential consequences of providing consent. At a minimum, this statement should explain that if the individual consents to the disclosure and the overseas recipient handles the personal information in breach of the APPs, the entity will not be accountable under the Privacy Act and the individual will not be able to seek redress under the Privacy Act.
400. *Ibid.*
401. *Ibid.*, also *see* Sending Personal Information Overseas, https://www.oaic.gov.au/privacy/guidance-and-advice/sending-personal-information-overseas.

personal information to an entity overseas with the consent of the data subject, following the data subject being informed, the APP entity expressly informs the individual that if they consent to the disclosure, this principle will not apply, and the individual then consents to the disclosure.[402] The formal and functional arrangements and operation of consent fall with APP 8.28 (express consent). It states that the 'APP entity should provide the individual with a clear written or oral statement explaining the potential consequences of providing consent. At a minimum, this statement should explain that if the individual consents to the disclosure and the overseas recipient handles the personal information in breach of the APPs the entity will not be accountable and the individual will not be able to seek redress under the PA'.[403] In APP 8.29, a consent statement should also be made at the time consent is sought, and not rely on assumed prior knowledge of the individual.[404] Furthermore, the statement could also explain any other practical effects or risks associated with the disclosure that the APP entity is aware of, or would be reasonably expected to be aware of. The office of the Information Commissioner states that this may include that the overseas recipient may not be subject to any privacy obligations or to any principles similar to the APPs; the individual may not be able to seek redress in the overseas jurisdiction; and the overseas recipient is subject to a foreign law that could compel the disclosure of personal information to a third party, such as an overseas authority.[405] Consent has been formed as an exception to an entity having to undertake an assessment to ensure they comply with the APPs. This, is arguably, an unusual exception where it is asserted that whether such an assessment is undertaken or otherwise, consent should not be an exception for the entity located outside of Australia. While this proposition adds to the already complex legal burden, it ensures there continues to be a high level of accuracy, accountability, transparency, and control to and for the data subject. However, it will provide a higher level of trust for data transfers.

Viewed this way, the legal framework in Australia has provided a level of data transfers, albeit not fully open. Arguably, and while it is a principle-based framework, it also aims to manage the risk of data transfers, and places significant obligations on the sending organisation. In part, this is similar to the EU position, whereby they require the controller to have responsibility for the transnational transfer of personal information. However, in Australia, it is not a mandatory requirement for an entity to appoint a controller or processor. Notably, Australia understands that organisations will enter into contractual arrangements to transfer personal information across international borders. This will ensure that an organisation is taking the necessary reasonable steps to control and, more importantly, to guarantee that the data recipient is complying with the APPs. This requires that the contract be specifically drafted in a way to ensure reasonable steps have been taken. The term 'reasonable steps' is widely

402. Australian Privacy Principles, 8.2(b).
403. Ibid., 8.28.
404. *Ibid.*, 8.29.
405. *Ibid.*, 8.30, Office of Information Commissioner, Chapter 8: APP 8-Cross-border disclosure of personal information, https://www.oaic.gov.au/privacy/australian-privacy-principles-guidelines/chapter-8-app-8-cross-border-disclosure-of-personal-information.

used in Australian legislation, and provides for flexibility and effective administration of the law. It aims not to restrict the function of the law, and it would be impractical for it to be defined specifically, so as to account for every possible scenario. Similar to the above terms though, it will be up to the Regulatory or the Judiciary to determine the extent to which reasonable steps constitute. Significant too, Australia is a member of APEC and actively participates in the APEC CBPRs.[406] However, this is limited to the member countries that participate in these CBPRs (*see* Chapter 1).

§2.02 BILATERAL AGREEMENTS

To date, as of January 2022, Australia had entered into a number of Bilateral Trade Agreements (BTAs) with many different countries. However, this section will only examine the FTAs that currently exist between Australia and the countries examined in this book, and not the FTAs currently under negotiation. More generally, FTAs are BTAs that contribute to a state's economy and job creation, while delivering opportunities for big and small Australian businesses to benefit from greater trade and investment.[407] A further formal functional benefit of these Agreements is their ability for governments to open markets and new economic activity. They promote the state's benefit for investing, such as a certain legal framework and access to services such as e-commerce. Moreover, since their establishment, they have benefited citizens and consumers, allowing them today, to efficiently access international markets and purchase goods and services over the Internet. This section will be limited to examining the Australia-US; China-Australia; Indonesia-Australia, India-Australia and Australia and Japan for an economic partnership, and trade agreements. To date, there is no recognition of cross-border data flows under the Australian – New Zealand Closer Economic Relations Trade Agreement (*see* section New Zealand).

Agreement Between Australia and Japan for an Economic Partnership[408]

Similar to the Singapore-Australia Digital Agreement (*see* below), the Agreement Between Australia and Japan for an Economic Partnership (AAJEP) has made provisions for personal data and its international transfers. A common definition of personal data or personal information has merged with FTAs. In this case, under Article 13.2 of the AAJEP, personal data means 'any information about an identified or identifiable individual'.[409] More specifically, the transfer and processing of information fall within Article 11.6, whereby, there has been a conscious effort to ensure both Parties do not invoke regulatory or other measures to prevent the transfer of data and information.

406. Asia Pacific Economic Cooperation, Cross Border Privacy Rules, 2022, http://cbprs.org As of January 2022, there were currently nine participating APEC CBPR system economies: US, Mexico, Japan, Canada, Singapore, the Republic of Korea, Australia, Chinese Taipei, Philippines.
407. Australian Government, *The Benefits of Free Trade Agreements*, https://www.dfat.gov.au/trade/about-ftas/Pages/the-benefits-of-free-trade-agreements.
408. Agreement Between Australia and Japan for an Economic Partnership, https://www.dfat.gov.au/sites/default/files/jaepa-chapters-1-to-20.pdf.
409. *Ibid.*, Article 13.2.

Centrally, the reference to data would take on a broad definition and include personal data. Article 11.6 also makes the point of allowing either state to establish relevant measures to protect personal data and privacy over the Internet, 'so long as such right is not used to circumvent the provisions of this chapter and Chapters 9 (Trade in Services) and 14 (Investment)'.[410] On this basis, the protection of personal data can be found in Article 13.8. It allows Australia and Japan to 'adopt or maintain measures to protect the personal data of electronic commerce users'.[411] 'In the development of protection standards for the personal data of electronic commerce users, each Party shall take into account relevant international standards and criteria of relevant international bodies.'[412] Arguably, this is in recognition of how both Australia and Japan have incorporated the OECD Principles on transnational data transfers into their respective national laws. This includes but is not limited to accountability, transparency, accuracy and data used for specific purposes.

Today, both states have adopted compressive national data protection laws. In a direct effort to shift the respective economies online, Article 13.9 provides and promotes the need to shift away from the traditional paper-based economy. While not stated, in part, this is a step to move the respective economies to the new digital world, whereby new jobs will be created and new economic activity will be undertaken. Importantly, in a potential sign that both states are wanting greater regional and multilateral input into not only broader electronic commerce matters but also data transfers, Article 13.10 calls for cooperation. However, it stops short on any reference to harmonisation or internationalising legal norms. It also makes no reference to creating an open system or environment for data flows. This is an area in my view that could be reconciled within this and other like Agreements.

Indonesia-Australia Comprehensive Economic Partnership Agreement

Indonesia-Australia Comprehensive Economic Partnership Agreement (IA-CEPA) came into effect in 2020 and is viewed as an important step towards deepening regional relationships for both countries. As one of Australia's closest neighbours, with a significantly higher population, 'Indonesia has been a growing market for Australian goods and services exporters. In 2018-19, total two-way trade in goods and services with Indonesia was worth A$17.8 billion, making Indonesia our 13th largest trading partner.'[413]

On this basis, Chapter 13 placed electronic commerce as an important economic driver for both states to cooperate. Similar to the other Agreements discussed in this section, Article 13 defines personal information to be 'any information, including data or opinions, about an identified or identifiable natural person'.[414] In developing the small- and medium-sized business sector, Article 13.1 encourages cooperation, to

410. *Ibid.*, Article 11.6.
411. *Ibid.*, Article 13.8.
412. *Ibid.*, Articles 13.1 and 13.2.
413. Indonesia-Australia Comprehensive Economic Partnership Agreement, Australian Government, https://www.dfat.gov.au/trade/agreements/in-force/iacepa/Pages/indonesia-australia-comprehensive-economic-partnership-agreement.
414. *Ibid.*, Article 13.

'overcome obstacles exchange information and share experiences on regulations, policies, enforcement and compliance regarding electronic commerce'.[415] Significantly, it promotes cooperation in the area of regulation for personal information protection and online consumer protection, including means for consumer redress and building consumer confidence. Arguably, these are two highly important areas where the government can gain trust in not only protecting the consumer but also governing personal information. In the same way as the Agreements examined above, the IA-CEPA promotes the idea of reaching a paperless trading environment. Thus, as there is a continual push to undertake more daily activities online, it will only heighten the transfer of data between the two countries - online. That is, the cross-border flow of data will only increase.

More importantly, Article 13.11 makes specific reference to the Cross-Border Transfer of Information. It 'recognises that each Party may have its own regulatory requirements concerning the transfer of information by electronic means. Further, each Party shall allow the cross-border transfer of information by electronic means, including personal information, when this activity is for the conduct of the business of a covered person'.[416] On the other side, Article 13.11.3 does not prevent Indonesia or Australia from adopting or maintaining 'a) measures inconsistent with paragraph 2 to achieve a legitimate public policy objective, provided that the measure is not applied in a manner which would constitute a means of arbitrary or unjustifiable discrimination or a disguised restriction on trade; or b) any measure that it considers necessary for protection of its essential security interests'.[417]

Article 13.7 deals with the Protection of Personal Information, and 'recognises the economic and social benefits of protecting the personal information of users of electronic commerce and the contribution that this makes to enhancing consumer confidence in electronic commerce'.[418] Furthermore, it provides that Indonesia and Australia are to 'adopt or maintain a legal framework that provides for the protection of the personal information of the users of electronic commerce. In the development of its legal framework for the protection of personal information, each Party should take into account the principles and guidelines of relevant international bodies'.[419] Under the current legal framework, data protection in Indonesia is by and large sectorial. Indonesia is one of those nation states that has been developing its laws for some time. Article 13.3 ensures that both states adopt non-discriminatory practices to protect users of electronic commerce from breaches of personal data security within their jurisdiction. Most noteworthy is that Article 13.4 formally recognises that these countries take different legal approaches to protect personal information. In doing so, it acknowledges that the two states are culturally, socially and ethnically different and that their laws will also differ, particularly since Australia is a common law country, while Indonesia is a civil law country.

415. *Ibid.*, Article 13.3.
416. *Ibid.*, Articles 13.11.1. and 13.11.2.
417. *Ibid.*, Article 13.11.3.
418. *Ibid.*, Article 13.7.1.
419. *Ibid.*, Article 13.7.2.

Given that Indonesia is a civil law country, the reference to 'these mechanisms may include the recognition of regulatory outcomes, whether accorded autonomously or by mutual arrangement, or broader international frameworks'.[420] It is argued that the seeking of a mutual arrangement suggests an emerging recognition of a level of interoperability, even though it is not explicitly stated. To this end, 'the Parties shall endeavour to exchange information on any such mechanisms applied in their jurisdictions and explore ways to extend these or other suitable arrangements to promote compatibility between them'.[421] Reaffirming the above, seeking a level of compatibility is leading the countries to not only accept their respective legal frameworks on data protection. More importantly, it provides a platform for both countries to develop a framework whether that be interoperability, convergence or harmonisation.

Nonetheless, there is a clear understanding of the promotion by Indonesia and Australia to maintain their respective legal frameworks governing electronic transactions in accordance with the principles set out under the '*UNCITRAL Model Law on Electronic Commerce 1996* or the *United Nations Convention on the Use of Electronic Communications in International Contracts,* done at New York, November 23, 2005'.[422] Apart from seeking a level of compatibility between the states' regulatory frameworks, the Australia and Indonesia agreement is similar to that of Japan and Singapore. Importantly, for Australia, Indonesia is a lot more culturally and religiously diverse, with Islam having a significant influence on daily life, and the understanding of privacy over the Internet and transnational data flows.

China-Australia Free Trade Agreement (ChAFTA)

Australia and China have had long-standing trade relations for a number of decades. In 2015, both countries established ChAFTA to further promote trade and economic relations between both countries. Chapter 12 deals with Electronic Commerce, 'recognising the economic growth and opportunities provided by electronic commerce, the importance of avoiding barriers to its use and development, and the applicability of relevant WTO rules'.[423] Of importance is the reference to the WTO (World Trade Organisation) rules. In Chapter 1, the WTO rules on GATS were outlined as having a significant role in enabling and facilitating e-commerce, or what might be referred to as the digital economy. Under both e-commerce and the digital economy, data is shaping and influencing economic activity and outcomes for the national and the global economy. Reflecting the importance of the WTO rules cannot be underestimated. They are arguably part of the foundational rules for trade and maintaining the rules-based system.

420. *Ibid.*, Article 13.4.
421. *Ibid.*
422. *Ibid.*, Article 13.9. Article 13.10: Transparency, each Party recognises that transparent regulations and policies are important for trade facilitation, creating a conducive environment for electronic commerce and promoting cross-border electronic commerce.
423. China-Australia Free Trade Agreement, Chapter 12, Article 12.1. Articles 12.2 and 12.3 provide the objective of this chapter is to promote electronic commerce between the Parties, including by encouraging cooperation on electronic commerce. The Parties shall endeavour to ensure that bilateral trade through electronic commerce is no more restricted than other forms of trade.

No different to the other Agreements examined above, personal information has been defined under Article 12.2 to mean, 'personal information means information about an individual whose identity is apparent, or can reasonably be ascertained, from the information'.[424] Similar to Indonesia, the agreement between China and Australia further reaffirms the need for transparency. Article 12.4 encourages both states to 'publish, or otherwise promptly make publicly available where publication is not practicable, all relevant measures of general application which pertain to, or affect, the operation of this Chapter'.[425] Further, both Parties should 'respond promptly to all requests by the other Party for specific information on any of its measures of general application'.[426] As a further sign, the current international rules on trade will be upheld. Article 12.5 requires that each state is able to 'maintain domestic legal frameworks governing electronic transactions based on the UNCITRAL Model Law on Electronic Commerce 1996 and taking into account, as appropriate, other relevant international standards'.[427] Building a strong relationship through this Agreement will benefit not only Australia and China but the entire world through trade. This section does not comment on the ongoing geopolitical tensions and competition between the countries. It will open up the digital economy, whereby these two states have much to gain both economically and socially. Furthermore, it will create environmental and human health benefits that are only beginning to be realised.

Article 12.8 deals with online data protection. China and Australia had very different legal frameworks related to data protection when this Agreement was drafted. In fact, until the end of 2021 when the Personal Information Protection Law 2021 was introduced,[428] China did not have any specific data protection laws.[425] Article 12.8.1 provides that 'notwithstanding the differences in existing systems for personal information protection in the territories of the Parties, each Party shall take such measures as it considers appropriate and necessary to protect the personal information of users of electronic commerce'.[429] Further, 'in the development of data protection standards, each Party shall, to the extent possible, take into account international standards and the criteria of relevant international organisations'.[430] However, the Agreement is silent on the cross-border transfer of data and personal information, generally. While the Agreement was established in 2015, arguably, it is in need of amending to reflect the importance and current status of data in the digital economy. While this is a major gap, Article 12.9 does reinforce the general theme of the above-mentioned Agreement, in that, it promotes the need for paperless trading. Thus, in part, the Agreement is moving the economy more generally to the online world.

---

424. *Ibid.*, Article 12.2.
425. *Ibid.*, Article 12.2.1.
426. *Ibid.*, Article 12.2.2.
427. *Ibid.*, Article 12.5. Each Party shall (a) minimise the regulatory burden on electronic commerce; and (b) ensure that regulatory frameworks support industry-led development of electronic commerce.
428. Privacy Commissioner for Personal Data, *Personal Information Protection Law of the Mainland*, https://www.pcpd.org.hk/english/data_privacy_law/mainland_law/mainland_law.html.
429. China-Australia Free Trade Agreement, Chapter 12, Article 12.8.1.
430. *Ibid.*, Article 12.8.2.

Australian and Singapore Digital Agreement

Notably, the Australian and Singapore Digital Agreement was established to amend the broader FTAs between the two countries, specifically Chapter 14 related to the Digital Economy.[431] It defines personal information to mean any information, including data, about an identified or identifiable natural person. Article 17 deals specifically with personal information and there is a general recognition that there are significant economic and social benefits to protecting the personal information of persons who conduct or engage in electronic transactions and commerce.[432] It calls for both Parties to take into account the principles and guidelines of relevant international bodies, such as the APEC CBPR System[433] and the *OECD Guidelines Governing the Protection of Privacy and Trans-border.* Article 17.3 specifically references the OECD Guidelines requiring each Party to take into account when developing its legal framework, including limitation on collection, data quality, purpose specification, use limitation, security safeguards, transparency, individual participation and accountability. Article 17.4 calls for 'non-discriminatory practices to be adopted in order to protect persons who conduct or engage in electronic transactions from personal information protection violations occurring within its jurisdiction'.[434] To provide a higher level of transparency, Article 17.5 requires each 'Party to publish information on the personal information protection along with information on how a data subject can pursue remedies and how businesses can comply with any legal requirements.'[435] In promoting transparency and accountability, Article 17.6 'encourages enterprises in its territory to publish, including on the Internet, their policies and procedures related to protection of personal information'.[436]

More generally, and not specific to personal information but wider information that is transferred by electronic means, Article 23, makes it clear that either Party has its own regulatory requirements. Every effort should be undertaken to ensure that there is no prohibition or restriction placed on cross-border transfer of information by electronic means, including personal information, provided the information is in relation to the business of a covered person.[437] However, Article 23.3 allows a level of restrictions to be established to protect from discrimination or not disguised any restriction on trade. Further any restrictions are not to impede transfers of information greater than are required to achieve the objective. Article 26 promotes the idea of data innovation so as to support the cross-border transfer of information by electronic means and promote data-driven innovation in the digital economy. Additionally, as

431. Australian and Singapore Digital Agreement, https://www.dfat.gov.au/sites/default/files/australia-singapore-digital-economy-agreement.pdf.
432. *Ibid.*, Article 17.
433. Articles 17.8 and 17.9, the Parties recognise that the CBPR System is a valid mechanism to facilitate cross-border information transfers while protecting personal information. The Parties shall endeavour to jointly promote the CBPR System, with the aim to improving awareness of, and participation in, the CBPR System, including by industry.
434. *Ibid.*, Article 17.4.
435. *Ibid.*, Article 17.5.
436. *Ibid.*, Article 17.6.
437. *Ibid.*, Article 23.2.

part of their respective data diplomacy programmes, Article 37 encourages cooperation in areas of capacity building across the Asia region in areas of the 'digital connectivity; small and medium business sector digital transformation; data protection regimes; and mechanisms to facilitate the cross-border transfer of information'.[438] Centrally, this bilateral agreement demonstrates how both states have embraced the current international principle-based framework. It promotes transparency, accountability, accuracy, and the use of personal information for a specific purpose.

Significant too, it takes significant steps for both countries to work together and open up the digital economy and the importance personal data will have across this new economy. Problematic though is that it stops short of taking this beyond the two states, other than promoting the idea that the digital economy and the data protection laws supporting this activity should be extended internationally. It does not promote nor encourage legal harmonisation or the development of international legal mechanisms. The only reference to a level of internationalisation is where both states can come together and develop capacity-building programmes for the respective data flows and data protection regimes. In my view, this should have been extended to cross-border data flows regulation. While it provides for dispute resolution, it restricts arbitrators' education and experience to come from the financial services discipline. This needs to be broadened to those experts in transnational data flows outside of the financial sector.

Australia India Comprehensive Economic Cooperation Agreement

The Australia-India Comprehensive Economic Cooperation Agreement (AICECA)[439] is the most recent trade agreement Australia has entered into, in April 2022. While it appears to be a trade agreement that will be built upon over the coming decades, to date, there is no mention of data flows, data protection or ensuring privacy over the Internet is afforded a high level of security and protection.

Australia and US established an FTA in 2005. *See* Chapter 9 in relation to this agreement. The next chapter examines the EU, which is arguably the benchmark in cross-border flows, data adequacy and data protection law.

§2.03 CONCLUSION

Australia is an island state located in Oceania. Currently, Australia has a number of trade agreements that do reflect varying approaches to the management and governance of personal data. Australia's data laws date back to the late 1980s and are structured very similarly to the data laws of New Zealand. The PA and accompanying APPs provide for the transfer of personal data to third countries outside of Australia. It is argued that FTAs do have an important role in providing a pathway to opening up the digital economy between Australia and Singapore. Even though this chapter has not

438. *Ibid.*, Article 37.
439. Australian Government, Australian-India ECTA official text, https://www.dfat.gov.au/trade/agreements/negotiations/aifta/australia-india-ecta-official-text.

analysed the benefits of past and current trade agreements between both states, it is further argued that without them, both countries would not have a deep level of trade relations today. On this basis, more work is needed by Australia and Singapore at the trade agreement level to account for and ensure that data flows form part of any future trade or digital agreements between both states.

Most noteworthy of the FTAs compared, Australia has recently implemented the Australian and Singapore Digital Agreement. Arguably, this agreement is the most advanced of all trade agreements to date and focuses on providing a pathway to opening up the respective state's digital economies. It calls for greater cooperation and engagement between both countries. As this chapter has demonstrated, Chapter 14 of the agreement is highly significant and relates directly to the digital economy. It defines personal data. However, the definition is broader than the definition of the same in both respective data-privacy legislation. Importantly, the agreement calls for both Australia and Singapore to uphold the current international and regional rules-based systems such as the APEC CBPR System and the OECD Guidelines Governing the Protection of Privacy and Trans-border.

Moreover, it is argued that in my view is fundamentally important to the ongoing governance of data in the emerging digital economy. It reinforces the overall argument of this book, by demonstrating that while nation states may take a different approach at a national level to regulating data flows and their security, there is a general consensus that, at an international and regional level, a consistent approach is required. The agreement is very specific in promoting data innovation so as to support the cross-border transfer of information by electronic means and promote data-driven innovation in the digital economy. By encouraging a deeper level of cooperation between both countries by building a higher level of capacity and skills through digital connectivity, both countries are informally implementing a level of data diplomacy. It is such a programme that, in the final Chapter 17, goes beyond what many scholars have not discussed in any depth thus far.

Problematic though is that the agreement in its current form does not promote or encourage legal harmonisation or the development of international legal mechanisms. The only reference to a level of internationalisation, is where both states can come together and develop capacity-building programmes for data protection regimes. To address this shortfall, the agreement should be extended to cross-border regulatory regimes and practices. Doing so will pave the way to set the current and future rules for data flows, beyond the current highly fragmented approach. It will strengthen economic outcomes, provide for more economic activity and certainty in a period of more contestability. Furthermore, taking this approach will provide for more skills and education opportunities between both states, which can be extended to other like-minded states in the Commonwealth and beyond.

Australia and India had the opportunity through the recent establishment of the 2022 trade agreement to expand on the above arguments. While it could be considered a lost opportunity, Australia was in an election year with the federal election being in

May 2022. Therefore, any further expansion of the Australia-India 2022 trade agreement needs to consider and include the digital economy, and ensure that data flows and their security are reflected.

Under the proposal(s) above, Australia is in a very strong position to work with the likes of the UK, US, EU, India, Singapore, New Zealand, Canada, Japan and Indonesia to shape, influence and direct the future of transnational data flows law. Australia, in my view, should further engage the OECD and UNCTIRAL to develop a pathway for international law for data flow regulation. Doing so will ensure that a pragmatic and agile approach can be implemented while determining what the international rules will be.

Australia needs to capitalise on its well-developed and mature data laws. It is one of a few countries that have had data laws in place for more than twenty years. They have the opportunity to leverage from this work, knowledge and high-level skill base, to further develop and foster growth and the development of transnational data flow law. This must be a priority for Australia. It will not only bring economic certainty and security but also address sovereign and national security concerns related to the weaponisation of data, within data flows/transfers, by nation states, state actors and private sector organisations and individuals.

CHAPTER 3

European Union

The EU has a long and complex history. It was established following the Second World War (WW II). The EU recently found that it was being challenged again when the UK decided to leave the bloc. Nonetheless, the EU and the implementation of the GDPR[440] *has had a profound impact on influencing and direction of data protection and data flows, and the law internationally.*

Under the GDPR, there are three main ways in which data can be transferred to a third country. First, a third country has been declared and assessed to have an adequacy level of similar protection to that of the EU. Second, where a third country does not have an AD, transfers can be undertaken via corporate binding rules, or, contractual arrangements. Third, is the ability for a transfer of data to take place, provided the data subject has consented. However, consent under the GDPR takes on a different role than that of the other jurisdictions examined in this book. It is multilayered and for a transfer to take place that consent has to be explicit.

The digital economy and the use of personal data from the environment, health, education, investment, trade and agriculture will transform the way the EU and its Member States operate over the coming decades. There is a significant opportunity for the EU and its Member States to grow their digital economy and provide the platform for data to underscore the varied economic activities. Even though the new economy and its economic benefits are not fully understood, it is projected to be up to EUR 2.2 trillion by 2030. If realised, this will unlock skills, jobs and economic activity whereby smaller

440. Regulation (EU) 2016/679 of the European Parliament and of the Council of 27 April 2016 on the protection of natural persons with regard to the processing of personal data and on the free movement of such data, and repealing Directive 95/46/EC (General Data Protection Regulation).

Member States can take full advantage and grow their economies in line with larger Member States.

§3.01 INTRODUCTION

The EU is a supranational political and economic Union made up of twenty-seven Member States[441] such as France, Italy, Netherlands, Germany, Slovenia, Spain, Austria and Croatia amongst others. The Union has a total area of 3,999, 6222, 429 km[442] and an estimated total population of about 447 million.[443] Through a number of treaties and conventions,[444] the Union has managed to create a single market and single currency and been a leader in harmonising economic, social, health and environmental law and policy. As such, all citizens of the EU enjoy rights, freedoms and protection of their right to move freely throughout the Union and have their personal data protected. It is out of the scope of this book to discuss the full legal process of legal integration dating back to the 1957 Community on Steel and Coal.[445] This chapter discusses the current-day data protection laws of the EU, as of January 2022.

In 2021, the European Commission (EC) released a report detailing the extent of how the 'digital transformation of Europe's economies and societies is accelerating'.[446] The EU and more broadly, society as a whole 'is entering a next phase, fuelled by a fusion of technologies that gradually blur the lines between the physical, digital, and biological spheres and push the frontier of what computers are capable of doing. These new technologies – and the new business models they create, building on the use of data – are progressively coming to maturity for at-scale deployment, and will increasingly impact all sectors of the economy'.[447] The extent of economic benefit, while not fully understood, has been estimated that 'by 2030, the cumulative additional GDP contribution of new digital technologies could amount to €2.2 trillion in the EU, a 14.1 per cent increase from 2017'.[448] The investment from this is expected to be significant. It has been estimated that to fully realise the economic benefit, 'European institutions and governments may need to contribute approximately EUR 75 billion per year in the coming decade to close the digital gap in Europe compared to the most digitally

441. European Union, Aims and Values, https://european-union.europa.eu/principles-countries-history/principles-and-values/aims-and-values_en, Austria, Belgium, Bulgaria, Croatia, Republic of Cyprus, Czech Republic, Denmark, Estonia, Finland, France, Germany, Greece, Hungary, Ireland, Italy, Latvia, Lithuania, Luxembourg, Malta, Netherlands, Poland, Portugal, Romania, Slovakia, Slovenia, Spain and Sweden.
442. World Bank, 2022, https://data.worldbank.org/indicator/AG.LND.TOTL.K2?locations = EU.
443. EUROSTAT, https://ec.europa.eu/eurostat/databrowser/view/tps00005/default/table?lang = en.
444. European Union, Founding Agreements, https://european-union.europa.eu/principles-countries-history/principles-and-values/founding-agreements_en.
445. Treaty establishing the European Coal and Steel Community, ECSC Treaty, 1957, https://eur-lex.europa.eu/legal-content/EN/TXT/?uri = LEGISSUM%3Axy0022.
446. European Commission, Shaping the Digital Transformation in Europe, https://www.standict.eu/sites/default/files/2021-02/McKinsey%20report.pdf.
447. *Ibid.*, p. 3.
448. *Ibid.*

advanced Member States'.[449] In addition to the above, 'education, upskilling and reskilling of the labour force to manage the digital transition, may require total investments of €42 billion per year'.[450] This is significant and provides an overview of where current and future investment is needed. The European Commission is continually trying to find the right balance between economic growth across the digital economy and the use of data while ensuring a high level of protection for that data. In its report in relation to Shaping the Digital Transformation in Europe, it identified up to nine initiatives to enhance and protect the EU 'economy and competitiveness societal challenges and climate democracy, trust and diversity sovereignty and security'.[451] Of the nine initiatives, three are critical to data flow and its protection. On the one side, there is the need for the EC to establish data platforms so that data can be shared such as health and transport data. On the other side, there is a need for the security of that data to be better protected, to mitigate against external intrusions and attacks by state and non-state actors. Importantly, there is a need to strengthen citizens' control of their data. That is, the EC will advance a 'citizens control of their personal data, by building on the GDPR 2016/679, to improve understanding, user-centricity, control and effective enforcement of citizens' data rights and enable innovation and new business models based on data portability'.[452]

On this basis, the GDPR, which was established in 2016 and came into effect in 2018,[453] will have a critical role in data flows while providing a pathway for the protection of personal data that form part of those cross-border transfers. The GDPR expressly notes that:

> flows of personal data to and from countries outside the Union and international organisations are necessary for the expansion of international trade and international cooperation. The increase in such flows has raised new challenges and concerns with regard to the protection of personal data. However, when personal data are transferred from the Union to controllers, processors or other recipients in third countries or to international organisations, the level of protection of natural persons ensured in the Union by this Regulation should not be undermined, including in cases of onward transfers of personal data from the third country or international organisation to controllers, processors in the same or another third country or international organisation. In any event, transfers to third countries and

449. *Ibid.*
450. *Ibid.*
451. *Ibid.*, p. 6.
452. *Ibid.* Also *see* Gregory Voss, 'Cross-Border Data Flows, the GDPR, and Data Governance' (2020) 29 Washington International Law Journal 485, 486-489, cross-border data flows are an important component of international trade and an element of digital service models. Cross-border data flows have been described as commerce-enabling 'hallmarks of 21st century globalisation' and 'the connective tissue holding the global economy together'. One estimate shows cross-border data flows added USD 2.8 trillion to world GDP since 2010. David Nguyen and Marta Paczos *Measuring the Economic Value of Data and Cross-Border Data Flows: A Business Perspective*, UK Economic Statistics Centre of Excellence, OECD Working Paper, No. 297 (2020), pp. 19-20.
453. Regulation (EU) 2016/679 of the European Parliament and of the Council of 27 April 2016 on the protection of natural persons with regard to the processing of personal data and on the free movement of such data, and repealing Directive 95/46/EC (General Data Protection Regulation).

> international organisations may only be carried out in full compliance with this Regulation.[454]

However, as noted by some scholars, the EU data protection laws prevent the export of data to countries with lower data privacy laws.[455] This law was introduced to address the different levels of data protection within the EU but also applies to the transfer of personal data to third countries. This law was introduced to address the different levels of data protection within the EU and applies to the transfer of personal data to third countries.[456] This position currently still exists. Yet, as highlighted in Chapter 1 there are gaps and tensions in the law where the EU has afforded a level of adequacy, based on the assumption that the third country does not have a lower level of protection than itself.

Nonetheless, essential to the transfer of data internationally is how personal data is defined. In accordance with Article 4, it provides for a broad definition and states that 'personal data breach' means 'a breach of security leading to the accidental or unlawful destruction, loss, alteration, unauthorised disclosure of, or access to, personal data transmitted, stored or otherwise processed'.[457] In addition to this general definition, other important personal data and information have also been identified to be defined as genetic, biometric and health data. It provides that:

> *genetic data* – means personal data relating to the inherited or acquired genetic characteristics of a natural person which give unique information about the physiology or the health of that natural person and which result, in particular, from an analysis of a biological sample from the natural person in question; and
>
> *biometric data* – means personal data resulting from specific technical processing relating to the physical, physiological or behavioural characteristics of a natural person, which allow or confirm the unique identification of that natural person, such as facial images or dactyloscopic data;
>
> *data concerning health* – means personal data related to the physical or mental health of a natural person, including the provision of health care services, which reveal information about his or her health status.[458]

Apart from the above, for personal data to be processed so that it can be transferred internationally, data subjects' consent is likely to be required from the controller or processor. However, it is out of the scope of this book to examine any consent requirements. Chapter 5 of the GDPR provides for the transfer of personal data

454. *Ibid.*, Preamble 101.
455. Joshua Meltze, 'The Internet, Cross-Border Data Flows and International Trade' (2014) 2(1) Asia & the Pacific Policy Studies 93. Also *see*, Joshua Meltzer and Peter Lovelock, *Regulating for a Digital Economy, Understanding the Importance of Cross-Border Data Flows in Asia*, Brookings Institute, 2018, https://www.brookings.edu/wp-content/uploads/2018/03/digital-economy_meltzer_lovelock_web.pdf.
456. *Ibid.*, p. 93.
457. Regulation (EU) 2016/679 of the European Parliament and of the Council of 27 April 2016 on the protection of natural persons with regard to the processing of personal data and on the free movement of such data, and repealing Directive 95/46/EC (General Data Protection Regulation), Article 4.
458. *Ibid.*, Article 4.

to a country outside of the EU and international organisations located in a nation state that is not a member of the EU. Article 44 allows for the transfer of personal data that is 'undergoing processing or is intended for processing after transfer to a third country or to an international organisation shall take place only if, subject to the other provisions of this Regulation, the conditions laid down in this chapter are complied with by the controller and processor. This also includes for onward transfers of personal data from the third country or an international organisation to another third country or to another international organisation'.[459] Underpinning the importance of Article 44 are Recitals 101 and 102. Recital 101 makes the point that 'flows of personal data to and from countries outside the Union and international organisations are necessary for the expansion of international trade and international cooperation. The increase in such flows has raised new challenges and concerns with regard to the protection of personal data'.[460] The EU undertakes to develop international agreements on trade and investment, and therefore, Recital 102[461] acknowledges that Member States can include international agreements that include data transfers to third countries, without the EU more generally. Yet, any Agreement must not affect the operation of the GDPR. The third element is to enable the transfer of personal data to a third country by the data subject providing explicit consent.

Consent

The concept of consent has begun to pervade most of the legal framework arising from the GDPR. For data transfers, consent is restricted to obtaining explicit consent. Article 9 states that '*the data subject has given explicit consent to the processing of those personal data for one or more specified purposes, except where Union or Member State law provides that the prohibition referred to in paragraph 1 may not be lifted by the data subject*'.[462] On this basis, data transfers to a third country or international organisation where there is no adequacy assessment decision in place, fall within Article 49. That is, Article 49 states:

> In the absence of an AD pursuant to Article 45(3), or of appropriate safeguards pursuant to Article 46, including BCR, a transfer or a set of transfers of personal data to a third country or an international organisation shall take place only on one of the following conditions:

459. *Ibid.*, Article 44.
460. *Ibid.*, Recital 101. General Principles on the International Data Transfers. However, when personal data are transferred from the Union to controllers, processors or other recipients in third countries or to international organisations, the level of protection of natural persons ensured in the Union by this Regulation should not be undermined, including in cases of onward transfers of personal data from the third country or international organisation to controllers, processors in the same or another third country or international organisation. In any event, transfers to third countries and international organisations may only be carried out in full compliance with this Regulation. A transfer could take place only if, subject to the other provisions of this Regulation, the conditions laid down in the provisions of this Regulation relating to the transfer of personal data to third countries or international organisations are complied with by the controller or processor.
461. *Ibid.*, Recital 102. International Agreements for an Appropriate level of Data Protection.
462. *Ibid.*, Article 9.

- the data subject has *explicitly consented* to the proposed transfer, after having been informed of the possible risks of such transfers for the data subject due to the absence of an AD and appropriate safeguards;
- the transfer is necessary for the performance of a contract between the data subject and the controller or the implementation of pre-contractual measures taken at the data subject's request;
- the transfer is necessary for the conclusion or performance of a contract concluded in the interest of the data subject between the controller and another natural or legal person;
- the transfer is necessary for important reasons of public interest;
- the transfer is necessary for the establishment, exercise or defence of legal claims;
- the transfer is necessary in order to protect the vital interests of the data subject or of other persons, where the data subject is physically or legally incapable of giving consent;
- the transfer is made from a register which according to Union or Member State law is intended to provide information to the public and which is open to consultation either by the public in general or by any person who can demonstrate a legitimate interest, but only to the extent that the conditions laid down by Union or Member State law for consultation are fulfilled in the particular case.[463]

The broad operation of Article 49 ensures that data can be transferred under the right conditions. It is restrictive. In other words, an individual or entity cannot freely transfer data internationally to an entity or country that does not have an appropriate level of safeguards in place to protect that data. In practice, what this means can be debatable, outside of BCR, contractual arrangements or an AD. Nevertheless, the data subject is to be provided with a level of information to make an informed decision that will either enable the data transfer or otherwise. It is only when the data subject is appraised of the risks that they can explicitly consent to the data transfer.

Against the backdrop of the above, the EU, unlike other states examined in this book, arguably has one of the most advanced legal frameworks for data protection. The EU has placed data protection as a fundamental human right to privacy over the Internet. The EU, in my view, has also been at the forefront of using the concept of interoperability to achieve a level of legal convergence with other nation states. On this basis, Article 45[464] becomes fundamental to the transfer of data to third countries. It

463. *Ibid.*, Article 49. *See also*, WP29 Guidelines 05/2020 on consent under Regulation 2016/679 Version 1.1, Adopted on 4 May 2020, explicit consent is required in certain situations where serious data protection risk emerge, that is, where a high level of individual control over personal data is deemed appropriate. Under the GDPR, explicit consent plays a role in Article 9 on the processing of special categories of data, the provisions on data transfers to third countries or international organisations in the absence of adequate safeguards in Article 49, and in Article 22 on automated individual decision making, including profiling. The GDPR prescribes that a 'statement or clear affirmative action' is a prerequisite for 'regular' consent. As the 'regular' consent requirement in the GDPR is already raised to a higher standard compared to the consent requirement in Directive 95/46/EC, it needs to be clarified what extra efforts a controller should undertake in order to obtain the explicit consent of a data subject in line with the GDPR, p. 20.

464. *Ibid.*, Article 45.

allows that the 'transfer of personal data to a third country or an international organisation may take place where the Commission has decided that the third country, a territory or one or more specified sectors within that third country, or the international organisation in question ensures an adequate level of protection. Such a transfer shall not require any specific authorisation'.[465] The proliferation of data and its ability to know no international borders has required the EU to establish a programme of Adequacy (*see* Chapter 1). However, as suggested earlier in Chapter 1, the ADs to date by the EU are a total of thirteen nation states.[466] With the small number of ADs, and the resulting effect of Convention 108, which does not require those states that have acceded to obtain adequacy,[467] a level of harmonisation or recognition that other nation states' laws provide a similar level of protection is far from settled. In determining a level of adequacy, the European Commission will consider the following as important elements to assess whether the state's laws will meet a standard of protection that is equivalent to the EU GDPR. Article 45.2 specifically requires that the third country seeking adequacy actively addresses and implements the 'rule of law, respect human rights and fundamental freedoms, public security, defence, national security and criminal law and the access of public authorities to personal data',[468] amongst others. It further requires that the third country has established supervisory authority, otherwise commonly referred to as a Regulator, with the appropriate level of power to undertake enforcement.

Despite this, one of the most important regulatory measures that has been established by the GDPR is Article 46. It requires that a 'controller or processor may transfer personal data to a third country or an international organisation only if the controller or processor has provided appropriate safeguards, and on condition that enforceable data subject rights and effective legal remedies for data subjects are available'.[469]

465. *Ibid.* Also *See* Recitals 103, 104, 105, 106, 107.
466. European Commission Adequacy decisions, https://ec.europa.eu/info/law/law-topic/data-protection/international-dimension-data-protection/adequacy-decisions_en.
467. *See* Chapter 1.
468. Regulation (EU) 2016/679 of the European Parliament and of the Council of 27 April 2016 on the protection of natural persons with regard to the processing of personal data and on the free movement of such data, and repealing Directive 95/46/EC (General Data Protection Regulation), Article 45.2. Additionally, a decision will be based on any international commitments the third country or international organisation concerned has entered into, or other obligations arising from legally binding conventions or instruments as well as from its participation in multilateral or regional systems, in particular in relation to the protection of personal data.
469. *Ibid.*, Article 46. Note that compared to many other nation states, the EU has adopted a multilayered approach to requiring the appointment of a Controller, Processor of Officer. Some states do not have the formal requirement within their respective data protection laws. The appropriate safeguards referred to in paragraph 1 may be provided for, without requiring any specific authorisation from a supervisory authority, by a legally binding and enforceable instrument between public authorities or bodies; binding corporate rules in accordance with Article 47; standard data protection clauses adopted by the Commission in accordance with the examination procedure referred to in Article 93(2); standard data protection clauses adopted by a supervisory authority and approved by the Commission pursuant to the examination procedure referred to in Article 93(2); an approved code of conduct pursuant to Article 40 together with binding and enforceable commitments of the controller or processor in the third country to apply the appropriate safeguards, including as regards data subjects' rights; or an

In addition, and although central to the private sector the EU, unlike other states has formally functionally approved the operation of corporate binding rules (CBRs *see* Chapter 11). On the one side, in order for the CBRs to be effective, they must comply with Article 47. That is, it requires all CBRs to be approved by the Regulator. For example, an EU Member State will appoint a Regulator who will oversee the implementation and enforcement of the GDPR, such as Slovenia which has a Commissioner.[470] Most third countries examined in this book have similar Regulators who carry out an enforcement function. The exceptions to this are Indonesia and India. Nonetheless, at the EU level, the European Data Protection Board (EDPB) was established to ensure a consistent approach to the implementation and oversight of the GDPR by the Member States. It also works with Member States Regulators. On this basis, the Regulator must in accordance with Article 47 ensure that any BCRs are 'legally binding and apply to and are enforced by every member concerned of the group of undertakings, or group of enterprises engaged in a joint economic activity, including their employees. They also must expressly confer enforceable rights on data subjects with regard to the processing of their personal data'.[471] The CBRs must also specify:

- the structure and contact details of the group of undertakings;[472]
- the data transfers or set of transfers, including the categories of personal data;[473]
- the application of the general data protection principles;[474]
- the rights of data subjects in regard to processing;[475]
- the acceptance by the controller or processor established on the territory of a Member State;[476]
- how the information on the BCR;[477]

approved certification mechanism pursuant to Article 42 together with binding and enforceable commitments of the controller or processor in the third country to apply the appropriate safeguards, including as regards data subjects' rights.

470. *Ibid.*, Articles 51-59.
471. *Ibid.*, Article 47. Also note Recital 110, Binding Corporate Rules.
472. *Ibid.*, Article 47(a), group of enterprises engaged in a joint economic activity and of each of its members.
473. *Ibid.*, Article 47 (b), the type of processing and its purposes, the type of data subjects affected and the identification of the third country or countries in question.
474. *Ibid.*, Article 47(d), in particular purpose limitation, data minimisation, limited storage periods, data quality, data protection by design and by default, legal basis for processing, processing of special categories of personal data, measures to ensure data security, and the requirements in respect of onward transfers to bodies not bound by the binding corporate rules.
475. *Ibid.*, Article 47(e), and the means to exercise those rights, including the right not to be subject to decisions based solely on automated processing, including profiling in accordance with Article 22, the right to lodge a complaint with the competent supervisory authority and before the competent courts of the Member States in accordance with Article 79, and to obtain redress and, where appropriate, compensation for a breach of the binding corporate rules.
476. *Ibid.*, Article 47(f), of liability for any breaches of the binding corporate rules by any member concerned not established in the Union; the controller or the processor shall be exempt from that liability, in whole or in part, only if it proves that that member is not responsible for the event giving rise to the damage.
477. Article 47(g), in particular on the provisions referred to in points (d), (e) and (f) of this paragraph is provided to the data subjects in addition to Article 13 and 14.

- the tasks of any data protection officer designated;[478]
- the complaint procedures;[479]
- the mechanisms within the group of undertakings;[480]
- the mechanisms for reporting and recording changes to the rules and reporting those changes to the supervisory authority;[481]
- the cooperation mechanism with the supervisory authority;[482]
- the mechanisms for reporting to the competent supervisory authority;[483] and
- the appropriate data protection training to personnel having permanent or regular access to personal data.[484]

In supporting the operation of the GDPR and CBRs, organisations are encouraged to develop codes of conduct, which can be approved in accordance with Article 40(3). While they are voluntary and set out rules and standards within the GDPR, they are a form of self, or otherwise, industry regulation of itself. The benefit of codes of conduct is that they can be industry-specific. For instance, such a code will have different requirements under the health sectors as it will for tourism. Another formal and functional arrangement has been the inclusion of certification schemes under Article 42(2). Certification schemes are nothing new and have been used very successfully across a number of industries such as agriculture and food production, such as the International Standards Organisation. They are effective along with contractual terms that can be used to facilitate the trade in goods and services. Therefore, under Article 46(2)(a), a signed contract providing a public authority is transferring data to another

478. *Ibid.*, Article 47(h), in accordance with Article 37 or any other person or entity in charge of the monitoring compliance with the binding corporate rules within the group of undertakings, or group of enterprises engaged in a joint economic activity, as well as monitoring training and complaint-handling.
479. *Ibid.*, Article 47(i).
480. *Ibid.*, Article 47(j), or group of enterprises engaged in a joint economic activity for ensuring the verification of compliance with the binding corporate rules. Such mechanisms shall include data protection audits and methods for ensuring corrective actions to protect the rights of the data subject. Results of such verification should be communicated to the person or entity referred to in point (h) and to the board of the controlling undertaking of a group of undertakings, or of the group of enterprises engaged in a joint economic activity, and should be available upon request to the competent supervisory authority.
481. *Ibid.*, Article 47(k).
482. *Ibid.*, Article 47(l), to ensure compliance by any member of the group of undertakings, or group of enterprises engaged in a joint economic activity, in particular by making available to the supervisory authority the results of verifications of the measures referred to in point (j).
483. *Ibid.*, Article 47(m), any legal requirements to which a member of the group of undertakings, or group of enterprises engaged in a joint economic activity is subject in a third country which are likely to have a substantial adverse effect on the guarantees provided by the binding corporate rules.
484. *Ibid.*, Article 47(n). Note also, Article 29 Data Protection Working Party, Working Document Setting Forth a Co-Operation Procedure for the approval of 'Binding Corporate Rules' for controllers and processors under the GDPR, 2018. Pursuant to Articles 64.1 and 64.4 GDPR, the BCR Lead will submit the draft decision to the EDPB on the 'final draft' of the BCRs along with all relevant information, documentation and the views of the concerned SAs. The EDPB will adopt an opinion on the matter in accordance with Article 64.3 GDPR and its Rules of Procedure.

public authority can be established provided it can be enforced.[485] Where a public authority does not have the requisite power to enter into contractual arrangements, they can use an enforceable administrative arrangement in accordance with Article 46(3)(b) - something not formally available under other common law countries although the same can apply under contract law, as long as there is a level of promissory obligations. Finally, Article 49, provides exemptions for the transfer of personal data under adequacy arrangements, in the absence of any particular safeguards, such as requiring explicit consent from the data subject.

Despite the importance placed on transnational transfers of personal data under the GDPR, to protect the data of the citizens of EU Member States, arguably, the EU has quite a flexible framework in place. That said, another feature of the GDPR that goes beyond the other states examined in this book is the disclosure requirements under Article 48. That is Article 48,[486] sets the framework for the disclosure of data that is required by the judiciary, tribunal or administrative authority, requiring a controller or processor to transfer the data, which can only be undertaken provided there is an international agreement in place.

However, while there is a robust framework in place for the transfer of data to third countries, it does not come without its challenges. The reality is that the data subject has a fundamental right to access their personal data, which is subject to the international transfer that they consented to. In other words, Article 15 allows a data subject to access their personal information. Apart from the ability of an organisation to transfer a data subject's data to a third country, under Article 15, the data subject has the right to access that data. It allows for the data subject to obtain their data from the controller information such as:

(a) the purposes of the processing;
(b) the categories of personal data concerned;
(c) the recipients or categories of recipients to whom the personal data have been or will be disclosed, in particular recipients in third countries or international organisations;
(d) where possible, the envisaged period for which the personal data will be stored, or, if not possible, the criteria used to determine that period;
(e) the existence of the right to request from the controller rectification or erasure of personal data or restriction of processing of personal data concerning the data subject or to object to such processing;
(f) the right to lodge a complaint with a supervisory authority;
(g) where the personal data are not collected from the data subject, any available information as to their source;
(h) the existence of automated decision making, including profiling, referred to in Articles 22(1) and (4) and, at least in those cases, meaningful information

485. *Ibid.*, Article 46.
486. *Ibid.*, Article 48.

> about the logic involved, as well as the significance and the envisaged consequences of such processing for the data subject.[487]

Further to the above, the data subject can also request access to their data that has been transferred to a third country to be informed of the appropriate safeguards that have been established to protect that data. The next section explores the work undertaken by the EU, under its adequacy programme. A notable difference that has emerged is that the EC issues an AD, outside of any other states acceding to Convention 108. Whereas, in states such as Australia, the Regulator has left it up to the private organisation to ensure that the receiving state has an adequacy level of protection for and of the data.

Adequacy

The current ADs by the European Commission (EC) are limited to Andorra, Argentina, Canada, (commercial organisation), Faroe Islands, Guernsey, Israel, Isle of Man, Japan, Jersey, New Zealand, Republic of Korea, Switzerland, and the UK.[488] Yet, those countries that are not members of the EU but have acceded to Convention 108 are also deemed to be adequate. Thus, there is a dual process and model operating concurrently in the EU. The complication of dual processes and systems is that the right hand may not know what the left hand is doing. While a question for the EU, it is asserted that a single framework be developed that raises the issue of adequacy above Convention 108, and the AD to the more formal framework of legal harmonisation. This section will discuss the most recent Adequate Decision between the UK and the EU.

In 2021, the EU issued its AD on data protection law for the UK.[489] First, the AD has been established to set out a framework for the transfer of data from third countries into and out of the EU. A third country is a nation state that is not a member of the EU. The UK is no longer a member of the EU, and throughout 2021, they were working with the EU to obtain a high level of adequacy for their data protection legal framework. While writing this book, the UK had not amended the Data Protection Act 2018, however, as the UK begins to move more formally away from the EU, this could change in the future. It is an area to watch closely, as it may affect the AD and future data transfers. The AD places the transfer of data and states that:

> Regulation (EU) 2016/679 sets out the rules for the transfer of personal data from controllers or processors in the European Union to third countries and international organisations to the extent that such transfers fall within its scope of application. The rules on international data transfers are laid down in Chapter V of that Regulation, that is in Articles 44 to 50. While the flow of personal data to and from countries outside the European Union is essential for the expansion of international cooperation and cross-border trade, the level of protection afforded

487. *Ibid.*, Article 15.
488. European Commission, Adequacy Decision, https://ec.europa.eu/info/law/law-topic/data-protection/international-dimension-data-protection/adequacy-decisions_en.
489. Commission Implementing Decision of 28 June 2021, pursuant to Regulation (EU) 2016/679 of the European Parliament and of the Council on the adequate protection of personal data by the United Kingdom.

to personal data in the European Union must not be undermined by transfers to third countries.[490]

Viewed this way, the baseline of data transfers is to expand international cooperation and cross-border trade. Both of these principles meet the Open Data concept, by bringing governments closer together. It is also an acknowledgement that data will play an important role in the digital economy and world trade. The legal framework for the protection of personal data in the UK after the end of the transition period had been set out in the UK under the EU (Withdrawal) Act 2018 and amended by the DPPEC Regulations [Data Protection, Privacy and Electronic Communications (Amendments, etc.) (EU Exit) Regulations 2019 (DPPEC Regulations)], and the DPA 2018 as amended by the DPPEC Regulations.[491] The overall process for the UK to obtain adequacy was significantly assisted as it was formally recognised that the 'UK GDPR is based on EU legislation, the data protection rules in the United Kingdom in many aspects closely mirror the corresponding rules applicable within the European Union'.[492] Unlike the other ADs, the EU has established that with other nation states, by and large, this AD would have been straightforward. A further dimension to this AD is that the UK has for decades been fully immersed in the development and implementation of data protection laws with the E and more broadly with Member States of the EU.

Based on the above, the overall AD is 92 pages long and consists of more than 290 paragraphs that include final considerations. Arguably, its extensive analysis highlights the extent to which the UK has incorporated the GDPR into its DPA. Therefore, this section will only discuss the key principles and concepts that are of notable importance when considering an AD. It will demonstrate how the EU has embraced the concept of interoperability, rather than requiring legal harmonisation. That said, on analysis, and because the UK was required to transpose the GDPR into national law, when a member of the EU, the level of legal harmonisation is arguably at the highest level possible. In future ADs, the EU should be encouraged to pursue more legal harmonisation rather than interoperability. Achieving a pragmatic and agile legal framework is needed, however, this can be achieved even in a climate of legal incoherence and inconsistency. The formal requirements of the AD are underscored by the following:

- material and territorial scope;[493]
- definitions of personal data and concepts of controller and processor;[494]
- safeguards, rights and obligations;[495]
- oversight and enforcement;[496]

490. *Ibid.*, p. 1.
491. *Ibid.*, p. 5.
492. *Ibid.*, p. 5.
493. *Ibid.*, pp. 6-7.
494. *Ibid.*, pp. 7-8.
495. *Ibid.*, pp. 8-12, Lawfulness and fairness of processing, Processing of special categories of personal data.
496. *Ibid.*, p. 22.

- oversight over the judiciary;[497]
- access and use of data transferred between public authorities;[498]
- access and use by UK public authorities for criminal law enforcement purposes;[499]
- investigatory powers for law enforcement purposes;[500] and
- access and use by UK public authorities for national security purposes.[501]

Due to the extensive comparative analysis undertaken as part of this AD, the discussion in this section will demonstrate the extent to which the EU considered the legal frameworks in deriving a level of adequacy. Therefore, this section will only discuss the material and territorial scope, definition of personal data and concepts of controller and processor, and safeguard, rights and obligations.

The formal and functional arrangements in relation to the material and territorial scope of the DPA were assessed as similar to that of the EU GDPR. In so doing, the AD made the point that 'similarly to Regulation (EU) 2016/679, the UK GDPR applies to the processing of Act or provide supplementary and additional rules only exercised the power under section 137 of the DPA 2018 to adopt the Data Protection (Charges and Information) (Amendment) Regulations 2019, which set out the circumstances in which data controllers are required to pay an annual charge to the UK's independent data protection authority, the Information Commissioner'.[502] Further, it highlighted how the:

> Secretary of State has so far personal data wholly or partly by automated means, or to other processing, if the personal data forms part of a filing system. The definition of 'personal data, of a data subject and of processing under the UK GDPR, are identical to those of Regulation (EU) 2016/679'.[503] On the other hand, the UK 'extends its scope also to the processing in the course of an activity which, immediately before the end of the transition period, fell outside the scope of European Union law (e.g., national security), or was within the scope of Chapter 2 of Title 5 of the Treaty on European Union (Common Foreign and Security Policy activities)'.[504]

---

497. *Ibid.*, p. 27.
498. *Ibid.*, p. 30.
499. *Ibid.*, p. 37.
500. *Ibid.*, p. 40.
501. *Ibid.*, p. 52.
502. *Ibid.*, pp. 6-7.
503. *Ibid.* In addition, the UK GDPR applies to the processing of manual unstructured personal data held by certain United Kingdom public authorities, although UK GDPR principles and rights that are not relevant to such personal data are disapplied by sections 24 and 25 of the DPA 2018. Similarly, to what is provided under Regulation (EU) 2016/679, the UK GDPR does not apply to the processing of personal data by an individual in the course of a purely personal or household activity.
504. *Ibid.* As in the European Union system, the UK does not apply to the processing of personal data by a competent authority for purposes of the prevention, investigation, detection or prosecution of criminal offences or the execution of criminal penalties, including the safeguarding against and the prevention of threats to public security (so called 'law enforcement purposes') – such processing is instead governed by Part 3 of the DPA 2018, as it is the case for Directive (EU) 2016/680 under European Union law – or the processing of personal data by intelligence

Central to understanding the extent of personal data is its definition within the respective laws. In the case of the EU, they have also defined what constitutes a controller, processor and pseudonymisation. The AD notes that the definitions provided by the DPA are consistent with those laid down by Regulation (EU) 2016/679. Importantly, the recognition of sensitive or a special category of data has been defined in Article 9(1) of the UK GDPR in the same way as under Regulation (EU) 2016/679 ('revealing racial or ethnic origin, political opinions, religious or philosophical beliefs, or trade union membership, and the processing of genetic data, biometric data for the purpose of uniquely identifying a natural person, data concerning health or data concerning a natural person's sex life or sexual orientation'). Section 205 of the DPA 2018 provides the definition of 'biometric data', 'data concerning health' and 'genetic data'.[505] This type of data has been determined to be highly important to individual data subjects. It discloses the most intimate of data about a human being that, without the current technology today, would never be available. For instance, biometric data such as facial recognition is only a recent addition and has only been made available because the technology has come onto the market that allows a computer to detect specific features of a person's face.

The AD acknowledges most of the OECD Principles, such as purpose limitation, accuracy, data minimisation, storage limitation, data security, transparency and accountability.[506] As highlighted earlier in this book, the OECD Principles have been the cornerstone of the development of policy and the law not only in data protection but also in cross-border data flows. Significantly, the UK has demonstrated over a long period that it has embraced these principles. They go some way to ensuring that 'personal data should be processed for a specific purpose and subsequently used only insofar as this is not incompatible with the purpose of processing. On the one side, data subjects should be informed of the main features of the processing of their personal data. On the other side, data subjects should have certain rights which can be enforced against the controller or processor, in particular the right of access to data, the right to object to the processing and the right to have data rectified and erased'.[507] A key feature of the EU framework is the ability for data subjects to hold the individual who is responsible for processing the personal data accountable. On this basis, the provisions of the GDPR and the DPA do allow for certain rights to be enforced against a controller or processor. The respective legal frameworks also allow for data subjects to access their personal data. Access is, arguably, becoming an increasingly important right for data subjects. It enables them to understand and know where and how their data is being used. Furthermore, the AD acknowledged that the UK allows its data subjects the 'right to object to the processing and the right to have data rectified and erased'.[508] The right to erasure or otherwise the right to be forgotten is also highly important. It allows

services (the Security Service, the Secret Intelligence Service and the Government Communications Headquarters) which is covered by Part 4 of the DPA 2018. The territorial scope of the UK is described in Article 3 and reflects the one taken in Article 3 of Regulation (EU) 2016/679.

505. *Ibid.*, p. 8.

506. *Ibid.*, pp. 11-12.

507. *Ibid.*

508. *Ibid.*

a person to request that their information be removed from a website, social media platform and other electronic use and storage systems.

In distinguishing substantive rights from those considered more important, generally, the UK grants individuals the same level of enforceable rights as those provided by Regulation 2016/679. In addition, they have ensured 'the right of access, rectification, erasure, restriction of processing, notification obligation regarding rectification or erasure of personal data or restriction of processing, data portability, and the right to object'.[509] These rights are often referred to as substantive rights, which reaffirm the high level of control intended to ensure that entities' personal data transmitted via the Internet is protected.

However, the AD formally places some restrictions on individual rights and makes other provisions for personal data processed for journalistic, artistic, academic and literary purposes, in addition to archiving and research.[510] This was emphasised in the case of *Baker v. Secretary of State for the Home Department*; it determined that it was unlawful to apply the national security exemption as a blanket exemption to access requests received by the intelligence services. Instead, the exemption had to be applied on a case-by-case basis by looking at each request on its merit and in view of the right of individuals to respect their private lives.[511] It also places a level of restrictions on onward transfers.[512]

In summary, the Commission considered that the UK guaranteed the same level of controls and protection surrounding the transfer of data between the two jurisdictions in accordance with Regulation (EU) 2016/679.[513] In maintaining that personal data and its protection thereof is a fundamental right, the AD concluded by requiring that the 'UK ensures an adequate level of protection within the meaning of Article 45 of Regulation (EU) 2016/679, interpreted in light of the Charter of Fundamental Rights of the European Union'.[514] However, the AD only lasts for a period of four years.[515] It will be up to the UK to determine whether they retain the current framework for transnational transfers or depart from it. Any departure may impact the forthcoming Adequacy Assessment, which is scheduled for 2025. Finally, and while the above discussion was brief, it highlighted the essential element of the AD. The entire AD is predicated on enabling the transfer of personal data between the two jurisdictions going forward and ensuring that the same level of protection is in place for data being transferred to the UK from an EU Member State. It has not departed from interoperability, and, in my view, and while both jurisdictions were probably under a lot of pressure to push this Decision through, the proposed assessment in 2025, should take interoperability to the next level, and begin to transition to legal harmonisation. It is further argued that these two jurisdictions are well placed to also include measures that

509. *Ibid.*, p. 12.
510. *Ibid.*, p. 16.
511. *Ibid.*, *See Baker v. Secretary of State for the Home Department* [2001] UKIT NSA2.
512. *Ibid.*, p. 18.
513. *Ibid.*, p. 88.
514. *Ibid.*
515. *Ibid.*, p. 90. It is therefore appropriate to provide that this Decision will apply for a period of four years as of its entry into force.

will begin to develop an international framework. Nonetheless, other forms of Adequacy have also been developed. *See* Chapter 9 on the discussion of the EU-US Privacy Shield. The next section examines some of the BTAs between the EU and nation states discussed throughout this book.

§3.02 BILATERAL AGREEMENTS

This section only examines the FTAs the EU has established with the states that have been discussed throughout this book. It does not comment on whether the EU is in negotiations with states. This is because such activities can take years to complete before they are formally adopted and implemented by nation states and the EU. At the time of writing the book, Japan and the EU had finalised a proposed trade agreement. However, it had not been approved by the European Council, and therefore will not be discussed in this section. Likewise, there are ongoing negotiations between Australia and the EU along with China and the EU on establishing similar agreements.

Free Trade Agreement between the European Union and the Republic of Singapore [FTA-EUSG]

The FTA-EUSG[516] is one of the most comprehensive trade agreements when compared with other states. Established in 2013, it did not come into force until 2019. It reinforces WTO-GATS rules that specifically allow for a 'free trade area to be established between the Parties; however, they must be consistent with Article XXIV of GATT 1994 and Article V of GATS.[517]

In the early sections of the agreement, there is an implied level of understanding that data will be transferred across national borders to third countries and between the EU and Singapore. Article 6.6.4 makes it clear that 'Parties shall promote the progressive development and use of systems, including those based upon information technology, to facilitate the electronic exchange of data among their respective traders, customs authorities and other related agencies.'[518] It provides that Singapore and the EU establish a pathway for data to be exchanged between the respective jurisdiction via electronic exchange - over the Internet.

Despite the extensive discussions on matters such as competition and intellectual property, there is little reference to cross-border data flows. The reference to data falls within Chapter 8. For example, Article 8.54 on Data Processing ensures that each Party is 'subject to appropriate safeguards on privacy and confidentiality, permit a financial service supplier of the other Party to transfer information in electronic or other form, into and out of its territory, for data processing, where such processing is required in the ordinary course of business of such financial service supplier'.[519] However, the emphasis is on the financial services sector, where large amounts of money are

516. Free Trade Agreement between the European Union and the Republic of Singapore, Official Journal of the European Union L 294/3.
517. *Ibid.*, Article 1.1.
518. Article 6.6.4.
519. *Ibid.*, Article 8.54.

transacted daily across international borders. With those transactions, the personal data of individuals are allowing the bank or the financial institution to transfer large quantities of this protected data to potentially all corners of the globe. Throughout this process, Article 8.54.2 requires each Party to 'maintain appropriate safeguards to protect privacy and personal data, including individual records and accounts, as long as these safeguards are not used to circumvent the provisions of this Agreement'.[520] In recognising that electronic commerce provides greater opportunity for trade to be enhanced, Article 8.57.4 ensures the 'Parties agree that the development of electronic commerce must be fully compatible with international standards of data protection, in order to ensure the confidence of users of electronic commerce'.[521] Given these developments, it could be assumed that there might have been more emphasis placed on PDP, and how it is a priority for the EU. On this basis, it is asserted that being a relatively young Agreement, with both Parties having implemented their respective data protection laws well before it came into force, lacks detail on cross-border data flows and the digital economy. It is asserted that going forward, states, including the EU, make provisions for specific chapters on cross-border data flows. Alternatively, there is a chapter on the digital economy that expands on the detail of regulating cross-border data flows and goes some way to standardising the international legal framework, rather than continually relying on interoperability. Doing so would bring many benefits, such as greater legal certainty, opening up the digital economy, setting international and regional rules-standards and norms and providing for more economic activity and jobs.

European Union, United Kingdom of Great Britain, Northern Ireland [EU-UK-NI TCA]

The European-United Kingdom-Northern Ireland Trade Cooperation Agreement,[522] referred to as the FCA, is a very recent Agreement as a result of BREXIT. It reaffirms each jurisdiction's commitment to 'democratic principles, to the rule of law, to human rights, to countering proliferation of weapons of mass destruction and to the fight against climate change, which constitute essential elements of this and supplementing agreements'.[523] The Preamble further states that in considering the importance of cross-border connectivity by air, road and sea, for passengers and for goods, there is a need to ensure a high standard in the provision of transportation services between the Parties.[524] This is the only mention of cross-border throughout the entire Agreement. That said, in Preamble 7, there is a wider understanding of how data protection and privacy have formed part of both jurisdictions' economic and political frameworks for a number of decades. It states:

520. *Ibid.*, Article 8.54.2.
521. *Ibid.*, Article 8.57.4.
522. Trade and Cooperation Agreement between the European Union and the European Atomic Energy Community, of the one part, and the United Kingdom of Great Britain and Northern Ireland, of the other part, Official Journal of the European Union L 149/10.
523. *Ibid.*, Preamble 1.
524. *Ibid.*, p. 19.

> Recognising the Parties' respective autonomy and rights to regulate within their territories in order to achieve legitimate public policy objectives such as the protection and promotion of public health, social services, public education, safety, the environment including climate change, public morals, social or consumer protection, animal welfare, privacy and data protection and the promotion and protection of cultural diversity, while striving to improve their respective high levels of protection.[525]

In addition to the above, and in underpinning Chapter 2 of the Agreement, Preamble 11 provides that:

> noting the importance of facilitating new opportunities for businesses and consumers through digital trade, and addressing unjustified barriers to data flows and trade enabled by electronic means, whilst respecting the Parties' personal data protection rules.[526]

Chapter 2, in my view, paved the way for the AD between the EU and the UK. It addresses the issues regarding cross-border data flows and PDP. In particular, Article 201 requires that each Party be committed to ensuring cross-border data flows to facilitate trade in the digital economy. Of all the Agreements examined, this is the most direct reflection of the UK and EU understanding that, in a digital economy, future activity inevitably involves data. This perception reinforces the importance of this book. Article 201 also requires that the respective Parties not restrict the 'use of computing facilities or network elements in the Party's territory for processing, including by imposing the use of computing facilities or network elements that are certified or approved in the territory of a Party'.[527] Additionally, it calls for no 'localisation of data in the Party's territory for storage or processing'.[528] Thus, the EU and UK discourage any form of data localisation or data nationalism and restrict the Parties from 'prohibiting the storage or processing in the territory of the other Party; or making the cross-border transfer of data contingent upon use of computing facilities or network elements in the Parties' territory or upon localisation requirements in the Parties' territory'.[529]

Moreover, Article 202 emphasises the need for the protection of personal data to be maintained at a high level. This is something that while historical to both jurisdictions, as the UK has been doing so since the establishment of Directive 46/95, it, in part, asserted the need for them not to dilute the protection arrangements that were well established when a member of the EU. On this basis, Article 202 requires that the Parties recognise 'that individuals have a right to the protection of personal data and privacy and that high standards in this regard contribute to trust in the digital economy and to the development of trade'.[530] Central to understanding Article 202 is that it promotes the WEF concept of trust, by connecting data with the digital economy

525. *Ibid.*, Preamble 7.
526. *Ibid.*, Preamble 11.
527. *Ibid.*, Article 201.
528. *Ibid.*
529. *Ibid.*
530. *Ibid.*, Article 202.

to the broader economy of trade. In a further sign that the EU and UK are fully committed to implementing the WEF Open Data concept, Article 210, makes provision for them to 'recognise that facilitating public access to, and use of, government data contributes to stimulating economic and social development, competitiveness, productivity and innovation'.[531] Even though there is no reference to the GDPR 1679/2018, it defines personal data to be 'any information relating to a data subject'.[532] This definition is arguably one of the broadest definitions provided and ensures that it is open enough to capture all of the elements that make up data under the GDPR. However, a challenge that might arise is whether the UK can set its own policy direction, and move away from the rights-based approach to a more liberal trade approach? While this is for the UK to determine, doing so, would and should require this Agreement to be revisited and amended accordingly.

Comprehensive Economic and Trade Agreement [CETA] Canada–European Union

The CETA[533] established in 2017, and similar to the UK-EU Agreement establishes a free trade area within the rules of 'Article XXIV of GATT 1994 and Article V of the GATS'.[534] There is no reference or chapter on cross-border data transfers. Article 13.15.2 on the processing of information requires that 'each Party shall maintain adequate safeguards to protect privacy, in particular with regard to the transfer of personal information'.[535] Yet this is limited to the financial sector. On the other side, there is no mention of the digital economy, however, it does promote the concept of trust and confidence in electronic commerce. That is, Article 16.4 requires Canada and the EU to 'adopt or maintain laws, regulations or administrative measures for the protection of personal information of users engaged in electronic commerce'.[536] Furthermore, Article 16.6 reinforces the above by noting that the protection of personal information and the protection of the consumer and business is a priority in e-commerce activities. However, it is left up to the national laws of Canada and the supranational polity of the EU to determine the level of protection. While this Agreement was established sometime before the EU and UK Agreement, it is arguably deficient in accounting for data in the new digital economy. It lacks any reference to cross-border data flows.

The next section discusses the laws of the UK. However, as highlighted above under the EU section, the UK has been determined to have the same level of protection and is rights-based as similar to that of the EU. Thus, the next section will not replicate the above provisions.

531. *Ibid.*, Article 210.
532. *Ibid.*, Article 6.
533. Comprehensive Economic and Trade Agreement (CETA) between Canada, of the one part, and the European Union and its Member States, of the other part, OJ L 11.
534. Article 1.4.
535. *Ibid.*, Article 13.15.2.
536. *Ibid.*

§3.03 UNITED KINGDOM

The UK exited the EU at the end of 2020. The EU remains the UK's largest trading partner. According to the UK House of Commons, in 2020, UK exports to the EU were GBP 251 billion (42% of all UK exports). UK imports from the EU were GBP 301 billion (50% of all UK imports).[537] In 2019, it was estimated that the UK exported GBP 234 billion in data-enabled services (74% of total UK services exports) and imported GBP 124 billion in data-enabled services (57% of total UK services imports).[538] However, as a member of the EU, they had transposed the EU GDPR into the national Data Protection Act 2018 (DPA) and UK GDPR. The DPA fully embraces the rights-based approach. In June 2021, the UK obtained Adequacy[539] with the EU. However, any future legislative changes would need to be considered in light of the AD. That is, provided the UK still wish to retain the AD. That is a decision for them.

Nonetheless, at the time of writing this book, the UK was exploring whether there was a need for the DPA to be amended to reflect their new trade and investment policy direction. The proposed amendments include:

- Enhancing the current structure of the overall legislation. Currently, the provisions for research are complex, dispersed and layered. To address this problem, the government is proposing to consolidate and bring together research-specific provisions, bringing greater clarity to the range of relevant provisions and how they relate to each other.[540]
- Incorporating a clearer definition of 'scientific research' into legislation.[541]
- Clarify the provisions surrounding access and the use of personal data for research purposes.[542]
- Clarifying consent of data subjects in relation to scientific research.[543]
- Allowing for further processing for an incompatible purpose may be permitted when it safeguards an important public interest.[544]
- Specifying personal data used by AI.[545]

537. Matthew Ward, *Statistics on UK-EU Trade, House of Commons Library*, CBP 7851, Briefing, 3 December 2021, https://researchbriefings.files.parliament.uk/documents/CBP-7851/CBP-7851.pdf.
538. Data: A New Direction, 2021, p. 86, https://assets.publishing.service.gov.uk/government/uploads/system/uploads/attachment_data/file/1022315/Data_Reform_Consultation_Document__Accessible_.pdf.
539. European Commission, Commission Implementing Decision 28 June 2021, pursuant to Regulation (EU) 2016/679 of the European Parliament and of the Council on the adequate protection of personal data by the United Kingdom, C(2021) 4800 final.
540. Data: A New Direction, 2021, p. 13, https://assets.publishing.service.gov.uk/government/uploads/system/uploads/attachment_data/file/1022315/Data_Reform_Consultation_Document__Accessible_.pdf. Navigating this web is a demanding task but a vital one for researchers to determine their legal obligations and whether any exemptions could apply. This complexity creates both real and perceived barriers for organisations.
541. *Ibid.*, p. 14.
542. *Ibid.*
543. *Ibid.*, p. 16.
544. *Ibid.*
545. *Ibid.*, pp. 24-38.

- AD to be risk-based.[546]
- Adoption of alternative transfer mechanisms, dining corporate rules, codes, standards and certification.[547]

Notwithstanding the above, the UK, having inherited a rights-based approach to data laws during its membership of the EU, will find it challenging to move away from that approach. The current proposal retains the rights-based approach so as to maintain its AD. It further expands on the concept of interoperability. The way forward prosed by the UK limits any harmonisation to standards, and not a broader or wider approach to the law. That said, what emerged in 2018, arguably placed the UK at the forefront of transnational data flow investigations. The next section highlights a case study and the challenges that emerged from the *Cambridge Analytica* (CA) case. It aims to ask more questions rather than resolve issues.

§3.04 REGULATOR: CASE STUDY

This section discusses the findings and challenges faced by Regulators when having to govern, regulate or more importantly develop the legal and policy framework to facilitate its flows. It will draw on two high-profile and widely reported *Cambridge Analytica* cases. This section does not discuss or pass comment on any political implications, only what evolved from the use of personal data and findings of the respective investigations decisions. It will identify the companies involved and not the individuals behind those companies. It will also attempt to align the issues that were highlighted by the Regulator with the current day cross-border data laws, and data protection laws more broadly. Moreover, this section will highlight gaps that will need to be addressed, in finding the right balance between protecting data and allowing it to flow freely across international borders.

In 2018, the Information Commissioner's Office (IOC) of the UK,[548] investigated the impact and use of personal data by Cambridge Analytica. A year earlier in 2017, there were a number of media reports in *The Observer* newspaper that claimed that CA worked for the Leave.EU campaign during the EU referendum, providing data services that supported micro-targeting of voters.[549] In March 2017, the Information Commissioner announced that the office (ICO) would begin a review of evidence as to the potential risks arising from the use of data analytics in the political process. Following that review of the available evidence, in May 2017 the ICO launched a broader formal investigation into the use of data analytics in political campaigns, and in particular

546. *Ibid.*, p. 89.
547. *Ibid.*, p. 92.
548. Information Commission Office, *Investigation into the Use of Data Analytics in Political Campaigns: A Report to Parliament*, 6 November 2018, https://ico.org.uk/media/action-weve-taken/2260271/investigation-into-the-use-of-data-analytics-in-political-campaigns-final-20181105.pdf.
549. Information Commissioner' Investigation into the use of data analytics in political campaigns Investigation update 11 July 2018, p. 5, https://ico.org.uk/media/action-weve-taken/2259371/investigation-into-data-analytics-for-political-purposes-update.pdf.

whether there had been any misuse of personal data and therefore breaches of data protection law by the campaigns, on both sides, during the referendum.[550] At the same time, the Information Commissioner committed to producing a policy report; that has been published alongside this update. What followed was a further inquiry into 'social media online platforms, data brokers, analytics firms, academic institutions, political parties and campaign groups. The nature of modern campaigning techniques and data flows means that some of these organisations of interest to the investigation are located outside the UK'.[551] In other words, personal data of foreign nationals from a third country, such as the US, had been transferred via servers to Cambridge Analytica (CA). CA was located in the UK, and at the time was subject to the EU GDPR.

It must be said that at the time of this entire investigation and decision, the UK were a full member of the EU. Therefore, the national laws of the UK, the Data Protection Act 2018, had transposed all of the elements of the GDPR on data protection and cross-border data flows. That said, 'Cambridge Analytica was a UK-based consulting firm that analysed data within the framework of data mining, data brokerage and strategic communication for elections.'[552] CA expertise had the ability to use modern technology to analyse personal data using behavioural sciences. This was undertaken through its subsidiary company of SLC Group in 2013, which would help organisations to identify/find target people and masses such as companies, parties, states, NGOs, etc. CA had offices in London, New York and Washington DC.[553]

Further to the background above, 'two Ph. D. students from The Psychology Center of Cambridge University in 2008 began to work on the theory of behaviour dating from the 1980s called The Great Five'.[554] The theory itself is a sophisticated technology that can identify the behaviour of individuals. In order to confirm its viability or otherwise, a test was developed through a social media platform, resulting in myPersonality,[555] which was an 'application created in 2007 that allowed users to take real psychometric tests and obtain their results instantly'.[556] Subsequently, an 'estimated 40% of the respondents also opted in to share data from their social media profile, resulting in one of the largest social science research databases in history'.[557] Up until its closure in 2012, that platform 'collected data from over 6 million volunteers during this time. This data was anonymised and samples of it were shared with registered academic collaborators around the world through the myPersonality project, resulting in over 45 scientific publications in peer-reviewed journals'.[558] The collected data when combined with additional information shared by users, included detailed

550. *Ibid.*
551. *Ibid.*
552. Pelin Vardarlıer and Cem Zafer, *Social Media and Crisis Management: The Case Study of Cambridge Analytica*, Social Media Crisis Management Cambridge Analytica Facebook, Celal Bayar University Journal of Social Sciences (2020) pp. 39-40.
553. *Ibid.*, pp. 39-40.
554. *Ibid.*
555. *Ibid.*
556. myPersonality, *The Psychometrics Centre Cambridge Judge Business School*, Cambridge University, https://www.psychometrics.cam.ac.uk/productsservices/mypersonality.
557. *Ibid.*
558. *Ibid.*

demographic profiles, a record of users' social media behaviour, interests, preferences, opinions, name, and date of birth. Because all of this data was personal, it enabled the construction of a detailed profile of the data subjects' likes and dislikes. More significantly, the 'personal data was part of 87 million social media users that was improperly shared with CA'.[559]

In 2015, a third-party application named 'this is your digital life' received information from Cambridge Analytica, which included the list of users who had permission to share information.[560] This enabled CA to analyse data pertaining to millions of individuals across the US in order to identify the most persuasive voters and identify the personal and political issues they have a low, medium or strong interest in. Having access to such important information, on a large scale, enabled targeted marketing, to influence the individuals' choice of vote. According to Vardarlıer and Zafer, the sophistication with which the data and information had been produced, enabled CA to:

- prepare speeches and messages according to personality, behaviour and needs evident in the datasets;
- test political messages By, for example, reporting a radical discourse such as 'Islam has no place in this country' and examining the reactions of the targeted population;
- produce other messages that might not have been factual such as stating that the cost of immigrants to the US is greater than that of military spending.[561]

This resulted in the data being used to 'identify those people who would or would not vote for a political party'. Unlike Australia, the US does not make voting compulsory. The data obtained by CA allowed undecided voters to be identified, which informed the content of messages sent to them to capture their votes.[562]

However, the ICO investigation identified probably one of the most important points from the data collected and used by CA and others. It was able to determine and identify individuals from 5,000 different data points per individual for 230 million adults.[563] Izabella Kaminska from the Financial Times noted the actual data points that the companies held consisted of the following:

- nationwide voter files from L2 (meaning Labels and Lists and DataTrust) (50 data points for 160 million individuals);

559. It's Facebook Again: 3 Million Users' Data Was Exposed by myPersonality app, Business Standard, 2018, https://www.business-standard.com/article/international/it-s-facebook-again-3-million-users-data-was-exposed-by-mypersonality-app-118051500216_1.html.
560. Pelin Vardarlıer and Cem Zafer, *Social Media and Crisis Management: The Case Study of Cambridge Analytica*, Social Media Crisis Management Cambridge Analytica Facebook, Celal Bayar University Journal of Social Sciences (2020) p. 39.
561. *Ibid.*, p. 41.
562. *Ibid.*
563. Izabella Kaminska, *ICO's Final Report into Cambridge Analytica Invites Regulatory Questions*, Financial Times, 2020, https://www.ft.com/content/43962679-b1f9-4818-b569-b028a58c8cd2.

- nationwide consumer data from entities such as Acxiom and Infogroup (500 data points for 160 million individuals);
- election return results from Magellen (20 data points from nation census tracks);
- nationwide consumer data from DataTrust (3000 data points from 100 million people);
- psychographic inventories (10 data points for 30 million individuals);
- social media accounts and likes of 30 million people;
- political party surveys up to 80,000;
- for America, member data (14.6 post comments, 240 likes of 31 million users); and
- emails from Infogroup and DataTrust.[564]

This indicates that a single individual data subject can produce a large quantity of data multiple times. The aforementioned data sources are possibly only a drop in the ocean, and it is plausible to assume that the number of data points is considerably higher than 5,000. This assumption is based on the number of platforms and applications available to people for their personal and professional use today would be much greater than five years ago when the CA issue surfaced. Relevant to this, Norris J. of the High Court of the UK stated:

> It was said at the hearing before me that Cambridge Analytica companies in the UK had access to some 700 terabytes of data (the equivalent of 52 billion pages of information). Public disquiet about the sourcing, aggregation and analysis of such vast quantities of data and its use for micro-targeting (not simply by Cambridge Analytica but also by others) dated back to newspaper articles published in December 2015.[565]

While the above matter centred on the insolvency and the administration of the insolvent companies in possession of the data mentioned, it highlighted the extent to which personal data, when aggregated, can be used not only to identify one individual thousands of times. It is quite possible, based on the 700 terabytes accounting for an estimated 52 billion pages of information, that the actual data points identifying one data subject could be in the hundreds of thousands. As stated at the outset of this section, this is not about taking a negative position against the companies and individuals involved. It is only to demonstrate that large quantities of data are being produced, and some of that data is being transferred across international borders. Therefore, the question arises as to whether the current policy and legal settings are appropriate and adequate. Do they balance the need for protecting data during transmission and receipt, with the requirements of the digital economy? A further important point to note is that throughout history, many industries initially operated with little regulatory oversight when a new economic activity emerged. Yet, as it matured, there was a need for regulation to minimise potential harm to people while

564. *Ibid. see also*, [2019] EWHC 954 (Ch), paragraph 2.
565. [2019] EWHC 954 (Ch), paragraph 2.

maintaining and increasing the economic benefits derived from the activity. As an example, various chemicals have been used in the agricultural and veterinary domains with few constraints initially, but which were either limited or made illegal subsequently as the risk of their manufacture and use (to humans, animals, environment and economy) became evident. What has emerged from the investigation into CA by the UK Government and others is the need to better understand the extent to which data is captured and used. It calls for more transparency and the application of the right to disclosure to ensure that data subjects actually do have access to this right in practice. It is argued that the extent of data points identifying an individual data subject be made a mandatory regulatory requirement. This is an area for further research.

§3.05 CONCLUSION

Arguably, the EU has been setting the benchmark around the world in every area of data laws. This chapter has examined the law applicable to data transfers outside the EU. It has demonstrated the complex issues that arose when the UK was a Member State of the EU. This chapter has raised other questions that not only require further research but also highlight the lack of information available to enable full transparency of data and its use under the current legal framework.

For data transnational data transfer to effectively operate from the EU there are three approaches. That is, outside of an AD, BCR or contractual arrangements, the data transfers can be undertaken provided that the data subject has provided full and explicit consent.

It is argued that another success coming out of the EU has been the ability of a third country to obtain an AD. The ADs, while limited to a few countries, have focused on interoperability of the respective data laws. As expected, the UK obtained an AD from the EU shortly after leaving the Union. However, for the other jurisdictions examined in this book, most do not make that list. A standout is New Zealand. This process has served data transfer very well, to date. However, it is questionable whether the gaps in the law created by ADs can ever be fully reconciled in a world of increasing conflict and legal incoherence.

The EU has had a long-standing relationship with the OECD Principles. They have been incorporated throughout the GDPR. Being one of the earliest adopters of data protection laws, the EU has reinforced the principles of the OECD data transfer guidelines.

In addition to the above, the EU is a party to a number of bilateral and multilateral trade agreements. While this chapter examined a limited number of these agreements, it demonstrated how more work is needed to fully utilise trade agreements in the future. That is, the most recent agreement between the EU, UK of Great Britain and Northern Ireland highlighted the importance of safeguarding Pre-BREXIT regulatory arrangements for the protection and use of data transnationally. It emphasises that the digital economy will be beneficial to all parties and cross-border data flows will be used to facilitate trade.

Problematic though is that there is no consistent approach to incorporating digital trade, economy and the data used in these agreements. Compatibility between agreements is creating another layer of fragmentation in the law. In part, agreements reflect the need for the protection of data, however, they lack any specifications in relation to data flows.

Despite the strength of the GDPR in governing data transfers, the investigation undertaken by the UK ICO highlighted the complex technical and technological components used to collect and transfer data internationally. It raised further questions than it resolved. This chapter demonstrated from this case study that 700 terabytes of data (the equivalent of 52 billion pages of information) were captured and used by an entity. In part, the 700 terabytes of data were mostly personal data. Therefore, how many additional data points can this create, where an individual can be identified over the Internet? This will largely depend on the level of engagement the individual has with and over the Internet. For example, is the data subject on social media platforms or only use search engines? This is another area of further research to understand the extent of data points that can be used to identify a person. More information is needed to inform the general public of the extent of the data points that can identify a data subject.

It is further argued that currently there is no requirement for these entities to report the use or transfer of data internationally. The only requirement for reporting in some jurisdictions is when an entity has breached the national laws. While this is an important feature to gain trust in the legal framework, it is not a silver bullet.

Law reform is required to develop a reporting system of all personal data being transferred internationally. For instance, if an entity in Australia transfers the personal data of 5 million Australian citizens to an entity (public or private) to the UK, that information should be provided to the Regulator. Doing so would enable data subjects to gain easier access to where their data has gone. It would add another layer of certainty and confidence to the otherwise inconsistent and highly fragmented legal framework. Further, it is argued that an International Organisation could be established not only to develop international laws but also to be a holding facility for all international transfers and trades in data. The next chapter examines the current approach taken by Canada to cross-border data flows.

Chapter 4
Canada

This chapter discusses the current-day PDP laws of Canada as they relate to data flows internationally. Where it has already been highlighted, there will be no examination of an FTA. For instance, as above, the Canadian and EU FTA have been discussed. The examination regarding FTAs is limited to Canada-ASEAN FTA; Canada-China FTA; Canada-EU Comprehensive Economic and Trade Agreement; Canada-India Comprehensive Economic Partnership Agreement (CEPA); and Canada, the US and Mexico.

The Personal Information Protection and Electronic Documents Act, S.C. 2000 (PIPEDA), and Privacy Act 1985 (PA) have been instrumental in providing the legal framework for the governance of personal data across Canada. The Canadian Consumer Privacy Protection Act (CPA) will replace the PIPEDA 2000. For some time, the Canadian legal framework has distinguished between the public and private sectors. In the new digital economy and the inevitable flow of data spanning both sectors, it will be highly complex to separate the two sectors going forward. At the time of writing, Canada was in the process of undertaking law reform. In part, the proposed changes address some of the issues related to data flows, such as the protection of data in the new digital economy. On the one hand, the proposed reforms are limited to Ontarians, and more needs to be done at the national level. The proposals recognise the significance of the collection and transfer of data, although they have stalled and are due to be reconsidered in late 2022. On the one hand, for Canada, there is a constant tension developing the need to embrace the digital economy and the benefits it will bring. On the other hand, it is creating the regulatory environment to allow data transfers to be efficient and protected. This in and of itself will be difficult to achieve while Canada continues to have separate rules for the public versus the private sector. Moreover, the concept of consent is another issue that Canada will need to resolve. Another problem faced by Canada is similar to that in the US where provinces are acting independently and developing local laws to deal with data flows and their protection.

§4.01 INTRODUCTION

For some time, Canada has been undertaking reform of its legal framework for data protection. At the time of writing (17 May 2022), the population of Canada stood at 38,360,271.[566] It has a population density of 4 people per km^2 (11 people per mi^2) and a total land area is 9,093,510 km^2 (3,511,022 sq. miles).[567] Since the 2000s, 'Canadians have embraced digital technologies at an unprecedented pace and breadth.'[568] Huju Liu, Julien McDonald-Guimond make the point that in 2018, '91% of Canadians were Internet users and 84% of Internet users shopped online to order digital goods and services and physical goods and other services – spending $57.4 billion, up from $18.9 billion in 2012'.[569] Similar trends have emerged worldwide, although online activity varies depending on the population and Internet connectivity.

The Canadian CPA will replace the former PIPEDA,[570] which regulates only the private sector. At the time of writing, the CPA had not fully passed through the Canadian Parliament. On that basis, Bill C-11, an Act to enact the CPA (the Personal Information and Data Protection Tribunal Act), was being further considered.[571] Furthermore, as of January 2022, the PA 1983 was also being reviewed. Unlike other jurisdictions that have developed a single Act to govern both the public and private sectors, Canada has opted to distinguish between the two sectors. The PA has been responsible for protecting all personal information held by the federal government and federal public-sector institutions. Currently, however under the PIPEDA, the EU has afforded an AD.[572]

However, note that this AD was under the former Directive 95/46/EC, and it is limited by and large to section 23.1 that allows for the disclosure of information to a

566. Worldometers, Canada, 2022, https://www.worldometers.info/world-population/canada-population/.
567. *Ibid.*
568. Huju Liu and Julien McDonald-Guimond, 'Measuring Digital Intensity in the Canadian Economy, Statistics Canada' (2021) 1(2) Economic and Social Reports Catalogue No. 36-28-0001, https //doi.org/10.25318/36280001202100200003-eng.
569. *Ibid.*
570. Personal Information Protection and Electronic Documents Act 2000, https://laws-lois.justice.gc.ca/PDF/P-8.6.pdf.
571. Government of Canada, Bill C-11: *An Act to enact the Consumer Privacy Protection Act and the Personal Information and Data Protection Tribunal Act and to Make Related and Consequential Amendments to Other Acts.* Tabled in the House of Commons, 2 December 2020, https://www.justice.gc.ca/eng/csj-sjc/pl/charter-charte/c11.html.
572. European Commission, Commission Decision, of 20 December 2001 pursuant to Directive 95/46/EC of the European Parliament and of the Council on the adequate protection of personal data provided by the Canadian Personal Information Protection and Electronic Documents Act (2002/2/EC), Official Journal of the European Communities L 2/13.

foreign state.[573] It provides powers to the Commissioner to disclose personal information that would be 'relevant to an ongoing or potential investigation or proceeding in respect of a contravention of the laws of a foreign state that address conduct that is substantially similar to conduct that would be in contravention of this Part, or is necessary to disclose in order to obtain from the person or body information that may be useful to an ongoing or potential investigation or audit under this Part'.[574] Professor Colin Bennett makes the point 'Canada has enjoyed the privilege of adequacy status with the EU.'[575] Bennett argues that the PIPEDA no longer provides a workable and balanced approach to privacy protection that has, in the past, served Canada well. Yet, he calls for change to bring the national framework of Canada in line with what other nation states have developed. In agreeing with Bennett, Canada should consider reforming their current data laws to a single specific data framework whereby the public and private sectors are regulated together and in a consistent manner.

Consent

Alex Cameron and Daanish Samadmoten make the point that an 'organisation is responsible for personal information in its possession or custody, including information that has been transferred to a third party for processing'.[576] They go on to say that, generally 'organisations must use contractual or other means, which usually include technical measures, to provide a comparable level of protection while the information is being processed by a third-party service provider or other entity'.[577] In referring to the Office of the Privacy Commissioner, '*consent* may be required for transfers to service providers, although this view is controversial, and no legislative amendment has been made. Additional considerations, including notice to individuals, are applicable regarding the use of service providers located outside of Canada. Certain provincial privacy laws impose additional obligations in relation to cross-border transfers'.[578] Significantly, unlike the EU and other states, consent is not a full legal requirement for the transfer of data internationally. It further highlights that broadly the data laws are inconsistent with each other. Noteworthy, that when comparing concepts and principles individually, they in and of themselves vary greatly. A further problem is that with such variation across national legal framework, it undermines confidence and trust in the law. Rather than create certainty, it creates a level of uncertainty.

573. Personal Information and Data Protection Tribunal Act 2000, section 23.1.
574. *Ibid.*, section 23.1.
575. Colin Bennett, *The Schrems II decision: Implications and challenges for Canada*, 2020, https://www.colinbennett.ca/canadian-privacy/the-schrems-ii-decision-implications-and-challenges-for-canada/.
576. Alex Cameron and Daanish Samadmoten, *Canada-Data Protection Overview*, https://www.dataguidance.com/notes/canada-data-protection-overview.
577. *Ibid.*
578. *Ibid.*

Aside from the national framework, provinces across Canada have prepared their own specific privacy laws. This section examines only the province of Quebec.[579] If and when enacted, Bill 64, while providing for cross-border data flows, has restrictions to ensure the assessment of sensitivity of personal information. Essentially, an assessment will drive the transfer process, whereby, the collection, use or communication of the data must have the same level of protection in the third country. Once an assessment has been finalised, there must be a written agreement in place between the relevant parties to mitigate any risks from the assessment. Despite the bill not coming into effect, it appears to provide wide enough reach to allow for the assessments, and written agreement to be and form part of the governance of data internationally. The next section examines a selection of FTAs Canada has entered into with nation states that form part of this book.

§4.02 BILATERAL AGREEMENTS

Canada-ASEAN FTA

In November 2021, Canada and ASEAN agreed to proceed with FTA negotiations.[580] The Association of Southeast Asian Nations (ASEAN) Member State economies represent Canada's sixth-largest trading partner as of 2020.[581] In 2020, merchandise trade between Canada and ASEAN reached USD 26.7 billion, and there is potential remaining to significantly enhance the relationship. According to the 2018 Joint Feasibility Study for a Canada-ASEAN FTA, the economic modelling projects that an FTA could increase Canada's GDP by USD 2.54 billion and boost exports to ASEAN countries to USD 2.67 billion.[582] While this Agreement is currently under negotiation, it offers a unique opportunity for the Parties to develop provisions specific to cross-border data flows. The proposed Agreement will cover areas such as e-commerce and trade-in services. More specifically, it will provide for cross-border trade-in services. Even though there is no mention at this early stage of data flows, data adequacy or data protection between the jurisdictions, consideration should be given to go beyond interoperability and include more on legal harmonisation.

Canada–China Free Trade Agreement

Similar to the above Canada-ASEAN Free Trade Agreement (CAFTA), the Canada-China Free Trade Agreement (CCFTA) is currently under consideration. While not discussing the political interventions as to why the proposed CCFTA has not been further developed, it provides an excellent opportunity for both states to come together

579. Bill 64 (2021, Chapter 25), An Act to Modernise Legislative Provisions as Regards the Protection of Personal Information, Http://Www2.Publicationsduquebec.Gouv.Qc.Ca/Dynamicsearch/Telecharge.Php?Type = 5&File = 2021C25A.PDF.

580. Government of Canada, *Canada-ASEAN Free Trade Agreement*, https://www.international.gc.ca/trade-commerce/trade-agreements-accords-commerciaux/agr-acc/asean-anase/fta-ale/negotiations-negociations.aspx?lang = *eng*.

581. *Ibid*.

582. *Ibid*.

and develop robust provisions that balance data flows in the digital economy. That is, on 22 September 2016, Canada and the People's Republic of China announced the launch of exploratory discussions for a possible Canada-China FTA.[583] Work on these discussions started in the fall of 2016. Face-to-face meetings took place from 20-24 February 2017, in Beijing and from 24-28 April 2017, in Ottawa. A third set of meetings took place in Beijing from 31 July to 4 August 2017. The discussions give both sides an opportunity to exchange information about each other's regulations and laws and to explore the details of a possible Canada-China FTA.

Canada-European Union Comprehensive Economic and Trade Agreement [CETA]

The EU is one of the largest economies in the world and Canada's second-largest trading partner.[584] The CETA presents Canadian businesses with preferential access to and excellent opportunities for growth in the EU. Learn about CETA and what it can do for your business. Chapter 13 deals with trade in financial services. Article 13.15.2, requires that on transferring and processing information for cross-border financial services, 'adequate safeguards to protect privacy, in particular with regard to the transfer of personal information'.[585] If the transfer of financial information involves personal information, such transfers shall be in accordance with the legislation governing the protection of personal information of the territory of the Party where the transfer has originated. On the other hand, Chapter 16 addresses electronic commerce. Article 16.4 promotes a level of trust and confidence in the e-commerce sector. Significantly, it allows for either Party to consider any 'international standards of data protection of relevant international organisations of which both Parties are a member'.[586] Further, Article 16.6, understanding that now e-commerce is global in nature; it requires a level of dialogue on 'the protection of personal information and the protection of consumers and businesses from fraudulent and deceptive commercial practices in the sphere of electronic commerce'.[587] The push for dialogue, unfortunately, does not address the broader issues pertaining to data flows, adequacy or data protection. How long can dialogue extend for and to? This can only be confirmed by the parties involved. Yet, Canada and the EU have an opportunity to reconsider the CETA and extend certain provisions to consider data flows.

Canada-India CEPA

India has emerged as a key trading partner not only for Canada but many other countries across the world. Negotiations began in 2010 negotiations, with the most recent in 2017 for the development of the Comprehensive Economic Partnership

583. Government of Canada, *Canada-China Free Trade Agreement*, https://www.international.gc.ca/trade-commerce/trade-agreements-accords-commerciaux/agr-acc/ceta-aecg/index.aspx?lang=eng&_ga=2.212181652.1664122841.1643725152-431525686.1643725152.
584. *Ibid.*
585. *Ibid.*, Article 13.15.2.
586. *Ibid.*, Article 16.4.
587. *Ibid.*, Article 16.6.

Agreement (CEPA).[588] More than a decade ago, in 2009, Canada was ranked the eighteenth largest services exporter globally, while India was ranked the twelfth largest services exporter.[589] India's two-way services trade value has increased from USD 36.7 billion in 2001 to USD 191.0 billion in 2008, with a compound annual growth rate of 26.6%.[590] Canada's two-way services trade also witnessed a substantial rise from USD 81.1 billion in 2001 to USD 151.4 billion in 2008, with a compound annual growth rate of 9.3%.[591] While the CEPA is currently in hibernation, it offers an excellent opportunity for both countries to develop a robust framework for transnational data flows. However, it may be beneficial for any progress to wait until India finally implements its proposed data protection laws.

Canada, the United States and Mexico

Canada, the United States and Mexico (CUSMA)[592] was signed in 2020 between Canada, US and Mexico. It replaced the North American Free Trade Agreement (NAFTA). That said, since NAFTA, the widespread use of the commercial Internet, for example, dramatically affected consumer habits and commercial activities, such as e-commerce, data flows, and supply chain management.[593] Financial services have grown and continue to grow into a global economic sector. The CUSMA 'distinguishes between financial services traded across borders and those sold by a provider with a commercial presence in the home country of the buyer'.[594] The review of NAFTA, affirmed how financial services firms rely on cross-border data flows to ensure data security, create efficiencies and cost savings through economies of scale, and utilise Internet cloud services that are often provided by US technology firms. Today, 'CUSMA strengthens the language to protect the free flow of data and removes the carve-out provided that a party's financial regulatory authorities have "for regulatory and supervisory purposes, immediate, direct, complete, and ongoing access" to data located in another party's territory'.[595] Moreover, it accounts for digital trade and is one of the only FTAs examined in this book that specifically addresses the digital economy. However, digital trade[596] excludes government and only constitutes the private sector. It does not include financial services, as highlighted above. Article 19.1 defines personal information to mean information, including data, about an identified or identifiable natural person. In relation to digital trade, it covers but is not limited to:

---

588. Government of Canada, *Canada-India Comprehensive Economic Partnership Agreement*, https://www.international.gc.ca/trade-commerce/trade-agreements-accords-commerciaux/agr-acc/india-inde/cepa-apeg/index.aspx?lang=eng&_ga=2.211805845.1664122841.1643725152-431525686.1643725152.
589. *Ibid.*
590. *Ibid.*
591. *Ibid.*
592. Congressional Research Services, *Canada, the United States and Mexico*, https://sgp.fas.org/crs/row/R44981.pdf.
593. *Ibid.*, p. 2.
594. *Ibid.*, pp. 22-24.
595. *Ibid.*
596. Canada-United States-Mexico Agreement, Chapter 19, Digital Trade, https://www.international.gc.ca/trade-commerce/trade-agreements-accords-commerciaux/agr-acc/cusma-aceum/text-texte/19.aspx?lang=eng.

- ensuring non-discriminatory treatment of digital products;
- prohibiting cross-border data flows restrictions and data localisation requirements;
- prohibiting requirements for source code or algorithm disclosure or transfer as a condition for market access, with exceptions;
- prohibiting customs duties or other charges for electronically transmitted products;
- requiring parties to have online consumer protection and anti-spam laws, and a legal framework on privacy;
- promoting cooperation on cybersecurity, risk-based strategies and consensus-based standards over prescriptive regulation in combating cybersecurity risks and events;
- prohibiting imposition of liability for harms against Internet services providers or users related to information stored, processed, transmitted, distributed, or made available by the service, with the exclusion of ISP liability for intellectual property rights infringement; and
- promoting publication of open government data in machine-readable format for public usage.[597]

Viewed this way, it addresses, in part cross-border data flows, however, it does not adopt the Open Data concept, discussed in chapter one. Rather, it accepts the notion that there will be restrictions placed on data flows, and localisation requirements. Put another way, CUSMA accepts that either nation state, may at some stage establish data localisation laws. On the other hand, it calls for collaboration in the area of cybersecurity, that each state is to have their own legal framework addressing privacy over the Internet. An accentuating issue that has arisen, is the lack of acknowledgement of interoperability. Further, the lack of any reference to harmonising the data flows laws amongst the three states. This could have been an opportunity for the three countries to set the policy and legal discourse internationally, in this area of the law.

Against the backdrop of the above, Article 19.8.1, goes into quite some detail in relation to personal information protection. It recognises the economic and social benefits of protecting personal information, and what that means to enhance consumer confidence in digital trade. Significantly, Article 19.8.2, requires that any legal framework implemented by either state, does so, provided that personal information of the users of digital trade is protected.[598] Most noteworthy is that it promotes the need for either state to take into account the *APEC Privacy Framework* and the *OECD Recommendation of the Council concerning Guidelines Governing the Protection of Privacy and Transborder Flows of Personal Data (2013)* when developing their nation laws.

In further espousing the international standard principles that many nation states have adopted, Article 19.8.3 states that the international principles include 'limitation

597. Congressional Research Services, *Canada, the United States and Mexico*, p. 24, https://sgp.fas.org/crs/row/R44981.pdf.
598. Canada-United States-Mexico Agreement, Article 19.8.2.

on collection; choice; data quality; purpose specification; use limitation; security safeguards; transparency; individual participation and accountability'.[599] Furthermore, 'Parties also recognize the importance of ensuring compliance with measures to protect personal information and ensuring that any restrictions on cross-border flows of personal information are necessary and proportionate to the risks presented.'[600] These additions, in my view, is the first Agreement that makes reference to the actual international standards. It could be argued that there is an implied level promoting international development of the law and more so, international harmonisation of their respective data laws. While, this would need to be clarified by the respective governments of Canada, the US and Mexico, it is a pivotal step in raising the standards set out in such Agreements. The CUSMA has a lot to offer other states that are developing FTAs-economic agreements, with specific provisions for digital trade and the digital economy that will use personal data in transnational flows. An additional provision/section worth considering is a definition of the digital economy, within the digital trade section. Likewise, a definition of cross-border data flows could also be inserted to provide greater certainty. Doing so would be the first step to internationalising additional concepts and principles, outside of what has already been provided for by the APEC Framework and OECD.

§4.03 CONCLUSION

The current legal landscape for data flows in Canada is in part fragmented. This is because data, as of January 2022, continues to be regulated differently for the private and public sectors. This chapter has examined five BTAs Canada has established with the US, EU, India, China and ASEAN.

The revised NAFTA and now the CUSMA provides the basis for further developing data flow law within trade agreements that will benefit Canada and its trading partners. Canada understands very well the need for them to continually transform themselves and their economy. They affirm the importance that data and the flows of data will have in the digital economy. Canada notes:

> Digital and data transformation has led to an explosion of data, with a large proportion of the world's data created recently. Data is helping to fuel innovations like AI, machine learning, and the Internet of Things throughout Canada. However, the rapid acceleration of data being created, and its use as a commodity

599. *Ibid.*, Article 19.8.3.

600. *Ibid.*, Article 19.8.3.2. Each Party shall publish information on the personal information protections it provides to users of digital trade, including how: (a) a natural person can pursue a remedy; and (b) an enterprise can comply with legal requirements. Recognising that the Parties may take different legal approaches to protecting personal information, each Party should encourage the development of mechanisms to promote compatibility between these different regimes. The Parties shall endeavour to exchange information on the mechanisms applied in their jurisdictions and explore ways to extend these or other suitable arrangements to promote compatibility between them. The Parties recognise that the *APEC Cross-Border Privacy Rules* system is a valid mechanism to facilitate cross-border information transfers while protecting personal information.

> means Canada must re-evaluate the frameworks it has in place. While the *Personal Information Protection and Electronic Documents Act* and other marketplace legal frameworks continue to provide important protections, particularly as they were situated as technologically neutral in orientation, there remain important questions about how to ensure these frameworks are transparent. Further questions arise whether the current approach taken by Canadians will over the long term establish a high level of 'trust in an increasingly data-driven world'.[601]

While Canada has a well-developed legal framework in relation to data protection, there is still some work to do, to enhance and strengthen its laws. The Canadian Office of the Privacy Commissioner in September 2021 acknowledged the importance of deeper international cooperation in the area of data flows. It stated 'to realise this ambition in a context where data flows seamlessly across borders and digital businesses reach customers globally – and build trust and confidence, underpinned by high standards of data protection – requires deeper and swifter international regulatory cooperation'.[602] Viewed this way, in my view, the statement arguably is calling for a shift from a national approach to an international approach for data flow regulation. While stopping short of calling for the internationalisation of data flow(s) law, it acknowledges that for trust to be achieved and standards to be strengthened, a pathway forward is the need for international law that would significantly benefit the Canadian and more broadly the world economy.

For Canada to fully realise the potential of data in the digital economy, they need to unlock the current barriers and obstacles that are created by the current national legal framework. The ongoing separation between the public and private sector regulation for data does not establish a high level of trust. There needs to be a deeper level of consistency and coherence within the country. They need to build on the current and their past work that, has been undertaken to support the implementation of global principles such as the OECD Principles and develop additional pathways to shaping an international legal framework.

This chapter has demonstrated that leading Canadian scholars argue that while the country has obtained an AD by the EU, under the former Directive 95/46/EC, it is somewhat outdated. It has been argued that the EU-AD that Canada has relied upon, no longer balances privacy with the flow of data, with the objectives of the PIPEDA. These leading scholars reinforce my view that Canada needs to further reform their data laws to regulate both the public and private sectors as a collective. Data flows and its security needs to be better balanced under the national legal framework, taking into consideration the economic benefits, with that of a high level of privacy protection. The next chapter examines India's legal framework for cross-border data flows.

601. Innovation, Science and Economic Development Canada, *Canada's Digital Charter in Action: A Plan*, (2016), pp. 9-10.
602. Office of the Privacy Commissioner, Data Free Flow with Trust, https://www.priv.gc.ca/en/opc-news/speeches/2021/communique-g7_210907/.

CHAPTER 5

India

India and its people are a remarkable country, located in South Asia, and have one of the highest populations in the world. This chapter examines the current-day cross-border data laws of India. It does not discuss any provisions of the proposed Data (Privacy and Protection) Bill. *While at the conclusion of 2021, the proposed Bill had entered Parliament, there has been no guarantee that it will pass in 2022. Nonetheless, the prosed Bill is partly modelled on the EU data protection legal framework. Today, India has taken a sectoral approach to data protection and cross-border data flow laws. They do not have an AD with the EU. This approach continues to be problematic for India and it can be argued that unless law reform is undertaken in the near future, the country may be restricting itself to the economic and social benefits that come from data flows in the new digital economy.*

Moreover, its current Information Technology Act 2000 is very limited in relation to transnational data flows. India has a limited number of FTAs with the other jurisdictions examined in this book. They currently rely on economic cooperation agreements, which lack any real meaningful provisions to support data flows in the digital economy. Even with this limited approach, there is a significant opportunity for India that any future developments of trade agreements could include specific provisions for data flows with their key trading partners.

Doing so will provide more certainty for their companies undertaking international business. Noteworthy too are the additional legislation and governance frameworks that do impact cross-border data transfers including the Digital Information Security in Healthcare Act 2017, and the Non-Personal Data Governance Framework. However, they do not form part of this chapter's discussion.

§5.01 INTRODUCTION

India is located in South Asia and has the second-highest population in the world as of January 2022. It is multi-racial, ethnic, and religious and comprises many different languages. India is a fascinating country and for more than a decade has been a leader in the technology outsourcing economy. As a country, it has been building the digital economy and has seen extraordinary growth in Internet connections[603] over the past five years. According to the McKinsey Global Institute, India is one of the 'largest and fastest-growing markets for digital consumers, with 560 million internet subscribers in 2018, second only to China. Indian mobile data users consume 8.3 gigabits (GB) of data each month on average, compared to 5.5 GB for mobile users in China and somewhere in the range of 8.0 to 8.5 GB in South Korea, an advanced digital economy. Indians have 1.2 billion mobile phone subscriptions and have downloaded more than 12 billion apps in 2018. The analysis of seventeen mature and emerging economies finds India is digitising faster than any other country in the study, save Indonesia - and there is plenty of room to grow: just over 40% of the populace has an internet subscription'.[604] Based on these estimates, the digital economy and the activity that will include the use of personal data will be significant.

McKinsey also states that digital sectors accounted for about 'USD 170 billion - or 7% - of GDP in 2017-2018.[605] This includes, but is not limited to, digital products and services, such as IT-BPM USD 115 billion; digital communication services USD 45 billion, and electronics manufacturing USD 10 billion. They estimate that the digital economy could climb to between USD 355 billion and USD 435 billion and account for 8%-10% of India's GDP by 2025-2026'.[606] On this basis, the potential for data flows within India is enormous, when considering the many other jurisdictions it will develop linkages to the digital economy with. What this does not explain is the estimated economic activity of transnational data flows into and out of India over the near, medium and longer term. Yet, it demonstrates the enormity of the digital economy. Further, those national states with high populations will naturally generate more data, as their citizens adopt technology and undertake activities (personal and professional) - online.

The current data legal framework in India can be best describes as being sectorial. At the time of writing this book, India had not implemented dedicated data protection laws, in the same way as many other nation states. The proposed draft *Data (Privacy and Protection) Bill,* had been under development for a number of years. The Joint Parliamentary Committee on 16 December 2021 'presented its report on the proposed data protection law, along with a revised version of the bill, the Data Protection Bill,

603. Noshir Kaka, Anu Madgavkar, Alok Kshirsagar, James Manyika, Kushe Bahl and Shishir Gupta, *Digital India: Technology to Transform a Connected Nation*, Mckinsey Global Institute, 2020, Preface. This Chapter draws on some of the earlier work undertaken by the author, particularly the book title Robert Walters, Leon Trakman and Bruno Zeller, *Data Protection Law: A Comparative Analysis of Asia Pacific and European Approaches*, Springer (2019), pp. 147-168.
604. *Ibid.*, p. vi.
605. *Ibid.*, p. 10.
606. *Ibid.*

2021 to Parliament'.[607] However, as of January 2022, the draft Bill was yet to be tabled for consideration and passing by the Parliament. Problematic, is if the draft proposal has to go out for further consultation with industry and the community. Doing so would further delay its implementation. Nonetheless, it has been prepared based on similar concepts and principles of the EU GDPR. If implemented in its current form, it will significantly add to the current legal framework by providing for transnational transfers of data. Under the current sectorial approach, international transfers can take place, however, the proposed draft laws[608] do take a different approach.

The Information Technology Act 2000 (IT Act)[609] is the principal legislation regulating data and privacy across India. They are supported by the Information Technology (Reasonable Security Practices and Procedures and Sensitive Personal Data or Information) Rules 2011 [the Rules].[610] In a period of growing Internet transactions and activity, the IT Act is somewhat limited. Its principal aim is to 'provide legal recognition for transactions carried out by means of electronic data interchange and other means of electronic communication, commonly referred to as electronic commerce, which involve the use of alternatives to paper-based methods of communication and storage of information and to facilitate electronic filing of documents with government agencies'.[611]

Nonetheless, this section will be examining both the IT Act and the Rules. Section 2 of the IT Act defines data to mean:

> a representation of information, knowledge, facts, concepts or instructions which are being prepared or have been prepared in a formalised manner, and is intended to be processed, is being processed or has been processed in a computer system or computer network, and may be in any form (including computer printouts magnetic or optical storage media, punched cards, punched tapes) or stored internally in the memory of the computer.[612]

Additionally, the IT Act defines information quite broadly to include 'data, message, [text,] images, sound, voice, codes, computer programmes, software and databases or micro film or computer-generated micro fiche'.[613] While information is not personal data, the term data, programmes, software and databases all provide the platform for personal data to be transferred internationally. The rules take the

607. Nishith Desai Associates, 'Privacy & Data Protection Capsule: India's Turn on the World Stage' (January 2022) XII(8) National Law Review, https://www.natlawreview.com/article/privacy-data-protection-capsule-india-s-turn-world-stage#google_vignette.
608. The Personal Data Protection Bill 2019, Chapter VII, Restriction on Transfer of Personal Data Outside India, Prohibition of processing of sensitive personal data and critical personal data outside India. Conditions for transfer of sensitive personal data and critical personal data.
609. The Information Technology Act 2008, https://www.indiacode.nic.in/bitstream/123456789/13116/1/it_act_2000_updated.pdf and https://police.py.gov.in/Information%20Technology%20Act%202000%20-%202008%20(amendment).pdf.
610. The Information Technology (Reasonable Security Practices and Procedures and Sensitive Personal Data or Information) Rules, 2011 obtain their power from clause (ob) of subsection (2) of section 87 and read with section 43A The Information Technology Act 2000, https://www.wipo.int/edocs/lexdocs/laws/en/in/in098en.pdf.
611. The Information Technology Act 2008, Preamble.
612. *Ibid.*, section 2.
613. *Ibid.*

definition of data one step further and define sensitive personal data or information to be a password; 'financial information such as Bank account or credit card or debit card or other payment instrument details; physical, physiological and mental health conditions; sexual orientation; medical records and history; biometric information; any detail relating to the above clauses as provided to body corporate for providing service; and any of the information received under above clauses by body corporate for processing, stored or processed under lawful contract or otherwise'.[614] Thus, there is a considerable amount of data that can form part of any international transfer.

With the definition of data clarified, that data can be transferred internationally to another country in accordance with Rule 7 of the Rules. Put another way, Rule 7 states that the 'transfer of information by a body corporate or any person on its behalf may transfer sensitive personal data or information including any information, to any other body corporate or a person in India, or located in any other country, that ensures the same level of data protection that is adhered to by the body corporate as provided for under these Rules'.[615] That said, the transfer may be allowed only if it is necessary for the performance of the lawful contract between the body corporate or any person on its behalf and provider of information or where such a person has consented to data transfer. This is somewhat limited to sensitive personal information. The processing and transfer of personal data under Rule 7 must be read in accordance with Rule 4 which requires a company which is handling personal data to prepare a privacy policy.[616]

However, sensitive personal data has been afforded a higher level of protection and control. On the one hand, any transfer involving sensitive personal data cannot be undertaken unless it meets the requirements of IS/ISO/IEC 27001. This international standard has been set by the International Organisation for Standards,[617] and 27001 specifically provides for information security management. Constituted this way, sensitive personal data comes with a further layer of governance.

Moreover, this addition under the current Indian framework has not been replicated by the other jurisdictions examined in this book. The ensuing question is whether national and FTAs should make specific reference to such international standards, as a matter of consistency and harmonisation? A further accentuating question is whether such standards retain and promote trust, and interoperability or go further and direct adoptees to see harmonisation?

In other words, a contract between an organisation and data subject that does not specify a transfer of data to another jurisdiction cannot be undertaken. On the one hand, this does not apply if the data subject has provided consent before the transfer occurs. In this current period, an entity is restricted from disclosing sensitive data to a third party. On the other hand, they can disclose this information provided they have

614. *Ibid.*
615. The Information Technology (Reasonable Security Practices and Procedures and Sensitive Personal Data or Information) Rules, 2011, Rule 7.
616. *Ibid.*, Rules 7 and 4. Also *see* Robert Walters, Leon Trakman and Bruno Zeller, *Data Protection Law: A Comparative Analysis of Asia Pacific and European Approaches* (2019), pp. 147-168.
617. International Organisation for Standards, https://www.iso.org/home.html.

obtained consent from the data subject.[618] Where there is a contract between the data subject and the company, consent is not necessarily required. In addition, if the company privacy policy adequately reflects that data subjects' consent and the privacy policy is understood by the data subject, the disclosure could occur.

Despite the above, cross-border data flows have been somewhat limited by the law. In other words, it has not been adequately addressed to date. On the other hand, with the challenges faced by India, economically and socially they have continued to follow the current sectorial approach. A question arises, does the current approach minimise or restrict their access to the digital economy in the future? More research is needed to understand whether the IT Act and Rules combined do achieve the economic outcomes for the country. However, in what appears to be a shift at some point in time to new legislation, the opportunities available to India in the digital could be expanded upon.

Nonetheless, India views the principle of territoriality as 'ordinarily connoting the jurisdiction of a state over an act committed both within its territory and can be exercised over the same acts which take place outside the state but have consequences within the State'.[619] Despite the above, there are other provisions with the ITA Act that, in part, need to be considered when an entity is transferring data outside of India. These include, but are not limited to:

- penalty and Compensation for damage to computer, computer system;
- compensation for failure to protect data;
- tampering with Computer Source Documents;
- computer Related Offences;
- power to issue directions for blocking public access of any information through any computer resource;
- national nodal agency;
- breach of confidentiality and privacy; and
- punishment for Disclosure of information in breach of lawful contract.[620]

However, the above predominantly deal with entities breaching the laws and not ensuring there is a level of security for the computer systems and in part infrastructure that facilitates the flow of data. Importantly, a breach of privacy is something that an entity will be penalised for if proven. That said, the next section examines the current-day FTAs India has with jurisdictions discussed throughout this book.

618. The Information Technology (Reasonable Security Practices and Procedures and Sensitive Personal Data or Information) Rules, 2011, Rule 3.
619. Ministry of Electronics and Information Technology, *White Paper of the Committee of Experts on a Data Protection* (2017), p. 24. *See also*, Robert Walters, Leon Trakman and Bruno Zeller, *Data Protection Law: A Comparative Analysis of Asia Pacific and European Approaches*, (2019), pp. 147-168.
620. The Information Technology Act 2008, sections 43, 43A, 65, 66, 69A, 70, 72, and 72A.

§5.02 BILATERAL AGREEMENTS

This section examines the bilateral trade-economic agreements India has with the other jurisdictions explored in this book. The agreements examined in this section are by and large investment agreements paving the way for further trade. India has adopted a minimalist approach to date in regard to trade agreements. This section only examines the ASEAN-India CECA; India-Australia CECA; India-Indonesia CECA between The Republic of India and the Republic of Singapore [India-Singapore CEC], India-New Zealand FTA, and India-Canada CEPA.

CECA between The Republic of India and the Republic of Singapore [India-Singapore CEC]

The CEC represents a long-standing trading relationship between India and Singapore. While established in the mid-2000s, before either Party had established form data protection laws, it lacks any reference to data flows. Chapter 7, Article 7.21 is the only provision that ensures anything undertaken as part of the Agreement is done so, that the protection of privacy in relation to the processing and dissemination of personal data and the protection of confidentiality of individual records and accounts is not compromised.

However, in any renegotiation of this agreement, it should be updated to expand on this protection and more so open up the provisions to include data transfers, legal harmonisation or interoperability. On the other side, Chapter 10 is specific to promoting e-commerce. However, it again lacks any reference to data transfers, or recognition of the digital economy and the economic and social benefits that data will bring to both India and Singapore.

ASEAN-India CECA

The ASEAN – India agreement is limited in its application to the following sectors including manufacturing; agriculture; fishery; forestry; and mining and quarrying.[621] It is predominantly focused on investment opportunities between both states. Noteworthy too, Article 21 does not exclude the 'protection of the privacy of individuals in relation to the processing and dissemination of personal data and the protection of confidentiality of individual records and accounts'.[622] This is against the backdrop that both states have a very limited approach to data transfers through their respective legal frameworks.

India-Australia CECA [IAC]

It began as negotiations between Australia and India in 2010-2011 to establish formal relationships between both countries regarding trade in goods, services and broader investment. However, according to the Indian government since 2013, negotiations

621. *ASEAN-India Comprehensive Economic Cooperation Agreement,* https://asean.org/wp-content/uploads/2016/04/ASEAN-India-Investment-Agreement-ASEAN-version.pdf.
622. *Ibid.,* Article 21.1(a)(ii).

regarding the IAC[623] have all stalled. It was placed in hibernation, and on 30 September 2021, Australia and India formally re-launched CECA negotiations and reaffirmed their commitment to conclude it by the end of 2022.[624] Importantly, and in recognition of the growing trade relations between both countries, it has been estimated that the trade in goods and services has grown in value from USD 13.6 billion in 2007 to USD 24.3 billion in 2020.[625] This marks the unique opportunity for both India and Australia to reset the policy discourse for cross-border data flows, and expand on the emerging international norms.

In adopting a 'winner takes some' rather than 'all' approach, could see both countries address the gaps in areas such as interoperability. It could and should provide a pathway to legal harmonisation. A further accentuating outcome could be for either India or Australia to reform their respective data laws, to make way for a deeper level of harmonisation on transnational data flows. Taking this approach would take away the need for adequacy provisions to be within national laws and other standards. It would reduce the regulatory burden on the private sector, as they would not be required to undertake exhaustive assessments.

India-Indonesia CECA

The CECA is another Agreement that had begun with much enthusiasm between India and Indonesia with extensive negotiations in 2011. However, similar to the negotiations with Australia, negotiations stalled and the Agreement has been in hibernation ever since. Indonesia is a key economic partner for India in Southeast Asia, and bilateral trade was estimated as being at more than USD 20 billion in 2017-18.[626] When the CECA is open again for negotiations, there is an opportunity similar to Australia to establish a robust framework for cross-border data flows.

India–New Zealand FTA/CECA

This is another agreement that since 2010 had negotiations for up to nine rounds for trade in goods, services, investment and related issues. Since 2013, it is all but been in hibernation. India and New Zealand both being Commonwealth nations have the opportunity to engage at a deeper level, particularly in relation to the digital economy and the use of data.[627] The most recent work has been a study undertaken by both countries to prepare 'economic profiles, trade policies and the trade and investment

623. Ministry of Commerce and Industry, India-Australia Comprehensive Economic Cooperation Agreement, https://commerce.gov.in/international-trade/trade-agreements/indias-current-engagements-in-rtas/india-australia-comprehensive-economic-cooperation-agreement-ceca/.
624. Australian Government, Australia-India Comprehensive Economic Cooperation Agreement (AICECA): About the Australia-India Comprehensive Economic Cooperation Agreement negotiations, https://www.dfat.gov.au/trade/agreements/negotiations/aifta/australia-india-comprehensive-economic-cooperation-agreement.
625. *Ibid.*
626. India-Indonesia Economic and Commercial Relations, December 2018, https://www.indianembassyjakarta.gov.in/users/assets/pdf/menu/ECRmenu.pdf.
627. *India – New Zealand Free Trade Agreement / Comprehensive Economic Cooperation Agreement [NZCEPA]*, https://commerce.gov.in/wp-content/uploads/2020/05/India_NewZealand_Joint_Study_Report_2009.pdf.

profiles of India and New Zealand'.[628] Both countries appear to be working towards building formal arrangements for the trade in goods and services. However, there is nothing in relation to e-commerce, digital economy, data flows, interoperability, international standard on data, protection of data nor privacy.

India-Canada CEPA

Similar to the above, India has been negotiating an agreement with Canada on bilateral trade. Its last negotiations took 'place in August 2017'.[629] At that time, constructive discussions were held on various issues, including cross-border trade in goods and services, e-commerce, telecommunications, sanitary and phytosanitary measures, as well as technical barriers to trade.

India-Japan CEPA

While India and Japan are at very different stages with regard to economic development, and the implementation of data laws, under this Agreement there is nothing that mentions data flows. According to Ram Upendra Das, 'India-Japan bilateral trade relations have strengthened over the years'.[630] From a baseline of USD 3.5 billion in trade between the two countries in 1990, bilateral trade stagnated until 2003-2004 before it rose to USD 14.6 billion in 2010.[631]

India went through a period of strong negotiations with a number of countries in relation to expanding their trade relations throughout the early 2000s. However, towards the end of that decade, most, if not all, negotiations were placed on hold. The reason for this is not fully understood. Although the answer might lie in the number of multilateral agreements it entered into with neighbouring countries (Pakistan, Sri Lanka, Bangladesh and others in the region). While this may be viewed as an obstacle for India in the digital economy, it should be viewed as an opportunity for future negotiations to include data flows, international norms and standards.

§5.03 CONCLUSION

India is a major emerging economy in South Asia. It has the second-largest population in the world and has much to offer not only to the region but also to the world. For more than a decade, they have emerged as a major participant in the technology and online economy, accounting for one of the largest outsourcing economies in the world.

However, India has not, to date, implemented specific data protection or privacy laws in the same way as many other nation states, including the EU. It has relied on a sectorial approach, that has been reliant on the ITA Act and the Rules. While it is for

628. *Ibid.*, p. vi.
629. *India-Canada Comprehensive Economic Partnership Agreement, 2021, https://www.international.gc.ca/trade-commerce/trade-agreements-accords-commerciaux/agr-acc/india-inde/cepa-apeg/index.aspx?lang=eng&_ga=2.127535374.286180289.1553878481-1377243369.1550408810.*
630. Ram Upendra Das, *India-Japan Comprehensive, Economic Partnership Agreement (CEPA) Some Implications for East Asian Economic Regionalism and RCEP*, (2014), p. 5-6.
631. *Ibid.*

India to decide if and when they implement their proposed Data Privacy and Protection) Bill, they have a significant opportunity to be leaders in cross-border data flow law. Under their current framework, they have not sought to obtain an AD from the EU. Yet, this should not deter them, as their proposed Bill is by and large based on the EU legal framework for data protection.

Today, the IT Act has a dual role. First, the laws protect personal data; however, this is limited. Second, it provides the basis for protecting elements of commercial and personal data from cybercrime. In taking a sectoral approach only because of the need for them to protect one of their main economic activities (outsourcing from other countries). In recognising its significance, India has been on the path to law reform for some time. Arguably, one of the dilemmas for India is the continued delay in establishing specific data protection laws, which may come at a cost to their Internet economy. This is because, India has one of the largest Internet economies in the world, that has developed from its online outsourcing industry. Arguably, India has sought and is seeking to continue to position itself as an 'attractive destination for business and data processing'.[632]

In developing a pathway forward, India should do more to consider the digital economy and the benefit that data will have in driving and developing the evolving economic activity. Doing so will enable it to develop innovative solutions to not only technology but also its trade and data laws. They need to consider stepping beyond the proposed Bill and developing a well-balanced legal framework for data flows, data adequacy, and data protection that will all form part of the digital economy.

The starting point is to review the current bill and ensure it meets its cross-border data flow needs. Second, the trade and economic agreements that have all but been in hibernation should be renegotiated, and a greater focus should be taken to establish provisions for data flows in the digital economy. Doing so will provide the foundation on which data-driven innovation and entrepreneurship can flourish throughout India. It can also place India as a leader in developing international law and standards that set the transnational policy and legal discourse for governing future data flows.

Without India's involvement in this area of law and policy, the world will be less effective in ensuring data flows and the use of data is undertaken under a governance framework that provides certainty and clarity for investment. Put another way, without India's intervention internationally, fostering such innovation and entrepreneurship which is essential for India may not be as successful as it could be. To achieve this, there is no better time for India to work more closely with its key international trading partners to enhance the trade agreements.

As highlighted earlier in this chapter, adopting a 'winner takes some' rather than 'all' approach could assist India in addressing the gaps related to legal interoperability. It could and should provide a pathway to legal harmonisation. While India has its own challenges in meeting its sovereign needs and the influence the many religious, racial and ethnic groups pose on data laws, generally, it should work closely with other states to further develop its legal framework. This is because there are a number of other

632. *Ibid.*, p. 4.

states such as the UK and Australia who have for a number of decades had well-established data laws in place. While not perfect, and it could be questioned whether their current legal frameworks actually address data flows in the digital economy, is not fully understood. They do offer India an excellent baseline.

Finally, in developing a pathway beyond the proposed Bill, India is encouraged to undertake further research of and for e-commerce, digital economy, data flows, interoperability, international standard on data, protection of data and privacy, to confirm or otherwise they be included into future trade agreements.

CHAPTER 6
Indonesia

Indonesia is Australia's largest neighbour and has a population of more than 250 million. It is located to the northwest of Australia and also borders Singapore and Malaysia. It is a democracy and the predominant religion is Islam. They have been heavily influenced by the Dutch and have predominantly adopted civil law.

Problematic though for Indonesia is the lack of specific data laws. To date, data is regulated on a sectorial basis, by the Law No. 11 of 2008 on Electronic Information and Transactions as amended by Law No. 19 of 2016. Additionally, there is also the Government Regulation No. 71 of 2019 on the Implementation of Electronic Systems and Transactions, and the Minister of Communications and Informatics Regulation No. 20 of 2016 on PDP in Electronic Systems. Nevertheless, since 2020, Indonesia has drafted a specific law which has been based on the EU framework. The PDP Bill was introduced in 2020.

Most noteworthy is that while the proposed new laws have been circulating for some time, they have been in the 2022 Prioritised National Legislation Programme.[633] *At the time of writing this book, there had been no further indication as to whether the Indonesian government would be implementing the proposed PDP in 2022. The proposed PDPD is very different from the current sectorial approach. Practitioners and technology experts will need to reconcile the proposed new rights-based approach with the need to allow the growth in data transfers, trade and economic activity.*

---

633. Glenn Wijaya, *Global Legislative Predictions 2022: Indonesia's Personal Data Protection Bill*, https://iapp.org/news/a/global-legislative-predictions-2022-indonesias-personal-data-protection-bill/ despite having not announced any expected date of entry into force, one of the officials from the Ministry of Communications and Informatics – quoted by a reliable news outlet at the end of January – said the government and the House of Representatives are 'finalising the bill', though they did not specify what this 'finalisation' actually entails.

Notwithstanding the above, Indonesia is a member of the Association of Southeast Nations (ASEAN). This, in part, does restrict how their data transfers may operate in the future. While Member States of ASEAN have not handed any sovereignty in the same way as Member States of the EU to a supranational polity, ASEAN is beginning to influence the development of data law. ASEAN[634] *has adopted a process of model contractual clauses and the Data Management Framework to facilitate data flows. As highlighted in Chapter 1 under ASEAN, there is a push towards developing a deeper level of legal harmonisation and legal convergence. Indonesia and Singapore, which are two of the ASEAN members discussed in this book, should consider expanding on this data management framework and other strategies to promote international legal harmonisation and the internationalisation of this area of the law.*

This chapter has only examined a selected number of trade agreements Indonesia has with other states such as Japan. The number of BTAs Indonesia has with other states in this book is limited. Other chapters have examined trade agreements that Indonesia has with them. Indonesia has also entered into a number of multilateral trade agreements, which have been discussed in this book. Yet, this is an opportunity for Indonesia to strengthen its governance of data flows, open up its digital economy further and influence regional and international law.

§6.01 INTRODUCTION

Indonesia is an archipelago in Southeast Asia, with Australia to its south and one of its nearest neighbours. Indonesia is a member of the association of Southeast Asian Nations and has a more than 250 million population.[635] The population density in Indonesia is 151 per Km (391 people per mi), and the total land area is 1,811,570 Km^2 (699,451 sq. miles).[636] According to a report by McKinsey Company in 2018,[637]

634. Personal Data Protection Commission Singapore, *ASEAN Data Management Framework and Model Contractual Clauses on Cross Border Data Flows*, On 22 January 2021, the 1st Association of Southeast Asian Nations (ASEAN) Digital Ministers' Meeting (ADGMIN) approved the ASEAN Data Management Framework (DMF) and Model Contractual Clauses for Cross Border Data Flows (MCCs), https://www.pdpc.gov.sg/help-and-resources/2021/01/asean-data-management-framework-and-model-contractual-clauses-on-cross-border-data-flows.
635. World Bank, Population Indonesia, 2020, https://data.worldbank.org/indicator/SP.POP.TOTL ?locations = ID.
636. Worldometer, Indonesia, https://www.worldometers.info/world-population/indonesia-population/, Associate Professor Sinta Dewi, of Information Technology Law/Data Privacy Law Universitas Padjadjaran, Indonesia has verified the contents in this chapter. Professor Dewi reviewed this chapter.
637. Kaushik Das, Toshan Tamhane, Ben Vatterott, Phillia Wibowo and Simon Wintels, *The Digital Archipelago: How Online Commerce Is Driving Indonesia's Economic Development*, McKinsey Company (2018), p. 3. This chapter will draw on earlier work of Robert Walters, Leon Trakman and Bruno Zeller, *Data Protection Law: A Comparative Analysis of Asia-Pacific and European Approaches*, Springer (2019), p. 169.

'Indonesians have embraced digital technology with enthusiasm and are among the world's most avid users of social media.'[638] They estimate that 'online commerce sales will grow to $65 billion by 2022. In addition to increasing revenue, we believe, online commerce can unlock broader social impact. We found that online commerce can facilitate women's participation in the economy – for example, 35% of online sales are generated by women'.[639] Significant too is how Indonesia has risen to have the 'largest online commerce market in Southeast Asia, generating roughly $2.5 billion in new consumption revenue'.[640]

This new consumption was before the outbreak of the coronavirus, and arguably this has increased since 2018. Indonesia is a civil law[641] country with significant influence from the Dutch. Irawan Soerodjo asserts that for Indonesia, 'source of law in the civil law system among other includes legislation, customs, and jurisprudence. Indonesia adopts a hierarchy system of legislation and the Constitution of the Republic of Indonesia of 1945 is the highest in the hierarchy of legislations in Indonesia'.[642] Soerodjo makes the point that the Republic of Indonesia is a country which adopts Civil Law system and as a former tributary of Continental Europe, the Netherlands, up until now, Indonesia is still bound by legislation of the colonial (Dutch). Article 1 transitional rule of the Constitution of the Republic of Indonesia of 1945 states that 'all existing legislations are still valid as long as a new one has not been enacted according this constitution'.[643]

While there has been significant growth in online activity across Indonesia over the past decade, they still lack specific data protection laws. They have, for some time, been developing the PDP Bill so as to close the gaps in the current sectorial 'regulatory framework on personal data protection'.[644] In 2021, the Bill along with the Cybersecurity and Resilience Bill were submitted to the Indonesian House of Representatives for consideration and decision. However, at the time of writing this book in the first half of 2022, neither the data nor cybersecurity Bill had been approved by the Parliament. That said, under the proposed PDP, data transfers since the 2018 draft have been of front and centre thinking in Indonesia because of the growing Internet economy.

Mark Innis[645] notes that under the future proposed data transfer arrangements, data controllers will have a greater role and higher level of obligation to manage any data international data transfer. Innis notes that under the proposal, controllers will need to obtain consent from data subjects 'in order to transfer the personal data to a

638. *Ibid.*, p. 3.
639. *Ibid.*
640. *Ibid.*, p. 5.
641. Irawan Soerodjo, 'The Development of Indonesian Civil Law' (30 September 2016) IV(IX) Scientific Research Journal (SCIRJ) 2201.
642. *Ibid.* Civil law in Indonesia is adopted from the Roman civil law covering both written law and unwritten law (customs).
643. *Ibid.*
644. Danny Kobrata and Rahma Atika, *The Privacy, Data Protection and Cybersecurity Law Review*, Indonesia, 2021, https://thelawreviews.co.uk/title/the-privacy-data-protection-and-cybersecurity-law-review/indonesia#footnote-028-backlink.
645. Mark Innis, Indonesia: Government Pushes Draft Data Protection Law, https://www.globalcompliancenews.com/2018/05/18/indonesia-draft-data-protection-law-20180518/.

third party within Indonesia'.[646] While this proposal is for the transfer of data within and across Indonesia, it demonstrates the higher level of responsibility that will be required for controllers to manage data. Moreover, where data is being transferred outside of Indonesia, consent will need to also be obtained from the data subject. The controller will need to ensure the receiving country has a level of protection to the same level as provided under the proposed PDP. However, this is not easy to achieve. Problematic, at this early stage, is that the proposal places the obligation on the controller to make this determination. This will add to the fragmented approach because different organisations will not be operating off a minimum standard set by the government as to what a similar level of protection constitutes. Data transfers will be administered under a contract or a bilateral arrangement. It is not clear whether BCR would fall within the proposal. Innis has called for international agreements to be established to ensure the proposal is supported adequately at the national level. To date, and while adopting most of the EU legal framework such as data rights into the proposed PDP, there is no requirement for Indonesia to establish a process of adequacy. On the one hand, there is the opportunity for Indonesia to review its current proposal and ensure that it will meet the needs of the new digital economy and the trade benefits it will bring. On the other hand, there is a need for Indonesia to expand the data transfer provisions to be more specific in setting a minimum standard that reflects the modern-day practice and encourages a greater level of legal harmonisation that will build in legal interoperability. Under the current sectorial approach, other concepts and principles will almost certainly change under the proposed PDP, such as the definition of personal data, and the right to access, disclosure and deletion of personal data. It will be important to reconcile whether these and other rights will impact data transfers.

Current Legal Framework – January 2022

Today, the collection, use, storage and dissemination of data are regulated by the Indonesian Parliament approved the Electronic Information and Transactions Law No. 11 of 2008 (EIT Law), and the Ministry of Communication and Informatics (MCI) Regulation No. 20 of 2016 on PDP in the Electronic System Regulation No. 20 of 2016, implements Regulation No. 82 of 2012 on the Implementation of Electronic Transactions and Systems.[647] Danny Kobrata and Rahma Atika, highlight that in 'May 2021, there was a technology breach that involved more than 200 million Indonesians' personal data being stolen from the National Health Insurance Agency.[648] While it is unknown whether any of the data left the Indonesian territory, the hackers offered

646. *Ibid.*
647. Aditya Rahman, 'Indonesia Enacts Personal Data Regulation, Privacy Laws and Business' (2017) 145 Data Protection and Privacy Information Worldwide, in Robert Walters, Leon Trakman and Bruno Zeller, *Data Protection Law: A Comparative Analysis of Asia-Pacific and European Approaches*, Springer (2019), pp. 169-170.
648. Danny Kobrata and Rahma Atika, *The Privacy, Data Protection and Cybersecurity Law Review*, Indonesia, 2021, https://thelawreviews.co.uk/title/the-privacy-data-protection-and-cybersecurity-law-review/indonesia#footnote-028-backlink.

access to such data for 2 bitcoins (roughly 1 billion rupiahs).[649] An investigation was opened, however, as of January 2022, there was no reported outcome of this significant breach. It demonstrates the vulnerability of data no matter where it is held. It further highlights that under the new digital economy, the technology intrusion could take place from any continent/country, and the data obtained could be rapidly transferred across multiple international borders. Furthermore, and according to Article 21, consent must be obtained for the display, announcement, transfer, dissemination or provision of access to personal data in an electronic system.

Centrally, all Electronic System Providers that are either part of, or service government or regional government agencies and are located within Indonesia or outside Indonesia must coordinate with the relevant Minister or agency.[650] Article 22 of MCI Regulation 20/2016 concerning PDP in Electronic Systems provides:

> Before transferring personal data overseas, an Electronic System Provider, whether a governmental institution, regional government or a company or private entity domiciled in the territory of Republic of Indonesia abroad, must coordinate with the MCI or authorized official/entity; and implement the laws and regulations applicable to cross-border transfer of personal data.[651]

Moreover, the requirement of coordination provided above can be satisfied in the forms by submitting the implementation plan of personal data transfer. The plan must contain the 'full name of the target country, the full name of recipient, the date of transfer, and the reasons/purpose of the transfer'.[652] Additionally, the 'Electronic Information Law provides for extraterritorial coverage, and is also applicable to any legal actions conducted outside the Indonesian jurisdiction that are potentially detrimental to Indonesia, and includes an Indonesian citizen, foreign citizen, an Indonesian legal entity and a foreign legal entity.'[653] It further seeks to protect the national interest, and includes, but is not limited to the losses in connection with the national economy, strategic data protection and the dignity, protection, defence and sovereignty of the nation, citizens and legal entities. The current approach has little relevance to the protection of personal data - of the data subject, but rather, seeks to protect state interests.[654] On that basis, under the current framework, data transfers have not taken on an economic approach. Rather, the controls over data transfers generally ensure Indonesia as a sovereign is protected. The current data transfer laws are limited and restrictive given the number of Indonesian citizens now online, and actively participating in parts of the digital economy.

In addition to the above, Article 15(1)(c) of Regulation No. 82 of 2012 on the Implementation of the Electronic Transactions and Information Law requires that any electronic system provider ensure that the collection, use and disclosure of personal

649. *Ibid.*
650. Protection of Personal Data in the Electronic System Regulation, Article 22.
651. *Ibid.*
652. *Ibid.*, Article 22.2.
653. Robert Walters, Leon Trakman and Bruno Zeller, *Data Protection Law: A Comparative Analysis of Asia-Pacific and European Approaches*, Springer (2019), pp. 178-179.
654. *Ibid.*

data is based on consent from the 'owner of personal data' (the data subject) unless otherwise provided by regulations.[655] Data may be disclosed to a third party only if that disclosure is in line with the original purpose for which the data had been originally collected from the data owner.

Nonetheless, any transfer of data can only be undertaken according to how such has been defined. That is, Article 1 of Regulation 20/2016 defines personal data as 'individual data that is stored, maintained and kept for correctness and protected for confidentiality'.[656] Additionally, the 'particular individual data' means any correct and actual information that relates to any individual and is identifiable directly or indirectly to be changed under the laws and regulations. This definition could be either viewed restrictively or very broadly and could include those other elements of personal data other countries have defined as sensitive personal data.[657] In addition to the above, a data subject may have the right to consent to their data being transferred internationally. To achieve this, according to MCI 20/2016 to obtain the individual's consent and verify the accuracy of personal data before transferring the data apply to both local and foreign electronic system providers.[658] MCI 20/2016 is an implementing measure of Law 11/2008, which expressly applies to Indonesian or foreign citizens, as well as Indonesian or foreign legal entities whose actions outside Indonesia have legal implications in, or harms the interests of, Indonesia in accordance with Article 2 of Law 11/2008.[659] The notion 'harms the interest of' is referred to as interests 'in connection with the national economy, strategic data protection and the dignity, protection, defence and sovereignty of the nation, citizens and legal entities' in the explanatory memorandum of Law 11/2008.[660]

Notwithstanding the above, according to Article 31 of Regulation Number 01/POJK 07/2013 that a financial service institution is not allowed to transfer consumer data and/or information to third parties, unless the consumer has provided consent in writing, or it is required by laws and regulations.[661] Importantly, this

655. Asian Business Law Institute, *Regulation of Cross-Border Transfers of Personal Data in Asia*, (2018), pp. 148-150, 'any Person, state agency, Business Entity, and community that provide, manage, and/or operate Electronic System individually or jointly to Electronic System User for its interest or other party's interest' according to Article 1(4).
656. MCI Regulation 20/2016, Article 1.
657. Robert Walters, Leon Trakman and Bruno Zeller, *Data Protection Law: A Comparative Analysis of Asia-Pacific and European Approaches*, Springer (2019), pp. 175-176. The process of collecting personal information is not voluntary, data collectors must disclose the information only to the authorised person/ institution. Second, there must be a mutual understanding between the owners of the personal information and the data collectors to use the information only for a specific purpose. In addition to requiring the confidentiality of personal information, transparency of information is also required to consider the public interest, so that the dissemination of personal information must align with the concept of confidentiality.
658. Asian Business Law Institute, *Regulation of Cross-Border Transfers of Personal Data in Asia*, (2018), pp. 148-149, https://cis-india.org/internet-governance/files/dp-compendium.
659. *Ibid.*
660. *Ibid.*
661. *Ibid.*, Financial Services Authority Regulation Number 01/POJK 07/2013 Concerning Consumer Protection in Financial Sector stipulates, Article 31. The Indonesian Financial Services Authority or 'Otoritas Jasa Keuangan' ('OJK') can impose sanctions in cases of non-compliance with the personal data rules.

restriction applies to both local and international data transfers.[662] Indonesia has much to offer the Asia region. As an emerging economy and home to ASEAN headquarters, it is well placed to develop its proposed data laws that reflect modern provisions to address the regional and international gaps in cross-border data flows. It has the opportunity, if it wishes, to move away from the traditional principles-based model to a more harmonised framework. However, this would probably mean further delay in their current proposed Bill being passed through parliament. Either way, it is in Indonesia's best interest for them to move away from the sectorial approach they currently operate under, sooner rather than later. The current framework is time-consuming and lacks a level of certainty that is required for data flows to prosper in and across the digital economy.

§6.02 BILATERAL AGREEMENTS

There are currently a limited number of Bilateral Agreements (BTAs) Indonesia has with other states. They are active in a multilateral setting, in particular as a member of ASEAN. This section examines only one trade agreement with Japan and a recent announcement with Canada.

Agreement Between Japan and the Republic of Indonesia for an Economic Partnership

Japan and the Republic of Indonesia for an Economic Partnership (JRIEP)[663] came into effect in 2008 and provides a framework for both states to facilitate, promote and liberalise trade in goods and services; increase investment opportunities and promote investment activities through strengthening protection for investments and investment activities.[664] In its capacity, there is a minimum data requirement for a certificate of origin in accordance with Article 41. That is, Article 41.1, 'a certificate of origin referred to in paragraph 1 of Article 40 shall be issued by the competent governmental authority of the exporting Party on request having been made in writing by the exporter or its authorised agent. Such certificate of origin shall include minimum data specified in Annex 3'.[665] The certificate itself requires the following information:

- exporter's name, address and country;
- importer's name, address and country;
- certification number;
- origin of good(s);
- invoice number and date;
- transport details (if known);
- HS tariff classification number;

662. *Ibid.*
663. *Agreement Between Japan and the Republic of Indonesia for an Economic Partnership,* https://www.mofa.go.jp/region/asia-paci/indonesia/epa0708/agreement.pdf, Annex 3 https://www.customs.go.jp/roo/english/text/indonesia3.pdf.
664. *Ibid.,* Article 1.
665. *Ibid.,* Article 41.

- marks, numbers, number and kind of packages;
- description of good(s);
- quantity (Unit);
- preference criterion.[666]

These certificates do provide a level of personal information. While not that exhaustive, they disclose the name, address and country of where the goods are being exported from. It is the information of the exporter's name specifically that can identify the individual. However, it must be noted that an exporter may well go under a company name. If this is the case, the individual owner of the entity may not be directly disclosed. Similarly, for the importer, the same applies. Nonetheless, directly or indirectly a data subject could be identified from these certificates.

Comprehensive Economic Partnership Agreement between Indonesia and Canada[667]

The Comprehensive Economic Partnership Agreement between Indonesia and Canada (CEPA) was established in 2021, to develop a pathway for Canada and Indonesia to promote bilateral trade. It states that:

> The pursuit of a CEPA represents a significant milestone in the longstanding bilateral relationship underpinned by a shared commitment to rules-based trade and open markets, and growing commercial and cultural ties. The Ministers recognised the potential for a CEPA to support long-term job creation and economic growth, reduce costs for businesses and consumers, and increase bilateral trade and investment. The Ministers underscored the importance of negotiating a CEPA that is comprehensive and provides benefits that are widely shared by the people of both countries. The Ministers agreed that, without prejudice to the final outcomes, the negotiations would cover mutually agreed areas of interest to both Indonesia and Canada, including market access, rules to facilitate trade and investment, and cooperation, taking into account each other's sensitivities and different levels of development. The Ministers agreed to commence negotiations towards a CEPA and instructed officials to hold the first round of negotiations at the earliest opportunity.[668]

While there is no reference to the digital economy, data flows, data protection or data adequacy, it reflects a strong commitment for both countries to come together and develop their trade relationship. It offers a unique opportunity for both states to come together and set the policy agenda and rules with like-minded countries and jurisdictions discussed in this book, to further develop trade agreements and include specific provisions on the digital economy, data flows and the internationalisation of this area of law.

666. *Ibid.*, Annex 3.
667. Joint Ministerial Statement for the Launch of Negotiations towards a Comprehensive Economic Partnership Agreement between Indonesia and Canada, June 2021, https://www.international.gc.ca/trade-commerce/trade-agreements-accords-commerciaux/agr-acc/indonesia-indonesie/cepa-apeg/joint_statement-declaration_commune.aspx?lang=eng.
668. *Ibid.*

§6.03 CONCLUSION

Indonesia is the most populous country in ASEAN. Indonesia is in the same way as many other countries are grappling with the concept of data flows, data protection, data adequacy and the digital economy. This is reflected by their delay in implementing specific data laws when compared to their regional neighbours of Australia, Singapore and Malaysia.

As a country, Indonesians are highly connected to the Internet and as the country and its citizenry continue to grow, this connectivity will also increase. This will generate significant more personal data that, will be exposed to transfers within and outside of the country.

For more than a decade Indonesia has been undertaking incremental steps to reforming relevant current-day laws to establish a level of protection for personal data. They are, after a number of years of review, about to implement specific data laws that, have by and large been based on the EU legal framework. Indonesia is another state that has used the EU as a benchmark as to how their proposed PDP laws will look. However, and even while writing this book, Indonesia had submitted the proposed PDP to the 2022 National Legislation Programme. It remains to be seen whether this will be passed by the Indonesian government and be implemented into law.

Problematic though, that the current proposed PDPD, falls short of the current international developments in the area of data flows. Essentially the proposal only provides a three-step process for data transfers through (1) consent of the data subject, (2), contractual arrangements, or (3), international agreement. The area of international agreement is very broad and it is argued that this could include an arrangement for adequacy or some other bilateral or multilateral arrangements. This would need to be clarified to provide investors with a level of clarity and certainty.

Moreover, and while the digital economy is expected to deliver significant economic, environmental and social benefits to Indonesia and its citizens, more work is needed in the area of data flows. Put another way, Indonesia has an opportunity to further reform its national and international legal mechanisms to enhance and strengthen the ability for data flows internationally. This must begin with its proposed national laws, and extend to bilateral and multilateral trade, investment and security agreements.

Against the backdrop of the above, further clarification on the extent to which the proposed rights-based approach will have to and on data flows. That is, today, under the current legal framework, the Electronic Information Law is limited in its scope and application to protecting personal data and data flows. Between the current and proposed new PDP, concepts and principles such as the definition of personal data, will need to be reconciled in their application and operation. The limited scope of the current day Electronic Information Law only extends to the right to enjoy a private life and to communication. Additionally, it allows for the right to monitor the access of information about a person's personal life and data. On this basis, it has a wide reach and enables the government to encroach on people's personal life. This is obviously necessary to curb illegal activity that is occurring over the Internet.

Meanwhile, data localisation has not been fully reconciled in and across Indonesia, and this will also need to be addressed under any future laws. Arguably, Indonesia is on the right path to strengthening its legal framework for data flows and its protection internationally. The proposed PDP will be critical in providing a pathway for this to occur. It will place obligations on controllers to perform specific assessments to ensure data transfers have the same level of protection in a third country like Indonesia.

The state will need to provide further guidance as to how this will be implemented to ensure there are no divergent processes being established by the public and private sectors. While specific sectors, such as health and education, may need to be slightly different in terms of data transfer and protection, a minimum level of standards needs to be established. Finally, it is unclear that while the proposed PDP has been based on the EU legal framework, there needs to be more clarification of how the proposal will compare with recently emerging laws in the US and other states in the region. This comparison will be important to understand the gaps and differences in controls and requirements for data transfers and trade.

CHAPTER 7

Japan

The Act on the Protection of Personal Information 2016 (APPI) came into effect on 30 May 2017. The right to privacy in Japan is not a recent right and can be traced back to the 1960s.[669] *The Japanese Constitution has confirmed that privacy in Japan is subject to protection. Article 13 of the Japanese Constitution provides that citizens' liberty in private life shall be protected against the exercise of public authority. The Japanese courts have reinforced this Constitutional status of privacy. Nevertheless, it can be confirmed that one of the liberties in private life is that every individual in Japanese society has the liberty to the protection of his or her own personal information from being disclosed to a third party, or made public without good reason.*[670]

The APPI establishes the framework for the transfer of personal data to a third country. Consent has an important function by the data subject in allowing their personal data being able to be transferred. Problematic though is that the current application of consent requires further clarification, as to its function within data transfers.

This chapter will briefly analyse a selected number of agreements that include, but are not limited to:

- *Japan–EU Adequacy.*
- *US–Japan Trade Agreement.*
- *US–Japan Digital Trade Agreement.*

669. Robert Walters, Leon Trakman and Bruno Zeller, *Data Protection Law: A Comparative Analysis of Asia-Pacific and European Approaches*, Springer (2019), p. 239.
670. *Ibid.* 1965 (A) No. 1187, Judgment of the Grand Bench of the Supreme Court of 24 December 1969, Keishu vol. 23, No. 12, at 1625, Graham Greenleaf, Country Studies – B5 Japan. In: Korff, D (ed.) *Comparative Study on Different Approaches to New Privacy Challenges, in Particular in the Light of Technological Developments*, European Commission, Directorate-General Justice, Freedom and Security (May 2010).

- *Japan–Australia Economic Partnership Agreement.*
- *Japan–Singapore Economic Partnership Agreement.*
- *Japan–EU Economic Partnership Agreement.*
- *The Japan–United Kingdom CEPA.*

This chapter will demonstrate how Japan can be considered a leader in the development of bilateral agreements that reflect the importance and inclusion of data in the economy. Yet, it will be argued that more work is needed to fully address the need for data flows within these agreements. Doing so will enable Japan to further develop its digital economy, and ensure data flows have minimal obstacles to achieving a deeper level of economic activity. This chapter will also call for further work to be undertaken by Japan to use the above instruments to develop an international legal framework for data flows, in partnership with Australia, the UK, the US, and the other countries compared. Japan has begun to embrace specific the Digital Trade Agreement as a framework. Arguably, it is a good first step to developing data flows in the digital economy. However, more work is needed to further develop these and the other agreements.

§7.01 INTRODUCTION

Japan has a rich history dating back many centuries. The current data modern state of Japan can be traced to the 'late nineteenth century saw the colonisation of the northern island where the Ainu people largely resided and the renaming of it as Hokkaidō in 1869.[671] The Ainu also lived in adjacent territories known as North Honshū, South Sakhalin, and the Kurile Islands. In 1875, the Treaty of St. Petersburg resulted in the drawing of borders between Russia and Japan right through Ainu territory. Kuril Ainu and Sakhalin Ainu were forced to relocate to Hokkaidō, give up hunting, and become farmers'.[672] Data protection and privacy over the Internet have not been a smooth transition for Japan and Japanese society. For instance, privacy has its foundations in a 1964 court decision.

The Tokyo District Court held in the 'After the Banquet' or *Utage no Ato* case that the 'the right to privacy is recognized as the legal or protection or the right so as not to be disclosed of private life based on section 709 of the Japanese Civil Code'.[673] Prior to this case, Dr Masami Ito, a former Professor at the University of Tokyo and later a Justice of the Japanese Supreme Court, published a book entitled *The Right to Privacy*.[674] The book referred to the After the Banquet case as 'proof that the right to

---

671. Morris Low, 'Physical Anthropology in Japan: The Ainu and the Search for the Origins of the Japanese' (2012) 53 Current Anthropology 57. This chapter draws on some of the earlier work undertaken by Robert Walters, Leon Trakman and Bruno Zeller, *Data Protection Law: A Comparative Analysis of Asia-Pacific and European Approaches*, Springer (2019).
672. *Ibid.*
673. Judgment of Tokyo District Court, 28 September 1964, *Hanrei-jiho* vol. 385, p. 12. In Hiroshi Miyashita, 'The Evolving Concept of Data Privacy in Japanese Law' (November 2011) 1(4) International Data Privacy Law 231, https://doi.org/10.1093/idpl/ipr019.
674. *Ibid.*

privacy, despite its various contents, is crystallized as a legal protection which indicates that its society shares a high standard culture'.[675]

Since then, Japan has become the 'world's third-largest economy'.[676] On the one hand, this has not been the case with its digital economy, as Japan does not have strong digital competitiveness. On the other hand, this country's 'relatively low level of digital competitiveness is in stark and unexpected contrast to the country's economic strength'.[677] Most noteworthy was that in 2020 Japan was ranked only '27th in digital competitiveness and 22nd in digital talent, and it has single-digit penetration in areas such as e-commerce, mobile banking, and digital government service usage'.[678] A somewhat surprising and possibly alarming statistic is that the 'country has produced only five of more than 500 unicorn start-ups globally (start-ups with a private or public valuation of more than USD$1B). On these estimates alone, the metrics fall far short of Japan's full potential'.[679] In part, there is a lack of skilled workers, and when coupled with an ageing population,[680] advancing the benefits of the digital economy is going to be challenging.

On the one hand, how they choose to grapple with this is a decision for Japan. On the other hand, they have well-developed data laws and have by and large embraced the Western concept of privacy. Nonetheless, the 'distribution of economic profit – profit after covering the cost of capital – in the global economy has been highly uneven: between 2014 and 2018, companies in the top quintile of the economic profit distribution captured nearly 90% of the economic profit, equivalent to $655 billion'.[681] Even amongst these challenges Japan face, the is optimism, as they continue to develop the online economy across sectors such as health, banking, retail, industrial manufacturing, education and government. They are a participant in the APEC CBPR since 2016.[682] Since then, a further and equally important development has been Japan obtaining observer status to the European Commission, Consultative Committee of Convention 108.[683]

Against this backdrop, personal data is regulated by a number of legal instruments and guidelines in Japan. These include the APPI 2016;[684] the APPI Held by

675. *Ibid.*
676. Mckinsey Digital, *How Japan Can Make Digital 'Big Moves' to Drive Growth and Productivity* (2021), p. 6, https://www.mckinsey.com/business-functions/mckinsey-digital/our-insights/how-japan-can-make-digital-big-moves-to-drive-growth-and-productivity.
677. *Ibid.*, p. 6.
678. *Ibid.*
679. *Ibid.*
680. *Ibid.*, pp. 6-9.
681. *Ibid.*, p. 12.
682. Ministry of Economy, *Trade and Industry, The Government of Japan Received Approval to Join the APEC Cross-Border privacy Rules System*, https://www.meti.go.jp/english/press/2014/0428_01.html.
683. Graham Greenleaf, 'How Far Can Convention 108+ 'Globalise'?: Prospects for Asian Accessions' (2020) 40 Computer Law & Security Review 1-12.
684. Act on the Protection of Personal Information, version 2, 2016 https://www.ppc.go.jp/files/pdf/Act_on_the_Protection_of_Personal_Information.pdf.

Administrative Organs;[685] and the APPI Held by Incorporated Administrative Agencies.[686] In addition to the above is the Ordinance on the Personal Information Protection of Rules for Local Governments, however, it is not considered in this discussion. However, this section will only deal with APPIs 2016.

Centrally, there are a number of definitions of personal information. Beginning with Article 2, Paragraph 1 of APPI, personal information has been defined to mean:

> information containing a name, date of birth, or other descriptions, etc. (meaning any and all matters (excluding an individual identification code) stated, recorded or otherwise expressed using voice, movement or other methods in a document, drawing or electromagnetic record (meaning a record kept in an electromagnetic form (meaning an electronic, magnetic or other forms that cannot be recognized through the human senses; the same shall apply in the succeeding paragraph, item (ii)); the same shall apply in Article 18, paragraph (2)); hereinafter the same) whereby a specific individual can be identified (including those which can be readily collated with other information and thereby identify a specific individual); or information containing an individual identification code.[687]

On the other side, and in addition to the above, Article 2(6) also provides a definition of personal data, to mean 'personal information constituting a personal information database, etc.'.[688] What could be described as a double definition of terms that are closely related, in the Japanese context, personal data directly relates back to personal information, however, extends that to such information as constitutes a database. The dichotomy would be determining what a personal information database constitutes.

Article 24 of the APPI prescribes one of the conditions for engaging in international transfers to a recipient in a foreign country provided there is consent. Article 24 states that:

---

685. Act on the Protection of Personal Information Held by Administrative Organs (Act No. 58 of 2003), https://www.cas.go.jp/jp/seisaku/hourei/data/APPIHAO.pdf.
686. Act on the Protection of Personal Information Held by Incorporated Administrative Agencies, Act No. 59 of 30 May 2003, https://www.kobe-u.ac.jp/documents/en/about_us/rules/Act_on_the_Protection_of_Personal_Information_Held_by_Incorporated_Administrative_Agencies.pdf.
687. Act on the Protection of Personal Information, 2020, Article 2. An 'individual identification code' in this Act means those prescribed by cabinet order which are any character, letter, number, symbol or other codes falling under any of each following item, (i) those able to identify a specific individual that are a character, letter, number, symbol or other codes into which a bodily partial feature of the specific individual has been converted in order to be provided for use by computers. Those character, letter, number, symbol or other codes which are assigned in regard to the use of services provided to an individual or to the purchase of goods sold to an individual, or which are stated or electromagnetically recorded in a card or other document issued to an individual so as to be able to identify a specific user or purchaser, or recipient of issuance by having made the said codes differently assigned or, stated or recoded for the said user or purchaser, or recipient of issuance.
688. *Ibid.*, Article 2, describes Retained personal data – in this Act means personal data which a personal information handling business operator has the authority to disclose, correct, add or delete the contents of, cease the utilisation of, erase, and cease the third-party provision of, and which shall be neither those prescribed by cabinet order as likely to harm the public or other interests if their presence or absence is made known nor those set to be deleted within a period of no longer than one year that is prescribed by cabinet order.

> A personal information handling business operator, except in those cases set forth in each item of the preceding Article, paragraph (1), shall, in case of providing personal data to a third party (excluding a person establishing a system conforming to standards prescribed by rules of the Personal Information Protection Commission as necessary for continuously taking action equivalent to the one that a personal information handling business operator shall take concerning the handling of personal data pursuant to the provisions of this Section; hereinafter the same in this Article) in a foreign country (meaning a country or region located outside the territory of Japan; hereinafter the same) (excluding those prescribed by rules of the Personal Information Protection Commission as a foreign country establishing a personal information protection system recognized to have equivalent standards to that in Japan in regard to the protection of an individual's rights and interests; hereinafter the same in this Article), in advance obtain a principal's consent to the effect that he or she approves the provision to a third party in a foreign country. In this case, the provisions of the preceding Article shall not apply.[689]

Importantly Article 23 provides for the transfer of personal data to a third party without obtaining in advance a principal's consent. A notable difference is how Article 23 pertains to personal data, while Article 24 pertains to personal information. This is why the definition of both personal data and personal information become highly significant. They constitute different things. Nonetheless, Article 23 also provides that any data transfers are to be considered in light of national and personal security, the outbreak of disease, and ensuring the health of children. However, this provision appears to apply to the transfer of personal data domestically within Japan, rather than to a third country. In a further observation Article 23 does not refer to Article 24. That is, unlike Article 24 which states that 'in this case, the provisions of the preceding Article shall not apply',[690] referring to Article 25. On this basis, further clarification is required to confirm or otherwise whether Article 23 pertains to international transfers. Should that be the case, only personal information can be transferred externally to Japan.

To ensure the security of personal information is undertaken specifically, Article 76 applies to all personal information including personal information from a foreign origin. Therefore, personal information that falls within the definition provided in Article becomes critically important because it is this data that can be transferred internationally. Also of note are Articles 36, 37, 38 and 39 that provide a level of security obligation on the personal information as part of any transfer. Also noteworthy is Article 16 of the Guidelines for Protecting Personal Information in the Field of Telecommunications, which establishes the rules for disclosing personal data to a third party located in a foreign country.[691] Article 16 states that:

> A telecommunications carrier, except in those cases set forth in each item of the preceding Article, Paragraph 1, shall, in case of providing personal data to a third

689. *Ibid.*, Article 24.
690. *Ibid.*
691. Guidelines for Protecting Personal Information in the Field of Telecommunications No. 152 of 18 April 2017, https://www.soumu.go.jp/main_content/000744054.pdf.

> party (excluding a person establishing a system conforming to standards prescribed by the next following paragraph as necessary for continuously taking action equivalent to the one that a personal information handling business operator shall take concerning the handling of personal data pursuant to the provisions of Chapter IV, Section 1 of the Act; hereinafter the same in this Article) in a foreign country, in advance obtain a principal's consent to the effect that he or she approves the provision to a third party in a foreign country. In this case, the provisions of the preceding Article (except for Paragraph 8 of the said Article) shall not apply.[692]

The formal and functional requirements of the Guidelines requires that organisation operating in this sector have a responsibility to manage personal information under the APPI and ensure a data subject's consent has been obtained before their data is transferred to a third country.

§7.02 BILATERAL AGREEMENTS

This section examines the BTAs established with those other jurisdictions examined in this book. However, where an agreement has already been discussed, it will be referenced accordingly. That is, Australia and Japan have long-standing bilateral trade relations. Chapter 2 discussed the Japan-Australia trade agreement.

Japan–EU Adequacy

The Personal Information Protection Commission (PPC) publicised its ADs on 23 January 2019. While the EU gave AD to the first third country under the GDPR, Regulation (EU) 2016/679 and the first Asian country, Japan issued its first equivalency decision under the APPI.[693] In making its decision, the European Commission concluded it carefully analysed Japanese law and practice. Based on the findings developed in Recitals (6) to (175), the Commission concludes that Japan ensures an

692. *Ibid.*, Article 16. Standards prescribed as necessary measures for continuously taking measures equivalent to those which shall be taken by a personal information handling business operator pursuant to the provisions of Chapter IV, section 1 of the Act with regard to the handling of personal data shall fall under any of each following item: (1) a telecommunications carrier and a person who receives the provision of personal data have ensured, in relation to the handling of personal data by the person who receives the provision, the implementation of measures in line with the purport of the provisions under Chapter IV, section 1 of the Act by an appropriate and reasonable method; (2) a person who receives the provision of personal data has obtained a recognition based on an international framework concerning the handling of personal information.

693. European Commission, Commission Implementing Decision (EU) 2019/419 of 23 January 2019 pursuant to Regulation (EU) 2016/679 of the European Parliament and of the Council on the adequate protection of personal data by Japan under the Act on the Protection of Personal Information, Official Journal of the European Union L76/1. European Commission, Commission Implementing Decision of 23 January 2019 pursuant to Regulation (EU) 2016/679 of the European Parliament and of the Council on the adequate protection of personal data by Japan under the Act on the Protection of Personal Information, https://ec.europa.eu/info/sites/default/files/draft_adequacy_decision.pdf Personal Information Protection Commission, Foreign countries which have the system of protection of personal information that ensure the

adequate level of protection for personal data transferred to organisations falling within the scope of application of the APPI and subject to the additional conditions referred to in this Decision. These conditions are laid down in the Supplementary Rules (Annex I) adopted by the PPC and the official representations, assurances and commitments by the Japanese government to the European Commission. This Decision has the effect that transfers from a controller or processor in the European Economic Area (EEA) to such organisations in Japan may take place without the need to obtain any further authorisation. This Decision does not affect the direct application of Regulation (EU) 2016/679 to such organisations when the conditions of its Article 3 are fulfilled.[694]
However, it has not been a smooth road towards obtaining adequacy. Hiroshi Miyashita notes that while:

> the original APPI was enacted in 2003 and took full effect in April 2005, there was almost no possibility to obtain adequacy from the EU. This was mainly because no independent supervisory authority existed. Furthermore, the original APPI reflected the 1980 OECD Privacy Guidelines instead of the EU Data Protection Directive. At least in the Diet, there were no substantive discussions on adequacy until the Consumer Affairs Agency published a study report on EU adequacy in March 2012.[695]

Since the APPI was implemented, it has undergone several amendments to strengthen the security and government of personal data for the Japanese people. Miyashita goes on to say the 'mutual adequacy decisions may be a successful political agreement, but one should note the extent to which it unites two systems with different philosophical ideas on data protection'.[696] Yet, obtaining a balance between data flows and the rights-based approach of the EU was problematic. There was tension between both frameworks because they were designed to achieve subtle different policy objectives. Miyashita further notes that the Japanese initiative of 'DFFT' is embedded in the WTO reform proposal. It is true that personal data can be discussed in the economic dimension, however, the EU's rationale for the AD stemmed from a human rights philosophy, which may be alien to the WTO solution. In this regard, He is of the view that it is too early to evaluate how the EU–Japan mutual AD will progress the convergence of data protection, whether it is taken as a human rights philosophy or an act of commercial reciprocity.[697]

---

equivalent level as Japan in protecting rights and interests of the individual (listing 31 EEA countries), 23 January 2019, https://www.ppc.go.jp/en/aboutus/roles/international/cooperation/20190123/.

694. European Commission, Commission Implementing Decision of 23 January 2019 pursuant to Regulation (EU) 2016/679 of the European Parliament and of the Council on the adequate protection of personal data by Japan under the Act on the Protection of Personal Information, https://ec.europa.eu/info/sites/default/files/draft_adequacy_decision.pdf.
695. Hiroshi Miyashita, *EU-Japan Mutual Adequacy Decision: The EU-Japan Relationship*, 2020, p. 3, https://blogdroiteuropeen.files.wordpress.com/2020/06/miyashita-redo.pdf.
696. *Ibid.*, p. 13.
697. *Ibid.*

Takayuki Kato is of the view that it is quite understandable that the EU takes an adequacy approach for the data protection of their residents.[698] However, he notes that the time when every country maintains an adequate level of data protection law is unlikely to come at least within the next couple of decades. Also, receiving the adequacy accreditation could not be a comprehensive solution since it has either a unilateral or a bilateral nature.[699] In addition, if our principal aim is to realise the international free flow of personal data in the private sector, raising the standard of data protection law is not the only means. He believes that when we narrow down the issues of data protection to the problem of cross-border data flow in the private sector, an international agreement or convention could be a preferable option. In doing so, Kato looks to the Council of Europe's Convention 108, OECD Recommendation on Cross-border Co-operation in the Enforcement of Laws Protecting Privacy, APEC, CBPR and so on,[700] for an international framework. Kato, along with Greenleaf underscores the same argument from this book that there is a need for data flow regulation to be internationalised. Kato further points to already existing frameworks that can be used as a starting point. The argument put forward by Kato is a viable option and something I agree with. The above regional instruments can be used to develop the beginnings of an international data flow(s) law.

US–Japan

In October 2019, the US and Japan signed the US–Japan Trade Agreement and the US–Japan Digital Trade Agreement (DTA), which entered into force on 1 January 2020.[701] The US–Japan Trade agreement eliminates or reduces tariffs on approximately USD 7.2 billion in US agricultural exports and the US–Japan DTA includes high-standard provisions that ensure data can be transferred across borders without restrictions, guarantee consumer privacy protections, promote adherence to common principles for addressing cyber security challenges, support effective use of encryption technologies, and boost digital trade.

US–Japan Trade Agreement

The US–Japan Trade Agreement (USJTA) was implemented in 2019,[702] paving the way for long-standing trade relations between both countries. However, it relates little to the trade in services and does not account for personal data, data floes, or data protection.

698. Takayuki Kato, 'Reflections on the GDPR Adequacy Assessment and Strategy of Japan: For the Enhancement of Transborder Data Flows' (2020) Global Privacy Review 161.
699. *Ibid.*
700. *Ibid.*, p. 162.
701. International Trade Administration, https://www.trade.gov/country-commercial-guides/japan-trade-agreements.
702. United States–Japan Trade Agreement, https://www.mofa.go.jp/policy/economy/fta/index.html.

US–Japan Digital Trade Agreement[703]

The DTA established a framework for both nation states to address barriers and obstacles to digital trade. The DTA is a relatively short Agreement only containing twenty-two Articles. It is separate from the above trade agreement and extends to ensuring economic growth and trade in the digital economy. Specifically related to personal data, it refers to personal information. The DTA defines personal information to mean information, including data, about an identified or identifiable natural person.[704] This is a broad definition. Most notably, it does not indicate in any way where and how the personal information relates. For instance, does it only relate to the Internet? Moreover, data captured used by the government and the private sector would constitute personal information.

Apart from restricting the level of customs duties that can be placed on digital products including tax measures, the DTA places a high-level emphasis on prohibiting data localisation. This measure alone departs from many other countries and highlights the strategic direction both Japan and the US are taking in relation to data flows. It reinforces the Open Data[705] concept and is designed to promote current and future financial services. It aims not to impose further obstacles to growth. Significant too, the DTA also prioritises the need for developing and implementing systems and infrastructure that ensure the highest level of data security,[706] so as to protect data, source code and algorithms. Further, the DTA ensures that consumers are protected and that privacy over the Internet is a high priority while maintaining and promoting the interoperability of enforcement regimes, such as the APEC CBPR.

Of note is Article 15 that, requires both countries to 'develop and maintain a legal framework for the protection of personal information and for the users of digital trade'.[707] Article 15 in my view has three important measures. First, it ensures that both Japan and US have a robust legal framework in place to protect data subject's personal data/information. Second, it requires that there is a high level of protection afforded to that information/data. Third, it ensures that the data is available for the digital economy and trade, expanding the digital economies of both countries.

Moreover, the DTA demonstrates the commitment Japan and the US have towards developing and implementing a similar data framework that provides for a high level of interoperability. Arguably, this is a good step. Yet, there is no mention of legal harmonisation or internationalisation of data rules or the law. Further work could be considered by both countries for any future amendments to the DTA, to ensure it promotes and provides for both countries to engage with other like-minded countries such as Australia and the UK to set the international rules for data flows in the digital

703. United States–Japan Digital Trade Agreement, https://ustr.gov/sites/default/files/files/agreements/japan/Agreement_between_the_United_States_and_Japan_concerning_Digital_Trade.pdf.
704. *Ibid.*, p. 6.
705. *Ibid.*, Article 20.
706. *Ibid.*, Article 19.
707. *Ibid.*, Article 15.

economy. Importantly, it is a good step and new addition to the trade agreement framework.

Japan–Australia Economic Partnership Agreement

The Japan–Australia Economic Partnership Agreement (JAEPA) was finalised in 2014. It provides financial and general services. Annex 9 while broad ensures a strategic relationship is developed for the development of cross-border financial services. It allows for the management and use of financial data and information. While not specifically stating the need to protect personal data/information, the reference to financial data would constitute personal data. That is, Annex 9 states banking and financial services provide for the 'provision and transfer of financial information, and financial data processing and related software by suppliers of other financial services'.[708] Of note is Article 2 of Annex 8, which states:
Provision of Information:

> Each Party shall designate one or more enquiry points that provide, on request of a service supplier of the other Party, information, including reference to the applicable legal basis, on: a) standards and criteria for the licensing and certification of professionals, which may include requirements regarding education, examinations, experience, conduct and ethics, professional development and re-certification, scope of practice, local knowledge, and consumer protection; b) the appropriate competent authority or other body to consult regarding the standards and criteria referred to in subparagraph (a); and c) requirements and procedures to obtain, renew or retain any licence or qualification requirements, at least for regulated services. Each Party shall provide the other Party with the contact details of such enquiry points. On request of the other Party, a Party shall hold consultations regarding its procedures for recognising qualifications and provide any relevant information regarding recognition to the other Party.[709]

Viewed this way, there is no reference to data flows or the security and protection of that data. The reference to certification, licencing, and standards, amongst others all constitute the probability that personal data will form part of this information. It is widely understood that a licence issued by a government or non-government organisation will contain some personal data that is protected under data law. In addition, Annex 3 establishes a process for the data elements for documentary evidence of a certificate of origin.[710] Again and while there is no reference to data flows or data protection, the information required on these certificates would include a level of personal data. However, to what extent that personal data is articulated on an individual certificate is unclear.

Japan–Singapore Economic Partnership Agreement

The Japan–Singapore Economic Partnership Agreement (JSEPA) signed in 2007, provides the pathway for Japan and Singapore to deepen their economic relationship.

708. Japan-Australia Economic Partnership Agreement, 2014, https://www.mofa.go.jp/files/000044331.pdf.
709. *Ibid.*, Annex 8, Article 2.
710. *Ibid.*, Annex 3.

In analysing this Agreement, Annex IV A[711] applies to 'measures affecting the supply of financial services. Reference to the supply of a financial service in this Annex shall mean the supply of a service as defined in subparagraph (o) of paragraph 6 of Article 58'.[712] Similar to the Australian-Japanese agreement there is no mention of personal data, data flows or its protection. It again takes a limited approach to even referring to data protection law, however, the reference to financial data would constitute a level of personal information being transferred between both states.

Noteworthy is section II. Domestic Regulation, whereby:

> Notwithstanding any provisions of Chapter 7, a Party shall not be prevented from taking measures for prudential reasons, including measures for the protection of investors, depositors, policy holders or persons to whom a fiduciary duty is owed by a financial service supplier, or to ensure the integrity and stability of the financial system. Where such measures do not conform with the provisions of Chapter 7, they shall not be used as a means of avoiding the Party's commitments or obligations under Chapter 7. Nothing in Chapter 7 shall be construed to require a Party to disclose information relating to the affairs and accounts of individual customers or any confidential or proprietary information in the possession of public entities.[713]

The reference to domestic regulation becomes important. It takes a broad approach and clarity is needed as to whether the above would include the national laws doe data flows and data protection? In my view, one could make the case that these laws would fall within the above. It can be argued that personal information and data fall within measures that in part go some way to protecting financial services and investors. This is because all this financial information would contain a level of personal data and information.

Japan-EU Economic Partnership Agreement

The Japan-EU Economic Partnership Agreement (JEPA) came into effect in 2019.[714] Specifically, Article 8.3 provides for general exceptions according to section B, Article XX of GATT 1994 that:

> Subject to the requirement that such measures are not applied in a manner which would constitute a means of arbitrary or unjustifiable discrimination between countries where like conditions prevail, or a disguised restriction on establishment or trade in services, nothing in Sections B to F shall be construed as preventing a Party from adopting or enforcing measures which are a) necessary to protect public security or public morals or to maintain public order; b) necessary to protect human, animal or plant life or health; c) necessary to secure compliance with laws or regulations which are not inconsistent with the provisions of this chapter including those relating to:

711. Japan-Singapore Economic Partnership Agreement, 2007, https://www.mofa.go.jp/region/asia-paci/singapore/jsepa-5.pdf.
712. *Ibid.*
713. *Ibid.*, II Domestic regulation.
714. Japan-EU Economic Partnership Agreement, 2021, https://www.mofa.go.jp/policy/economy/page6e_000013.html.

(i) the prevention of deceptive and fraudulent practices or dealing with the effects of a default on contracts;
(ii) the protection of the privacy of individuals in relation to the processing and dissemination of personal data and the protection of confidentiality of individual records and accounts.[715]

This provision in and of itself requires further clarification of its meaning and application. It appears to be counter to the ADs, above. Further, it also appears to be against the general approach and direction of both countries towards achieving an open data legal landscape. In other words, it is argued that the above can be read that privacy is an important feature of the trading landscape between both countries. The above would not undermine or dilute the effectiveness of the EU-Japan AD. The importance of the above allows for the promotion and trade in general that involves data while ensuring that the current level of protection is not reduced. Finally, the reference to the dissemination of personal data would include the international data flows between both states.

In reinforcing the above, Article 8.63 provides for the transfers of information and processing of information, whereby:

> A Party shall not take measures that prevent transfers of information or the processing of financial information, including transfers of data by electronic means, or that, subject to importation rules consistent with international agreements, prevent transfers of equipment, if those transfers of information, processing of financial information or transfers of equipment are necessary for the conduct of the ordinary business of a financial service supplier. Nothing restricts the right of a Party to protect personal data, personal privacy and the confidentiality of individual records and accounts so long as that right is not used to circumvent Sections B to D and this Sub-Section.[716]

While broad, the language used in the above Article 8.63 clearly relates to personal data that is being transferred between each state under financial transactions. This is because of the requirement for personal data and privacy to be afforded the highest level of protection possible. It is another acknowledgement that personal data is of high value and is an important component of financial transactions, whether that be through the traditional banking sector or the emerging FinTech sector. Of the trade agreements analysed thus far, the JEPA is the most comprehensive in recognising data flows and data protection outside of the data adequacy arrangements with the EU.

The Japan–United Kingdom CEPA

Since leaving the EU, the UK has embarked on formulating trade agreements and engagement with countries around the world. This initiative has resulted in Japan very quickly reaching an agreement on a Japan–United Kingdom Comprehensive Economic

715. *Ibid.*, Article 8.3.
716. *Ibid.*, Article 8.63.

Partnership Agreement (JUEPA) in 2020.[717] The JUEPA comprises twenty-four chapters and up to eleven Annexes. Similar to the JEPA, the JUEPA paves the way for trade between the two countries. Article 8.3 ensures that PDP and the processing or dissemination of personal data are not contrary to Article XX of GATT 1994. Thus, reinforcing the point made in Chapter 1 whereby WTO-GATS rules do play a role in opening up the economic activity of data flows. Moreover, Article 8.7 defines personal information to be 'any information, including data, about an identified or identifiable natural person'.[718] In addition. Article 8.8, ensures there is a high level of protection afforded to personal information/data. Article 8.80.1, states that 'the Parties recognise the economic and social benefits of protecting the personal information of users of electronic commerce and the contribution that this makes to enhancing consumer confidence in electronic commerce'.[719] In one of the most comprehensive provisions within a trade agreement, Article 8.80 further states:

> To this end, each Party shall adopt or maintain a legal framework that provides for the protection of the personal information of the users of electronic commerce. In the development of its legal framework for the protection of personal information, each Party should take into account protection of the personal information of the users of electronic commerce. principles and guidelines of relevant international bodies. Each Party shall endeavour to adopt non-discriminatory practices in protecting users of electronic commerce from personal information protection violations occurring within its jurisdiction. Each Party shall publish information on the personal information protections it provides to users of electronic commerce, including how a) individuals can pursue remedies; and b) business can comply with any legal requirements. Recognising that the Parties may take different legal approaches to protecting personal information, each Party should encourage the development of mechanisms to promote compatibility between these different regimes. These mechanisms may include the recognition of regulatory outcomes, whether accorded autonomously or by mutual arrangement, or broader international frameworks. To this end, the Parties shall endeavour to exchange information on any such mechanisms applied in their jurisdictions and explore ways to extend these or other suitable arrangements to promote compatibility between them.[720]

Viewed this way, the JUEPA certainly places the protection of personal data at the forefront of trade. It recognises the increasing role that data is playing in transnational trade arrangements. While mentioning the exchange of personal data and information that will be part of the digital economy. The JUEPA promotes the Open Data concept, even though it appears to be limited to government-to-government activity. That is, Article 8.82 states that 'Open government data applies to facilitate public access to and use of government information fosters economic and social development, competitiveness and innovation'.[721] It does not fully embrace the Open Data concept espoused in

717. The Japan-United Kingdom Comprehensive Economic Partnership, 2020, https://www.mofa.go.jp/ecm/ie/page24e_000270.html.
718. *Ibid.*, Article 8.7.
719. *Ibid.*, Article 8.80.1.
720. *Ibid.*, Articles 8.80.2, 3, 4, 5.
721. *Ibid.*, Article 8.82.

Chapter 1. However, it stops short of mentioning data flows. It could be improved to specify data flows form an integral component of the new digital economy, and establish rules for how these flows can benefit both states. As the UK was quick to obtain an EU Data AD, a similar AD should be established between Japan and UK. This is because Japan also has an AD with the EU. Therefore, Japan and a UK AD could be achieved relatively with ease. Further, it could the above could be expanded to provide a pathway for Japan, the UK, Australia, the US, the EU and Singapore, amongst others to rapidly develop an international legal framework and set the rules for data flows. This is an urgent policy and legal matter and will ensure that data is not weaponised into a trade or national security threat.

§7.03 CONCLUSION

Japan has been significantly progressive in developing data laws and was one of the first countries in Asia to do so. Being one of the first countries in Asia to obtain an AD from the EU, has been a major accomplishment. It has paved the way for data flows to be transferred with a high level of ease between the two jurisdictions.

One of the dichotomies with this AD is that appears to be in favour of the EU and commercial entities located in the EU. It requires Japanese commercial entities to comply with the EU GDPR. Yet and conversely, it does not require EU commercial entities to comply with Japanese data law. Whether this is palatable for the longer term is unknown. While it is up to states to determine what is best for them, taking this approach only further heightens the complicated and inconsistent approach to data flows and the law. There must be the same rules to apply to all. It creates certainty and economic investment. It establishes a deeper level of economic activity that will result in more jobs.

Centrally, Japan can be considered a leader in the development of transnational principles and rules for data flows and its security. The recent agreement with the UK appears to be one of the most comprehensive, along with the recently developed DTA. The DTAs have begun to emerge as the agreement of choice for nation states to develop the digital economy and complement FTAs. The DTA underpins and reinforces the Open Data concept, however, in this situation it is limited to the financial sector. It places consumers at the forefront to ensure there is a high level of protection of their personal data that is used in online transactions between both states.

Nonetheless, a strong level of progress has been made in relation to enhancing the transnational response to data flows and data protection law in relation to transnational trade. The APPI requires a high threshold such as consent from the data subject to which the data applies and will be transferred internationally. There are obligations for a business to ensure data subjects are properly informed of where their personal data is being transferred. For instance, information must be provided with regard to the name of the country or region where a receiving third party is located. There must be a description of the personal information protection system in such country or region, which the business confirmed by an appropriate and reasonable method.

Additionally, there must be a level of information to the data subject of the level of protection that will be afforded to the data subject, when their data is in a third country. While these measures could be considered onerous, this reporting mechanism ensures there is a level of accountability and transparency for and to the data subject. It goes some way to reinforcing the OECD Principles on transparency and accountability. In further underpinning the information to be provided to data subjects, the business is obligated to also establish audit measures to ensure there remains a high level of protection for the data, once transferred.

In summary, Japan has a well-established legal framework for data flows. They are in a strong position to influence and shape the future regulation of data flows in the digital economy, regionally and around the world. It continues to be one of the first states to adopt a high level of protection for data flows.

Chapter 8

New Zealand

New Zealand is one of Australia's closest neighbours and has taken a similar approach to data law. It is a Commonwealth country, located in Oceania. New Zealand and Australia enjoy a long-standing economic, social and security partnership that goes back many decades.

Similar to Australia, New Zealand has had a well-mature data legal framework that dates back to the early 1990s.

In 2020, the PA was amended to include specific provisions for protecting personal data used in cross-border data transfers. The reforms clarified the law and imposed new obligations relating to cross-border flows of information to support New Zealand businesses to operate effectively internationally. The amendments reinforced the commitment New Zealand has made to implement and grow its digital economy. As a country they see the many economic, social and security benefits data transfers bring to the state. In addition to these reforms, New Zealand is another country that enjoys the status of obtaining Data Adequacy with the EU. It has established an advantage over Australia, which has not obtained Adequacy with the EU.

In adopting a similar approach to other country chapters, this chapter analyses a number of trade agreements New Zealand has established. The most recent agreement has been the 2020 Digital Economy Partnership Agreement (the DEPA). It is arguably the most comprehensive of agreements that promote trade, the digital economy and data flows. It also ensures there is a high level of protection retained. This chapter will argue that such agreements promote the need for international cooperation, particularly in relation to trade harmonisation. This call for harmonisation is something that is argued that also needs to be extended to include data laws. Importantly, it reinforces the principle-based approach under the OECD Guidelines.

It encourages participants to include the following principles in their respective legal frameworks (a) collection limitation; (b) data quality; (c) purpose specification; (d) use limitation; (e) security safeguards; (f) transparency; (g) individual participation; and (h) accountability.[722] *Most, if not all, of these principles are well-grounded in the international response to data flows, by the OECD. Of the agreements compared, this chapter argues that further work is needed to expand upon data flows and their protection.*

§8.01 INTRODUCTION

New Zealand is a Commonwealth nation and is often forgotten about in the discussion in relation to data, privacy, international trade and investment. It is located in the South Pacific and its closest and largest neighbour is Australia. It is a common law country and inherited its legal framework from the UK, in the same ways as Australia. As highlighted above under Australia, New Zealand has for a long time relied on the traditional resource economy[723] to fuel its economic growth. Both countries have a unique and special connection. They have a similar history and were colonised by the British. They both have challenging stories in relation to their indigenous communities. Yet, New Zealand has the opportunity to collaborate with Australia and become even more innovative and develop a pathway to establish a data flow framework that is harmonised. Pralong et al., wrote in 2015, that over the long term, economic growth will partly hinge on the two nations' full participation in global flows. Australia and New Zealand, 'can strengthen their performance in the three areas of opportunity identified above. There have been successful efforts to boost flows and connectivity in each of these areas - some in Australia and New Zealand - that can point the way ahead'.[724] However, even today, more needs to be done. Their respective data legal frameworks are very similar, in a lot of ways, however, in the area of data flows, there are significant differences.

Against the backdrop of the above, the data laws of New Zealand (NZ) date back to the early 1990s, whereby the *PA 1993* was established. Nearly thirty years later, it was revised and the *PA 2020*, came into effect on 1 December. The 2020 PA[725] was amended to include specific provisions on protecting personal data used in cross-border data transfers. The reforms specifically focused on clarifying the law and imposing new obligations relating to cross-border flows of information to support New Zealand businesses to operate effectively internationally. Arguably, this new reform package is aimed at allowing NZ businesses to operate effectively in the digital economy. NZ realises the importance of allowing its business to access international

722. *Ibid.*, Article 4.2.3.
723. David Pralong, James Manyika, Sree Ramaswamy, Ben Fletcher and Kate Yang, *Companions Abroad: Australia and New Zealand's Participation in Global Flows*, 2015, pp. 2-3 https://www.mckinsey.com/~/media/McKinsey/Locations/Pacific/Australia/flows.pdf.
724. *Ibid.*, p. 5.
725. Privacy Act 2020, No. 31. New Zealand.

markets. Without that access, businesses throughout NZ would not have the economic activity that they currently enjoy. Nonetheless, one of the major gaps that was to be addressed, as part of the reform package was to reconcile the tension between privacy with cross-border data flows. It stated that the 1993 'Act does not address the privacy issues associated with cross-border flows of data, goods and services that are now routine for private sector businesses and some public sector agencies'.[726]

NZ, similar to other jurisdictions around the world, has arguably been challenged by having to strike the right balance between privacy over the Internet and data transfers and the economic benefits this brings. In their Report on Reforming the PA 1993, this challenge was that:

> the Act generally requires agencies to handle personal information in accordance with 12 information privacy principles. The principles govern personal information at all points of its data life cycle, from its collection to destruction. The principles are intended to be flexible enough to enable agencies to develop their own information-handling policies, tailored to the needs of the agency and its users or customers. The principles can be overridden by any other enactment. Second, the privacy principles are designed to prevent harm occurring to individuals, and under the Act the Commissioner has an important role to play in 'educating agencies about their responsibilities and providing guidance on how to meet them'.[727]

Clearly, there were problems with this flexible and agile approach. Importantly, where a complaint was made by a data subject to the Commissioner, under the 1993 arrangements, there was only the ability for a recommendation to be made. For instance, it did not fully address a breach of privacy. Furthermore, in reforming the privacy laws of NZ, it also focused on developing provisions to 'streamline the complaints resolution process to build trust in the system and increase efficiency and effectiveness'.[728] NZ is yet another nation state to develop a framework that instils a high level of trust not only in the legislation but also in the digital economy, and the use of data. Without a high level of trust, NZ citizens would not have confidence in their country's ability to protect their data over the Internet, or when transferred outside the borders of the state. Another area of reform was compliance,[729] whereby, under the previous 1993 framework, compliance was not effective.

Moreover, the reforms were designed to meet the 'revised OECD Privacy Guidelines (adopted in July 2013, replacing the 1980 Guidelines on which New Zealand's

726. Reforming the Privacy Act 1993, Office of the Minister of Justice, Cabinet Social Policy Committee, pp, 2-3, https://www.justice.govt.nz/assets/Documents/Publications/cabinet-paper-reforming-the-privacy-act-1993.pdf.
727. *Ibid.*, p. 3.
728. *Ibid.*, p. 1.
729. *Ibid.* Enhanced own motion investigations – strengthening the Commissioner's existing own motion investigation powers to investigate emerging issues before serious harm occurs and for proactive assessment of agencies' systems and practices where privacy concerns have been identified, by increasing the penalty for non-compliance with requests for information from the Commissioner and allowing urgent requests to be made. compliance notices – the power to issue compliance notices for privacy breaches as a result of a complaint, own motion investigation, data breach notification or other avenue.

Privacy Act was based)'.[730] It noted that like-minded countries such as Canada, the UK and Australia either have broadly similar functions/powers in place or will have in the near future. Implementing these proposals will add to New Zealand's reputation as a good place to do international business, and will contribute to economic growth and prosperity. The proposals will help ensure, for example, that New Zealand continues to enjoy its EU Adequacy status which is a major advantage to New Zealand business.[731] Having Adequacy with the EU would be significantly advantageous for NZ. It paves the way for the ease of data transfers while acknowledging that NZ has a level of protection in place to ensure there is a high level of privacy protection for data. The baseline to achieve a balance between privacy and data flows is complex, and ultimately, it is significantly important for NZ to retain the EU Adequacy status.

Against the backdrop of the above, the NZ PA 2020, in part, replicates the Australian data laws That is, similar to the Australian Privacy Principles, NZ's version is the IPPs (Information Privacy Principles).[732] Section 7 defines personal information to mean 'information about an identifiable individual and includes information relating to a death that is maintained by the Registrar-General under the Births, Deaths, Marriages, and Relationships Registration Act 1995 or any former Act (as defined in section 2 of the Births, Deaths, Marriages, and Relationships Registration Act 1995)'.[733] While out of the scope of this book, the comparative differences in this definition to that of Australia, the US, the UK and the EU is the reference to information retained by the Registrar-General under the Births, Deaths, Marriages. None of the other states mentioned makes specific reference to an organisation, rather they identify the data/information that can identify an individual. Another addition to the NZ PA is how it defines a unique identifier in section 7, in relation to an individual, which means an identifier other than the individual's name that uniquely identifies the individual. Although this is a very broad definition, under IPP 13, it constitutes 'individual numbers, references, or other forms of identification allocated to people by organisations, such as driver's licence numbers or passport numbers, among others'.[734]

However, and unlike other states examined in this book, the concept of consent under the PA is all but non-existent. In other words, IPPs 10 and 11 require that an agency that collects personal information for one purpose, should not use or disclose that personal information for any other purpose unless an exception to that overarching principle applies. Arguably, not having consent from the legal framework removes a barrier to international transfers. Nonetheless, this book is not advocating that other jurisdictions follow the same approach to NZ, it could be of consideration. This consideration is predicated on the need for further research because consent, in my view, while not perfect, ensures a layer of control for the consumer. Take this away and privacy protections are diluted.

730. *Ibid.*, p. 6. *See also* Privacy Act, Schedule 8.
731. *Ibid.*, p. 6.
732. Privacy Act 2020, section 22.
733. *Ibid.*, section 7.
734. Information Privacy Principles, 13. An organisation cannot assign a unique identifier to a person if that unique identifier has already been given to that person by another organisation. Organisations must take reasonable steps to protect unique identifiers from misuse.

Rather than provide for a direct pathway to international data transfers, NZ has taken the path of prohibiting onwards transfers received in NS from another country.[735] Additionally, IPP 12 provides for the disclosure of personal information outside of NZ. However, section 23 restricts the application of the IPPs, in so far as 'an action taken by an agency in relation to information held overseas does not breach any of the IPPs if the action is required by or under the law of any country other than New Zealand'.[736] Furthermore, section 24 goes on to reflect the relationship between the IPPs and other New Zealand laws. It states that nothing in IPP 6, 11, or 12 limits or affects a provision contained in any New Zealand enactment that authorises or requires personal information to be made available; or a provision contained in any other New Zealand Act that:

(i) imposes a prohibition or restriction in relation to the availability of personal information; or
(ii) regulates the manner in which personal information may be obtained or made available.[737]

On closer reading of the above, it is a further sign that NZ is willing to make personal data more open a free on the international market. It is argued this is yet another barrier reduction of the flow of personal information. On the other side, it is difficult to conclude how section 24 impacts privacy over the Internet. Such variability, from other similar laws discussed throughout this book, only reinforces the significance of the fragmentation in cross-border data flows, data adequacy and data protection law(s).

Nonetheless, section 192 supports section 193 with the use of a transfer prohibition notice. The formal requirements under section 193, prohibit the transfer of personal information outside of NZ. The power rests with the Commissioner. In other words, the Commissioner can refuse to allow the transfer of personal data beyond the borders of NZ, on the basis that the 'information has been, or will be, received in New Zealand from another country and is likely to be transferred to a third country where it will not be subject to a law providing comparable safeguards to those in the PA'.[738] Additionally, the transfer contravenes the principles of the OECD Guidelines, Schedule 8. While an important and additional requirement, this is another but subtle departure from other nation states data laws. It is a good initiative, and, arguably, could be something that should be inserted into FTAs and other international agreements or legal mechanisms. Further section 193 provides that 'in determining whether to prohibit a transfer of personal information, the Commissioner must also consider whether the transfer affects, any individual; and the general desirability of facilitating

735. Privacy Act 2020, Part 8.
736. *Ibid.*, section 23.
737. *Ibid.*, section 24.
738. *Ibid.*, section 193. Subsection (1) does not apply if the transfer of the information, or the information itself, is (a) required or authorised by or under any enactment; or (b) required by any convention or other instrument that imposes inter- national obligations on New Zealand.

the free flow of information'.[739] This also extends to having to consider existing or developing international guidelines relevant to transborder data flows, including the OECD Guidelines and the GDPR. The reference to the EU GDPR is arguably to retain NZs AD.

Moreover, IPP 12 takes the transfer of data outside of NZ a step further. It specifically places controls and obligations around the disclosure of personal information to a country outside of NZ, for example, India. On this basis, the disclosure of personal data can be undertaken by a foreign individual or entity according to IPP 11 where the data subject authorises the disclosure to B after being expressly informed by A that B may not be required to protect the information in a way that, overall, provides comparable safeguards to those in NZ.[740] Put another way, the safeguards that are overall espoused by the NZ PA, are somewhat diluted from IPP12, because it does not require the receiving entity located in India, for example, to have the same level of safeguards for personal data. While it is for NZ to have a policy setting that serves their sovereign needs, the question arises how far does this dilute NZ citizens' privacy over the Internet once the data has arrived in another country?

A further development is that prohibition on any transfer can take place where the individual concerned authorises the disclosure to 'B after being expressly informed by A that B may not be required to protect the information in a way that provides comparable safeguards to those in NZ, or B is carrying on business in New Zealand and, in relation to the information, A believes on reasonable grounds that B is subject to the PA'.[741] On the other side, prohibition on disclosure may also occur when 'A believes on reasonable grounds that B is subject to privacy laws that, overall, provide comparable safeguards to those in this Act, or, A believes on reasonable grounds that B is a participant in a prescribed binding scheme, or A believes on reasonable grounds that B is subject to privacy laws of a prescribed country. Finally, section 193 applies where there is another type of agreement in place that provides comparable safeguards to those in NZ. While out of the scope of this chapter, Regulations can also be prepared in relation to prescribed binding schemes'.[742]

739. *Ibid.*
740. *Ibid.*
741. *Ibid.*
742. *Ibid.*, sections 223 and 224. 213 Regulations: prescribed binding schemes. The Governor-General may, by Order in Council made on the recommendation of the responsible Minister given after consultation with the Commissioner, make regulations prescribing binding schemes for the purpose of IPP 12(1)(d). The Minister may recommend the making of regulations under subsection (1) only if the Minister is satisfied that the binding schemes require a foreign person or entity to protect personal information in a way that, overall, provides comparable safeguards to those in this Act. 214 Regulations: prescribed countries (1) The Governor-General may, by Order in Council made on the recommendation of the responsible Minister given after consultation with the Commissioner, make regulations prescribing countries for the purpose of IPP 12(1)(e).

§8.02 FREE TRADE AGREEMENTS

New Zealand has established a number of bilateral and participates in multilateral trade agreements. This section does not examine the bilateral agreement in place with Australia (*see* chapter 2). Additionally, it does not examine the RCEP or the AANZFTA. Beginning with the Digital Economy Partnership Agreement (DEPA), which is a new initiative in digital trade that was only recently established.

Digital Economy Partnership Agreement [DEPA]

The DEPA was signed in an entirely online virtual signing ceremony by New Zealand, Chile and Singapore on Friday 12 June 2020 NZT and has entered into force for New Zealand and Singapore on 7 January 2021.[743] It is arguably the most recent and up-to-date trade agreement that provides for the protection of personal data and cross-border transfers. The DEPA defines personal information to mean 'any information, including data, about an identified or identifiable natural person'.[744] Importantly, Article 2.1 mentions, in my view, one of the most important international institutions that have been working on legal trade harmonisation as being UNCITRAL. Article 2.2 promotes the idea of trading partners working towards paperless trading. In pushing forward with the development of the digital economy, Article 3.3 places a level of control over the non-discriminatory treatment of digital products. That is, Parties to the DEPA affirm their level of commitments relating to non-discriminatory treatment of digital products, in particular, but not exclusively whereby:

> No Party shall accord less favourable treatment to digital products created, produced, published, contracted for, commissioned or first made available on commercial terms in the territory of another Party, or to digital products of which the author, performer, producer, developer or owner is a person of another Party, than it accords to other like digital product.[745]
>
> Viewed this way, the Parties of DEPA are prioritising their approach to the digital economy, and opening up this new and emerging area of economic activity. Most noteworthy is Module 4, which provides for the management of data. In other words, Article 4.2 requires a level of protection to be afforded to personal information. It aligns personal information with the economic and social benefits for its continued protection, to enhance confidence in the 'digital economy and development of trade'.[746] On that basis, Article 4.2.2, ensures that Parties to the

743. Digital Economy Partnership Agreement, https://www.mfat.govt.nz/en/trade/free-trade-agreements/free-trade-agreements-in-force/digital-economy-partnership-agreement-depa/overview/, also see, Text of DEPA, https://www.mfat.govt.nz/assets/Trade-agreements/DEPA/DEPA-Signing-Text-11-June-2020-GMT.pdf. DEPA is a living agreement, and its membership may grow – the DEPA will be open to WTO members. Canada has expressed interest in joining. Negotiations have commenced with the Republic of Korea to join.
744. *Ibid.*, Article 1.3.
745. *Ibid.*, Article 3.3. 3.3.2 Paragraph 1 shall not apply to the extent of any inconsistency with a Party's rights and obligations concerning intellectual property contained in another international agreement a Party is party to. 3.3.3. The Parties understand that this Article does not apply to subsidies or grants provided by a Party, including government-supported loans, guarantees and insurance. 3.3.4. This Article shall not apply to broadcasting.
746. *Ibid.*, Article 4.2.1.

agreement adopt a legal framework for the protection of personal data. Undoubtedly, promotes the policy approach that countries participating in DEPA do develop national laws that protect personal data. However, it does not describe how that should be undertaken. In an important development, the DEPA, however, encourages participants to include the following principles in their respective legal frameworks:

(a) collection limitation;
(b) data quality;
(c) purpose specification;
(d) use limitation;
(e) security safeguards;
(f) transparency;
(g) individual participation; and
(h) accountability.[747]

The importance of these principles being expressed within the DEPA, cannot be underestimated. Arguably, it represents a small but major step towards international harmonisation, not of the law, but of the principles themselves. However, encouraging participants to include these principles within national laws provides a layer of legal harmonisation, as the provisions develop, to implement them. Problematic though, there is no mandatory requirement to have these principles within national laws. Article 4.2.4 requires participants not to adopt non-discriminatory practices in 'protecting users of electronic commerce from personal information protection violations occurring within its jurisdiction'.[748] In achieving a level of transparency, participants are to 'publish information on the personal information protections it provides to users of electronic commerce, including how individuals can pursue remedies; and businesses can comply with any legal requirements'.[749] A further development was, from the outset, by the participants that the respective legal frameworks are different, however, they are encouraged to 'pursue the development of mechanisms to promote compatibility and interoperability between their different regimes for protecting personal information'.[750] On the one hand, DEPA is promoting a level of international harmonisation by and through the adoption of the OECD principles. On the other hand, the DEPA promotes compatibility and interoperability of legal frameworks. Arguably, providing for both at this early stage enables a level of agility in the development of legal frameworks, so that participants can continue to operate, while their laws vary from other participants. It is an acknowledgement of the fragmented approach taken by

747. *Ibid.*, Article 4.2.3.
748. *Ibid.*, Article 4.2.4.
749. *Ibid.*, Article 4.2.5.
750. *Ibid.*, Article 4.2.6. These mechanisms may include: (a) the recognition of regulatory outcomes, whether accorded autonomously or by mutual arrangement; (b) broader international frameworks; (c) where practicable, appropriate recognition of comparable protection afforded by their respective legal frameworks' national Trustmark or certification frameworks; or (d) other avenues of transfer of personal information between the Parties. Article 4.2.7. The Parties shall exchange information on how the mechanisms in paragraph 6 are applied in their respective jurisdictions and explore ways to extend these or other suitable arrangements to promote compatibility and interoperability between them.

nation states, in meeting their sovereign needs for protecting personal data. Yet, a new concept, Trustmarks, has been introduced within the DEPA that, to date, has not been included in other trade agreements examined in this book. Trustmarks can be used to 'verify conformance with privacy standards. It has modules on e-invoicing and e-payments and has specified rules on non-discrimination for digital products. Other modules are forward-looking to cover regulatory sandboxes for testing new ideas in data innovation'.[751] How effective these Trustmarks are in practice is yet to be fully determined. Hence, it is an important area of future research, as their application needs to be fully understood by parties to this agreement.

Of most importance is Article 4.3 that specifically deals with cross-border data flows. Article 4.3 states that *Cross-Border Transfer of Information by Electronic Means* that participants affirm their level of commitments relating to cross-border transfer of information by electronic means, in particular, but not exclusively:

> The Parties recognise that each Party may have its own regulatory requirements concerning the transfer of information by electronic means. Each Party shall allow the cross-border transfer of information by electronic means, including personal information, when this activity is for the conduct of the business of a covered person. Nothing in this Article shall prevent a Party from adopting or maintaining measures inconsistent with paragraph 2 to achieve a legitimate public policy objective, provided that the measures:
>
> a) do not apply in a manner which would constitute a means of arbitrary or unjustifiable discrimination or a disguised restriction on trade; and
> b) do not impose restrictions on transfers of information greater than are required to achieve the objective.[752]

Arguably the above is attempting to strike a balance between the free flow of data and ensure that there are appropriate safeguards in place to protect a level of privacy over the Internet. While there is no mention of the digital economy, the reference to the conduct of business by electronic means, forms part of that economic activity. Therefore, it is, in part, pro-business and indirectly of the new digital economy. Critically though, rather than encourage a level of legal convergence, it maintains the status quo, recognising that nation states have gone it alone and developed their own legal frameworks. For the participants in this Agreement, they do have diverging legal frameworks. A further accentuating issue is a reference to the public policy objective. There is nothing in the Agreement that defines public policy and would arguably have a wide reach. Of further note is that there is no mention of data nationalisation or localisation. This, in my view, is one of the key elements being described in the reading

751. *Ibid.*, Article 4.2.8. The Parties shall encourage adoption of data protection trustmarks by businesses that would help verify conformance to personal data protection standards and best practices. The Parties shall exchange information on and share experiences on the use of data protection trustmarks. The Parties shall endeavour to mutually recognise the other Parties' data protection trustmarks as a valid mechanism to facilitate cross-border information transfers while protecting personal information. Digital Commerce and Modern Trade Agreements, *International Economics, Strategic Analysis for Growth & Development*, https://www.tradeeconomics.com/digital-commerce-and-modern-trade-agreements/.
752. *Ibid.*, Article 4.2.8.

of unjustifiable disguised discrimination or restrictions. Nation states today, in adopting data nationalism have by and large communicated those restrictions to the world. On the other side, the DEPA is to date one of the most advanced agreements for the protection of personal data over the Internet, and balancing those protections with cross-border data flows. The obvious question arises: could DEPAs replace FTAs? A further and more important question is: has the DEPA gone far enough to manage cross-border data flows? In responding to these questions, it is for the relevant governments of each participating state to determine their effectiveness or otherwise. In my view, they are an excellent initiative and could be attached to FTAs as an Appendix. They could be further enhanced by having specific provisions for personal information/data and general information.

Pacific Agreement on Closer Economic Relations [PACER]

The PACER, in accordance with Article 2, is to ensure predictability, consistency and transparency in the application of customs laws and regulations. It further promotes efficient, economical administration of customs procedures and the expeditious clearance of goods. One of the most important objectives of PACER is to simplify and harmonise customs procedures. The reference to harmonise procedures is a good starting point to further legal harmonisation and convergence. Furthermore, it reaffirms New Zealand's commitment to the implementation of Article VII of GATT 1994, the Agreement on Customs Valuation and other relevant WTO provisions relating to customs matters.[753] Even though there is no reference to or definition of personal information/data, nor cross-border data flows, it goes some way to protect privacy. That is, according to Article 12.1(b), in providing information between Parties, any disclosure of information should be undertaken to be contrary to those laws protecting privacy.

On the one hand, privacy, in this context, has been provided with a broad application. There is no specific reference to data, the Internet, or some other form of Privacy. On the other hand, it is assumed that while PACER predominantly pertains to customs information (shipments, goods),[754] over time as systems are automated, they will capture large quantities of personal data. In reaffirming the use of automation, Article 6 requires that 'each Party shall take into account relevant international standards and best practices, taking into consideration its available infrastructure, capabilities and needs'.[755] Arguably, as technology automation expands and evolves, the standards referred to in Article 6 could include those international standards on cross-border data flows, data adequacy and data protection. The limited examination of the PACER suggests that in the future, it is argued that with technological

753. Pacific Agreement on Closer Economic Relations, https://www.mfat.govt.nz/assets/Trade-agreements/PACER-Plus/PACER-Plus-consolidated-legal-text.pdf.

754. *Ibid.*, Article 1, customs law means such laws and regulations administered and enforced by the Customs Administration of a Party concerning the importation, exportation, and transit/transhipment of goods, as they relate to customs duties, other taxes and other charges, or to prohibitions, restrictions and other similar controls with respect to the movement of controlled items across the boundary of the customs territory.

755. *Ibid.*, Article 6.

advancement in and across the customs sector, the instrument could be reviewed and amended to ensure that cross-border data flows are included.

New Zealand-Hong Kong, China Closer Economic Partnership [CEP]

The CEP[756] came into force in 2011[757] and underscored the excellent long-term trading relationship both jurisdictions have enjoyed. As of 2020, New Zealand was Hong Kong's forty-first largest trading partner. Merchandise trade between New Zealand and Hong Kong amounted to HKD 8.7 billion. In terms of services trade, New Zealand has been Hong Kong's twenty-ninth largest trading partner, with bilateral services trade amounted to HKD 3.5 billion in 2019.[758] Article 6, in minimising barriers to the trade in services, restricts the requirement that a Party supplying a service must establish an office in the jurisdiction.[759] Put another way, an entity in NZ, supplying a service to an entity in Hong Kong, does not have to have an established office on the territory of Hong Kong. Of importance are Chapters 10 and 15. Chapter 10 promises the need for electronic commerce not to be restricted in any form or way. Article 1 also promotes the need for participants in the CEP not to impose unnecessary tariffs or other limitations or costs, and encourages that e-commerce transactions have the same equivalence as traditional paper transactions.

Arguably, this is to promote the economies of both NZ and Hong Kong to transition away from the paper-driven economy. Against the backdrop of Article 1, Article 2 expands on the need to strengthen e-commerce between both Parties. Article 2 requires that both Parties agree to cooperate in promoting the use of e-commerce, and the maintenance of an open trading environment for the free flow of information and services. It is asserted that the reference to the free flow of information, while the overall Agreement does not specifically state personal information or personal data, it could conceivably include personal information data. In my view, this can be justified as e-commerce continues to grow and the number of transactions that cross international borders expands. Although to formally and functionally clarify this position, clarification is needed from either Party, and it is argued that an amendment is needed for CEP. On the one hand, Article 2 goes on to ensure that transaction costs are minimised as far as possible; there is international alignment of laws, regulatory coordination, and interoperability of infrastructures. However, it can be determined that these provisions do in part consider the wider impacts of the operation of technology in transferring information and data across international borders. Under these bilateral arrangements, there is a push for technical interoperability and not legal interoperability. International alignment of laws and regulatory coordination are stand-outs under this Agreement. It could be argued that they do promote a level of internationalisation of legal and regulatory frameworks.

756. New Zealand-Hong Kong, China Closer Economic Partnership (CEP),https://www.mfat.govt.nz/assets/Trade-agreements/Hong-Kong-China-CEP/NZ-HK-CEP.pdf.
757. *Ibid.*, also *see* Hong Kong, China – New Zealand Closer Economic Partnership Agreement, https://www.tid.gov.hk/english/ita/fta/hknzcep/index.html.
758. *Ibid.*
759. *Ibid.*, Article 6.

The obstacles provided by interoperability, can in part be resolved through transparency. However, transparency cannot be viewed as a silver bullet. Therefore, Chapter 15, Article 3 brings together an important feature of the Agreement, by requiring a level of cooperation of business law. That is, according to Article 3, there is a concerted effort from Hong Kong and NZ to make available information on their respective business laws. In going further, it allows each other to provide comments on any legal reform and cooperate in the area of business law, for any future law reform. Moreover, the article defines the term business law to mean the domestic law of a Party which relates to security markets, insurance markets, insolvency, corporate governance or other similar business activities.[760] That said, data does cut across all these areas of the law. Nonetheless, the data protection laws of both jurisdictions do involve securities, insurance sector, insolvency, corporate governance and similar business activities. Similar business activities could include the digital economy and any new laws that are developed in that area. However, the data protection laws by their very title and definition are not yet categorised as business law.

New Zealand-Malaysia FTA [NZM]

The NZM came into effect in 2010, and at the time of its development, Malaysia was one of NZ's fastest expanding export markets, and its sixth-largest goods trading partner.[761] Importantly, it expanded upon the ASEAN Australia New Zealand FTA.[762] Article 1.1 establishes an FTA between the Parties, consistent with Article XXIV of GATT 1994 and Article V of GATS, based upon the principles of common interest and cooperation and the goals of free and open trade and investment.[763] Further, Article 1.2 aims to strengthen trade and economic partnerships, liberalise trade in goods and services and establish a framework conducive to investment. It also aims to establish a framework to enhance socio-economic cooperation, exchange of information, skills and technology and improve the efficiency and competitiveness of their goods and services sectors by promoting conditions for competition cooperation, innovation and mutually beneficial business collaboration. Importantly, it aims to facilitate trade and investment by establishing transparent rules and minimising transaction costs.[764] While there are no specific chapters or provisions in relation to the trade-in services.

Centrally, Article 8.2 seeks to facilitate the expansion of trade-in services under conditions of transparency and progressive liberalisation. Additionally, Article 8.3 ensures that there are appropriate measures in place for investment in accordance with Article 7, Transfers, Article 10.8 Expropriation; Article 10.9 Compensation for Losses.

760. *Ibid.*, Chapter 15, Article 3.
761. New Zealand-Malaysia Free Trade Agreement, https://www.mfat.govt.nz/en/trade/free-trade-agreements/free-trade-agreements-in-force/nz-malaysia-free-trade-agreement/ Also *see*, New Zealand-Malaysia Free Trade Agreement, https://www.mfat.govt.nz/assets/Trade-agreements/Malaysia-NZ-FTA/mnzfta-text-of-agreement.pdf.
762. *Ibid.*
763. *Ibid.*, Article 1.1.
764. *Ibid.*, Article 1.2.

Most noteworthy is Article 10.10[765] which ensures the development and application of minimum standards of treatment. It goes on to provide a pathway to a higher level of certainty based on investments, fair and equitable treatment and full protection and security. Yet, while it is promoting the trade-in services between the two countries, it lacks any reference to data protection, cross-border data flows or data adequacy. The reason for this is likely when it began to be developed and negotiated back in 2005 when Malaysia did not have any data protection laws. In addition, and at the time of its implementation in 2010, data protection laws were only being conceptualised by many nation states in and across Southeast Asia. Thus, it is argued that in any review of this Agreement in the future, there should be consideration of data flows, protection and adequacy to be included. It should also be reviewed in light of developing provisions to expand on adequacy to achieve legal harmonisation.

New Zealand-Thailand Closer Economic Partnership [NTCEP]

The NTCEP has emerged as an important agreement, because Thailand is NZ's tenth largest trading partner, with the total trade in goods between the two countries reaching more than 'NZD 2.5 billion in 2014'.[766] Even though 'the value of our exports to Thailand fluctuates from year to year, since the 'Closer Economic Partnership (CEP) came into force in 2005, total exports have almost doubled'.[767] Article 1.1, sets out the framework by establishing a free trade area that is consistent with the rules of the WTO. It further seeks to attain a stronger trade and economic relationship, along with liberalising trade and investment and stimulating trade and investment flows. These trade and investment flows would also include but not be limited to data flows that are attached to trade, investment and services. Significant too is Chapter 10 in relation to electronic commerce. Article 10.5 applies to PDP and ensures that both Thailand and NZ take the necessary steps to protect the personal data of their respective citizens.[768] Moreover, Article 10.5.2 goes on to require that 'in the development of data protection standards, each Party shall, to the extent possible, take into account international standards and the criteria of relevant international organisations'.[769] Yet, and more critically, there is no reference to cross-border data flows, data adequacy or legal harmonisation. Thus, along with the other FTAs examined in this book, there should be further research undertaken to ensure such agreements are effective in the new digital economy. Nevertheless, Article 3.4 of Chapter 3, on customs cooperation,

---

765. *Ibid.*, 10.10, for greater certainty: (a) fair and equitable treatment requires each Party not to deny justice in any legal or administrative proceedings; (b) full protection and security requires each Party to take such measures as may be reasonably necessary to ensure the protection and security of the covered investment; and (c) the concepts of 'fair and equitable treatment' and 'full protection and security' do not require treatment in addition to or beyond that which is required under customary international law, and do not create additional substantive rights.
766. New Zealand – Thailand Closer Economic Partnership, https://www.mfat.govt.nz/en/trade/free-trade-agreements/free-trade-agreements-in-force/nz-thailand-closer-economic-partnership/ and, https://www.mfat.govt.nz/assets/Trade-agreements/Thailand-NZ-CEP/thainzcep-agreement.pdf.
767. *Ibid.*
768. *Ibid.*, Article 10.5.
769. *Ibid.*, Article 10.5.2.

ensures that the transmission of information between countries should not be undertaken that would breach the local data protection or privacy laws. Arguably, this includes privacy over the Internet. Constituted in this manner, there is the need for NZ and their bilateral partners to revise these Agreements, so as to bring them in line with the new digital economy.

New Zealand-Korea FTA [NZK]

The NZK came into effect in 2015 to strengthen trade relations between the two countries. Korea is NZ's sixth-largest export destination. Total trade in 2016 reached NZD 4.3 billion, with a fairly even split between exports and imports.[770] It facilitates the movement of goods and services, removes trade barriers, provides greater certainty to investments, and establishes a framework for resolving trade-related issues. Furthermore, it provides a pathway for more cooperation in the areas of agriculture, education, trade facilitation, science and technology, and film and television.[771] However, there is nothing in this Agreement that corresponds to cross-border data flows, data adequacy, data protection or privacy over the Internet. Chapter 8 of the Agreement deals with the cross-border trade in services. Yet, there is nothing in relation to transnational data flows and their protection.

New Zealand-China FTA [NZC]

Since the signing of the NZC in 2008, New Zealand goods' exports to China have quadrupled since the FTA.[772] Today, China is now New Zealand's largest trading partner with two-way trade valued at over NZD 28 billion in 2018.[773] Significant too is that 'New Zealand exports to China total $20.1 billion, comprising $16.7 billion in goods and $3.4 billion in services'.[774] However, similar to the NZK, there is nothing in this Agreement that corresponds to cross-border data flows, data adequacy, data protection or privacy over the Internet.

New Zealand-Singapore Closer Economic Partnership [NZSEP]

The NZSEP is one of the most recent Agreements NZ has entered into, with it coming into effect in 2020.[775] In recognition. Of their long-standing mutual partnership, NZ and Singapore under the NZSEP do not consider the digital economy or data flows. However, Part 5 provides for services and opens up new opportunities within the financial sector. Article 14 provides that:

770. New Zealand-Korea FTA, https://www.mfat.govt.nz/en/trade/free-trade-agreements/free-trade-agreements-in-force/nz-korea-free-trade-agreement/.
771. *Ibid.*
772. New Zealand-China FTA, https://www.mfat.govt.nz/en/trade/free-trade-agreements/free-trade-agreements-in-force/nz-china-free-trade-agreement/new-zealand-china-fta-overview/.
773. *Ibid.*
774. Using the New Zealand-China FTA, https://www.mfat.govt.nz/en/trade/free-trade-agreements/free-trade-agreements-in-force/nz-china-free-trade-agreement/using-the-new-zealand-china-fta/.
775. New Zealand-Singapore Closer Economic Partnership, https://www.youtube.com/watch?v=bCJjpAzDDFE.

> expanding trade in services is to be undertaken on a mutually advantageous basis, under conditions of transparency and progressive liberalisation through successive reviews, with the aim of securing an overall balance of rights and obligations, while recognising the rights of both Parties to regulate, and to introduce new regulations, giving due respect to national policy objectives including where these reflect local circumstances.[776]

Viewed this way, it can be argued that there are elements of the digital economy that have been considered. Centrally, securing a balance of rights and obligations under national laws could include data flows and data protection. Nonetheless, Article 15 goes on to provide for the inclusion of financial services into the overall Agreement. This would include FinTech. Yet, the only reference to Privacy falls within Article 77, whereby the disclosure of information should not be undertaken if such disclosure is contrary to 'laws protecting personal privacy or the financial affairs and accounts of individual customers of financial institutions'.[777] The financial services sector, particularly the emerging area of FinTech, is another area of further research. The protection of privacy is a good step in understanding the amount of data that forms part of cross-border financial transactions. On the other side, and while it is up to NZ and Singapore to decide, with this sector alone developing at a significant rate, further additional provisions could be included in this Agreement. Doing so would strengthen the governance of data flows between both countries, even though, it has by and large been addressed in the DEPA and to a lesser extent multilateral agreements.

§8.03 CONCLUSION

This chapter has demonstrated the advanced position New Zealand has taken in developing its legal framework for data flows to third countries. While not perfect, it is one of the most advanced. The Agreements analysed and compared include the:

- Digital Economy Partnership Agreement.
- Pacific Agreement on Closer Economic Relations.
- New Zealand-Hong Kong, China Closer Economic Partnership.
- New Zealand-Malaysia FTA.
- New Zealand-Thailand Closer Economic Partnership.
- New Zealand-Korea FTA.
- New Zealand-China FTA.
- New Zealand-Singapore Closer Economic Partnership.

Viewed this way, the Digital Economy Partnership Agreement is arguably the most advanced of the agreements established to date. It affirms the principle-based approach under the OECD Guidelines. This is important in any international law that could be developed for data, in the future. Nevertheless, the above agreements all in part complement the national data laws that allow for data transfers. Some go a lot

776. *Ibid.*, Article 14.
777. *Ibid.*, Article 77.

further than others. This chapter went further and compared other countries that New Zealand has established agreements with that do not form a part of this book. Doing so, further demonstrated the ad hoc approach towards developing trade agreements, and the lack of consistency, particularly towards data law.

However, this chapter did not consider the following Codes that would need to be consulted in relation to whether there are obligations required to be implemented where data is being transferred internationally. These include: Credit Reporting Privacy Code; Health Information Privacy Code; Justice Sector Unique Identifier Code; Superannuation Schemes Unique Identifier Code; Telecommunications Information Privacy Code; and the Civil Defence National Emergencies (Information Sharing) Code.

In transferring personal data to a third country, the organisation would need to ensure that there is a high level of protection of that data. However, this is subject to the powers of the Privacy Commissioner who can step in and impose restrictions on data transfers. Similar to other states, data transfers can form part of contractual arrangements between entities located in New Zealand and that of another state. What is emerging is additional agreements that have the potential to further fragment trade and the digital economy, along with data flow regulations. The next chapter examines the approach taken by the US.

CHAPTER 9

United States

The US has a complex history, yet they have emerged as a leader in data law. While they have a sectoral approach that is very different from that of many other like-minded countries. In other words, they are considered the leaders in the development of technology, bringing most if not all modern-day technological advances to the world. They have for more than a century understood the importance of the right to privacy. The digital economy is a significant component of the US economy. It is driving economic growth and advancements in skills, technology and the capacity to evolve and lead the world.

This short chapter focuses on the Privacy Shield between the US and the EU, which has not been a smooth framework for data flows between both states. It had emerged as a leading framework for data flows between the two jurisdictions. However, recent judicial decisions in the EU have highlighted its invalidity. It poses a significant challenge between the two. Moreover, it highlights how complex it is to maintain a balance between the EU rights-based approach and the high-level threshold required to ensure a similar level of protection for personal data. This is against the backdrop of the US consumer-based approach.

Additionally, a further and accentuating problem is the sectoral approach the US has taken to regulating data, more generally. It applies data law very differently across a number of national laws. This includes trade, health, consumer and child protection law. This chapter does not compare the individual states' data laws, such as California.

Of the trade agreements compared, the US, similar to the other states compared throughout this book, has an opportunity to undertake a lot more work in this area. This chapter discusses three trade agreements. The most advanced is the agreement with Australia. The US are encouraged to explore and further consider the benefits of trade agreements in establishing the broader rules related to data flows. It will benefit them in future trade negotiations. It will provide a platform for the development of international rules that are urgently needed so that like-minded countries that share the same values are directing this new area of the economy. Failure to do so will enable other nation states to step in and fill the gaps in the law that may be contrary to how countries such as Australia, the UK and the US view data flows.

§9.01 INTRODUCTION

The US has a long and complex history, similar to Australia, and New Zealand as they were all colonised. Dating back to the 1600s, and in 1697, British colonists settled permanently on the American continent.[778] While the Internet had not even been thought of in the late 1800s, let alone computer technology, elements of privacy were important to the US. In other words, Samuel Warren and Louis Brandeis put forward the right to privacy in 1890; however, it took until 1965 for the Supreme Court to find a right to privacy in the '*penumbras*' and '*emanations*' of other constitutional protections.[779] However, the right to privacy in the US has faced similar challenges, obstacles and debates, as it has, in other nation states. For Warren and Brandies meant that 'much of the force of their argument for legal recognition and enforcement of the right to privacy derives from their ingenious evocation of a broad historical sweep in which such legal recognition and enforcement appear as natural and inevitable developments'.[780]

The US International Trade Commission (ITC) 2014 calculated the 'productivity gains from the Internet by surveying US businesses and converting the results into an economic model. The productivity gains from the Internet have increased US real GDP by 3.4 to 3.5 %'.[781] Move forward nearly a decade and 'digital trade has become prominent on the global trade and economic policy agenda'.[782] This has been further heightened by the global pandemic. According to the US Department of Commerce, the

778. Luis Grau, *An American Constitutional History Course for Non-American Students* Carlos III University of Madrid, https://core.ac.uk/download/pdf/29403732.pdf. This chapter draws on the work of Robert Walters and Marko Novak, *Cyber Security, Artificial Intelligence, Data Protection & the Law*,1st ed., Springer (2021), p. 360.
779. Samuel Warren and Louis Brandeis, 'The Right to Privacy' (1890) 4(5) Harvard Law Review 192-196. In Robert Walters and Marko Novak, *Cyber Security, Artificial Intelligence, Data Protection & the Law*,1st ed., Springer (2021), pp. 360-361.
780. Dorothy Glancy, 'The Invention of the Right to Privacy' (1979) 21 Arizona Law Review. In Robert Walters and Marko Novak, *Cyber Security, Artificial Intelligence, Data Protection & the Law*, 1st ed. Springer (2021), p. 361.
781. United States International Trade Commission, *Digital trade in the US and global economies, part 2*, August 2014.
782. Congressional Research Service Digital Trade and U.S. Trade Policy, 2021, R44565 https://sgp.fas.org/crs/misc/R44565.pdf.

'digital economy' accounted for 9.6% of US GDP in 2019 (pre-pandemic) and supported 7.7 million US jobs or 5.0% of total US.[783] employment in 2019. It was estimated that between '2005 to 2019, real value added for the US digital economy grew at an average annual rate of 5.2% per year, outpacing the 2.2% growth in the overall economy each year. Digital trade has been growing faster than traditional trade in goods and services, with the pandemic further spurring its expansion'.[784] Furthermore in 2020, for the US, 'exports of information and communications technologies services increased to $84 billion, while services exports totalled $ 520 billion. Digital trade is growing on a global basis, contributing more to GDP than financial or merchandise flows'.[785]

Viewed this way, the digital economy has been important to the overall growth of the US, providing significant jobs, and domestic and international activity. In the US, digital trade has been defined as:

> The delivery of products and services over the internet by firms in any industry sector, and of associated products such as smartphones and internet-connected sensors. While it includes provision of e-commerce platforms and related services, it excludes the value of sales of physical goods ordered online, as well as physical goods that have a digital counterpart (such as books, movies, music, and software sold on CDs or DVDs).[786]

Central to this definition is data. Without data whether commercial or personal, the digital economy cannot thrive and grow. Without personal data smartphones and other personal technology ceases to function. The point made with regard to any industry can be assumed that the digital trade expands across and includes every industry sector. For the US they understand that for the digital trade to expand, it must include most aspects of e-commerce. However, and interestingly, digital trade excludes the value of sales of physical goods ordered online. The reasoning behind this exclusion is unclear when the physical goods mentioned require a level of personal data in order for the online order and trade to be activated and completed.

Voss notes that two government organisations of the US Department of Commerce – the Economics and Statistics Administration and the National Telecommunications and Information Administration – place data flows into four categories. These include:

(1) *Purely non-commercial data traffic*, including government and military communications.
(2) *Transaction data flows between buyers and sellers at a market price*, including direct purchases between buyers and sellers, such as in online banking or

783. *Ibid.*
784. *Ibid.*
785. *Ibid.*
786. *Ibid.*, p. 1. United States, International Trade Commission, *Global Digital Trade 1: Market Opportunities and Key Foreign Trade Restrictions*, August 2017, p. 33, at: https://www.usitc.gov/publications/332/pub4716.pdf.

advertising, and services transactions that involve digital platforms acting as intermediaries between buyers and sellers.

(3) *Commercial data and services exchanged between or within businesses or other related parties at USD 0 market price*, including supply chain, personnel, or design information.

(4) *Digital data and services delivered to and from end-users at USD 0 market price*, including free email, search engine results, maps and directions, and information via social media.[787]

Based on the above, data has developed into a commercial and non-commercial activity. Data interacts between consumers and organisations, data subjects and government, commercial entities and government, amongst others.

Although, the current day data laws at the federal level in the US are highly fragmented. They have been segregated and established sectorial for health, consumer, children and trade. For example, the following is a list of federal legislation that regulates data:

- Gramm-Leach-Bliley Act (GLBA) imposes several data protection obligations on financial institutions.[788]
- The Fair Credit Reporting Act (FCRA) covers the collection and use of information bearing on a consumer's creditworthiness.[789]
- The Telecommunications Act of 1996 amended the Communications Act to impose data privacy and data security requirements on entities acting as common carriers.[790]
- Video Privacy Protection Act (VPPA) was enacted in 1988 in order to preserve personal privacy with respect to the rental, purchase, or delivery of videotapes or similar audiovisual materials.[791]
- Family Educational Rights and Privacy Act of 1974 (FERPA) creates privacy protections for student education records.
- Children's Online Privacy Protection Act (COPPA) and the FTC's implementing regulations regulate the online collection and use of children's information. Specifically, COPPA's requirements apply to: (1) any operator of a website or online service that is directed to children, or (2) any operator that has any actual knowledge that it is collecting personal information from a child (covered operators).[792]
- Consumer Financial Protection Act (CFPA) prohibits covered entities from engaging in certain unfair, deceptive, or abusive acts. Enacted in 2010 as Title

787. Gregory Voss, 'Cross-Border Data Flows, the GDPR, and Data Governance' (2020) 29 Washington International Law Journal 485 488.
788. U.S.C. §§ 6801-6809. In Data Protection Law: An Overview Congressional Research Service 25 March 2019, https //fas.org/sgp/crs/misc/R45631.pdf.
789. *Ibid.*
790. *Ibid.*
791. *Ibid.*
792. *Ibid.*

X of the Dodd-Frank Wall Street Reform and Consumer Protection Act, the CFPA created the Consumer Financial Protection Bureau (CFPB) as an independent agency within the Federal Reserve System.[793]
- Federal Trade Commission Act (15 U.S.C. §§41-58).[794]

However, the list is not exhaustive and does not include state laws. While out of the scope of this book, it does not examine all below to confirm their role in data transfers. Rather, there will be an examination of the Federal Trade Commission Act. The FTC enforces key international privacy frameworks, including the EU and US. It also enforces the Swiss and US Privacy Shield Framework.[795] The EU and US Privacy Shield Framework provide a legal mechanism for companies to transfer personal data from the EU to the US. This Framework, administered by the Department of Commerce, protects consumers' privacy and security through an agreed set of Privacy Shield Principles.[796] The FTC also serves as a privacy enforcement authority in the APEC CPBR system. The APEC CBPR system is a voluntary, enforceable code of conduct designed to enhance the privacy and security of consumers' personal information transferred amongst the US and other APEC members. Under the system, participating companies can be certified as compliant with APEC CBPR programme requirements that implement APEC's nine data privacy principles.[797] However, the Safe Harbor and the Privacy Shield have come under significant judicial scrutiny in the EU. The next section briefly looks into the EU-US former Safe Harbor and the Privacy Shield, along with the challenges it has faced from the judiciary.

US–EU, Safe Harbour Framework

In 2000, the European Commission handed down a Decision that provided legal adequacy between the US and EU Safe Harbor Framework.[798] However, fifteen years on and in 2015, the CJEU ruled that the 2000 decision was invalid. This section will explore the developments of the decision and the CJEU decision, and what both the EU and the US have undertaken since. First, the 2000 Decision set out a number of Principles that included:

- Notice – an organisation must inform individuals about the purposes for which it collects and uses information about them, purposes other than that for

793. *Ibid.*
794. Federal Trade Commission Act (15 U.S.C. §§41-58) https://uscode.house.gov/view. xhtml?req =granuleid%3AUSC-prelim-title15-chapter2-subchapter1&edition=prelim.
795. *Ibid.*, §§57.
796. Robert Walters, Marko Novak, *Cyber Security, Artificial Intelligence, Data Protection & the Law*, 1st ed. (2021), p. 388.
797. *Ibid.*
798. 2000/520/EC: Commission Decision of 26 July 2000 pursuant to Directive 95/46/EC of the European Parliament and of the Council on the adequacy of the protection provided by the safe harbour privacy principles and related frequently asked questions issued by the US Department of Commerce (notified under document number C (2000) 2441) OJ L 215.

which it was originally collected or processed by the transferring organisation or discloses it for the first time to a third party.[799]

- Choice – an organisation must offer individuals the opportunity to choose (opt out) whether their personal information is (a) to be disclosed to a third party, or, to be used for a purpose that is incompatible with the purpose(s) for which it was originally collected or subsequently authorised by the individual.[800]
- Onward Transfer – to disclose information to a third party, organisations must apply the Notice and Choice Principles.[801]
- Security – organisations creating, maintaining, using or disseminating personal information must take reasonable precautions to protect it from loss, misuse and unauthorised access, disclosure, alteration and destruction.[802]
- Data Integrity – consistent with the Principles, personal information must be relevant to the purposes for which it is to be used. An organisation may not process personal information in a way that is incompatible with the purposes for which it has been collected or subsequently authorised by the individual.
- Access – individuals must have access to personal information about them that an organisation holds and be able to correct, amend, or delete that information where it is inaccurate, except where the burden or expense of providing access would be disproportionate to the risks to the individual's privacy in the case in question, or where the rights of persons other than the individual would be violated.[803]
- Enforcement – effective privacy protection must include mechanisms for assuring compliance with the Principles, recourse for individuals to whom the data relate affected by non-compliance with the Principles, and consequences for the organisation when the Principles are not followed.[804]

Viewed this way, these Principles reflect many of those of the OECD, beginning with notice and requiring a data subject to be informed of the purpose (purpose

799. *Ibid.*, how to contact the organisation with any inquiries or complaints, the types of third parties to which it discloses the information, and the choices and means the organisation offers individuals for limiting its use and disclosure. This notice must be provided in clear and conspicuous language when individuals are first asked to provide personal information to the organisation or as soon thereafter as is practicable, but in any event before the organisation uses such information.
800. *Ibid.*, Individuals must be provided with clear and conspicuous, readily available, and affordable mechanisms to exercise choice. For sensitive information (i.e., personal information specifying medical or health conditions, racial or ethnic origin, political opinions, religious or philosophical beliefs, trade union membership or information specifying the sex life of the individual), they must be given affirmative or explicit (opt in) choice if the information is to be disclosed to a third party or used for a purpose other than those for which it was originally collected or subsequently authorised by the individual through the exercise of opt in choice.
801. *Ibid.*, where an organisation wishes to transfer information to a third party that is acting as an agent, as described in the endnote, it may do so if it first either ascertains that the third party subscribes to the Principles or is subject to the Directive or another adequacy finding or enters into a written agreement with such third party requiring that the third party provide at least the same level of privacy protection as is required by the relevant Principles.
802. *Ibid.*
803. *Ibid.*
804. *Ibid.*

specification principles) for which their personal data is to be used. Giving a data subject the choice to opt out accords with the openness principle, which offers transparency to data subjects. The disclosure and security of personal data are also fundamental to the integrity of the overall framework as they provide a high level of trust. Arguably, security has become one of the highest valued principles, due to the ease with which cyber systems and infrastructures can be infiltrated in order to acquire personal information. Disclosure, on the other hand, imposes some accountability on the organisation handling the data. In the AU, in particular, data subjects have the right to access their data. It is an important right that is essential to the implementation of OECD Principles. Finally, enforcement allows both the Government and the Regulator to enforce and hold individuals and entities accountable for any alleged or confirmed breach of the laws.

Central to the success of this framework was the ability of both jurisdictions to collaborate on highly sensitive areas of data governance. They had been able to develop a new process and system that would later be extended to other countries, which the EU has established a level of adequacy with. However, in 2015, the CJEU would be required to intervene in the case of *Maximillian Schrems v. Data Protection Commissioner*[805] ruled that the Safe Harbour framework between the EU and the US was in fact invalid.[806] The Court noted that:

> Maximillian Schrems, an Austrian citizen, has been a Facebook user since 2008. As is the case with other subscribers residing in the EU, some or all of the data provided by Mr Schrems to Facebook is transferred from Facebook's Irish subsidiary to servers located in the United States, where it is processed. Mr Schrems lodged a complaint with the Irish supervisory authority (the Data Protection Commissioner), taking the view that, in the light of the revelations made in 2013 by Edward Snowden concerning the activities of the United States intelligence services (in particular the National Security Agency ('the NSA')), the law and practice of the United States do not offer sufficient protection against surveillance by the public authorities of the data transferred to that country. The Irish authority rejected the complaint, on the ground, in particular, that in a decision of 26 July 2000, the Commission considered that, under the 'safe harbour' scheme, the United States ensures an adequate level of protection of personal data transferred (the Safe Harbour Decision).[807]

The Court in ruling the Safe Harbour Decision invalid further stated:

> Article 25(6) of Directive 95/46/EC of the European Parliament and of the Council of 24 October 1995 on the protection of individuals with regard to the processing of personal data and on the free movement of such data as amended by Regulation (EC) No. 1882/2003 of the European Parliament and of the Council of 29 September 2003, read in the light of Articles 7, 8 and 47 of the Charter of

805. Case C-362/14 *Maximillian Schrems v. Data Protection Commissioner*, https://curia.europa.eu/juris/document/document.jsf;jsessionid=691E609B392962CDBD7AC854FF56C6F2?text=&docid=169195&pageIndex=0&doclang=EN&mode=lst&dir=&occ=first&part=1&cid=343865.
806. *Ibid.*, at 107.2.
807. *Ibid.*, at 27-36. Also *see*, Court of Justice of the European Union, https://curia.europa.eu/jcms/upload/docs/application/pdf/2015-10/cp150117en.pdf.

> Fundamental Rights of the European Union, must be interpreted as meaning that a decision adopted pursuant to that provision, such as Commission Decision 2000/520/EC of 26 July 2000 pursuant to Directive 95/46 on the adequacy of the protection provided by the safe harbour privacy principles and related frequently asked questions issued by the US Department of Commerce, by which the European Commission finds that a third country ensures an adequate level of protection, does not prevent a supervisory authority of a Member State, within the meaning of Article 28 of that directive as amended, from examining the claim of a person concerning the protection of his rights and freedoms in regard to the processing of personal data relating to him which has been transferred from a Member State to that third country when that person contends that the law and practices in force in the third country do not ensure an adequate level of protection.[808]

Clearly, the CJEU was reinforcing first, that the protection of personal data is a fundamental right under EU law. The court went further by also reinforcing the operation of the safe harbour rules, and how a Member State's Supervisory Authority examines the claim of a data subject that has lawfully applied according to the law. While the decisions by the court were made under the former Directive 46/95. The US not being a Member State of the EU must at all material times ensure that there is an adequate level of protection of that data. The Court was arguably referring not only to the US but also to other third countries.

US–EU, Privacy Shield

Since then, in 2016, the European Commission and the US established the US-EU Privacy Shield. In 2020, the Privacy Shield would also be invalidated by the CJEU.[809] A material difference between Schrems I and Schrems II is that the decision in 2020 was based on the recently introduced GDPR. In reinforcing its decision in Schrems I – protecting personal data is a fundamental right and there should be an adequate level of protection in data transfers to and from third countries. Centrally, the Court was required to address whether there were any gaps between EU Directive 95/46 that was relied upon in Schrems I, with that of Regulation (EU) 2016/679. In determining the invalidity of the Privacy Shield, the Court determined there were five core elements of the law that needed to be addressed. The Court ruled that first:

> Article 2(1) and (2) of Regulation (EU) 2016/679 of the European Parliament and of the Council of 27 April 2016 on the protection of natural persons with regard to the processing of personal data and on the free movement of such data, and repealing Directive 95/46/EC (General Data Protection Regulation), must be interpreted as meaning that that regulation applies to the transfer of personal data for commercial purposes by an economic operator established in a Member State to another economic operator established in a third country.[810]

808. *Ibid.*, at 107.1.
809. Case C-311/18 *Data Protection Commissioner v. Facebook Ireland Limited and Maximillian Schrems*, Judgment of the Court (Grand Chamber) of 16 July 2020.
810. *Ibid.*, at 203.1.

By determining the above, it paved the way for the Court to reconcile what was meant by Article 46(1) and Article 46(2)(c) of Regulation 2016/679. Second, the Court argued that:

> Article 46(1) and Article 46(2)(c) of Regulation 2016/679 must be interpreted as meaning that the appropriate safeguards, enforceable rights and effective legal remedies required by those provisions must ensure that data subjects whose personal data are transferred to a third country pursuant to standard data protection clauses are afforded a level of protection essentially equivalent to that guaranteed within the European Union by that regulation, read in the light of the Charter of Fundamental Rights of the European Union.[811]

Viewed this way, the Court reaffirmed that an appropriate level of safeguards, enforceable rights and effective legal remedies had to be available to ensure that a data subject's data could be transferred from a third country to an EU Member State. That said, third, the Court made the point that:

> Article 58(2)(f) and (j) of Regulation 2016/679 must be interpreted as meaning that, unless there is a valid European Commission adequacy decision, the competent supervisory authority is required to suspend or prohibit a transfer of data to a third country pursuant to standard data protection clauses adopted by the Commission.[812]

Nonetheless, the Court also looked beyond the interpretation of the new Regulation 2016/679, to the operation of contractual clauses. The Court made the point that:

> Examination of Commission Decision 2010/87/EU of 5 February 2010 on standard contractual clauses for the transfer of personal data to processors established in third countries under Directive 95/46/EU of the European Parliament and of the Council, as amended by Commission Implementing Decision (EU) 2016/2297 of 16 December 2016 in the light of Articles 7, 8 and 47 of the Charter of Fundamental Rights has disclosed nothing to affect the validity of that decision.[813]

On this basis, fifth, the Court in concluding clearly stated that the 'Commission Implementing Decision 2016/1250 of 12 July 2016 pursuant to EU Directive 95/46/EC of the European Parliament and of the Council on the adequacy of the protection provided by the EU-US Privacy Shield is invalid'.[814] At the time of writing this book, the

811. *Ibid.*, at 203.2. To that end, the assessment of the level of protection afforded in the context of such a transfer must, in particular, take into consideration both the contractual clauses agreed between the controller or processor established in the European Union and the recipient of the transfer established in the third country concerned and, as regards any access by the public authorities of that third country to the personal data transferred, the relevant aspects of the legal system of that third country, in particular those set out, in a non-exhaustive manner, in Article 45(2) of that regulation.
812. *Ibid.*, at 203.3. Note, if, in the view of that supervisory authority and in light of all the circumstances of that transfer, those clauses are not or cannot be complied with in that third country and the protection of the data transferred that is required by EU law, in particular by Articles 45 and 46 of that regulation and by the Charter of Fundamental Rights, cannot be ensured by other means, where the controller or a processor has not itself suspended or put an end to the transfer.
813. *Ibid.*, at 203.4.
814. *Ibid.*, at 203.5.

US and EU had begun further negotiations on an adequacy framework, whatever that will look like. The twc cases demonstrate that the CJEU takes seriously that there is not just a mere adequate level of protection in the, or from a, third country. It continues to reaffirm how data protection in, and across the EU remains rights-based, even as the digital economy grows and the need to open up the flow of data is under increasing pressure. Should there be another iteration of Safe Harbour of Privacy Shield, it is obviously going to come under a lot of scrutiny by the courts, particularly the CJEU. Every effort must be made to ensure that the protection from the US meets the level of protection according to Regulation (EU) 2016/679. It is precisely this tension that, as the digital economy evolves that will pose the most significant challenges to reconciling the balance between the current rights-based approach, with that of having to open up the digital economy. Opening up is imperative and will allow data to be transferred internationally with ease. What this might look like is unknown. The ensuing question is whether, if at all, this can be achieved for the EU and US, without having to give up or compromise on the current rights-based approach. While this will be, and is, a question for the European community; however, a further accentuating question is how can they maintain the current rights-based approach when they have adopted the policy of Open Data? A starting point, in my view, is for the EU to work through their current FTAs.

The next section discusses a selected few FTAs that the US has established with a trading partner to determine how transnational flow of data has been addressed. This is against the backdrop that in 2020 alone, the EU and US trade and investment relationship was extensive and according to the US Bureau of Economic Analysis, US-EU trade-in ICT services and potentially technology-enabled services were estimated to be more than USD 264 billion in 2020.[815] On this basis alone, it is asserted that there is an urgent need for the US and the EU to work with other like-minded nation states to develop a framework of harmonisation and more towards establishing an international legal framework for transnational data flows. The next section examines select BTAs the US has established with jurisdiction discussed in this book.

§9.02 BILATERAL TRADE AGREEMENTS

This section examines the BTAs in the US that are currently operational. Where an Agreement has already been discussed in a previous chapter, it will only be referred to here.

United States–Australia Free Trade Agreement [US-AUFTA]

The US has for many decades viewed Australia as a key trade, investment and security partner. In 2005, both states established the US-Australia FTA. That is, the Government

815. Kirstin Archchick and Rachel Feher, *Congressional Research Services, US – EU Privacy Shield and Transatlantic Data Flows*, 22 September 2021, https://crsreports.congress.gov/product/pdf/R/R46917.

of the United States of America and the Government of Australia resolved to reinforce the long-standing ties of friendship and cooperation between them and strengthen their economic relations and further liberalise and expand bilateral trade and investment.[816] Established at a time when data was an emerging part of the digital economy, and many states around the world had not developed specific data laws – it makes minimal reference to data. It does not define personal information or personal data. Chapter 10 relates to cross-border trade-in services. Article 10.1 pertains specifically to governing transnational trade-in services; however, it does not apply to financial or air services. Importantly, there is no mention of personal data, personal information, its management or protection. The protection of this data information over the Internet has also not been featured. Yet, Article 12.5 defines public telecommunications service and refers to data transmission involving customer-supplied information, by and through telecommunications services.[817] Arguably, customer-supplied information would in part also include personal information of individuals engaged in telecommunications services. That said, this type of information is limited to telecommunications services between both countries such as the telephone. It does not extend to Internet traffic. At issue is the exchange of data within the financial services. This may be regulated by other national laws, and in my view, the agreement should include data used across this sector. This is because the financial sector alone is expected to generate large quantities of data flows.

Against the backdrop of the above, Chapter 13 becomes important in dealing with financial services. This is a growing area of the economy for both states. Article 13.1 applies to financial institutions involved in cross-border trade in financial services. Furthermore, Article 13.5.1 also refers to data used within financial services. It states that 'with respect to the provision and transfer of financial information and financial data processing and related software as referred to in Article 13.19.5(o), and advisory and other auxiliary services, excluding intermediation, relating to banking and other financial services as referred to in Article 13.19.5'.[818] That information will, in part, include personal data. However, overall, the Agreement makes no reference to national laws, standards or norms in relation to the privacy of the governance of data. Considering that when this Agreement was established, both states had data protection-privacy laws in place, more needs to be done in this area. Understandably, it is very commercially oriented, although any review of the Agreement should consider those areas of the digital economy that will pervade the trade-in services. On this basis, it is argued that data will need to be considered as well.

816. United States – Australia Free Trade Agreement 2005, Preamble, https://ustr.gov/sites/default/files/uploads/agreements/fta/australia/asset_upload_file148_5168.pdf *see also* Existing US Trade agreements, https://www.state.gov/trade-agreements/existing-u-s-trade-agreements/.
817. *Ibid.*, Article 12.5.
818. *Ibid.*, Article 13.5.1.

United States–Canada FTA [USC]

The USC[819] was established in 1994 and has expired. Canada, the US and Mexico trade agreement[820] was signed in 2020 between Canada, US and Mexico, which replaced the former NAFTA Agreement. There appears to no longer be a trade agreement in place between the two countries alone.

United States–Singapore FTA [USS]

The USS agreement was established in 2004,[821] sometime before data was recognised as an issue to regulate in Singapore. It does not define personal information or personal data. Article 9.2 regulates the access to and use of public telecommunications transport networks and services. Article 9.2.4 goes on to state that a Party may take such measures as are necessary to ensure the security and confidentiality of messages, or protect the privacy of customer proprietary network information.[822] Annex 10D governs the operation of the Financial Services Committee. One of its responsibilities is to protect the 'privacy of individuals in relation to the processing and dissemination of personal data and the protection of confidentiality of individual records and accounts'.[823] This Agreement was established at a time when Singapore had no data protection laws. The notion of privacy under this Agreement is somewhat ambiguous and vague. On the one hand, it can be argued that there is a level of protection of personal data that is limited to financial accounts. This position is reasonable and protecting the financial records of individuals is important to provide trust and confidence in the sector. On the other hand, it only applies to financial data that is between the US and Singapore, as the Agreement suggests. However, it lacks clarity on what personal data constitutes and the meaning and application of privacy under the Agreement. More explanation is needed by both parties to confirm how these concepts operate.

§9.03 CONCLUSION

The US has been formidable at directing and developing the rules for international trade since World War II. They have a robust but complex national framework for data flows and data protection. Yet, data flows at an international level are a priority for the country. For the US, it is the digital economy that is driving innovation and economic growth. Within their economy, similar to every other economy discussed throughout

819. Office of the united States Trade Representative, United States – Canada Free Trade Agreement, https://www.international.gc.ca/trade-commerce/trade-agreements-accords-commerciaux/agr-acc/united_states-etats_unis/fta-ale/background-contexte.aspx?lang=eng The Canada-US Free Trade Agreement was brought into force on 1 January 1989 and is superseded by NAFTA.
820. Congressional Research Services, *Canada, the United States and Mexico*, https://sgp.fas.org/crs/row/R44981.pdf.
821. United States – Singapore Free Trade Agreement https://ustr.gov/trade-agreements/free-trade-agreements/singapore-fta/final-text.
822. *Ibid.*, Article 9.2.4.
823. *Ibid.*, Annex 10D.

this book, data flows extend to supply chains, research, national security, trade in goods and services and technology development. Today, it must be a central feature of current and future trade policy at the national level.

The US has a formidable opportunity to utilise its well-established trade agreement process and frameworks to establish a high level of international rules for data flows and its security. It is argued that there is an urgent and significant need for the US to establish a comprehensive framework that works closely with Australia and the UK, amongst others, to make data flow regulation a national priority. Failure to do so, the US risk losing their status as being able to set and direct trade rules and laws.

As the consumers of the US increasingly engage in online transactions, the growth in the collection and use of citizens' data across international borders has the potential of becoming a major risk to the US if not managed appropriately. The increased international tensions and pressure on trade and economic activity will place further obstacles to data flows and the digital economy. While the US has embraced the OECD framework for data flows, they need to build on this and express them within trade agreements. They need to develop a pathway for the internationalisation of data flows law. In further making, the case that the US must urgently develop more in this area of policy and law was emphasised in the following:

> The US has traditionally supported open data flows and has regulated privacy at a sectoral level to cover certain types of data, such as health records, although Congress is currently debating potential comprehensive national policy. That said, US trade policy has sought to balance the goals of consumer privacy, security, and open commerce, including eliminating trade barriers and opening markets. Other countries are developing data privacy policies that affect international trade as some governments or groups seek to limit data flows outside of an organization or across national borders for a number of reasons. Blocking international data flows may impede the ability of a firm to do business or of an individual to conduct a transaction, creating a form of trade protectionism.[824]

The point is that every regulation that is established that provides an obstacle to data flows takes away from nation states to fully realise the economic potential of data in the digital economy. They should use their experience and influence to establish and reshape bilateral and multilateral trade agreements. This work should be undertaken to expand the rules for data flows internationally, with a view to developing an international legal instrument for data flows and their protection. Finally, it should be viewed as an opportunity rather than an obstacle for the US to move and shift rapidly to provide world and regional leadership in this complex area of the law. Doing so will enable many other countries to rapidly follow and embrace the international rules.

824. United States Congress, Data Flows, Online Privacy, and Trade Policy, 2020, p. 2, https://sgp.fas.org/crs/misc/R45584.pdf.

CHAPTER 10
Multilateral: Free Trade Agreements and Other Mechanisms

Multilateral FTAs are nothing new and have been servicing the world economy very well for decades. This brief chapter examines those multilateral FTAs in which the states examined throughout this book are a participant. Multilateral agreements allow a number of nation states to come together, form trading partnerships and set the rules on trade. Provided all participants adhere to the Agreements, they can be effective in developing common standards, principles and concepts, particularly in the area of transnational data flows.

However, it is argued that these Agreements should not depart from any bilateral Agreements states have that deal with the same issues. It is an opportunity to pave the way for the internationalisation of cross-border data flows and begin to develop a framework for legal harmonisation. This chapter only examines the Trans-Pacific Partnership [TPP], Regional Comprehensive Economic Partnership [RCEP] and the ASEAN-Australia-New Zealand Free Trade Area [AANZFTA]. Further research is needed to fully understand the breadth and depth of other multilateral agreements that these jurisdictions are participants of. Doing so will provide an extensive evidence base to identify current and future gaps and threats that need to be reconciled for data flows in the digital economy.

§10.01 INTRODUCTION

Trans-Pacific Partnership [TPP]

This section identifies the key FTAs that reflect the nation states examined throughout this book. Beginning with the CPTPP is an FTA between Australia, Brunei Darussalam,

Canada, Chile, Japan, Malaysia, Mexico, Peru, New Zealand, Singapore and Vietnam.[825] The CPTPP incorporated most of the provisions of the previous Trans-Pacific Partnership (TPP) Agreement until the US withdrew. As a high-level strategic document, it provides that countries will 'guarantee the free flow of data across borders for service suppliers and investors as part of their business activity'.[826] This 'movement of information' or 'data flow' is relevant to all kinds of businesses – from an Australian hotel which relies on an 'international online reservation system, to an Australian telecommunications company seeking to provide data management services to businesses across a number of TPP markets'. TPP countries have retained the ability to maintain and amend regulations related to data flows, but have 'undertaken to do so in a way that does not create barriers to trade'.[827]

Chapter 14 of the TPP is the most important of the entire agreement in relation to cross-border data flows. Article 14.8 is specific to Personal Information Protection.[828] Article 14.8.1 makes the point of the importance of the economic and social benefits of protecting personal information. One of the direct benefits is enhancing consumer trust. It further understands that nation states will have developed their own protection framework. Importantly, each Party shall endeavour to adopt non-discriminatory practices in protecting users of electronic commerce from personal information protection violations occurring within its jurisdiction.[829] Article 14.8.4: each Party should publish information on the personal information protections it provides to users of electronic commerce, including how: (a) individuals can pursue remedies; and (b) business can comply with any legal requirements.

Moreover, Article 14.8.5 recognises that the 'Parties may take different legal approaches to protecting personal information, each Party should encourage the development of mechanisms to promote compatibility between these different regimes. These mechanisms may include the recognition of regulatory outcomes, whether accorded autonomously or by mutual arrangement, or broader international frameworks. To this end, the Parties shall endeavour to exchange information on any such mechanisms applied in their jurisdictions and explore ways to extend these or other suitable arrangements to promote compatibility between them.'[830] The similarities emerging from the TPP can also be seen in the Singapore-Australia Digital agreement whereby, both international instruments encourage the states party to the agreement to publish information on the personal information protections it provides to users of electronic commerce, including how: (a) individuals can pursue remedies; and (b) business can comply with any legal requirements.

825. The Comprehensive and Progressive Agreement for Trans-Pacific Partnership (CPTPP), https://www.dfat.gov.au/trade/agreements/in-force/cptpp/comprehensive-and-progressive-agreement-for-trans-pacific-partnership.
826. Australian Government, TPP outcomes: trade in the digital age, https://www.dfat.gov.au/trade/agreements/not-yet-in-force/tpp/Pages/outcomes-trade-in-the-digital-age.
827. *Ibid.*
828. Trans-Pacific Partnership, Chapter 14, https://ustr.gov/sites/default/files/TPP-Final-Text-Electronic-Commerce.pdf.
829. *Ibid.*, Article 14.8.3.
830. *Ibid.*, Articles 14.8.4, 14.8.5.

Nevertheless, Article 14.11 goes into more specific regarding cross-border data flows and recognises that each Party may have its own regulatory requirements concerning the transfer of information by electronic means. More specifically, Article 14.11.2 provides that each 'Party shall allow the cross-border transfer of information by electronic means, including personal information, when this activity is for the conduct of the business of a covered person'.[831] Importantly, and while it allows for some restrictions to be established, any restrictions should not be more than is necessary. Thomas Streinz is of the view that the TPP:

> constrains states' ability to restrict cross-border data flows or to require the use of domestic computing facilities by requiring a legitimate public policy objective that must be pursued in a non-arbitrary or not unduly discriminatory manner, is not a disguised restriction on trade, and does not exceed what is necessary to achieve the objective. Such language is inspired by the WTO's General Agreement on Trade in Services (GATS) but it is unclear how dispute settlement panels are going to interpret and apply the TPP's new rules if states' regulation of the digital domain impacts cross-border data flows. The TPP charted new ground by creating binding rules for 'free data flows' and against 'data localization' that are not directly tied to trade in goods or services. States that sign and ratify agreements like the TPP subject their regulation of the digital economy to external scrutiny.[832]

Viewed this way, I agree with the position taken by Streinz. Most significant is the external scrutiny of countries that have ratified the TPP face in relation to creating and establishing barriers to data flows, such as data localisation. The mandatory obligations that have arisen from the TPP arguably meet the Open Data concept (*see* Chapter 1), strengthening the accountability and transparency of those states participating in the TPP. Conversely, it fails to mention or encourage legal harmonisation or internationalise elements of laws for cross-border data flows.

In making the case for the internationalisation of cross-border data flows and the law, Article 14.15 makes a pertinent and compelling statement. It requires that when states engage in domestic electronic transactions, 'each Party shall maintain a legal framework governing electronic transactions consistent with the principles of the UNCITRAL Model Law on Electronic Commerce 1996 or the United Nations Convention on the Use of Electronic Communications in International Contracts'.[833] Although the TPP has not called for any international law on data flows, in making reference to the international legal instruments and the institutions responsible for them, it argues that UNCITRAL should consider undertaking work on developing a convention or model law for cross-border data flows.

---

831. *Ibid.*, Article 14.11.2. Note that at 14.11.3. Nothing in this article shall prevent a Party from adopting or maintaining measures inconsistent with paragraph 2 to achieve a legitimate public policy objective, provided that the measure is not applied in a manner which would constitute a means of arbitrary or unjustifiable discrimination or a disguised restriction.
832. Thomas Streinze, 'Digital Megaregulation Continued: the Regulation of Cross-Border Data Flows in International Economic Law' 2020, pp. 1-2, https://www.jef.or.jp/journal/pdf/232nd_Cover_Story_11.pdf.
833. Trans-Pacific Partnership, Chapter 14, Article 14.15, https://ustr.gov/sites/default/files/TPP-Final-Text-Electronic-Commerce.pdf.

Regional Comprehensive Economic Partnership [RCEP]

A further important and recent addition to trade agreements has been RCEP, which came into force in January 2022.[834] Chapter 12 of RCEP provides for Electronic Commerce. Online personal information protection is covered in accordance with Article 12.8.1 and ensures that each 'party can adopt or maintain a legal framework which ensures the protection of this important data'.[835] In drawing similarities with the TPP, Article 128.2 requires that 'in the development of its legal framework for the protection of personal information, each Party shall take into account international standards, principles, guidelines, and criteria of relevant international organisations or bodies'.[836]

Further, each Party shall 'publish information on the personal information protection it provides to users of electronic commerce, including how: (a) individuals can pursue remedies; and (b) business can comply with any legal requirements'.[837] Article 12.8.4 also requires that the Parties 'shall encourage juridical persons to publish, including on the internet, their policies and procedures related to the protection of personal information'.[838] In promoting privacy over the Internet, Article 12.8.5, 'encourages Parties to protect personal information transferred from a Party'.[839] While not expressly referring to cross-border transfers, it could mean both domestic and international transfers.

While the above takes a privacy protection focus, more specifically, Section D promotes the idea of cross-border electronic commerce. On that basis, Article 12.14 requires Parties to take particular steps in relation to the location of computing facilities. Importantly, it allows a degree of flexibility for the parties to use or locate such facilities in a Party's own territory and develop their own measures to protect information and confidential communications. Further, Article 12.15 provides for the cross-border transfer of information. Article 12.15.1 makes it clear that countries understand that each will have its own regulatory requirements that need to be met with regard to transferring information. This accords with the current fragmented approach taken by nation states that are Party to RCEP. It also acknowledges that each member has its own sovereign needs for regulating data flows/transfers. However, Article 12.15.2 goes on to say that 'no one should prevent cross-border transfer of information in the conduct of business'.[840] Thus, two matters arise here. First, it is

---

834. Regional Comprehensive Economic Partnership (RCEP) agreement to enter into force on 1 January 2022, https://asean.org/regional-comprehensive-economic-partnership-rcep-to-enter-into-force-on-1-january-2022/.
835. *Ibid.*, Article 12.8.1.
836. *Ibid.*, Article 12.8.2.
837. *Ibid.*, Article 12.8.3.
838. *Ibid.*, Article 12.8.4.
839. *Ibid.*, Article 12.8.5.
840. *Ibid.*, Article 12.15.2. Nothing in this Article shall prevent a Party from adopting or maintaining: any measure inconsistent with paragraph 2 that it considers necessary to achieve a legitimate public policy any measure inconsistent with paragraph 2 that it considers necessary to achieve a legitimate public policy objective, provided the measure is not provided in a manner which would constitute a means of arbitrary or unjustifiable discrimination or a disguised restriction

asserted that there is a clear acknowledgement that information (data) is a fundamental requirement of the digital economy. Second, it promotes the idea for states not to place restrictive measures in place to prevent transfers. In reality, this is far from what has occurred to date, by the states party to this agreement.

While out of scope to detail the exact restriction nation state by nation state. Australia and China amongst others have established levels of data location laws that, in part, are a restrictive measure. Finally, in recognition of the importance of the new digital economy, Article 12.5 promotes the adoption of paperless trading as far as possible. Doing so reinforces how this book has demonstrated that data will only increase as less and less paper is used. It will heighten the growth in data transfers and trade in goods and services that rely on personal data. In my view, Chapter 12 of RCEP is very similar to that of the TPP. Surprisingly, countries did not take a broader view and recognise interoperability as a means of enhancing data transfers. Moreover, Chapter 12 makes no reference to regionalisation, internationalisation or harmonisation of cross-border data transfer law. It has by and large retained the status quo, which it is argued was a missed opportunity by all who are participants in RCEP.

ASEAN-Australia-New Zealand Free Trade Area [AANZFTA]

The AANZFTA is a multilateral trade agreement between Australia, New Zealand and all ASEAN[841] Member States, which was signed in 2009.[842] Its principal aim was to bring the countries together through trade, investment and development. More broadly, it has a desire 'to minimise barriers and deepen and widen economic linkages among the Parties; lower business costs; increase trade and investment; enhance economic efficiency; create a larger market with more opportunities and greater economies of scale for business'.[843] Of importance to the evolving digital economy is Chapter 10. While it does not define personal information or data, it calls on each party to provide a high level of transparency.[844] It refers to UNCITRAL Model Law on Electronic Commerce 1996[845] and thus demonstrates how the countries consider the importance of such a multilateral organisation to international trade.

Despite not discussing cross-border data flows, Article 7 refers to Data Protection. Interestingly, the provision predates most of the ASEAN countries' data protection laws. In other words, at the time of this multilateral agreement, none of the member countries of ASEAN had established specific data/privacy laws. Australia and New Zealand have a long history of privacy legislation. For instance, New Zealand's first laws were established in 1993, while Australia's laws came five years earlier in 1988.

---

on trade; or any measure that it considers necessary for the protection of its essential security interests. Such measures shall not be disputed by other Parties.

841. Association of South East Nations, ten member countries including, Brunei, Cambodia, Indonesia, Laos, Malaysia, Myanmar, the Philippines, Singapore, Thailand, and Vietnam.
842. ASEAN-Australia-New Zealand Free Trade Area, https://www.dfat.gov.au/trade/agreements/in-force/aanzfta/official-documents/Pages/official-documents.
843. *Ibid.*, Preamble, https://www.dfat.gov.au/sites/default/files/aanzfta_preamble.PDF.
844. *Ibid.*, Chapter 10, Article 3, https://www.dfat.gov.au/trade/agreements/in-force/aanzfta/official-documents/Pages/chapter-10-electronic-commerce.
845. *Ibid.*, Article 4.

However, it is a very different picture across ASEAN. Singapore and Malaysia have been leaders in establishing their respective data laws in 2012 and 2010 respectively. On the other side, as of July 2022, Indonesia is still yet to establish specific data laws. Nonetheless, Article 7 goes on to provide that personal data is to be protected over e-commerce. However, there is an exception to this rule, as Article 7.2. provides that a Party is not obliged to protect personal data before the date 'on which that Party enacts domestic laws or regulations to protect the personal data of electronic commerce users'.[846] Thus, for Australia and New Zealand, this applied at the time of signing the agreement. However, the ASEAN Member States who had not established specific laws and had not done so in 2022 are not obligated by this provision. Positively, Article 7.3 promotes the idea of international standards, the rule of law and arguably the rules-based system. It ensures that the OECD Principles and other international standards that are developed in the future form part of national domestic standards.

§10.02 CONCLUSION

This brief chapter highlights a few examples of the current multilateral trade agreements to which the jurisdictions compared in this book are a party. This chapter examined the Trans-Pacific Partnership, Regional Comprehensive Economic Partnership [RCEP] and the ASEAN-Australia-New Zealand Free Trade Area.

The chapter determined that further research is needed to fully understand the breadth and depth of other multilateral agreements and the contribution they can make to the evolving legal landscape of data flows. It provides an important opportunity for nation states to come together and develop international rules for data flows. Doing so will provide an extensive evidence base, to identify current and future gaps and threats that need to be reconciled for data flows in the digital economy.

Arguably there is a significant amount of work that can be undertaken in this area alone. The above agreements, by and large, lack any detail on data laws and the digital economy. Any reference to data protection, personal information or personal data, lacks any significant detail. Of the agreements compared, the RCEP is the most advanced, however, it largely focuses on transnational e-commerce with a view to ensuring steps are in place to protect computing facilities and information along with communications. Such communications and information would invariably include personal data. Similarly, to the overall discussion in this book, it further highlights the inconsistent and fragmented approach that has been adopted by states to establish rules for transnational data law in the digital economy.

The complexity in achieving anything meaningful in multilateral agreements is the competing geopolitical views and sovereign needs of the nation states involved. In any case, the TPP provide an example of where it promotes the idea of embracing the internationalisation of technology law. This Chapter has demonstrated how such an agreement can be used, even in its infancy, to influence and direct the future development of law and call for the internationalisation of data flow law. By adopting

846. *Ibid.*, Article 7.2.

an international approach, industry sectors can further develop their respective self-regulation frameworks over and above government regulation. Such an approach will provide greater certainty for investment in the use, trade and transfer of personal data internationally. A wider and more in-depth research is needed on other multilateral trade agreements to which the jurisdictions compared throughout this book is a party. This will confirm the extent of data governance, and achieve a faster rate of internationalisation of this area of the law because there are more countries involved in multilateral agreements. The next chapter explores some of the cross-border standards and rules that have emerged that assist in governing data flows.

CHAPTER 11

Cross-Border Standards and Rules

The evolving nature of data protection law and data flows has resulted in standards (certification) and rules being established across the private sector to implement government regulation. This chapter examines one of the most common industry standards: the International Organisation for Standardisation, Binding Corporate Rules and contractual clauses. This chapter does not provide an exhaustive comparison of the countries examined throughout the book. Rather it focuses on the EU framework, and where appropriate, it highlights how other jurisdictions have implemented standards that have possibly been the catalyst for the development of national data laws.

This chapter will highlight how these standards and rules do go some way to harmonising elements of the framework for the governance of data – outside the national and supranational laws. In demonstrating this proposition, it will be argued that such standards and rules are only as good as the industry sector, and more specifically, the organisation that develops and implements them. Problematic though is that these tools are generally voluntary and have minimal or in many cases no legal obligations to adopt them.

They are technically based at a level of internal policy, procedures and guidelines so that offices located in different countries establish a single system of governance. The downside to this approach is that under the current fragmented approach of data laws, complying with multiple country laws may be missed. A further accentuating problem is how they are specific to an organisation, which makes them non-binding. It is the choice of the organisation as to whether they are binding or otherwise. This will depend on the resources available within an organisation itself. Put another way, being internal to an organisation poses another challenge to data subjects, knowing and understanding to what extent the standards or rules are developed, what they achieve, and how are they implemented. More pervasively, they can act as a strategic marketing tool to convey best practice management for data and their transnational flows by an organisation.

§11.01 INTRODUCTION

There have been a number of international standards that have emerged, and today 'are of paramount importance to the information and communication technology industry'.[847] This chapter only discusses International Organization for Standardization (ISO) and not others that have also been established to manage and govern data. The ISO has published over 22,000 international standards that range from the company's management system to domestic and commercial equipment standards.[848] Di Luozzo, Varisco, and Schirald are of the view that these standards are crucial for the economic activity of a company since compliance to a certain standard could be a requirement either for public/private sectors or for the penetration of a marketplace. Agreeing with these authors, data and the digital economy are interrelated and require the marketplace to open for this economic activity to thrive. They further note that the relationship between standards and innovation demonstrated that without a level of standardisation innovation is significantly diluted. ISO standards can be found across many governments and private sectors, such as the airline industry, health, primary production, food processing, education, shipping and manufacturing.

Against the backdrop of the above, agreed international standards 'serve to facilitate interoperability by allowing various devices to communicate with one another'.[849] Standards help to address the 'complex technological system that involves communication and computing functions, there must be appropriate interfaces through which signals can pass'.[850] Most, if not all, ICT devices and components cannot work unless they can connect to and interoperate with other devices and components. Some examples include but are not limited to Wi-Fi:

847. There is no universally agreed definition on ICT industries amongst legal scholarship. Nor does the WTO provide an answer about the scope of the ICT industries, http://www.oecd.org/science/sci-tech/oecdguidetomeasuringtheinformationsociety2011.htm, In Han-Wei Liu, 'International Standards in Flux: A Balkanized ICT Standard-Setting Paradigm and Its Implications for the WTO' (2014) 17(3) Journal of International Economic Law 551-600, https://doi.org/10.1093/jiel/jgu034.
848. International Organisation for Standardisation, We're ISO: we develop and publish International Standards, 2018, https://www.iso.org/standards.html. In Sebastiano Di Luozzo, Martina Varisco and Massimiliano M Schirald, 'The Diffusion of International Standards on Managerial Practices' (2020) 12 International Journal of Engineering Business Management 1, DOI: 10.1177/1847979020921611.
849. There is no universally agreed definition on ICT industries among legal scholarship. Nor does the WTO provide an answer about the scope of the ICT industries, http://www.oecd.org/science/sci-tech/oecdguidetomeasuringtheinformationsociety2011.htm, In Han-Wei Liu, 'International Standards in Flux: A Balkanized ICT Standard-Setting Paradigm and Its Implications for the WTO' (2014) 17(3) Journal of International Economic Law 551-600, https://doi.org/10.1093/jiel/jgu034.
850. *Ibid.*

which stands for 'wireless fidelity', enables greater distance between wireless devices and fosters use of the Internet in a variety of daily tasks. Universal Serial Bus, better known as 'USB', allows users to connect smart and iPhones, keyboards, printers, and many other peripheral devices to their computers. HTML, an acronym for 'Hyper-Text Markup Language', is the primary markup language used by web designers to create web pages and information that can be displayed in a web browser. Wi-Fi is based on the 802.11 standard first introduced by the Institute of Electrical and Electronics Engineers (IEEE), while USB and HTML standards are established by the USB Implementers Forum, Inc. (USB-IF) and World Wide Web Consortium (W3C), respectively.[851]

While the above are standards that are used to assist in regulating technology, it is this technology that enables data flows. Moreover, some standards have emerged to be included in national and supranational law. For data, ISO has been used to develop a framework of security for the data collected and stored.

International Organization for Standardisation [ISO]

In diverging to other technology that is used to save lives and enhance a human's life expectancy, the use of international standards to achieve this has been in the area of cardiovascular implants. For instance, 'the approval of a heart valve for the European market takes place in accordance with European and international (ISO) standards (ISO 5840 and the old EN 12006-1).[852] The basis for the new European ISO 5840 served the American ISO/CD 5840 which is also the basis for the approval of the US by the Food and Drug Administration'.[853] What can be demonstrated under this example is how the two jurisdictions of the US and EU have established a level of compatibility under the ISO standards. This is not new and ISO standards are used across a number of different government and business sectors. That is, ISO is a worldwide federation of national standards bodies.[854]

Increasing data breaches are a concern for most organisations.[855] With the constant changes in technology, there is an increasing need for individuals and entities to keep pace with the environment and adapt a process of change to enable the use of these new technologies in a safe manner.[856] This type of standard is used across many industries and is a form of self-regulation unless national laws specifically require that ISO be used. This chapter will only examine one of ISO's standards as they generally have the same key concepts and elements of data and its governance. Implementing an ISMS for certification under ISO/IEC 27001 is one way to ensure that your organisation follows a process for its information systems to provide an assurance to its vendors and third parties that the systems and data are appropriately protected.

851. *Ibid.*
852. Walter Eichinger, Sabine Däbritz and Rüdiger Lange, 'Update of the European Standards for Inactive Surgical Implants in the Area of Heart Valve Prostheses' (2007) 32(5) European Journal of Cardio-Thoracic Surgery 690, https://doi.org/10.1016/j.ejcts.2007.08.015.
853. *Ibid.*, p. 690.
854. ISO/IEC 27000:2018 Information Technology - Security Techniques - Information Security Management Systems, https://www.iso.org/obp/ui/#iso:std:iso-iec:27000:ed-5:v1:en.
855. Accedere, ISO/IEC 27 Certification Service, https://accedere.io/iso-certification-services.html.
856. *Ibid.*

The ISO/IEC 27001 certificate provides evidence of an audit of Confidentiality, Integrity, and Availability (CIA) of an organisation that follows an internationally recognised process to manage their customer's information or data.[857] The ISO/IEC 27017 demonstrates Cloud Service Providers' (CSPs') control over their cloud services. The ISO/IEC 27018 is used for personal data in the cloud. ISO 27001 combined with Cloud CSA CCM4 can enable an organisation to achieve the CSA STAR Level 2 Compliance.[858] On that basis, with the use of the Information Security Management system (ISMS) of standards, organisations can develop and implement a framework for managing the security of their information assets, including financial information, intellectual property, employee details, or information entrusted to them by customers or third parties. These standards can also be used to prepare for an independent assessment of their ISMS applied to the protection of information.[859] It enables a series of quarterly and annual audits. The resulting effect from the audits is that gaps are identified to be addressed. It is a continuous improvement life cycle.

A further and ensuing aspect of the quality management system is that it provides terms and definitions commonly used in the ISMS family of standards. It is applicable to all types and sizes of organisations (commercial enterprises, government agencies, not-for-profit organisations).[860] It further plays a significant role in enabling organisations to gauge the scope and limitations of the security programmes they have in place. Centrally, the security standard includes asset management, operational security, access control, and incident management. Operationally, an organisation would need to document and safeguard their physical assets. Procedures are to be established in relation to securing data, to control data sets that are more sensitive than others. It promotes and encourages entities to develop and maintain internal processes and procedures to report on and manage data. That is, have a procedure in place to rapidly respond to a breach and loss of data.

Richard Zarbo makes the point that 'systems do not produce quality, people do. According to Zarbo, management systems are required to guide people in their daily focus to lead, manage, and work toward consistent execution of quality goals'.[861] The benefit of their application is how the 'management structures hardwire human intention and behaviours at all levels of the enterprise because they form the underlying business system for leaders, managers, and employees. In this way, culture is transformed so that quality is the basis of management'.[862] The Fukushima incident in 2011 reminded the world community of how accidents can occur and have devastating impacts on human health, the economy and the environment. A consequence of this incident was the reliability that scientific laboratories reverted to current international standards such as ISO to direct and guide their investigations and analysis. Put another

857. *Ibid.*
858. *Ibid.*
859. *Ibid.*
860. *Ibid.*
861. Richard J Zarbo, 'MD, DMD, Management Systems to Structure Continuous Quality Improvement' (2022) 157(2) American Journal of Clinical Pathology 159-164, https://doi.org/10.1093/ajcp/aqab109.
862. *Ibid.*

way, radiological protection from this disaster needed to be measured across the environment and continues to be a 'matter of concern for members of the public and thus authorities likely to trust the quality of radioactivity data provided by accredited laboratories using common standards'.[863] Calmet et al. note that to assist in the management of laboratories investigating radioactivity, there are more than '150 international standards, most of which are published by ISO'.[864] The authors go on to say that:

> ISO is a worldwide federation of national standardisation bodies which has developed for years a full set of international standards on metrology including those on radioactivity test methods. Some of these standards are the result of collaboration with other international bodies such as the Bureau International des Poids et Mesures (BIPM), the International Electrotechnical Commission (IEC), the International Federation of Clinical Chemistry and Laboratory Medicine, the International Laboratory Accreditation Cooperation (ILAC), the International Union for Pure and Applied Chemistry (IUPAC), the International Union for Pure and Applied Physics, the International Commission on Radiation Units and Measurements (ICRU) and the International Organization of Legal Metrology. The international standards on test methods for radionuclides are reference documents to address the technical concerns that arise repeatedly from economic, scientific, technical and social stakeholders, both nationally and internationally.[865]

Viewed this way, there are a number of benefits that international standards can serve. They ensure that each entity is operating according to a set of agreed principles, concepts, norms and standards. The standards are international and form a level of international harmonisation. However, they are not laws unless they have been inserted into the national laws or EU law, and they are binding. By and large, ISO standards can also be categorised as a level of certification that is voluntary. Yet, of the jurisdictions examined in this book, such as India, under their current legal framework does legislate for the transfer of data to be undertaken according to ISO/IEC 27001.[866] The EU in accordance with Article 43 of the GDPR detail certification requirements requires Member States to ensure that those certification bodies are accredited by the supervisory authority which is competent pursuant to Article 55 or 56, or the national accreditation body named in accordance with Regulation (EC) No. 765/2008 of the European Parliament and of the Council in accordance with EN-ISO/IEC 17065/2012 and with the additional requirements established by the supervisory authority which is competent pursuant to Article 55 or 56.[867] However, the reference to ISO under Article

863. D. Calmet, et al., 'International Standards on Food and Environmental Radioactivity Measurement for Radiology Protection: Status and Perspectives' (2017) 173(1-3) Radiation Protection Dosimetry 55, https://doi.org/10.1093/rpd/ncw342.
864. *Ibid.*, p. 55.
865. *Ibid.* the Fukushima accident dramatically reminded the need during an accidental situation to rapidly check the radionuclide activity concentrations in the environment and foods, including drinking water, to ensure radiological protection of the public as well as to control food traded internationally. In these situations, the major constraint for a testing laboratory is how rapidly the data can become available, rather than the accuracy of the results.
866. The Information Technology Rules 2011, 7 and 8.
867. Regulation (EU) 2016/679 of the European Parliament and of the Council of 27 April 2016 on the protection of natural persons with regard to the processing of personal data and on the free

43 is limited to the powers of the supervisory body. In other words, the specification of ISO in this situation has no relevance to data transfers. Arguably, more could be done by the EU to harmonise certification of standards, particularly with third countries as they have by and large achieved internally amongst the Member States.

In another example, according to Kamesh Bajaj, the Japanese Standards Association released the Japanese Industrial Standards Q 15001, which adapted the Environmental Management Standard, ISO 14001 to PDP (Japanese Industrial Standards Committee).[868] This again led to the establishment of their privacy legislation. Bajaj further notes that 'privacy codes' of practice are administered in these countries by the industry bodies in the co-regulation model. They also perform crucial functions within the framework of statutory data protection regimes in countries such as Australia, New Zealand, Ireland, and the UK. Bajaj is correct if referring to codes that these countries and many others have included in their respective national laws for data governance. However, codes are not international standards and are generally up to the national or local organisation's approach to develop them for their own needs. Codes, even when they are included in national laws, are not necessarily described as to what and how they are to govern the data. That is, the laws do not specify the exact contents of a code and they are managerial and less technical. In accordance with Articles 40 and 41, the EU GDPR provides for Codes and specifies the content of this legal mechanism. Article 40.4(j) requires that the Codes specify data transfers to third countries outside of the EU. However, not all nation states have taken this approach, and it is an area of further research. Whereas international standards specify a consistent approach to managing a specific function that is attributed to data.

However, Tricia Sherer[869] notes that there are many similarities between ISO 27001 and the EU GDPR. While out of the scope of this chapter to examine all jurisdictions, it will highlight some of the similarities and gaps related to data transfers. Sherer is of the view that the GDPR is responsible for how personal data is collected and who is involved (the controller-processor has a level of responsibility). On the other side, ISO 27001 is a guidance tool that directs users about how the data is collected and ways to secure that data.[870] Sherer further asserts that under both ISO 27001 and the GDPR, 'companies must notify supervisory authorities of a breach of personal data within 72 hours of discovering it. ISO 27001 also contains standards designed to assure that information security incidents are handled in a consistent way. The difference is that the GDPR stipulates consumers be notified when the breach poses a high risk of infringing upon their individual rights'.[871] The GDPR focuses on protecting personal data, data confidentiality, and managing the risks to the rights of EU citizens and

movement of such data, and repealing Directive 95/46/EC (General Data Protection Regulation) (Text with EEA relevance) OJ L 119, Article 43.

868. Kamlesh Bajaj, 'Promoting Data Protection Standards through Contracts: The Case of the Data Security Council of India' (2012) Review of Policy Research 132-133, https://doi.org/10.1111/j.1541-1338.2011.00541.x.
869. Tricia Sherer, *Difference Between GDPR and ISO 27001*, 2020 https://reciprocity.com/difference-between-gdpr-and-iso-27001/.
870. *Ibid.*
871. *Ibid.*

residents. Whereas ISO 27001 is a framework that offers guidance on how organisations can implement clear and actionable policies for reducing risks that generate security incidents.[872]

Furthermore, to obtain ISO 27001 certification, organisations must make all legislative and contractual requirements related to their business and their customers available to auditors, so that the audit team can confirm compliance. It allows an entity to establish a preventative approach to managing data security, by forcing organisations to foresee risk. That is, foreseeing the risk to the data once collected and stored. How is that collection and more so storage going to be undertaken and by what? For instance, the EU GDPR manages the risk of personal data before it has been collected by an organisation, by providing a high level of protection of privacy over the Internet. The EU GDPR similarly mandates that all statutory and contractual requirements be made available to ensure compliance. ISO 27001 treats personal data as information security, and not so much on data flows. As such, those assets are subject to constraints around storage, length of storage, collection, and access. Those are also requirements of the EU GDPR.[873] Therefore, those legal frameworks that have by and large followed the EU model, would have a number of similarities with the ISO 27001. This is arguably a further area of research. The brief comparison undertaken by Sherer highlights that standards do provide a level of both interoperability and harmonisation. In my view, it is a step closer to a level of legal harmonisation because it is harmonising the operational implementation of the law. In this case, ISO 27001 is largely ensuring that there is a level of consistent and harmonised operational approaches to securing the data once collected from the data subject. This is a step beyond protecting privacy over the Internet and is somewhat removed from that process. Securing the data once collected is ensuring that the data is stored appropriately. The gap in the current ISO framework is two-fold. First, there is no standard specifically for transnational data flows. The benefits of development will strengthen the technical governance of data flows between systems and infrastructure and better manage its storage. Second, there are no standards specifically for privacy over the Internet internationally. This is something that Bajaj also identified.

That said, other scholars view ISO as a managerial rather than technical governance framework. If it holds true that data is the 'new oil', then a 'substantial increase in the research effort is needed to understand how organisations may secure information assets and what role major international standards play in providing guidance against an ever-increasing complexity'.[874] Culot et al. make an important point that 'a further motivation mentioned in the studies refers to the presence of governmental regulatory and promotion activities fostering ISO/IEC 27001 diffusion'.[875] Culot and others argue that:

872. Data Privacy Manager, *What Is the Difference Between GDPR and ISO 27001*, 2021, https://dataprivacymanager.net/what-is-the-difference-between-gdpr-and-iso-27001/.
873. *Ibid.*
874. Giovanna Culot, Guido Nassimbeni, Matteo Podrecca and Marco Sartor, 'The ISO/IEC 27001 Information Security Management Standard: Literature Review and Theory-Based Research Agenda' (2021) TQM Journal, 2021, DOI: 10.1108/TQM-09-2020-0202.
875. *Ibid.*

> The past decade has seen a progressive intensification of national (e.g., in the USA, the 'National Strategy to Cyberspace Security') and international initiatives (e.g., the Organization for Economic Cooperation and Development – OECD guidelines, European-level initiatives such as the recent EU Cybersecurity act). Overall, these initiatives have been contributing to the dissemination of ISS awareness; some of them have fostered explicitly the ISO/IEC 27001 certification, as in the case of Japan. The Australian Government preferred ISO/IEC 27001 over other ISS standards because of its flexibility in accommodating local legal requirements.[876]

To conclude, ISO enables an organisation to develop and apply flexible controls to suit a business. Importantly, it enables risks to be identified and control mechanisms to be established so that risks are managed and minimised as far as possible. They add a further layer of trust, confidence and certainty to an otherwise highly fragmented legal framework, by establishing some operational harmonisation. It achieves a level of compliance that can and would complement national, regional and international law. That said, binding corporate laws have emerged as another area of non-government regulation or soft law instrument that assists with the management of cross-border data transfers as Binding Corporate Rules. The next section will examine how they have been applied to transnational data movements.

§11.02 BINDING CORPORATE RULES

BCRs are generally authorised by national DPAs in the EU for transfers of personal data outside of the EU but within a corporate group, and the APEC CBPR system.[877] BCRs, similar to most other regulatory tools examined in this book, are nothing new. However, in the 'digital age, data protection is of increasing concern to governments, individuals, and companies alike'.[878] Lokke Moerel wrote in 2012, was of the view that by then, most advanced industrial societies face essentially the same dilemma of how to regulate these vast flows of personal information, but their governments have chosen substantially different solutions to do so. A decade on and nothing has generally changed. It could be argued that increasingly, there is divergence rather than convergence. As highlighted earlier in chapter 1, countries are at very different stages of developing and implementing data laws. For instance, many African nations, which are not represented in this book are only relatively newcomers to the data protection legal landscape. In the past decade, most countries in Asia are in a similar position. Yet, the EU, the UK, Australia, New Zealand, the US and Canada, amongst others, have been operating in this area of the law for more than twenty years. Moerel further notes that 'government regulation in the area of data protection needs to balance the interests

876. *Ibid.*
877. Joint work between experts from the Article 29 Working Party and from APEC Economies, on a referential for requirements for Binding Corporate Rules submitted to national Data Protection Authorities in the EU and Cross Border Privacy Rules submitted to APEC CBPR Accountability Agents, p. 5, https://www.apec.org/docs/default-source/groups/ecsg/20140307_referential-bcr-cbpr-reqs.pdf.
878. Lokke Moerel, *Binding Corporate Rules: Corporate Self-Regulation of Global Transfers*, Oxford Scholarship Online (2012), p. 37.

of organisations that use personal data against the potential harm such use could cause individuals'.[879] This section will use the EU as an example of how BCRs operate under the GDPR.

Nonetheless, they were first introduced back in 2003 under Article 29 Data Protection Working Party ('A29WP'). Upon the implementation of the GDPR in 2018, BCRs were reaffirmed by:

> personal data protection policies which are adhered to by a controller or processor established on the territory of a Member State for transfers or a set of transfers of personal data to a controller or processor in one or more third countries within a group of undertakings, or group of enterprises engaged in a joint economic activity.[880]

These rules are different from international standards, as they have not been established by an international institution. They are generally internal to an organisation that develops the framework to suit its own internal needs. This is particularly the case when transnational entities have offices located in multiple countries and are required to comply with local national and supranational laws. In this fragmented environment, BCRs can assist an organisation to achieve compliance across multiple jurisdictions. In this situation, organisations look to the government to set the minimum standard for data flows and their protection, while the organisation itself establishes international corporate rules that go beyond government regulation. Conversely, they may work in reverse and could be used by an organisation to avoid complying with the laws of multiple jurisdictions. Arguably though, as data laws have become more mainstream, the willingness and need for organisations to comply with government regulations are significantly greater today. Thus, and similar to international standards, BCRs are voluntary in terms of development, implementation and compliance. They are subject to an organisation's resources for undertaking necessary action to review, audit and improve their function. Arguably, in times of financial stress, this is often an area that is neglected while the company focuses on staying economically viable.

Article 47(2) of the EU GDPR sets the minimum requirements for the content of BCRs, while A29WP provides detailed guidance on the elements and principles to be contained in BCRs for controllers and processors separately through Working Documents. More broadly, in relation to data transfers, Article 47(2)(b) states that: BCR are to specify at least: the data transfers or set of transfers, including the categories of personal data, the type of processing and its purposes, the type of data subjects affected and the identification of the third country or countries in question.[881] The approval of BCRs is to be undertaken by the supervisory authority in accord with the consistency

879. *Ibid.*, p. 37.
880. Regulation (EU) 2016/679 of the European Parliament and of the Council of 27 April 2016 on the protection of natural persons with regard to the processing of personal data and on the free movement of such data, and repealing Directive 95/46/EC (General Data Protection Regulation) (Text with EEA relevance) OJ L 119, Article 47. Also *see* Christopher Kuner, *Transborder Data Flows and Privacy Law*, Oxford University Press (2013), p. 93.
881. *Ibid.*, Article 47(2)(B).

rules set out in Article 63. Therefore, Article 63 requires that in order to contribute to the consistent application of this Regulation throughout the Union, the supervisory authorities shall cooperate with each other and, where relevant, with the Commission, through the consistency mechanism.[882] While silent on the level of consistency, it is nevertheless, a level of harmonisation that is being achieved. In practice, not having a harmonised set of BCRs adds no value to an organisation's management of data. Therefore, consistency or harmonisation is the best option because it established economic and administrative efficiencies. For example, an entity located in the UK with an office in Australia, India, Singapore, Indonesia, the US and Canada has no incentive to establish BCRs that are as fragmented as the national data laws of these countries. BCRs can at a technical level ensure each office operates in a consistent and harmonised way. Australia is another state that has established BCR, [883] according to APP 8.2(a). However, the Privacy Commissioner's Guidelines provide a level of support to the use of BCRs by international organisations, at least where the BCRs reflect 'the intercorporate global privacy policy that satisfies EU standards'.[884] Problematic though is that under the Guidelines they take a minimalist approach, whereby, there is no requirement as to the contents required of the BCRs. Thus, for a country such as Australia which does not have an AD with the EU, any transfer of data from Australia to a Member State of the EU, such as Slovenia, BCRs are the appropriate tool, within a multinational organisation. Problematic though is the lack of accountability or oversight of the BCRs.

For multinational companies, BCR can serve as an 'effective global policy, of an internal standard for PDP within the group. Indeed, they apply indiscriminately to the whole corporate group, regardless of the establishment of the subsidiaries or of data subjects' citizenship'.[885] In reinforcing the above, Proust and Bartoli are of the view that BCRs contribute to harmonising practices and alleviate the risks associated with the processing of personal data, in particular within the entities of the group established in countries lacking PDP legislation. Yet, their contribution to harmonisation cannot be over-stated. BCRs do not operate beyond a single organisation. They are international and any level of harmonisation achieved is limited to the organisation that adopted them. While not legally binding, they do come with an internal binding factor. Proust and Bartoli argue that if implemented correctly, they can be binding on employees. Therefore, BCRs do provide a level of trust to data subjects that their personal data is being handled within an organisation to a level, providing protection from the misuse of that data. The authors in espousing their benefits make the point that BCRs bring a globalised response to the issues associated with international data

882. *Ibid.*, Article 63.
883. Anna von Dietze and Anne-Marie Allgrove, 'Australian Privacy Reforms – An Overhauled Data Protection Regime for Australia' (November 2014) 4(4) International Data Privacy Law, 333, https://doi.org/10.1093/idpl/ipu016.
884. Australian Privacy Commissioner's Guidelines, 2019, p. 8, https://www.oaic.gov.au/__data/assets/pdf_file/0009/1125/app-guidelines-july-2019.pdf.
885. Olivier Proust and Emmanuelle Bartoli, 'Binding Corporate Rules: A Global Solution for International Data Transfers' (2012) 2(1) International Data Privacy Law 36, https://doi.org/10.1093/idpl/ipr023.

transfers within the same corporate group. They also enable companies to communicate more openly with their clients, suppliers, and employees regarding their data processing activities and the protection of personal data. Beyond a legal obligation, BCRs are nowadays perceived as a competitive advantage.[886] Moreover, their development can extend to also include compliance arrangements in relation to infrastructure, training, communication, audits and assessments.[887]

That being the case, the rise of BCRs will only add to the already complex toolbox for the governance of data across international borders. It is argued that while this discussion has been limited to the EU, under the GDPR, there are minimum requirements for what BCRs are to contain, although somewhat limited in relation to data transfers. In fact, this is an area that requires urgent attention by legal and policy scholars to ensure there is a consistent and coherent approach taken by nation states to ensure that BCRs do not create a further regulatory burden, but rather, reduce compliance costs. The next section examines SCC.

§11.03 STANDARD CONTRACTUAL CLAUSES

SCC in addition to BCRs have also emerged as another tool in the toolbox to manage cross-border data flows, in the absence of any data AD.[888] Regional institutions including the EU and ASEAN have developed comprehensive models and examples of SCCs. Thus, this section will only discuss the EU and ASEAN. This section does not examine the clause or compare the current-day standardised clauses. Importantly, it highlights how they came under intense scrutiny by the courts. The subtle but important comparison is how the respective institutions refer to clauses that function for the same outcome. That is, in the EU, they are referred to as SCCs; throughout ASEAN they are called MCCs[889] – *see* Appendix One for standard MCC.

In highlighting their importance in transnational data flows, according to a 2020 study by 'European trade associations, SCCs are the most widely used mechanism for data transfers, and 90% of the SCCs are used for business-to-business data transfers'.[890] 'The study found that 70% of SMEs used SCCs. Of significance was that the costs associated with using SCCs are higher than those associated with participating in

---

886. *Ibid.*, p. 39.
887. Hutton and Williams LLP, *Cross-Border Data Transfer Mechanisms,* Center for Information Policy Leadership (2015), Center for Information Policy Leadership, p. 4. Also *see* Organisation for Economic Co-operation and Development, Mapping commonalities in regulatory approaches to cross-border data transfers, TAD/TC/WP, (2020)15/FINAL.
888. European Commission, European Commission adopts new tools for safe exchanges of personal data, https://ec.europa.eu/commission/presscorner/detail/en/ip_21_2847 Also *see*, Commission Implementing Decision, on standard contractual clauses for the transfer of personal data to third countries pursuant to Regulation (EU) 2016/679 of the European Parliament and of the Council, https://ec.europa.eu/info/system/files/1_en_annexe_acte_autonome_cp_part1_v5_0.pdf.
889. ASEAN Model Contractual Clauses for Cross Border Data Flows, 2021, p. 4, https://asean.org/wp-content/uploads/3-ASEAN-Model-Contractual-Clauses-for-Cross-Border-Data-Flows_Final.pdf.
890. Congressional Research Services, *Data Flows, Online Privacy, and Trade Policy* (2020), p. 16, https://sgp.fas.org/crs/misc/R45584.pdf.

Privacy Shield.'[891] The Privacy Shield had been a long-standard mutual arrangement between the EU and the US to allow for the transfer of data between the two jurisdictions. Yet, in relation to cost, it varied 'depending on how many SCCs an entity may need (depending on the number of third parties to which it transfers data) and how much information it already has regarding its data collection, management practices, and data flows'.[892] However, there may be situations where transfers are not possible using SCCs because there are not sufficient supplemental measures in place to eliminate the risks of foreign intelligence surveillance, such as when the recipient needs to have access to the unencrypted data.

Nonetheless, while they have arguably served the business sector well, these clauses have not come without their own challenges and scrutiny. Since 2020, the EU GDPR SCCs,[893] an unassuming set of default contractual terms for data transfer, have drawn the attention of companies around the world. On that basis, in its decision in *Data Protection Commissioner v. Facebook Ireland Ltd and Maximillian Schrems* ('*Schrems II*')[1] the European Court of Justice (CJEU) abruptly redrew the landscape for exchanging personal data across borders.[894] The CJEU struck down the EU-US Privacy Shield, the limited 'AD' that had allowed free commercial data flows between Europe and the USA under Article 45 of the GDPR. The Court upheld the validity of SCCs, the other main avenue for cross-border transfers, but set major conditions on their use.[895] Laura Bradford, Mateo Aboy and Kathleen Liddell are of the view the CJEU missed the 'opportunity to clarify how to transfer data safely using "accountability" when local and EU law conflict'.[896] For Bradford et al., 'the court repudiated or made unstable the two principal mechanisms for data transfers to the USA'.[897] As noted by the authors, the resulting effect was to 'reduce the available channels for transferring personal data from the EU to third countries'.[898] Bradford and others make a further point that three sets of clauses have been approved: two between an EU controller and a controller in a third country, and one between an EU controller and a non-EU EC processor.[899] Moreover, for Bradford Aboy and Liddell:

> Each of these versions requires the data importer's agreement to the data protection law of the exporter in processing the data, to name data subjects as third-party beneficiaries under the contract, and to agree to answer for breaches in a court of a member state. These clauses must be used exactly in the approved form unless an amendment is approved in advance by a data protection authority. The EC

891. *Ibid.*, p. 16.
892. *Ibid.* One investigation found that most firms will need to hire specialist data compliance and consulting firms to assist with data mapping, data management and auditing. Specifically, data mapping is the biggest challenge cited, as most SMEs lack the knowledge and tools to do so themselves.
893. Laura Bradford, Mateo Aboy and Kathleen Liddell, 'Standard Contractual Clauses for Cross-Border Transfers of Health Data after Schrems II' (2021) 8(1) Journal of Law and the Biosciences 1, https://doi.org/10.1093/jlb/lsab007.
894. *Ibid.*
895. *Ibid.*
896. *Ibid.*
897. *Ibid.*
898. *Ibid.*
899. *Ibid.*

> released new SCC 2.0 clauses that have a dual nature as both private contract and public instrument granting enforceable rights to third parties under domestic law. The Clauses contain three sets of interlocking obligations for the parties to (i) abide themselves by GDPR fundamental principles (Appendix 1/Annex 1) (ii) extend enforceable rights and remedies to data subjects under the law of the exporter, (main body) and (iii) adopt technical and organizational measures, tailored to the specific risks of the transfer, to ensure security of processing (Appendix 2/Annex 2). Once the exporter chooses to transfer under the clauses, the parties are in effect opting into an additional set of default legal requirements calibrated to ensure continuous protection to data subjects.[900]

Viewed this way, the SCCs have evolved as the law, society, and judiciary have had to resolve data transfers. Arguably, there is an increasing awareness of the impacts of personal data being transferred around the world. The resulting effect is that regulators and the judiciary will be called upon to determine whether the law has been complied with, and amend the law where there are gaps to balance the economic needs with that of protecting the data. In addition to the above, Barbara Sandfuchs makes the point from Schrems-II that SCCs function at two levels. First is from controller to controller, and the second is from controller to processor.[901] Claire Jervis, also commenting on the case of Schrems-II, notes that the SCC (adopted under Article 46(2)(c) GDPR[47]) (which were, in fact, the focus of the case) were not declared invalid as opposed to the Privacy Shield, their use did require adjustment in order to address analogous concerns around compliance.[902] Jervis notes the 'obligation on controllers to ensure that the undertakings contained in such clauses could be fulfilled in practice was, therefore, amplified'.[903] Jervis is of the view that as a result of this case, 'controllers must now conduct their due diligence with reference to the factors prescribed by the EDPB and in the UK, the Information Commissioner. It is clear from these proceedings that the preoccupation of the Regulation, and those responsible for its enforcement, is with compliance in practice'.[904] Arguably there has been a greater risk-based (transfer risk assessments) approach adopted in requiring controllers to undertake further due diligence. They are complex, and as there is increasing interest by the public as to what and how their data is being transferred and under what mechanisms and controls, contractual clause will be reviewed when challenged in the judiciary. This is because they have become a tool of convenience and choice for organisations to transfer data internationally.

900. *Ibid.*, p. 20.
901. Barbara Sandfuchs, 'The Future of Data Transfers to Third Countries in Light of the CJEU's Judgment C-311/18 – Schrems II' (March 2021) 70(3) GRUR International246, https://doi.org/10.1093/grurint/ikaa204.
902. Claire E M Jervis, International Transfers: *Johnson v. Secretary of State for the Home Department*, 2020 and Diplomatic Missions, *International Data Privacy Law*, 2021; p. 5, https://doi.org/10.1093/idpl/ipab026.
903. *Ibid.*, p. 5.
904. *Ibid.*

§11.04 CONCLUSION

This chapter has briefly outlined one international standard that has been introduced that achieves a level of management over operational aspects of securing data. It is arguably a step further than government regulation, which in my view sets the minimum standard. ISO builds on that standard. It also gives effect to transnational trade laws such as GATS. Article XVI in relation to Market Access stipulates that the 'country must provide access to foreign supplies of a particular sector to its market if it lists a particular sector on its Schedule of Specific Commitments. A market-access commitment made in a member's Schedule of Specific Commitments constitutes that member's commitment to the open flow of related services'.[905]

Centrally international standards while having many benefits are often beneficial to medium and larger organisations that have the resources and capital to purchase the service. As the chapter has discussed, they are often voluntary unless national governments have enshrined them into law. For example, India, as part of managing data has enshrined ISO standards into their current-day national laws. Whether this is retained in the forthcoming data laws, remains to be seen. Nonetheless, standards when adopted require organisations to change the way they do things, such as having highly visible international policies, procedures, guidelines and processes to ensure that the requirements of ISO are met. They can act as a level of interoperability and/or harmonisation.

However, it is argued their value in either is somewhat limited in relation to the law. They serve as a managerial and technical tool for government data beyond the GDPR or Australian PA for example. An ensuing question arises: is there a reference to such standards within FTAs at the technical level? A further ensuring question is: should they be inserted into all data national laws? It is argued that a seamless pathway to internationalisation needs to occur, from international law, national law reform, inclusions of standards such as ISO into all national laws, and FTAs.

They are in my view a valuable tool for managing cross-border data flows, and national laws should specify either ISO or some other highly regarded international standard. The important point to make is that whatever standard is adopted it should provide a level of harmonisation by building on interoperability. Doing so will provide another layer of trust and confidence, and help to unlock data flows within and across the digital economy.

In addition to standards, the emergence of BCRs and SCCs has been instrumental in adding a further layer to the otherwise complex but important governance of data flows. BCRs similar to standards are voluntary and are technically based within an organisation that is located in one or more or multiple jurisdictions. As an internal tool, they are effective in ensuring employees not only follow the law but also, implement consistent approaches whether in Singapore or the UK.

---

905. Joshua Blume, 'Reading the Trade Tea Leaves: A Comparative Analysis of Potential United States WTO-GATS Claims Against Privacy, Localization, and Cybersecurity Laws' (2018) Georgetown Journal of International Law 809.

Yet, they can be problematic, where the national laws diverge significantly, making them complex and difficult for organisations to comply with because a single BCR would need to address the gaps in both national laws. Conversely, problems can arise where an organisation uses them to diverge away from the national laws, and gaps in compliance emerge. In this case, they can be used as a mere marketing tool to show the world they have a robust framework in place to manage data flows. In practice though, this is far from the actual reality. In part, they do harmonise internal practices and procedures, at a national and international level.

Therefore, it is argued more needs to be undertaken by nation states to ensure BCRs are addressed similarly to the EU GDPR, for example, expressing the contents required with a BCR. The current minimum requirements need to be reviewed to ensure they meet the current day requirements of data flows and their economic benefit, along with a high level of protection of that data. Positively, it has been reported that BCRs when developed properly can reduce regulatory burden, even though there is an administrative cost to their implementation.

SCCs, are another tool that has emerged as one of the leading mechanisms of choice used by organisations to transfer data internationally. Contractual arrangements for goods and services have been effective in international trade for decades. This is nothing new. What is new, is the area being contracted. SCCs have been established at the regional level within the EU and ASEAN. Subsequently, as with any contractual arrangement they have not come without their challenges. This chapter highlighted how in the recent *Shrems* case, the court highlighted the proper function of the SCCs, and consequently the EU has revised its SCC.

These provide a higher level of certainty than standards and the BCRs because they can be enforced by the court, their move towards a risk-based approach has in my view been a welcomed introduction. Standards can be enforced when incorporated into a code that has legislative backing to be enforced. It is this risked based approach that needs to be enshrined all the way through the life cycle of data governance. Nonetheless, SCCs perform an important function in different organisations. For instance, entity A located in Australia can under an SCC transfer data to entity B located in Slovenia, Europe.

Finally, and even though this book it arguing for the internationalisation of data flows law specifically, this does not mean that the standards, BCRs or SCCs, should be discarded and they no longer have a place within the data landscape. They do and will continue to play an important function at an international and technical level, supporting and underpinning the operation of national and international law.

PART III Data Flows and Other Developments

CHAPTER 12

Obstacles to Data Flows and Digital Economic Development

This chapter explores the obstacles to data flows. It will highlight how apart from the lack of a coherent and consistent legal framework at the national and international level, data sovereignty is significantly influencing this area of the law. This chapter does not discuss the national security obstacles that have been imposed by jurisdictions that can restrict the movement of data across international borders.

Against *the backdrop of the above, there are a number of obstacles that have been imposed by regulators to govern data flows. Centrally, there are control obligations imposed by national laws that require the user of the data to obtain a level of consent from the data subject for their data to be transferred internationally. Second, in some jurisdictions, there is the regulation of BCR and in the private international law sphere, there are SCC. In addition to these legal mechanisms, the rise in the use of standards or codes highlights other mechanisms available that, in part place another level of obstacles on the free flow of data. Some of these are enforceable, while others are not. However, this chapter examines the increasing importance that is being placed on data localisation. It diverges from the law briefly and examines the area of a digital-data tax. While not often thought of as an obstacle to data flows, taxes are an economic and regulatory burden to businesses. However, it does not argue that this sector should not be taxed in the future. It does not discuss national security.*

Nonetheless, other forms of obstacles that are imposed on businesses by the government are licensing and certification regimes. This is a common response to industry sectors that require a level of regulation. However, this will not be examined in any depth. Importantly, this chapter reinforces the need for the internationalisation of systems, policy and the law. It will propose an international organisation be established to manage the call for a Global Tax. Such an organisation can have a dual role, to manage data flows and the tax, which will find its operation. Such an organisation could not only collect tax but could also act as a repository and collector of all international data transfers. While many will argue that it would not be palatable to establish either, the conversation needs to take place. Of the jurisdictions examined in this chapter, it will be demonstrated how India, to date, has established a higher level of localisation control than any other jurisdiction. This in part can be attributed to its reliance on the Internet outsourcing economy, and it along with Indonesia has not established specific data laws.

§12.01 INTRODUCTION

Data in the digital age will bring many economic, social, health and environmental benefits. As far back as 1998, it was identified by Peter Swier and Robert Litan[906] that data flows were increasing', due to the continued spread of information technologies such as client-server systems and corporate intranets'.[907] The authors note that data laws generally 'limit transborder data flows directly and confront organisations' expectations to be able to circulate information freely inside their firewalls and other security arrangements'.[908] Viewed this way, the current data laws examine all, at various levels place restrictions and obstacles to data flowing freely around the world over the Internet. As highlighted in previous country chapters, there is a level of restrictions already placed on data transfers such as requiring data subjects' consent, contractual obligations, BCR or ADs in the case of the EU.

This has been reinforced by the OECD applying the services trade restrictiveness index (STRI).[909] The STRI (services trade restrictiveness index) highlights how 'burdensome domestic regulations that increase the costs of obtaining a license to operate or lower regulatory transparency hamper trade in services'.[910] This is the case for data flows. The varied legal approach taken domestically by national governments imposes a significant level of regulatory burden on business. These specific restrictions include that the cross-border transfer of personal data is possible when certain private-sector safeguards are in place.[911] Additionally, restrictions that have also been established impose an obligation on the receiving country to have a similar level of protection for

906. Peter Swier and Robert Latin, *World Data Flows, Electronic Commerce, and the European Privacy Directive*, Brookings Institute Press (1998).
907. *Ibid.*, p. 91.
908. *Ibid.*
909. Organisation for Economic Development and Cooperation: *OECD Services Trade Restrictiveness Index: Policy Trends up to 2022*, February 2022. The STRI scores countries by assessing various aspects of regulation that affect cross-border trade.
910. *Ibid.*, p. 14.
911. Frontier Economics, *The Value of Cross-Border Data Flows to Europe: Risks and Opportunities*, 2021, pp. 21-22.

that data, and in some circumstances is subject to approval on a case-by-case basis.[912] Importantly, the growing requirement for specific data to be stored locally, and in some cases a total prohibition of the transfer of specific data.[913] Moreover, the OECD note that developing a pathway for streamlining regulation would 'reduce the time and cost required for complying with administrative barriers and regulatory red tape'.[914] On the one hand, it is widely acknowledged that streamlining regulation reduces the cost of doing business. On the other hand, and while not calling for legal harmonisation, further streamlining regulation of national domestic laws pertaining to data flows would go some way to a level of harmonisation. The ensuing question is whether such an approach would extend interoperability? This could be undertaken through a pilot project to research the extent of how such a proposal would benefit data in the digital economy – outside of the current legal framework. It is argued that taking this step would be a move to a deeper level of harmonisation of the data laws.

However, just as there is this increasing acknowledgement has many benefits, and in addition to the above, there are obstacles and barriers emerging that as they begin to be implemented by nation states, data flows are being restricted. This chapter will discuss the emerging issue of data localisation, otherwise, known as data nationalism or data sovereignty. The terms will be used interchangeably in this chapter. However, the ensuing question is what does data localisation constitute? John Selby asserts that data localisation has two meanings:

> The first is a policy whereby national governments compel Internet content hosts, to store data about Internet users, in their country on servers located within the jurisdiction of that national government (localised data hosting). The data stored in the local jurisdiction may be either the sole copy of the data or a required local copy of data sent for storage or processing in another jurisdiction. The second form of data localisation is a policy, whereby national governments compel Internet service providers to 'route data packets sent between Internet users located in their jurisdictions across networks located only within their jurisdiction (localised data routing)'.[915]

The introduction of these policy initiatives into law is only beginning to be fully understood by regulators around the world. While the first definition of what Selby argues can be seen across a number of countries, which will be explored later in the chapters. The second point made by Selby is far from understood by policymakers, regulators and governments, including the broader business community. In referring to Chander and Lê,[916] Selby argues that it is these data packets that have to be routed

912. *Ibid.*, p. 21.
913. *Ibid.*
914. Organisation for Economic Development and Cooperation: *OECD Services Trade Restrictiveness Index: Policy Trends up to 2022*, February 2022, p. 14.
915. John Selby, 'Data Localization Laws: Trade Barriers or Legitimate Responses to Cybersecurity Risks, or Both?' (2017) 25(3) International Journal of Law and Information Technology 214, https://doi.org/10.1093/ijlit/eax010.
916. Anupam Chander and Uyên P. Lê, 'Data Nationalism' 64 Emory Law Journal 677 (2015), https://scholarlycommons.law.emory.edu/elj/vol64/iss3/2.

through domestic servers. This chapter will examine what countries examined in this book have established or otherwise as localisation rules.

Nonetheless, and against the backdrop of the above, Nigel Cory notes that:

> Data localisation can be explicitly required by law or is the de facto result of a culmination of other restrictive policies that make it unfeasible to transfer data. That is, an organisation's policy requires companies to store a copy of the data locally, requiring companies to process data locally, and mandating individual or government consent for data transfers. These policies represent a new barrier to global digital trade. Cutting off data flows or making such flows harder or more expensive puts foreign firms at a disadvantage. This is especially the case for small and solely Internet-based firms and platforms that do not have the resources to deal with burdensome restrictions in every country in which they may have customers. In essence, these tactics constitute 'data protectionism' because they keep foreign competitors out of domestic markets.[917]

Viewed this way, data in the digital economy is going to face headwinds. As countries around the world being to implement such a policy approach, data will be restricted. It will dilute economic activity. However, central to the debate on data localisation is that some governments are wanting to protect citizens' personal information. Conversely, it is argued that data localisation policies and laws have emerged as a result and response to ongoing and increasing security breaches of technology and obtaining personal data. Later, in 2020, Nigel Cory and Luke Dascoli, leading scholars wrote on data localisation.

The spread of data localisation policy and legal initiatives to other countries and data types poses a growing threat to the potential for an open, rules-based, and innovative global digital economy. Data localisation makes the Internet less accessible and secure, more costly and complicated, and less innovative. Surprisingly, as geopolitical tension rises across the world, both democratic and non-democratic countries are embracing the idea of data localisation. It is estimated that a 'one-unit increase in a country's data restrictiveness index (DRI) results (cumulatively, over a five-year period) in a 7% decrease in its volume of gross output traded, a 1.5% increase in its prices of goods and services among downstream industries, and a 2.9% decrease in its economy-wide productivity'.[918]

917. Nigel Cory, 'Cross-Border Data Flows: Where Are the Barriers, and What Do They Cost?' (2017) Information Technology & Innovation Foundation 1-2.

918. *Ibid.*, pp. 1-2. Forced data localisation also undermines the potential for shared governance. Countries can work together to address legitimate concerns about data transfers, such as to prevent espionage, to maintain financial oversight, and to conduct law enforcement investigations, while still allowing data to flow freely. Of course, countries should create robust data privacy frameworks that protect consumers and address national security concerns, but policymakers should do so in a transparent, targeted, and balanced way to avoid unnecessarily costly and restrictive policies given their economic and trade impacts. This is a crucial distinction to differentiate policymakers in those countries that try to misuse data localisation as a legitimate data protection tool, when it is not.

Australia

In 2012, Australia passed the Personally Controlled Electronic Health Records (PCEHR) Act, section 77 of which prohibits the transfer of health records outside of Australia, with certain exceptions. Subsection 1 provides:

> The System Operator, a registered repository operator, a registered portal operator or a registered contracted service provider that holds records for the purposes of the PCEHR system (whether or not the records are also held for other purposes) or has access to information relating to such records, must not: '(a) hold the records, or take the records, outside Australia; or (b) process or handle the information relating to the records outside Australia; or (c) cause or permit another person: (i) to hold the records, or take the records, outside Australia; or (ii) to process or handle the information relating to records outside Australia'.[919]

Subsection 77(2) permits the transfer, processing, or handling of data outside of Australia if such records do not include 'personal information in relation to a consumer' or 'identifying information of an individual or entity'. On this basis, a foreign company that is in possession of Australian health data can only store that data on the territory of Australia.

Canada

Canada's PIPEDA[920] does not prohibit the transfer of personal data outside of Canada. It does not require that personal data be stored locally on the territory of Canada. However, as highlighted earlier in the book, businesses are responsible for all the data collected, processed, transferred, and stored. Additionally, they are mandated to provide protection of that data at all times.

EU–UK

Specifically, the EU-UK do not have data localisation laws, in the same way as Australia and the other states discussed in this chapter. However, the data subject has certain rights pertaining to their personal data being transferred outside of the EU. That is, a data subject's consent is required before their data can leave the EU. Additionally, contractual obligations, BCR or an AD can be used to transfer data. While this book has only focused on the transfer of data, there are other rights a data subject is entitled to in relation to their personal data. That is the right to access, disclosure and deletion of their data. Yet, these additional rights are not consistently established by many other jurisdictions.

919. *Personally Controlled Electronic Health Records Act 2012* (Cth), No. 63, section 77.

920. *Personal Information Protection and Electronic Documents Act*, S.C. 2000, c. 5. However, at the local level, British Columbia and Nova Scotia in Canada both require personal information maintained by 'public bodies' (hospitals) to be stored locally unless the explicit consent to transfer such data outside of Canada and be accessed by non-Canadians is obtained from the data subject.

Martina Ferracane, argues that conditional data flows are common and can only be undertaken if certain conditions are fulfilled.[921] Ferracane makes the point that the conditions can apply to the recipient country, to the company, or to both the recipient country and the company. In most cases, it is enough that one of the alternative options is fulfilled in order for the company to transfer data abroad. If the conditions are stringent and cannot be fulfilled by the recipient country or the company, the measure results in a ban on the transfer of data abroad.[922] Ferracane states that:

> The European regime of data protection is typical example of a conditional regime. Under European law, conditions apply to both the recipient country and the transferring entity. In the first case, the company can transfer data abroad to countries with an 'adequate level of protection'. In the second case, even when the recipient country is not deemed adequate, data can be transferred and processed overseas if the transferee fulfils certain conditions. The most common condition is the consent of the data subject for cross-border transfer. This condition, as is also the case for most of the conditions, can be more or less strict, and its interpretation or enforcement may vary. For example, the General Data Protection Regulation (GDPR) requires that the data subject has 'explicitly' consented to the data transfer abroad, while the previous EU directive allowed controllers to rely on an 'unambiguous' consent by the data subject.[923]

In addition to the above, an 'alternative means to fulfil the conditions under EU law and other conditional regimes include the use of BCR or the condition that the transfer is necessary to complete the contract concluded with the data subject. There are also exceptions for cases where a transfer is necessary for medical treatment, or where transfers serve the public interest; or when a transfer falls within the scope of international judicial cooperation. Also, the 'information transferred may already be in the public domain – e.g., already published and available legally on the internet'.[924] Thus, apart from the general discussion surrounding data localisation being the most significant impediment to data flows, the conditional approach has also imparted a level of restrictions on data transfers. The level of economics is not fully understood. However, these conditions and any future additional conditions will only dilute the economic activity and outcomes data will bring to the digital economy.

India

Generally, it is understood that most jurisdictions impose conditions on when and how data can be transferred (commonly called data export restrictions) and very few resort to physical data localisation requirements.[925] Justification in support of data localisation by the governments varies from citizen's privacy, checks on freedom of speech,

921. Martina Ferracane, *Restrictions on Cross-Border Data Flows: A Taxonomy*, European Center for international Political Economy, Working Paper No. 1/2017, p. 5.
922. *Ibid.*, p. 5.
923. *Ibid.*
924. *Ibid.*
925. Arya Tripathy, *Cross Border Data Transfer: India's Attempt at Data Localisation* https://www.psalegal.com/cross-border-data-transfer-indias-attempt-at-data-localization. Note this section comes from earlier work undertaken by the author Robert Walters, along with Professor, Dr Shanthakumar, Professor, Dr Mamata Biswal, Professor, Dr Ranita Nagar, Dr Deesha Khaire,

protecting local business, and corporate accountability, to data security, surveillance and national security. Table 12.1 highlights the complex and fragmented approach to data localisation in and across India.

Table 12.1[926] *Data Localisation Laws Throughout India*

Sr No.	*Policy/Act/Initiative*	*Mandate*
	Direct and Explicit Localisation	
1	Reserve Bank of India (RBI), Amendment to the Master Direction (MD) on KYC, (RBI, 10 May 2021)[927]	Revised regulations on electronic know your customer (eKYC) requirements which state that the technology infrastructure should be housed on the Regulated Entity's own premises and the video-based customer identification process connection and interaction (to do digital due diligence and verification of a customer) shall necessarily originate from its own secured network domain.
2	Securities and Exchange Board of India (SEBI), Circular No: SEBI/HO/MIRSD2/DOR/CIR/P/2020/221, (SEBI, 3 November 2020)[928]	Cybersecurity-related circular-Financial institutions should ensure complete protection and seamless control over ... critical systems ... while keeping the critical data within the legal boundary of India.

Ms Harasha Rajwanshi, Mr Soaham Bajpai: *Cross Border Data Flows and Data Adequacy United Kingdom & India,* A Government Report, ISBN 978-86272-837-0 (2022).

926. Robert Walters et al., *Cross Border Data Flows and Data Adequacy United Kingdom & India,* A Government Report, ISBN 978-86272-837-0 (2022), pp. 20-21.

927. Reserve Bank of India (RBI), Amendment to the Master Direction (MD) on KYC, (RBI, 10 May 2021), https://rbidocs.rbi.org.in/rdocs/notification/PDFs/NT354BE2BCC23B344982BD57937 37940EFF3.PDF.

928. Advisory for Financial Sector Organisations regarding Software as a Service based solution, https://www.sebi.gov.in/legal/circulars/nov-2020/advisory-for-financial-sector-organizati-ons-regarding-software-as-a-service-saas-based-solutions_48081.html (https://www.sebi.gov .in/legal/circulars/nov- 2020/advisory-for-fi nancial-sector-organizations-regarding-software-as-a-service-saas-basedsolutions_ 48081.html).

Sr No.	*Policy/Act/Initiative*	*Mandate*
	Direct and Explicit Localisation	
3	Different RBI Notifications.[929]	Rules force all payments to be stored in India. No bar on processing the data outside India, but data should be stored only in India after processing. the data should be deleted from the systems abroad and brought back to India no later than one business day or twenty-four hours from payment processing, whichever is earlier. To store payment data locally also applies to banks operating in India.
4	The Ministry of Electronics and Information Technology released Guidelines for Government Departments on Contractual Terms Related to Cloud Services.	Any government contracts contain a localisation clause mandating that all government data residing in cloud storage networks be located on servers in India.
5	FDI Policy 2017.	Requires all FDI-receiving entities in the broadcasting sector to ensure local storage and processing of subscriber data. It also prohibits the transfer of subscriber data outside India.
6	The Insurance Regulatory and Development Authority of India of 2017.	All original policyholder records should be maintained in India and obtain express consent from the data subject to transfer data outside India.
7	The Companies (Accounts) Rules, 2014.[930]	If financial information is primarily stored abroad, its backups must be stored in India.

929. Reserve Bank of India (RBI), Storage of Payment System Data, (RBI, 6 April 2018), https://rbi.org.in/scripts/NotificationUser.aspx?Mode = 0&Id = 11244: Reserve Bank of India (RBI), Statement on Developmental and Regulatory Policies, (RBI, 5 April 2018), https://rbi.org.in/Scripts/BS_PressReleaseDisplay.aspx?prid = 43574: Reserve Bank of India (RBI), First Bi-monthly Monetary Policy Statement, 2018-19, (RBI, 10 April 2018), https://rbi.org.in/scripts/BS_ViewBulletin.aspx?Id = 17479; Reserve Bank of India (RBI), Storage of Payment System Data, (RBI, 6 April 2013), https://m.rbi.org.in/Scripts/FAQView.aspx?Id = 130 (https://rbi.org.in/scripts/Notifi cation User.aspx?Mode = 0&Id = 11244) (https://rbi.org.in/Scripts/BS_PressReleaseDisplay.aspx?prid = 43574) (https://rbi.org.in/scripts/BS_ViewBulletin.aspx? Id = 17479) (https://m.rbi.org.in/Scripts/FAQView.aspx?Id = 130).

930. Rule 3(5) Companies (Accounts) Rules, 2014 mandates that: 'the back-up of the books of account and other books and papers of the company maintained in electronic mode, including at a place outside India, if any, shall be kept in servers physically located in India on a periodic basis'. Stephen Mathias and Naqeeb Ahmed Kazia, 'Collection, Storage and Transfer of Data in

Sr No.	*Policy/Act/Initiative*	*Mandate*
	Direct and Explicit Localisation	
8	National Data Sharing and Accessibility Policy (NDSAP).[931]	Mandates localisation of all government-related data, and allows sharing of all non-sensitive data for legitimate and registered use.
9	India's Unified Telecom License Agreement for Telecom Service Provider.[932]	Requires local storage and local processing of subscriber information and prohibits the transfer of (*i*) accounting information related to the subscriber and (*ii*) user information.
10	The Public Records Act 1993.[933]	Prohibits public records from being transferred out of India except for official public purposes.
	Indirect and De facto *Localisation*	
11	India's new Intermediary Guidelines and Digital Media Ethics Code, 2021.[934]	Includes a very short time period (seventy-two hours) to respond to government orders to remove illegal content that would create a de facto data localisation requirement for online intermediaries as it would otherwise be hard, if not impossible, for them to comply (and thus avoid fines and other penalties)

India' (8 February 2017) Lexology, http://www.lexology.com/library/detail.aspx?g=00e56cb6-b0ea-46b7-ab1b-1d52de3646d0.

931. National Data Sharing and Accessibility Policy, Indian Ministry of Science and Technology, 2012, https://dst.gov.in/national-data-sharing-and-accessibility-policy-0.
932. Amendments in Unified Access Service License Agreement, issued by the Ministry of Communications and IT, Government of India. As per Clause 1G(iv). Vikram Singh, Klaindhi Bhatia, *India: What's Driving Data Localisation in India?* 2020, https://www.mondaq.com/india/data-protection/928916/what39s-driving-data-localisation-in-india.
933. The Public Records Act 1993, section 4.
934. Ministry of Electronics and Information Technology Notification, The Gazette of India, 25 February 2021, https://egazette.nic.in/WriteReadData/2021/225464.pdf, Daniel Castro, *India's Intermediary Liability Law Out of Step With Global Norms* (ITIF, 11 May 2021), https://itif.org/publications/2021/05/11/indias-intermediary-liability-law-out-step-global-norms, https://egazette.nic.in/WriteReadData/2021/225464.pdf, https://itif.org/publications/2021/05/11/indias-intermediary-liability-law-outstepglobal-norms.

Sr No.	*Policy/Act/Initiative*	*Mandate*
	Direct and Explicit Localisation	
12	The Information Technology (Reasonable Security Practices and Procedures and Sensitive Personal Data or Information) Rules 2011 (Privacy Rules).[935]	Limited the transfer of data in cases only if it is necessary for the performance of the lawful contract or when the data subject consents to the transfer. However, the necessity requirement is not adequately explained, effectively limiting the transfer of data only when consent is given. Prohibits the transfer of sensitive personal data by a body corporate outside the country unless the other party can match the same level of data protection mandated under the IT Rules.

Over the years, the Indian government has passed sector-specific data localisation measures, however, it is now contemplating passing a more expansive, economy-wide proposal.[936] Major sector-specific localisation measures in India broadly cover matters relating to personal data, financial, tax, banking, payment data, mapping data, health and genomic data, ICT/Telecom data, govt. records and cloud services as well as something as recent as the non-personal data framework.[937] Restricting data flows has a statistically significant impact on a nation's economy, by reducing its total volume of trade, lowering its productivity, and increasing prices for downstream industries that increasingly rely on data.[938] Whether this current approach to data localisation will change when the proposed new data laws are implemented, is uncertain. It could go either way. That is, there could be further restrictions imposed. If so, this may significantly restrict the growth of India's digital economy and data flows into and out of the country.

Indonesia

Generally related to the public sector, the Indonesian government requires service providers providing 'public services' to store that data in the country. That is, Regulation 82 concerning Electronic System and Transaction Operation states 'Electronic System Operator for the public service is obligated to put the data centre and disaster recovery centre in Indonesian territory for the purpose of law enforcement,

935. Rules 3 & 7 The Information Technology (Reasonable Security Practices and Procedures and Sensitive Personal Data Information) Rules 2011.
936. Robert Walters et al., *Cross Border Data Flows and Data Adequacy United Kingdom & India*, A Government Report, ISBN 978-86272-837-0 (2022), pp. 20-21.
937. *Ibid.*, pp. 20-21.
938. *Ibid.*

protection, and enforcement of national sovereignty to the data of its citizens'.[939] Under the current framework, ESOs (electronic system operators) are divided into two groups: (1) public ESOs, and (2) private ESOs.[940] Public ESOs are government authorities and their appointed parties, while private ESOs include companies.[941] To date, only public ESOs are required to process and store data in Indonesia. Therefore, private ESOs are allowed to process and store data offshore, provided that they maintain the effectiveness of legal monitoring and enforcement in Indonesia.[942]

Japan

In Japan, the provision of personal information to a third party in a foreign country is restricted by Article 24 of the APPI and states that:

> A personal information handling business operators, except in those cases set forth in each item of the preceding Article, paragraph (1), shall, in case of providing personal data to a third party (excluding a person establishing a system conforming to standards prescribed by rules of the Personal Information Protection Commission as necessary for continuously taking action equivalent to the one that a personal information handling business operator shall take concerning the handling of personal data pursuant to the provisions of this Section; hereinafter the same in this Article) in a foreign country (meaning a country or region located outside the territory of Japan; hereinafter the same) (excluding those prescribed by rules of the Personal Information Protection Commission as a foreign country establishing a personal information protection system recognized to have equivalent standards to that in Japan in regard to the protection of an individual's rights and interests; hereinafter the same in this Article), in advance obtain a principal's consent to the effect that he or she approves the provision to a third party in a foreign country. In this case, the provisions of the preceding Article shall not apply.[943]

In addition to the above, there are restrictions placed on medical records.[944] On this basis, where there is a transfer of data to a third country, and the data subject has provided consent, the data subject must be informed as to the jurisdiction the data is going. While a good initiative, it again provides another layer of complexity for individuals and entities to understand their rights with the many subtle but important differences. Singapore, New Zealand along the US do not agree with data localisation. However, note that under the respective country chapters, Singapore, New Zealand

939. Regulation Concerning Electronic System and Transaction Operation, Law No. 82 of 2012, Article 17(2) (Government Gazette of the Republic of Indonesia Year 2012 No. 189), verified by Professor Sinta Dewi, Information Technology Law/Data Privacy Law, Fakultas Hukum Universitas Padjadjaran, Indonesia.
940. Baker McKenzie, 11 Things to Know: Data Centers Indonesia, p. 6, https://insightplus.bakermckenzie.com/bm/attachment_dw.action?attkey = .
941. *Ibid.*
942. *Ibid.*
943. Act on the Protection of Personal Information (APPI), Amended Act on the Protection of Personal Information, Personal Information Protection Commission, Japan, 2020, https://www.ppc.go.jp/files/pdf/APPI_english.pdf.
944. The Safety Management Guideline for Providers of Information Systems and Services that Handle Medical Information (version 1), and the Guideline on Safety Management of Medical Information System (version 5).

and the US have different levels of obligatory requirements to be met by the data users for a data transfer to occur.

There are no winners in and across the digital economy where countries continue to develop and establish data localisation laws. Data localisation makes impossible the forms of global business that have appeared over the last two decades, allowing the provision of information services across borders.[945] Moreover, protectionist policies 'barring access to foreign services only invite reciprocal protectionism from one's trading partners, harming consumers and businesses alike in the process by denying them access to the world's leading services'.[946] It further highlights the various directions jurisdictions are taking from each other. In data localisation alone, they have diverged significantly from each other that, providing a high level of legal certainty for data flows has become inhibited. This is likely to change if and when they implement their proposed data protection laws.

Should more states continue to implement these measures, the possibility of achieving an Open Data landscape will be diluted. Of the limited jurisdictions compared in this book, India, has to date implemented a complex layer of laws that all, in their own specific way have a level of data localisation. Meriem Rafik makes the point that what has emerged is a level of digital sovereignty.[947] It is a new form of conflict not often discussed that includes controlling personal data at a state level. Rafik highlights two examples whereby India has exerted their sovereignty over digital technology and data. According to Rafik, India, which banned TikTok in early 2020, as Narendra Modi's government discovered that the application steals and clandestinely transmits the data of Indian Internet users outside the country. Rafik argues that African nations find themselves facing a level of digital colonisation. As these forms of control become even more pronounced and visible, citizens may force the government to establish more localisation initiatives.

Data localisation along with the already existing rights and restrictions that entities must implement such as obtaining consent from the data subject, right to access, disclosure and deletion all dilute the economic benefits and outcomes from data flows across the digital economy. These conditions have been described as conditional flows. Even though there has been considerable emphasis placed on the current legal frameworks and the introduction of data localisation as being a major barrier to data flows, another emerging area is digital taxation.

§12.02 DIGITAL TAXATION

Apart from the controls national laws have placed on data flows, another area of restriction not often discussed is taxation. This is because, by and large, taxes on transactions undertaken over the Internet have not been attributed by any country until

945. Anupam Chander, Uyên P. Lê, Data Nationalism, 64 Emory L. J. 677 (2015), p. 714, https://scholarlycommons.law.emory.edu/elj/vol64/iss3/2.
946. *Ibid.*
947. Meriem Rafik, *Data Sovereignty: New Challenges for Diplomacy*, p. 40. In Fatima Roumate, *Artificial Intelligence and Digital Diplomacy, Challenges and Opportunities*, Springer (2021).

recently. This has been considered another barrier to opening up data and the digital economy. However, over the past five years, there has been a significant shift by nation states, which has resulted in the rise of 'digital taxation'.[948] This section will briefly highlight the progress that has been made towards introducing a digital tax. It will further demonstrate how jurisdictions are implementing such an initiative at different stages. It does not negate the need for governments to impose a level of tax on data transfers and data transactions, internationally, where there is an economic need to do so.

Centrally, the introduction or reform of the tax system is complex for any nation to undertake. It is a policy area that usually invokes debate amongst industry, community and government. Yet, the increasing development and availability of digital platforms provide the world with a new area of commercial and economic activity that, if treated the same as every other area of the economy, can also be subject to tax. Therefore, according to the OECD, including at the minimum '(i) network effects that generate market power, (ii) two- or multi-sided business models that involve complex pricing choices in profit maximization, (iii) negligible marginal cost, and (iv) geographic mobility in the location of service delivery and profit recognition'.[949] However, any such digital tax does not come without its challenges. Cristian Óliver Lucas-Mas, Raúl Félix Junquera-Varela, believe the 'first challenge is to understand what digital means. Digital refers to binary-digit data-encoding technology'.[950] For Lucs-Mas and Junquera-Varela a 'binary code represents text, computer processor instructions, or other data using a two-symbol system of zeros and ones. Something is said to be digital if it uses such data-encoding technology, which enables the transfer of data worldwide in practically real time at zero marginal cost'.[951] The authors go on to further state that:

> any economic transaction and, by extension, any business model that comprises one or more digital elements (digital communication, digital content, digital automation, digital distribution, digital payment) is categorized as digital for taxonomical purposes and is considered part of the digital economy. For tax purposes, special emphasis is placed on the analysis and impact of economic transactions and digital business models that have digital elements with tax-disruptive aspects.[952]

Viewed this way, the question arises where can such a tax be assigned. Put another way, where along the life cycle of the digital transaction should or can be taxed? A further accentuating question is what, if any role does data have in the taxing

948. Gloria Pasadilla, Yann Duval and Witada Anukoonwattaka, *Next Generation Non-Tariff Measures: Emerging Data Policies and Barriers to Digital Trade*, ARTNeT Working Paper Series No. 187, (2020), p. 23, January 2020, Bangkok ESCAP.
949. Organisation for Economic Co-operation and Development, *Tax Challenges Arising from Digitalisation: Interim Report 2018: Inclusive Framework on BEPS, OECD/G20 Base Erosion and Profit Shifting Project*, OECD Publishing, (2018).
950. Cristian Óliver Lucas-Mas and Raúl Félix Junquera-Varela, *Tax Theory Applied to the Digital Economy: A Proposal for a Digital Data Tax and a Global Internet Tax Agency*, World Bank Group (2021), p. 17.
951. *Ibid.*, p. 17.
952. *Ibid.*

of a digital transaction? In other words, the digitalisation of the economy is a new phenomenon, and it clearly poses challenges for taxation in all states.[953] On this basis, the authors propose a digital data tax (DDT). The DDT would be administered by the government at the federal level, similar to Australia's current taxation model. In proposing such a tax, the authors go one step further in proposing a Global Internet Tax Agency (GTA). This is something in my view that should be established, to ensure that for once and for all there is a coherent approach to taxation, particularly to the new digital economy. While it is acknowledged that there are significant issues with such a proposal, in terms of how and who would administer the organisation, it is not insurmountable. In fact, this form of taxation is not new. The further question is whether an international tax would be agreed upon by nation states. In this current period of heightened geopolitical and economic tension, such a proposal would not be agreed upon by all nation states.

For instance, while it was proposed to reduce volatility in the market, the Tobin tax was put forward in the 1970s. That is, Professor James Tobin first suggested a level of a global tax in 1972.[954] While it has never been implemented, the Tobin proposal sought to charge between 0.1% and 1% on the conversion of one currency into another. On its face, such a taxation charge appears to be negligible to the consumer or financial institutions. However, the estimated revenue that could be raised from such a tax would make available significant tax revenues in the billions that could have been used globally. Importantly the design of the tax is not too dissimilar to the DDT. That is, the Tobin tax would have had a 'broader benefit to reduce exchange-rate volatility by reducing currency speculation; raise revenue for international organisations; and make national economic policies less vulnerable to external shocks'.[955] In providing the 'collection of 0.1%, it has been calculated that more than USD 50 billion a year in revenue could be raised. Furthermore, even assuming that the number of current foreign exchange transactions fell by half, that 20% were exempt and that another 20% of the tax was evaded. This is over double the total now spent on stabilisation programmes, development and humanitarian aid, peace-keeping operations and other activities by the UN and its agencies'.[956] This sizeable allocation of revenue can be used by international organisations to strengthen local and international economic, social, health and environmental programmes.

Nonetheless, while a DDT would not have the same effect as the Tobin model in stabilising volatility in the market, its potential stabilising effect would have an impact on digital trade. The problem with the Tobin proposal is the same as with the DDT, that there is a need for an international tax agency. If established, the GTA could be extended to monitor data transfers and record those transfers. Thus, there are proposals available that can assist in strengthening the governance of data flows

953. Allison Christians and Tarcisio Diniz Magalhaes, 'A New Global Tax Deal for the Digital Age' (2019) Canadian Tax Journal1176.
954. Ben Patterson, Mickal Galliano, 'The Feasibility of an International "Tobin Tax" European Parliament' (1999) Economic Affairs Series iii.
955. *Ibid.*
956. *Ibid.*, p. iv.

around the world. On the one hand, problematic though is that should an organisation be established it will add to the current regulatory and business burden of organisations. On the other hand, consumers are unlikely to oppose such a proposal where there is a broader societal benefit. In 2021, the International Bar Association[957] noted that apart from the EU, countries were beginning to accept that such a digital tax would be necessary.

Problematic though is the 'mismatch in the current distribution of internet users and the location of digital production, changing tax rules to reflect where users are located would change where businesses owe and pay taxes'.[958] The resulting effect as noted by the author is that one of the greatest challenges is the need to undertake comprehensive law reform. Nevertheless, there have been attempts and some states have begun to implement their own level of tax on the digital economy. A digital tax, while a possible obstacle to data flows, is the data that accompanies the flow of other information or a consumer transaction that creates the economic activity and revenue outcome.

The European Commission (EC) in 2018 put a proposal forward for the establishment of a digital tax.[959] The Proposal has noted that 'the current corporate tax rules were conceived for traditional businesses. They were mainly conceived in the early 20th century for traditional "brick and mortar" businesses and define what triggers a right to tax in a country (where to tax) and how much of corporate income is allocated to a country (how much to tax) largely based on having a physical presence in that country'.[960] Centrally, such rules fail to capture the global reach of digital activities where physical presence is not a requirement anymore in order to be able to supply digital services.[961] For the EC and other nation states, the problem with the digital economy and the transactions that are created over the Internet, they are increasingly located in third countries. Put another way, a data subject residing in Slovenia (EU) may make a purchase of a good or a service over the Internet and the actual supplier is located in the US. Likewise, a data subject making an online purchase of a good or service from Singapore is actually interacting with a supplier located in Indonesia and Australia. These types of transactions are only recent and were heightened throughout 2020 to 2022 and the global pandemic. Yet, it is these transactions that have not been traditionally taxed.

---

957. International Bar Association, *Tech Giants: UK Leads the Way with Digital Services Tax*, https://www.ibanet.org/article/1c73aade-96cd-43fe-a8cd-b42cb40de4cb *See also* Marcel Olbert and Christopher Spengel, 'International Taxation in the Digital Economy: Challenge Accepted?' (2017)World Tax Journal 4. With regard to digital business models, the main tax challenges in the digital economy stem from the decreasing relevance of a physical presence in the market of the customers, the increasing importance and mobility of intangibles and the high degree of integration of the value chain.
958. Daniel Bunn Elke and Asen Cristina Enache, 'Digital Taxation Around the World', (2020)Tax Foundation 4, https://files.taxfoundation.org/20200527192056/Digital-Taxation-Around-the-World.pdf.
959. Proposal for Council Directive, on the common system of a digital services tax on revenues resulting from the provision of certain digital services {SWD (2018) 81} – {SWD (2018) 82}.
960. *Ibid.*, p. 2.
961. *Ibid.*

Under the existing international tax rules, the EC is of the view that 'the application of the current corporate tax rules to the digital economy has led to a misalignment between the place where the profits are taxed and the place where value is created, notably in the case of business models heavily reliant on user participation'.[962] For the EC this poses two sets of challenges:

> Firstly, the input obtained by a business from users, which actually constitutes the creation of value for the company, could be located in a tax jurisdiction where the company carrying out a digital activity is not physically established (and thus not established for tax purposes according to the current rules) and where therefore the profits generated from such activities cannot be taxed. Secondly, even where a company has a permanent establishment in the jurisdiction where the users are located, the value created by user participation is not taken into account when deciding how much tax should be paid in each country.[963]

Against the backdrop of the above, and while the EC has gone no further with the digital tax proposal, other states have begun to implement a system. In 2020, Singapore has been one of the first nation states to move in this area of law reform. Their system of tax was reformed to ensure that any 'foreign digital companies with customers in the city-state to register, collect, and remit 7% GST rate on their sales there'.[964] It has a two-tier threshold. First, the OVR (Overseas Vendor Registration) system applies to foreign suppliers of digital services whose annual global turnover exceeds SGD 1,000,000 and whose sale of digital services to consumers in Singapore exceeds SGD 100,000. Second, the latter threshold is included to minimise the compliance burden on overseas vendors which do not make significant sales to Singapore consumers.[965]

However, even though Australia has investigated whether such a tax is needed, it decided that a digital tax is not required[966] at this stage. New Zealand[967] at the time of writing this book in 2022, was undertaking a review to determine the viability of such a tax. France, being one of the largest economies within the EU has implemented such a tax. The French DST (digital services tax), when introduced in 2020, imposed a 3% cash flow tax on the revenue of large multinationals that provide digital advertising and digital platform services.[968] Member States of the EU are responsible for setting taxes. To date, there is no EU-wide tax system in place. India is another state that has also introduced a digital tax.

962. *Ibid.*
963. *Ibid.*
964. Vertex, Singapore taxes foreign digital companies with new registration regime, https://www.vertexinc.com/resources/resource-library/singapore-taxes-foreign-digital-companies-new-registration-regime.
965. *Ibid.*
966. BDO Global, Australia Digital Services Tax, https://www.bdo.global/en-gb/microsites/digital-services-taxation/countries-cit-map/australia-digital-services-tax.
967. BDO Global, New Zealand Digital Tax service, https://www.bdo.global/en-gb/microsites/digital-services-taxation/countries-cit-map/new-zealand-digital-services-tax.
968. Andrew Maslaris, France's Digital Services Tax, 2019, Australian Parliament, https://www.aph.gov.au/About_Parliament/Parliamentary_Departments/Parliamentary_Library/FlagPost/2019/August/Digital_Services_Taxation.

The Indian Finance Act 2020 added a 2% gross receipts tax on the consideration received for 'e-commerce supply or services', which goes well beyond online advertising and does not exempt business-to-consumer transactions. Robert Goulder is of the view that under the Indian model, the dual facets of the equalisation levy differ so greatly that they deserve to be spoken of as two distinct taxes. Over the last year, we've been in the habit of distinguishing between the original 6% 'advertising' levy (which was never repealed) and the expanded 2% 'e-commerce' levy.[969] Goulder argues that to 'avoid overlap, the e-commerce levy does not apply to transactions covered by the original advertising levy. Additionally, it does not apply when the non-resident e-commerce operator has an Indian company as long as the supply of goods or services is effectively connected with that company. On this basis, the term "e-commerce supply" has been defined to mean the sale of goods owned by the operator; the provision of services by the operator; or the sale of goods or provision of services facilitated by the operator'.[970] Already, and without undertaking a comprehensive comparison, this is another area of fragmentation. Thus, the obstacles imposed on data flows through various taxation, or a lack thereof, places a further burden on businesses to understand the tax obligations. Understandably, governments around the world are, more than ever, needing to identify new areas of tax. Taxing the online sector is one area that could alleviate financial stress for the government. Importantly, it must be measured and carefully introduced so as not to impose too great a barrier to the Internet economy.

§12.03 CONCLUSION

Data flows have been restricted by the implementation of the emerging control rights and data localisation rules. They can be grouped as controls that restrict storage or conditional requirements depending on the jurisdiction. As highlighted earlier in Chapter 1, the WTO-GATS rules promote and encourage free trade and where possible nation states should not develop barriers to that trade.

However, data flows constitute a new area of the digital economy. Governments and Regulators have struggled with balancing the needs of the new economic activity, and the protection of the data. Some of the obstacles that have been identified in this chapter that, have emerged as having implications for online trade over the longer term. The restrictions discussed in the chapter go against the commitments of GATS.

That said, data and the digital economy are different from other traditional sectors of the economy such as primary industries and food processing. These long-standing industries alone have over a long period of time been subject to significant law reform, to ensure the safety of humans and the environment while allowing for economic growth. Data transfers are personal. This is because they involve moving personal information of individuals from one jurisdiction to another. It is this

969. Robert Goulder, India's Evolving Solution To Digital Taxation, 2021, Forbes, https://www.forbes.com/sites/taxnotes/2021/04/26/indias-evolving-solution-to-digital-taxation/?sh=713c53db1428.
970. *Ibid.*

personal data that can identify the most intimate information of an individual. On the other side, there is a continual push at the international and national levels to open up the digital economy and allow data to flow freely.

Centrally, this chapter has again demonstrated the incoherent approach that has been undertaken by the jurisdictions compared to data localisation. Data localisation has attracted a lot of attention over the past five years and is only a recent addition to the data laws. India, for example, has some of the most extensive data localisation laws. While, at the other end of the spectrum, Canada at the national level, Singapore, the US and New Zealand have not established any such controls. In between these jurisdictions, Australia has selected a level of localisation requirement, predominantly attributed to health data. Indonesia also has a level of localisation requirements. Yet, this could change in the future for India and Indonesia, particularly if and when they implement their data-specific laws.

This chapter has confirmed that the current level of divergence related to data localisation alone will only continue to create gaps in the law and trust along with confidence for future investment within the digital economy. Should governments establish restrictions that limit the movement of data, it could create an environment where businesses reduce their online exposure. Should this occur, economic activity will slow and there will likely be a reduction in jobs. Significantly too, it is the new regime of data localisation along with the already existing rights and restrictions that entities must implement such as obtaining consent from the data subject, right to access, disclosure and deletion all dilute the economic benefits and outcomes from data flows across the digital economy. These conditions have been described as conditional flows. While there has been considerable emphasis placed on the current legal frameworks and the introduction of data localisation as being a major barrier to data flows, another emerging area is digital taxation. In other words, another impediment or restriction that is not often discussed is tax.

Tax is both an economic and legal barrier to data flows. There have for some time been discussions about what a tax might look like in relation to Internet transactions and activities. Viewed as a benefit, a tax can be diverted and used to grow innovation in the digital economy, providing broader social, economic and environmental benefits across the world. What has emerged is the various terms such as Digital Tax, Digital Data Tax, or Digital Services Tax. While subtly different, they all espouse the need for transactions over the Internet to be taxed in the same way as transactions of goods and services in most countries. That is, when a person purchases a good or a service in person, upon payment, there is a tax. Problematic to imposing such a tax on digital activity involving data is the need to understand the life cycle of the transaction over the Internet. For example, where along the cycle of the transaction is it appropriate to impose the tax? A further question is: should there be an international approach or, leave it up to individual nation states to determine?

At this stage, some states have chosen to go it alone, even after a review by the OECD. This chapter calls for an international body or organisation to be established to manage and develop international tax. The responsibility of any such organisation should, or could also be extended to monitoring and reporting on data flows around the world. The benefits, while complex to implement, would allow a central depository of data flows, so that any data subject can access their personal information to ascertain where and how it is being used. The problem with this approach is a large number of nation states that are likely to oppose any such proposal.

CHAPTER 13
Cyber Security

One of the biggest challenges for organisations both public and private is ensuring there is a high level of security of personal data before, during and post an international transfer. This challenge is not isolated to a single country, region or jurisdiction. Security issues pervade the Internet, at every step in the input, transmission and receipt of personal data. This chapter will discuss the current data security issues for cross-border data transfers. It does not examine or compare the cybersecurity laws of each of the jurisdictions. In analysing the security risks to data transfers, this chapter examines the balance that is sometimes not being struck between protecting and securing data transfers in accordance with that of WTO-GAT rules. Furthermore, there is a brief but important examination of the current approach to Impact Assessments (IAs). While often referred to as Privacy IAs, they have taken on an important role in performing risk assessments of the recipient organisation of the data transfer. It demonstrates yet again the different approaches taken by the limited jurisdictions compared to adopting this area of the law.

The Chapter then diverges and examines the vulnerability of IP addresses to cyber security intrusions. The IP address is a critical feature not often discussed in data transfers and data protection law. The IP address itself can identify a data subject when they are accessing information over the Internet. Even though they are generally not specifically defined in privacy or data laws, the IP address is an extension of personal data, as it forms part of the overall information that can identify an individual. This data can locate a personal-persons location.

On this basis, data transfers are significantly aligned to and linked with cyber security. Today, they have become an integral part of any business model, and entities increasingly engage with data and the Internet. Problematic today is the unknown illegal cyber intrusions that are compromising data transfers. In other words, as the digital economy continues to grow, more and more data will be used. Therefore, it is argued that with more data being transferred around the world, the scale and potential for increased cyber security breaches are likely to rise. The reported and unreported surge in cyberattacks does highlight the vulnerable position of data when transferred internationally.

As the digital economy continues to expand, and there is more connectivity across the world, the cyber threat to data transfers could become even more pronounced. As this book continually reinforces that data laws alone are highly fragmented. Cybersecurity law, while often constituting elements of criminal activity, has by and large been dealt with under criminal law. Despite the legal landscape not often connected between the two functions, practically it is hard for them to be separated. On the one hand, the ability for individuals and entities to secure the confidentiality of their personal data when transferred comes down to the technology used and the competence of the individual user. On the other hand, small- and medium-sized businesses do not have the same level of resources available to invest in data security. Thus, in many situations, older technology could be used in transferring data, which makes it increasingly vulnerable to state and non-state actor intrusions. More needs to be undertaken to reconcile the alignment of data laws, with that of cybersecurity law to ensure there are not only a high level of safeguards for data transfers but also ensure that any safeguards do not dilute the WTO-GATS rules. Doing so will significantly restrict the open data concept and economic development of the digital economy.

§13.01 INTRODUCTION

The proliferation of cross-border data flows does not and will not come without security issues and challenges. In other words, the sophistication of data flows, and how it can be secure may never be settled. This chapter briefly examines the current security issues related to transnational data flows. Special emphasis will be on the extent of how IP Addresses are dealt with under the law. Similar to other chapters, it will use the EU as the benchmark in responding to data security issues. Emily Laidlaw argues that data flows create three overlapping challenges.[971] These include:

> First, the flow of data can risk the security of the data, systems and networks. This would be the data security or cybersecurity challenge. From an information security perspective, the focus is on the CIA triad of confidentiality, integrity and availability of data. Concerns are different and include authentication, access

971. Emily B. Laidlaw, *Privacy and Cybersecurity in Digital Trade: The Challenge of Cross border Data Flows Canada*, Research Chair in Cybersecurity Law and Associate Professor, Faculty of Law, University of Calgary, *Global Affairs Canada* (2021), p. 3. *See also*, Jeff Kosseff, *Cybersecurity Law*, 2nd ed. Hoboken, NJ: Wiley & Sons, Inc., (2020) p. 361. Benjamin Wittes et al. discuss this idea in the context of sextortion: *Sextortion: Cybersecurity, Teenagers, and Remote Sexual Assault*' (2016) Brookings Institute.

> control, cryptography, malware, social engineering and communications and network security. Second, data flows create privacy challenges, which overlap with the above, but pose unique challenges in themselves. Privacy concerns range from the data that is collected, who controls it, the narratives spun, or inferences made from the data and uses made of it. Third, data flows create information challenges. Data is information, and the same attack vectors can be used to bully children and even adults today, by spreading misinformation and exploiting sensitive health or financial data.[972]

Laidlaw goes on to say that one of the great challenges of living in a data-driven economy is that data is embedded in all aspects of our lives. From a regulatory perspective, this means that data is an issue in all areas of the law from competition law, to financial services regulation, criminal law, tort law, contract law, arbitration, primary industries, health and environment, to name a few.[973] Most, if not all these areas of the law will need to balance the inevitable need for an open market for data to flow while ensuring that there are enough privacy protections in place so that the data subjects have a high level of trust in the governance, technology and legal framework. It cannot be left to one area to secure data flows. Technology is unlikely to be the silver bullet to address the security issues of loss or illegal collection, storage and use of data in the digital economy as it flows from the UK to Singapore, for instance.

Technology has changed increasingly over the past decade; governments and the private sector have been moving towards the use of the Cloud. Ali Sunyaev is of the view that 'cloud computing is a model for enabling access to computing resources that evolved in information technology and has become a dominant business model for delivering IT infrastructure, components, and applications'.[974] Sunyaev makes the point that this technology while being in use since 2007, is a 'product-centric model for IT provisioning is transformed into a global, distributed, service-centric model, leading to a disruptive shift from IT-as-a-product to IT-as-a-service'.[975] Centrally, the technology 'enables individuals and organizations to access IT resources on-demand, from any device, and at any time, as a measured service'.[976] There are a number of benefits from the technology. First, Sunyaev believes that it 'lowers the entry point to high-performance computing'.[977] Second, it has 'led to a rapid increase of online services and applications'.[978] These applications are now pervasive across iPhones and smartphones and provide access to individuals and entities such as financial services, purchasing services and goods from around the world. For its immediate benefits, its size and accessibility have allowed for data flows to pervade international borders at a rapid rate. This includes large quantities of personal data. Angeliki Zavou et al.

972. *Ibid.*, p. 3.
973. *Ibid.*
974. Ali Sunyaev, Cloud Computing. In: *Internet Computing*, Springer, Cham (2020), p. 196 https://doi.org/10.1007/978-3-030-34957-8_7 Also *see* Alexander Benlian and Thomas Hess', Opportunities and Risks of Software-as-a-Service: Findings from a Survey of IT Executives' (2011) 52(1) Decis Support System 232-246.
975. *Ibid.*, p. 196.
976. *Ibid.*, p. 106.
977. *Ibid.*, p. 196.
978. *Ibid.*

highlight that some of the 'personal information collected, used and stored over Cloud ranges from credit card numbers, private files, and other kinds of sensitive data are temporarily or permanently stored in back-end databases and file systems, beyond user control'.[979] Savou and others note that while Cloud has bought many efficiencies to business, it had in the early days of operation, also been compromised. They argue that 'data confidentiality becomes one of the primary concerns for users of these cloud-hosted services, especially when taking into account the recent security incidents and data breaches, witnessed even on major and reputable online services'.[980]

To overcome security vulnerabilities, Zavou et al. are of the view that auditing and making the technology more transparent, will address a level of security concerns. They point out that, 'auditing has been long employed with success as an added security measure in alleviating user security concerns in domains like banking, where information security is mission critical'.[981] The authors do not view this process as being too onerous. Such a process would not prevent data flows. Rather for them, having a robust policy framework in place enhances transparency and would strengthen data flows. While this is one tool in the overall toolbox that can be implemented to ensure data flows are facilitated so that barriers are reduced. On the other side, more internal policies do add another layer of administrative burden and cost. However, many other industry sectors such as primary industries and medical have operated under a similar framework for decades.

In supporting the position taken within this book, Laidlaw in her assessment of the multilateral trade agreements noted a number of similarities and issues. Laidlaw examined the Canada-United States-Mexico Agreement (CUSMA), the Comprehensive and Progressive Agreement for Trans-Pacific Partnership (CPTPP), the Agreement between the European Union and Japan for an Economic Partnership (EPA) and the Digital Economy Partnership Agreement between Singapore.[982] In her observations, it was demonstrated that all 'agreements focus on promoting open and secure digital trade in acknowledgment of the importance of digital commerce'.[983] While Laidlaw did not examine or compare provisions of the agreements in the same way this book undertakes, she found that states participant in these agreements are generally 'geared toward enabling the free flow of cross-border data'.[984] Technology today such as the Internet of Things (IoT) and AI, while offering many benefits, can have a devastating effect on individuals and entities. Nowadays, AI can be used to analyse big data and provide solutions in health, transportation, organisational management and so on. Hence, the use of technology is a consumer experience, and thus online harm becomes

979. Angeliki Zavou et al., *Cloudopsy: An Autopsy of Data Flows in the Cloud*, Springer (2013), pp. 366-367.
980. *Ibid.*, pp. 366-367.
981. *Ibid.*
982. Emily B. Laidlaw, *Privacy and Cybersecurity in Digital Trade: The Challenge of Cross border Data Flows Canada*, Research Chair in Cybersecurity Law and Associate Professor, Faculty of Law, University of Calgary, *Global Affairs Canada* (2021), p. 62. *See also* Gregory Shaffer, 'Globalization and Social Protection: The Impact of EU and International Rules in the Ratcheting up of U.S. Privacy Standards' (2000) 25 Yale Journal of International Law 1, 4.
983. *Ibid.*, pp. 62-63.
984. *Ibid.*

intimately connected with consumer protection and vice versa,[985] which is either domestic or international trade. Laidlaw posits that there has been too great a focus on soft law when addressing the many issues related to data flows and their security, and there is too much of a reliance on technology to solve the problems related to breaches. Despite international law being viewed as soft law, it is urgently needed. Multilateral trade and investment agreements are one area in need of improvement, amongst others.

Notwithstanding the above, Joshua Meltzer argues that there is a 'commonly agreed definition of cybersecurity'.[986] Meltzer, in referencing the International Telecommunication Union, broadly defines cybersecurity as:

> the collection of tools, policies, security concepts, security safeguards, guidelines, risk management approaches, actions, training, best practices, assurance and technologies that can be used to protect the cyber environment and organisation and user's assets. Organisation and user's assets include connected computing devices, personnel, infrastructure, applications, services, telecommunications systems, and the totality of transmitted and/or stored information in the cyber environment. Cybersecurity strives to ensure the attainment and maintenance of the security properties of the organisation and user's assets against relevant security risks in the cyber environment.[987]

Central to the above quotation is that there is no mention of data, whether personal or commercial. While there is a reference to 'assets include connected computing devices, personnel, infrastructure, applications, services, telecommunications systems, and the totality of transmitted and/or stored information in the cyber environment',[988] all these devices are not only connected to the Internet but all transmit data flows. Despite focusing on the infrastructure and systems that support the connectivity to the Internet, today more than ever cybersecurity has to include data flows and its protection. Meltzer further notes that the US National Institute of Standards and Technology defines cybersecurity as 'the prevention of damage to, unauthorized use of, exploitation of, and – if needed – the restoration of electronic information and communications systems, and the information they contain, in order to strengthen the confidentiality, integrity and availability of these systems'.[989] In turn, the White House National Cyber Strategy focuses on increasing the security and resilience of the nation's information and information systems. Again, there is no reference to data, which would make up most if not all that requires security.

For Meltzer, there are five key areas of cyber risk with implications for global data flows in a digital economy. The first is the national defence, which includes branches of the military and intelligence services. The second is the critical infrastructure. The

985. *Ibid.*
986. Joshua Meltzer, *Cybersecurity, Digital Trade, and Data Flows: Re-Thinking a Role for International Trade Rules*, Working Paper 132 Global Economy and Development Brookings Institution (2020), p. 7.
987. *Ibid.*, p. 7. *See also*, International Telecommunication Union, p. 20, https://www.itu.int/net/itunews/issues/2010/09/pdf/201009_20.pdf.
988. *Ibid.*
989. *Ibid.*, p. 7.

third area comprises trade secrets and IP with commercial value. Online information is fourth, and the fifth area is access to data and technology through international investment.[990] No matter how one interprets Meltzer's observations, in all of these areas, personal data will be contained in transnational data flows. Further underscoring the urgency of this book, Meltzer highlights how the US has identified the 'collection of personal data as "sensitive personal data" is a cybersecurity risk and more broadly a risk to national security'.[991] Such is this concern in the US and other states around the world, that nations have begun pressuring foreign entities with investments in a technology company, to exit the country and the market, in order to protect the data and its flows. The resulting effect of the Internet is a convergence of policy issues that have otherwise been dealt with by governments and regulators separately. We are in a period where trade and national security are intertwined more than at any other time in history. What this means for data flows, open data, and the digital economy is unknown. Will states revert to additional inward policies that restrict data flows?

To overcome online trade, Meltzer proposes the need for greater use of the WTO Technical Barriers to Trade (TBT) Agreement (S).[992] This is an important point, because, TBTs could be used where states are increasingly developing ways to keep trade as open as possible. They promote transparency and ensure that technical regulations, standards, and conformity assessment procedures are non-discriminatory and do not create unnecessary obstacles to trade.[993] Arguably they are another tool at the international level that can, in part, be used to unlock the digital economy. Despite the lack of reference to the digital economy, they do promote harmonisation. That is Article 2.3 states that 'with a view to harmonising technical regulations or standards on as wide a basis as possible, Parties shall play a full part within the limits of their resources in the preparation by appropriate international standardizing bodies of international standards for products for which they either have adopted, or expect to adopt, technical regulations or standards'.[994] While not calling for the internationalisation of trade law. The reference to harmonising technical regulations or standards, is in part, promoting a level of international harmonisation of technical regulation. It is argued that interpreting this as broadly as possible includes data regulation for data flows because they are technical regulation(s). However, others may interpret this narrowly, and therefore, its scope may be limited to only purely technical regulation that sits outside of government regulation. That said, calling for harmonisation of standards, also reinforces the position this book takes. Moreover, as highlighted earlier in the book, some states regulate the use of certain international standards such as ISO, whereas others do not. A problem though is that this further adds to the multiple layers

990. *Ibid.*, p. 8.
991. *Ibid.*, p. 12.
992. World Trade Organisation, *Technical Barriers to Trade Agreement*, https://www.wto.org/english/tratop_e/tbt_e/tbt_e.htm.
993. *Ibid.*
994. Agreement to Technical Barriers to Trade, https://www.wto.org/english/docs_e/legal_e/tokyo_tbt_e.pdf.

that regulate trade generally and the digital economy. Meltzer asserts that there are two challenges here to applying this to cybersecurity measures. He states:

> One is that as cybersecurity measures will be risk-based, in many instances a WTO panel will need to assess whether the regulation appropriately calibrates the discriminatory aspects with the cybersecurity risk. Yet, the higher the risk, the more deference will be given to the government decision and how to address such a risk. When it comes to high-risk cybersecurity, then this assessment of whether the regulatory distinction is appropriately calibrated could cash out as extensive deference. When dealing with lower risk products, the TBT could require a high level of calibration.[995]

Arguably, in my view today, data flows and the personal data involved in those transfers internationally, do constitute a high risk. In other words, the more sensitive the data used, the increasing high risk it becomes and security becomes even more important. For instance, it has emerged that health data is considered the most personal of all personal data. In most states, it has been afforded the highest level of control and protection possible. Therefore, having the right balance is assessing the risk to the data, while enabling it to be transferred must be struck. In part, the current legal framework for data requires a level of risk assessment. In keeping with the theme of this book Meltzer also notes that recent FTAs include digital trade commitments not found in the WTO, and which commitments may also be at odds with cybersecurity measures.[996] Therefore, what has emerged is many competing areas of policy and the law, trying to be converged so as to enable digital trade to expand.

Notwithstanding the above, Meltzer makes an important point that even though TBTs exist, there are exceptions to the WTO rules. He further argues that 'the security exception in the GATT and GATS is identical and allows members to adopt measures for security purposes, which would otherwise be inconsistent with these agreements. The following addresses the security exception in GATS Article XIV bis, but the analysis would also apply to GATT article XXI. The security exception in GATS Article XIV *bis* is as follows: nothing in this Agreement shall be construed (a), to require any Member to furnish any information, the disclosure of which it considers contrary to its essential security interests; or (b) to prevent any Member from taking any action which it considers necessary for the protection of its essential security interests:

> (i) relating to the supply of services as carried out directly or indirectly for the purpose of provisioning a military establishment;

995. Joshua Meltzer, *Cybersecurity, Digital Trade, and Data Flows: Re-Thinking a Role for International Trade Rules*, Working Paper 132 Global Economy and Development Brookings Institution (2020), p. 19. *See also*, World Trade Organisation, Russia – Measures Concerning Traffic in Transit Panel Report, *Action by the Dispute Settlement Body* At its meeting on 26 April 2019, the Dispute Settlement Body adopted the Panel report on *Russia – Measures concerning Traffic in Transit* (WT/DS512/R and WT/DS512/R/Add.1), https://www.wto.org/english/tratop_e/dispu_e/cases_e/ds512_e.htm and https://docs.wto.org/dol2fe/Pages/FE_Search/FE_S_S006.aspx?Query=(@Symbol=%20wt/ds512/*)&Language=ENGLISH&Context=FomerScripte dSearch&languageUIChanged=true#.
996. *Ibid.*, p. 20.

(ii) relating to fissionable and fusionable materials or the materials from which they are derived;
(iii) taken in time of war or other emergency in international relations; or
(c) to prevent any Member from taking any action in pursuance of its obligations under the United Nations Charter for the maintenance of international peace and security. The Council for Trade in Services shall be informed to the fullest extent possible of measures taken under paragraphs 1(b) and (c) and of their termination'[997] (*see* Chapter 1).

The provisions require careful interpretation and consideration of an exemption. Importantly, in the modern day of technology, the ensuing question is to what extent can cybersecurity or privacy or data protection be considered, if at a security matter, where it can invoke Article XIV.

Meltzer goes on to point out that according to GATS Article XIV *bis* can admit to a range of interpretations, from fully self-judging - where it is up to each government to determine its security needs, through to various roles for a WTO panel, including determining whether a measure was taken in good faith and complies with objective standards. Moreover, key terms in GATS Article XIV bis are undefined, including what is meant by 'essential security interest' or 'emergency in international relations'.[998] Referring to a WTO Decision of Russia - Measures Concerning Traffic in Transit - involved a challenge by Ukraine to restrictions imposed by Russia on Ukrainian imports and exports transiting through Russian territory. The dispute:

> concerned Ukraine's challenge to Russian bans and restrictions on traffic in transit by road and rail, from Ukraine, across Russia and destined for Kazakhstan and the Kyrgyz Republic, as well as to the alleged de facto extension of these bans and restrictions to Ukrainian traffic in transit destined for Mongolia, Tajikistan, Turkmenistan and Uzbekistan. Ukraine claimed that these transit measures are inconsistent with Russia's obligations under Article V (freedom of transit), Article X (publication and administration of trade regulations) and with related commitments in Russia's Accession Protocol. Russia asserted that the measures were among those that it considered necessary for the protection of its essential security interests, which it took in response to the emergency in international relations that occurred in 2014, and which presented threats to Russia's essential security interests. Russia therefore invoked the provisions of Article XXI(b)(iii) of the GATT 1994, arguing that, as a result, the Panel lacked jurisdiction to further address the matter.[999] Notably, the matter was not specifically trade related but, had an indirect impact on trade. In other words, the restriction on road and rail would ultimately have an impact on the trade in goods.[1000]

997. *Ibid.*, p. 21.
998. *Ibid.*, pp. 24-25.
999. *Ibid.*, Articles 7.3-7.4.
1000. World Trade Organisation, Russia - Measures Concerning Traffic in Transit Panel Report, *Action by the Dispute Settlement Body* At its meeting on 26 April 2019, the Dispute Settlement Body adopted the Panel report on *Russia - Measures concerning Traffic in Transit* (WT/DS512/R and WT/DS512/R/Add.1), https://www.wto.org/english/tratop_e/dispu_e/cases_e/ds512_e.htm, paragraphs 7.1, 7.2, 7.3, 7.4.

Viewed this way, the dispute was based on national security grounds. While cybersecurity did not form part of the overall dispute, it nevertheless is front and centre in modern way trade and national security disputes. Nonetheless, Meltzer justifiably argues that cybersecurity, unlike more traditional security issues, does challenge how to distinguish legitimate concerns from disguised protectionism. Cybersecurity policy is increasingly risk-based and hidden behind computer screens. He further argues that addressing high-risk potentially catastrophic cyberattacks by restricting data flows and trade in digital products, would likely be considered an 'essential security interest'.[1001] In my view, as the digital economy and the trade-in data grow, the security issues arising from this activity, once compromised by a cyberattack, would warrant the incident being categorised as an exception. However, he makes that point to proceed with a level of caution because 'in many cases cybersecurity measures are not in response to imminent catastrophic attack, nor are they observable in the way which help ground national security claims',[1002] until well after the event. He notes that the approach taken by the WTO Panel in the Russia-Transit case to define what constitutes an 'emergency in international relations' as well as the temporal link in the text that requires the measure to be 'taken in time of' the emergency in international relations, would seem to exclude from the scope many of the risk-based. This is just one example where it has been difficult to confirm with a high level of certainty that this outcome would apply in other cyberattacks.

In support of Meltzer, Panos Delematsis and Thomas Cottier believe that 'Article XIVb is intended to achieve a proper balance between members' prerogative to pursue their security interests and the multilateral interest in securing the realisation and implementation of WTO rights and obligations.'[1003] They go on to say that open markets are an important prerequisite for peaceful relationships, and an illustration list of where derogation from the GATS rules under Article XIV would exist. On the one hand, while not exhaustively examining WTO decisions, it is a matter of time before data in the digital economy and the cybersecurity threats posed by that trade activity will find their way to the WTO.

On the other hand, Nesha Misha asks the question of whether GATS Article XIV does achieve a balance between trade and Internet policy - focusing on privacy and cybersecurity.[1004] Misha takes a broader view under the general exception provisions of Article XIV. That is, according to Article XIV, General Exceptions provide that subject to the requirement that such measures are not applied in a manner which would constitute a means of arbitrary or unjustifiable discrimination between countries where like conditions prevail. They can also disguise any restriction on trade in

1001. Joshua Meltzer, *Cybersecurity, Digital Trade, and Data Flows: Re-Thinking a Role for International Trade Rules*, Working Paper 132 Global Economy and Development Brookings Institution (2020), p. 19.
1002. *Ibid.*
1003. Panos Delematsis and Thomas Cottier, Article XIV bis GATS: Security Exceptions. In: Rudiger Wolfrum, Peter Stoll and Clemens Feinäugle (eds), *WTO – Trade in Services*, Max Planck Commentaries on World Trade Law, No. 6, Martinus Nijhoff Publishers (2008), pp. 329-348.
1004. Neha Mishra, 'Privacy, Cybersecurity, and GATS Article XIV: A New Frontier for Trade and Internet Regulation?' (2020) World Trade Review 343, DOI: 10.1017/S1474745619000120.

services, nothing in this Agreement shall be construed to prevent the adoption or enforcement of measures:

> (a) necessary to protect public morals or to maintain public order; (b) necessary to protect human, animal or plant life or health; (c) necessary to secure compliance with laws or regulations which are not inconsistent with the provisions of this Agreement including those relating to: (i) the prevention of deceptive and fraudulent practices or to deal with the effects of a default on services contracts; (ii) the protection of the privacy of individuals in relation to the processing and dissemination of personal data and the protection of confidentiality of individual records and accounts; (iii) safety; (d) inconsistent with Article XVII, provided that the difference in treatment is aimed at ensuring the equitable or effective imposition or collection of direct taxes in respect of services or service suppliers of other Members; (e) inconsistent with Article II, provided that the difference in treatment is the result of an agreement on the avoidance of double taxation or provisions on the avoidance of double taxation in any other international agreement or arrangement by which the Member is bound.[1005]

The above Article XIV is different to that of Article XIVbis. Article XIV is wider in its scope and takes into consideration privacy and data protection. Misha asserts that the 'protection of privacy of individuals' in GATS Article XIV(c)(ii) can be interpreted in the context of the internet and online services, thus covering restrictions on 'data transfer contained in data protection laws, or other compliance requirements on service providers such as obtaining informed consent from internet users and preventing unauthorized use of personal data'.[1006] Misha goes further by arguing that where 'measures necessary to achieve compliance with domestic laws dealing with "default on service contracts" (with reference to contracts in the online environment) under GATS Art. XIV(c)(i). data protection laws concerns, GATS Art. XIV(c)(ii) should also be interpreted to include domestic laws addressing privacy concerns in the online context'.[1007] However, Misha does not say that not all data and cybersecurity laws would be consistent with WTO rules. She is of the view that Article XIV(a) is broad enough to cover security threats to the IoT that pose a 'serious threat' to security. Furthermore, and due to the strategic position that data and cybersecurity are now taking place with the digital economy, Misha believes that increasingly these issues will find their way into trade disputes.[1008] She cautions on the role of GATS in the regulation of data flows in the digital economy. Moreover, for Misha, GATS do not recognise cybersecurity and privacy as preconditions for digital trade but rather limits their relevance to GATS Article XIV (and also, GATS Article XIV bis, when national security issues are involved). WTO members are divided on the role of cybersecurity and privacy in international trade law.[1009] Arguably, the ambiguity and lack of

1005. World Trade Organisation, General Agreement on Trade in Services, https://www.wto.org/english/docs_e/legal_e/26-gats_01_e.htm.
1006. Neha Mishra, 'Privacy, Cybersecurity, and GATS Article XIV: A New Frontier for Trade and Internet Regulation?' World Trade Review (2020), p. 351-352, DOI: 10.1017/S1474745619000120.
1007. *Ibid.*, pp. 351-352.
1008. *Ibid.*, p. 354.
1009. *Ibid.*

certainty in relation to the application of WTO-GATS is far from settled in the digital economy. There will be a significant transition over the coming decades that could see disputes on trade grounds arise for data and cybersecurity. Because of the nature and the speed at which the digital economy is evolving and the breadth and depth of issues it is challenging the current trade rules that have served transnational trade well for more than half a century. It is certainly an area to watch closely. When coupled with the restrictive measure such as data localisation in data flows and the law, the exception provisions of the WTO will be possibly called upon for Panels to use to resolve trade disputes.

The next section examines the assessment process under the EU GDPR. It will compare some of the other jurisdiction's approach to these assessments and confirm or otherwise their applicability to securing data with transnational transfers.

§13.02 IMPACT ASSESSMENTS, CYBER LAWS

Nation states refer to Impact Assessment differently. They also differ in their application and how jurisdictions have viewed them as an essential tool to manage risk in data transfers and the protection of that data. They act as, and provide, a level of security of the data in an international transfer. This is because generally, IAs require the recipient state or organisation to have a similar level of protection for that data. This section does to a limited extent discuss and compare IAs that are required for the private or public sector. This is because government organisations are and will increasingly engage in the transfer of data internationally. In some jurisdictions, there will be variables in the development and application of IAs for the public and private sectors. IAs are commonly referred to as privacy IAs. This section will use the term IAs, which is often defined as the 'methodology for assessing the impacts on privacy of a project, policy, programme, service, product or other initiative which involves the processing of personal information and, in consultation with stakeholders, for taking remedial actions as necessary in order to avoid or minimise negative impacts'.[1010] David Wright and Paul De Hert in referring to Roger Clarke who defined a 'privacy impact assessment as a systematic process that identifies and evaluates, from the perspectives of all stakeholders, the potential effects on privacy of a project, initiative or proposed system or scheme, and includes a search for ways to avoid or mitigate negative privacy impacts'.[1011] Wright and De Hert further argue that 'privacy risks may flow from any number of sources. Risks may arise from vulnerabilities within the organisation or the design and implementation of a project. They may also arise from 'external threats, e.g., from evil-doers who engage in social engineering to con personnel into giving them the information they want or who exploit weaknesses in the organisation's access

1010. David Wright and Paul De Hert, *Privacy Impact Assessment*, Springer, (2012), p. 5.
1011. Roger Clarke, 'An Evaluation of Privacy Impact Assessment Guidance Documents' (2011) International Data Privacy Law, http://idpl.oxfordjournals.org/content/early/2011/02/15/idpl.ipr002.full or http://www.rogerclarke.com/DV/PIAG-Eval.html In David Wright, Paul De Hert, *Privacy Impact Assessment*, Springer (2012), p. 5.

control procedures'.[1012] It is this management of risk that, today is fast becoming the number one priority for government and business in times of geopolitical tension. In managing such risks, the security of that data provides for a higher level of privacy protection. This section will explore whether IAs are mandatory across the jurisdictions examined. It only focuses on Australia, the EU, India, Indonesia, Japan, New Zealand, Canada and the US.

Australia

For Australia, a starting point has to be whether they are an APP entity. That said, in accordance with APP 1.3, such an entity must 'have a clearly expressed policy about the management of personal information by the entity'.[1013] To underscore this point, an APP entity 'must take such steps as are reasonable in the circumstances to implement practices, procedures and systems relating to the entity's functions or activities that: (a) will ensure that the entity complies[1014] with the Australian Privacy Principles and a registered APP code (if any) that binds the entity; and (b) will enable the entity to deal with inquiries or complaints from individuals about the entity's compliance with the Australian Privacy Principles or such a code'.[1015] The issue though is highlighted that while there is a mandatory requirement where APP 1.2 refers to 'must', however, this is somewhat diluted when reading further to 'take such steps as are reasonable in the circumstances'.[1016] This is ambiguous and not entirely clear. Furthermore, there is an obligation to comply with a registered code under the APPs, if one exists.

On this basis, the Commissioner may be involved in directing an APP entity to undertake such an assessment, whether they are a private organisation or otherwise.[1017] Moreover, it is the Commissioner who has the ultimate power to conduct the assessment for the handling and storage of personal data. This pertains to health, tax and data matching systems. On its face, it appears that the provision is broad enough to include the data which form part of cross-border transfers. In addition, under section 33D, the Commissioner also has the discretion to require an IA where the government organisation is engaged in 'the handling of personal information about individuals. Noteworthy, is that a privacy impact assessment is not a legislative instrument'.[1018]

European Union

This section gives a brief outline of the extent of IAs under the EU GDPR. It does not comprehensively discuss or compare the EU approach with other jurisdictions discussed in this book. The instrument for an IA can be found in accordance with Article 35 of the GDPR.[1019] Article 35 provides that 'where a type of processing in particular

1012. *Ibid.*, p. 11.
1013. Australian Privacy Principles, 1.3.
1014. Privacy Act 1988, section 33D.
1015. Australian Privacy Principles, 1.2.
1016. *Ibid.*
1017. Privacy Act 1988, section 33C.
1018. *Ibid.*, section 33d(5).
1019. Regulation (EU) 2016/679 of the European Parliament and of the Council of 27 April 2016 on the protection of natural persons with regard to the processing of personal data and on the free

using new technologies, and taking into account the nature, scope, context and purposes of the processing, is likely to result in a high risk to the rights and freedoms of natural persons, the controller shall, prior to the processing, carry out an assessment of the impact of the envisaged processing operations on the protection of personal data. A single assessment may address a set of similar processing operations that present similar high risks'. On this basis, the controller shall seek the advice of the data protection officer, where designated, when carrying out a data protection impact assessment. Centrally, an IA is a systematic and extensive evaluation of personal aspects relating to natural persons which are based on automated processing. This includes profiling, and on which decisions are based that produce legal effects concerning the natural person or similarly significantly affect the natural person; 'processing on a large scale of special categories of data referred to in Article 9(1), or of personal data relating to criminal convictions and offences referred to in Article 10; or a systematic monitoring of a publicly accessible area on a large scale'.[1020] On this basis generally, an IA must always be conducted when the processing could result in a high risk to the rights and freedoms of natural persons.[1021] In order to specify the open-ended wording of the law regarding the basic obligation to perform a privacy impact assessment, the supervisory authorities are involved. In a first draft, the Article 29 Working Party created a catalogue of ten criteria which indicate that the processing bears a high risk to the rights and freedoms of a natural person.[1022] Importantly, Article 35(7) requires that such an assessment shall contain:

- a systematic description of the envisaged processing operations and the purposes of the processing, including, where applicable, the legitimate interest pursued by the controller;
- an assessment of the necessity and proportionality of the processing operations in relation to the purposes;
- an assessment of the risks to the rights and freedoms of data subjects referred to in paragraph 1; and
- the measures envisaged to address the risks, including safeguards, *security measures* and mechanisms to ensure the protection of personal data and to demonstrate compliance with this Regulation taking into account the rights and legitimate interests of data subjects and other persons concerned.

Viewed this way, Article 35(7) becomes critically important to the security of personal data. In part, it requires that security measures are established to ensure a high level of safeguards is established to address the risks associated with illegal intrusions. In addition to the above, 'as part of the accountability principle, every data

movement of such data, and repealing Directive 95/46/EC (General Data Protection Regulation) (Text with EEA relevance) OJ L 119, Article 35.

1020. *Ibid.*, Article 2.

1021. Privacy Impact Assessment, https://gdpr-info.eu/issues/privacy-impact-assessment/, *See also*, Guidelines on Data Protection Impact Assessment (DPIA) and determining whether processing is 'likely to result in a high risk' for the purposes of Regulation 2016/679, (2017).

1022. *Ibid.*

controller "shall maintain a record of processing activities under its responsibility" including *inter alia* the purposes of processing, a description of the categories of data and recipients of the data and "where possible, a general description of the technical and organisational security measures referred to in Article 32(1)" (Article 30(1)) and must assess whether a high risk is likely, even if they ultimately decide not to carry out an impact assessment'.[1023] Importantly, the primary use and application of IAs in the EU are not to address cybersecurity concerns. They do provide the basis for the assessment of personal data being transferred to a third country that, compliance with the EU GDPR is achieved. Therefore, indirectly, they have become an important tool for ensuring a high level of security of personal data from cybersecurity intrusions.

India, Indonesia, Japan

Under current India, Indonesia or Japan's legal landscape, there is no formal legal requirement for an impact assessment to be undertaken to ensure the protection and security of that data when transferred to a third country.

New Zealand

New Zealand in accordance with their Privacy Principle 11 entities are encouraged to undertake an IA. The IA is to outline aspects of the transfer including details of the receiving country. Explain steps to be taken to protect the information and the interests of the people concerned.[1024]

Canada and US

In Canada, because the privacy laws have been separated between the public and private sectors, IAs have thus far only pertained to the public sector. For Canada, to date, IAs concentrate on privacy compliance as well as risks to 'privacy posed by programmes and activities, other assessments have different areas of focus'.[1025] Such an assessment similar to other jurisdictions requires an assessment of security to ensure that levels of controls are in place to establish what risks if any are attributed to the use of the data. Similarly, in the US such assessment is required, particularly between government organisations. Thus, the E-Government Act of 2002[1026] requires federal agencies to conduct an IA for any information electronic collections and information technology systems that contain personally identifiable information. This

1023. Guidelines on Data Protection Impact Assessment (DPIA) and determining whether processing is 'likely to result in a high risk' for the purposes of Regulation 2016/679, (2017), p. 12. *See* Annex 2, criteria for acceptable IA.

1024. Privacy Impact Assessment Handbook, https://www.privacy.org.nz/publications/guidance-resources/privacy-impact-assessment-handbook/.

1025. Office of Privacy Commissioner Canada, OPCs Guide to Privacy Impact Assessment Process, https://www.priv.gc.ca/en/privacy-topics/privacy-impact-assessments/gd_exp_202003/#fn 1 *See also*, Directive on Privacy Impact Assessment, https://www.tbs-sct.gc.ca/pol/doc-eng .aspx?id = 18308. This directibe applies to government institutions as defined in section 3 of the Privacy Act, including parent Crown corporations and any wholly owned subsidiary corporations.

1026. United States Department of States, Privacy Impact Assessments, https://www.state.gov/ privacy-impact-assessments-privacy-office/.

section does not assess whether IAs are required under health, child, federal trade and other laws that provide for the protection of privacy.

This short brief section has highlighted again the inconsistent approaches to obtaining a level of security for personal data in transnational or other transfers. It further demonstrated that some jurisdictions require a high level of assessment, whereas, in other jurisdictions, there is no requirement at all. The discussion concerning IAs is important because it further highlights that the security of data in transnational transfers is vulnerable. It is this level of vulnerability created by the lack of coherence and consistency in the law that, has established gaps which need to be closed, to minimise the occurrence of future cyber intrusions. The next section discusses a technical area that is not often addressed in data flows. That is, IP addresses have emerged as an important feature of data flows, data protection and security.

§13.03 IP ADDRESSES

In today's highly connected society everything from our iPhones, laptops, and tablets to desktops can be connected to the Internet. In so doing, it will connect with a globally unique address to identify itself over the Internet.[1027] This section draws upon selected jurisdictions as part of the examination of IP Addresses and whether they constitute personal data. It does not compare every jurisdiction that forms part of this book. It uses the EU as the benchmark. IP addresses are increasingly important as they can be used to identify a person over the Internet and their specific activity. It is that level of intrusion that poses a risk to data subjects of their data being illegally used. It also poses other direct and indirect risks to personal data flows and their security. This is because depending on the settings of a computer, particularly a laptop, the location of the computer can be easily identified.

Generally, the IP Address constitutes 132.146.100.100. The 132.146.100.100 address would have a subnet mask of '255.255.0.0', the 255s indicating which numbers represent a network, and the zeros indicating which numbers represent the hosts on that network, the 194.72.10.10 example would have the subnet mask '255.255.255.0'.[1028] Thus, the question arises – what is an IP Address? So far, we know that it constitutes a series of numbers, however, it is more than that. Further, what does this mean for personal data flows? Centrally, Roberts and Challinor assert that an IP Address consists:

> of 32 bits, written as four 8-bit numbers (thus in the range 0 to 255) separated by a decimal point. Every IP address is invisibly divided into two parts, the first part identifies a particular network, and the second part identifies a particular machine on that network (called a 'host'). The point at which the first part, the network part, of the address ends and the second part, the host part, of the address begins depends upon the size of the network.[1029]

1027. P.A. Roberts, S. Challinor, 'IP Address Management' (2000) 18 BT Technology Journal 127, https://doi.org/10.1023/A:1026749131441.
1028. *Ibid.*, p. 127.
1029. *Ibid.*

The authors go on to say that network is very large, with many hosts, the:

> division point is nearer the beginning of the address than it would be in a smaller network with fewer hosts. For instance, with the address 132.146.100.100, the first two numbers (132.146) may refer to a single large network, leaving address space from 0.0 through to 255.255 (65 000 addresses). Whereas the address 194.72.10.10 may be the address of a host on a smaller network represented by the numbers 194.72.10 which leaves only 255 addresses on that network (0 to 255). The exact position of this division point is denoted by the 'subnet mask', which indicates which part of the address represents the network, and which represents the host. The 132.146.100.100 address would have a subnet mask of '255.255.0.0', the 255s indicating which numbers represent network, and the zeros indicating which numbers represent the hosts on that network, the 194.72.10.10 example would have the subnet mask '255.255.255.0'.[1030]

Viewed this way, they are a set of complex arrangements of numbers that are either configured for small or larger networks. Therefore, how can and does such an address constitute personal data? On 19 October 2016, the CJEU ruled in Case 582/14 *Patrick Bayer*,[1031] whereby the Court held that IP addresses are personal data in certain circumstances. While this case was before the implementation of the current GDPR, it referred to the previous Directive 95/46/EC.[1032] The Court in referring to the former Article 2 noted that the definition of personal data constituted:

> (a) 'Personal data' shall mean any information relating to an identified or identifiable natural person ('data subject'); an identifiable person is one who can be identified, directly or indirectly, in particular by reference to an identification number or to one or more factors specific to his physical, physiological, mental, economic, cultural or social identity; (b) 'processing of personal data' ('processing') shall mean any operation or set of operations which is performed upon personal data, whether or not by automatic means, such as collection, recording, organisation, storage, adaptation or alteration, retrieval, consultation, use, disclosure by transmission, dissemination or otherwise making available, alignment or combination, blocking, erasure or destruction; (c) 'controller' shall mean the natural or legal person, public authority, agency or any other body which alone or jointly with others determines the purposes and means of the processing of personal data; where the purposes and means of processing are determined by national or Community laws or regulations, the controller or the specific criteria for his nomination may be designated by national or Community law; (d) 'third party' shall mean any natural or legal person, public authority, agency or any other body other than the data subject, the controller, the processor and the persons who, under the direct authority of the controller or the processor, are authorised to process the data.[1033]

Notably, in its analysis, the court did not include paragraphs (c) or (e). That is, paragraph 'c' refers to data filing systems and paragraph 'e' refers to a processor.

1030. *Ibid.*
1031. Case 582/14 *Patrick Bayer v. Germany*, ECLI:EU:C:2016:779.
1032. *Ibid.*, Directive 95/46/EC of the European Parliament and of the council of 24 October 1995 on the protection of individuals with regard to the processing of personal data and on the free movement of such data, Official Journal of the European Communities No L 281/31.
1033. Case 582/14 *Patrick Bayer v. Germany*, ECLI:EU:C:2016:779, paragraph 5.

Understandably, the Court at the time did not need to include these provisions as part of its analysis and determination of whether an IP Address fell within the overall definition of personal data. In its analysis, the court confirmed that IP Addresses are a series of numbers that are assigned to networked computers. The Court further stated that:

> IP addresses are series of digits assigned to networked computers to facilitate their communication over the internet. When a website is accessed, the IP address of the computer seeking access is communicated to the server on which the website consulted is stored. That connection is necessary so that the data accessed maybe transferred to the correct recipient. Internet service providers allocate to the computers of internet users either a 'static' IP address or a 'dynamic' IP address, that is to say an IP address which changes each time there is a new connection to the internet. Unlike static IP addresses, dynamic IP addresses do not enable a link to be established, through files accessible to the public, between a given computer and the physical connection to the network used by the internet service provider.[1034]

Against the backdrop of the above, the Court went further and questioned whether 'the situation in which it is the online media services provider, namely the Federal Republic of Germany, which registers IP addresses of the users of a website that it makes accessible to the public, without having the additional data necessary in order to identify those users'.[1035] The Court confirmed that an IP address does not necessarily identify a data subject. The Court argued that:

> IP address and the date and time that a website was accessed from that IP address registered by an online media services provider do not, without more, give the service provider the possibility to identify the user who consulted that website during that period of use and, second, the internet services provider has additional data which, if combined with the IP address would enable the user to be identified. Such an address does not directly reveal the identity of the natural person who owns the computer from which a website was accessed, or that of another person who might use that computer.[1036]

However, in paragraph 39, the Court asserted that an:

> IP address constitutes personal data within the meaning of Article 2(a) of Directive 96/45 in relation to an online media services provider, it must be ascertained whether such an IP address, registered by such a provider, may be treated as data relating to an 'identifiable natural person' where the additional data necessary in order to identify the user of a website that the services provider makes accessible to the public are held by that user's internet service provider.[1037]

Importantly the Court went further and clearly argued that where such an address can identify a person or data subject, it must fall within the meaning of personal data. The Court argued that:

1034. *Ibid.*, paragraphs 15-16.
1035. *Ibid.*, paragraph 35.
1036. *Ibid.*, paragraphs 37-38.
1037. *Ibid.*, paragraph 39.

> Article 2(a) of EU Directive 95/46 must be interpreted as meaning that a dynamic IP address registered by an online media services provider when a person accesses a website that the provider makes accessible to the public constitutes personal data within the meaning of that provision, in relation to that provider, where the latter has the legal means which enable it to identify the data subject with additional data which the internet service provider has about that person.[1038]

In conclusion, the Court held that an 'IP address registered by an online media services provider when a person accesses a website that the provider makes accessible to the public constitutes personal data within the meaning of that provision, in relation to that provider, where the latter has the legal means which enable it to identify the data subject with additional data which the internet service provider has about that person.'[1039] This case is an excellent example of how the court has had to grapple with technology and its operational impact and then determine whether it meets the law. The court demonstrated and confirmed that where an IP Address identifies a data subject, that IP Address will then fall within the meaning of personal data. It must be able to identify the data subject. The point to note under this scenario is that the definition of personal data is fragmented around the world, and an IP Address may not be covered by such a definition. This is something that would need to be confirmed and reconciled in any investigation of IP Addresses.

More recently, the CJEU in *Mircom*[1040] was required to determine the identification data of its customers on the basis of IP addresses collected. That is, the Court was requested to confirm whether Telenet had to produce the identification data of its customers on the basis of IP addresses collected, by a specialised company, on behalf of Mircom. The Internet connections of Telenet's customers have been used to share films in the Mircom catalogue, on a peer-to-peer network, using the BitTorrent protocol. Telenet challenges that request. While this was generally related to intellectual property, the court had to also consider whether the GDPR was also applicable. The Court determined that:

> IP addresses of persons whose Internet connections have been used to upload pieces of files containing protected works on peer-to-peer networks, for the purposes of filing a request for disclosure of the names and postal addresses of the holders of those IP addresses, can be regarded as lawful by satisfying the conditions laid down by Regulation (EU) 2016/679.[1041]

The Court ruled that:

> Point (f) of subparagraph 1 of Article 6(1) of Regulation (EU) 2016/679 of the European Parliament and of the Council of 27 April 2016 on the protection of natural persons with regard to the processing of personal data and on the free movement of such data, and repealing Directive 95/46/EC (General Data Protection Regulation), read in conjunction with Article 15(1) of Directive 2002/58/EC of

1038. *Ibid.*, paragraph 49.
1039. *Ibid.*, paragraph 65.
1040. Case C597/19 *Mircom International Content Management & Consulting (M.I.C.M.) Limited v. Telenet BVBA, Proximus NV, Scarlet Belgium NV*, ECLI:EU:C:2021:492.
1041. *Ibid.*, paragraph 118.

> the European Parliament and of the Council of 12 July 2002 concerning the processing of personal data and the protection of privacy in the electronic communications sector (Directive on privacy and electronic communications), as amended by Directive 2009/136/EC of the European Parliament and of the Council of 25 November 2009, must be interpreted as meaning that it precludes in principle, neither the systematic recording, by the holder of intellectual property rights as well as by a third party on his or her behalf, of IP addresses of users of peer-to-peer networks whose Internet connections have allegedly been used in infringing activities, nor the communication of the names and postal addresses of those users to that right holder or to a third party in order to enable it to bring a claim for damages before a civil court for prejudice allegedly caused by those users, provided, however, that the initiatives and requests to that effect of that right holder or of such a third party are justified, proportionate and not abusive and have their legal basis in a national legislative measure, within the meaning of Article 15(1) of Directive 2002/58, which limits the scope of the rules laid down in Articles 5 and 6 of that directive, as amended.[1042]

In drawing the connection between intellectual property and copyright(s) with the identifying information of a data subject, the Court demonstrated that IP Addresses that fall within the meaning of personal data do not preclude those activities under other EU laws. On the other side, the Court did conclude by stating that any departure must be proportionate and not abusive to the existing legal basis, for example, the GDPR. Even though there was no confirmation of the definition of personal data as they relate to IP Addresses, this is yet another example of the cross-over of the law and data protection - cross-border data flows. It follows that under intellectual property and copyright an IP Address that identifies a data subject could be disclosed under limited circumstances. Nonetheless, at all material times, it would be up to the organisation who is claiming the property right to demonstrate they have taken the appropriate measures to conform with the GDPR.

Demonstration of the fragmented approach that has been afforded the definition of personal data and its relationship to IP Addresses can be seen in the recent implementation of the US state of California - California Consumer PA 2018.[1043] Section 1798.140(A) defines identifiers broadly. It lists out identifiers such as a real name, alias, postal address, unique personal identifier, online identifier, IP address, email address, account name, social security number, driver's license number, passport number, or other similar identifiers.[1044] The reference to a unique personal identifier, more so an online identifier and IP address, can all constitute an IP Address. Similarly, the UK GDPR and the EU GDPR itself provide a non-exhaustive list of identifiers, including name; identification number; location data; and an online identifier.[1045] Yet, Australia's section 5 of the PA 1988 is far from specific in its definition of personal or sensitive information. it provides a broad definition of these

1042. *Ibid.*, paragraph 133.
1043. California Consumer Privacy Act 2018, https://leginfo.legislature.ca.gov/faces/codes_displayText.xhtml?division = 3.&part = 4.&lawCode = CIV&title = 1.81.5.
1044. *Ibid.*, 1798.140 (A).
1045. United Kingdom GDPR, Article 4, https://www.legislation.gov.uk/eur/2016/679/article/4, Regulation 2016/1679, Article 4.

concepts which do not include unique personal identifiers, online identifiers, or IP addresses. This needs to be reconciled. Arguably, an online identifier constitutes an IP Address.

What has emerged post the 2016 case of *Patrick v. Germany* is that arguably the law has changed to accommodate IP Addresses into the meaning of personal information. At the time, an IP Address had to be able to specifically identify the data subject. Today it has been defined more specifically in some jurisdiction's laws. In the EU context, and while specifically not stated from the original personal data definition to only provide for an identification number, it has been broadened, in some jurisdictions to include a wider recognition of identifiable information. Today, in some jurisdictions, the inclusion of a unique personal identifier, online identifier, and IP address ensures that an IP Address is part of the overall definition of personal data/information.

Notwithstanding the above and in addressing the security issues surrounding IP Addresses has many similarities with security issues for broader cross-border data flows. These types of intrusions are not new and can be traced back to the emergence of Internet activity in the 1990s. That is, in a Berkeley version of UNIX, the attacker can exploit this attack to gain access to the target host from an untrusted host.[1046] The 'host was 'target.com' had an IP address 190.190.190.190, the attacker's host is 'attack.com' with IP address 180.180.180.180, and the target host trusts 'trust.com'. Before the attack, the attacker changes the inverse mapping so that the attacker's IP address is associated with 'trust.com'.[1047] When the attacker attempts to 'rlogin' to 'target.com' from the attacker's machine, the target machine will try to validate the name of the attacker's machine, that is, it sends the DNS server a query with the attacker's IP address.[1048] However, because the DNS has been modified by the attacker, the DNS server will reply to the target host that 180.180.180.180 is associated with the domain name 'trust.com'. The authors, not the target host, believe that one of its trusted hosts, i.e., 'trust.com', is trying to connect. The remote login is accepted and the attacker obtains access. Thus, once inside, the individuals or entities can then access the personal data and information of everybody on the network. More recently in 2021, Amnesty International in a study found that Innefu Labs IP address, 122.160.158.3, was exposed in Android screenshots on the Android spyware test server.[1049] The authors go on to say that:

> While this IP address is not registered directly to Innefu Labs, it is being used by the company. A subdomain for authshieldserver.com has pointed to the Innefu Labs IP address since 2016. AuthShield is an Innefu Labs product. Additionally,

1046. Steven Bellovin, *Using the Domain Name System for System Break-ins, Proceeding of the 5th UNIX Security Symposium* (1995), pp. 199-208. In Qijun Gu, Peng Liu, Chao-Hsien Chu, *Hacking Techniques in Wired Networks*, https://s2.ist.psu.edu/paper/hack-wired-network-may-04.pdf.
1047. *Ibid.*
1048. *Ibid.*
1049. Amnesty International, *Hackers-For-Hire-In West Africa: Activists in TOGO attacked with Indian-Made Spyware* (2021) pp. 20-22, https://www.amnesty.org/en/wp-content/uploads/2021/10/AFR5747562021ENGLISH.pdf.

> the PassiveTotal service has also recorded TLS certificates containing the innefu-.com domain on the same IP address. Such web service at neighbouring IP address 122.160.158.4 is titled 'Intelligence Collation and Analysis System'. The service is 'Powered by Innefu Labs'. The same Innefu Labs IP address also appeared in the SQL databases Amnesty International discovered on the URL shortener and Android spyware distribution servers. These SQL databases also contain records from previous spyware distribution servers which were no longer active at the time of discovery.[1050]

The ensuing problem demonstrates that even nearly twenty years later, technology has not managed to fully protect IP Addresses from illegal intrusions. It is a further demonstration of a sector that may never be settled. Furthermore, it highlights how the identifying information of individuals and entities engaged in data flows can be subject to sophisticated hacking. This issue continues to be challenging. While this chapter has not, and cannot identify every area of the data, or, technology life cycle where data flows are subject to security breaches, the limited discussion confirms it is likely to be an ongoing issue in the future. Moreover, and even though there was no examination of the respective jurisdictions' criminal laws that would penalise actors for these types of intrusions, it is argued that this is another area of further research. In other words, the criminal laws have to be aligned with this activity and the penalties provided must be high enough so as to ensure there is a high level of deterrence.

§13.04 CONCLUSION

Today, the Internet is a critical platform that has significantly contributed to the growth in transnational trade in goods and services. This proliferation of economic activity has resulted in personal data being transferred across national borders at a significant rate. For instance, for a person to download an application onto their iPhone or laptop and purchase something from France, while located in Singapore, is a very simple activity to undertake. This was not possible more than a decade ago. With that rise in activity has seen a rise in cybersecurity breaches and personal data has been exposed to significant illegal actors collecting it for economic and other uses.

This chapter demonstrated the current legal framework for data flows and data protection when coupled with cybersecurity law, is contrary to the WTO-GATS rules. What and how this will evolve, no one really knows or understands. On the one side, would there be continued pressure from the community on the government to protect their personal data online, further barriers and cybersecurity restrictions may be imposed.

On the other side, the more states open up their digital economies and allow data to flow, this creates an even level playing field whereby all data is vulnerable to similar attacks. The problem with this proposition is that it is unlikely in the near term that people will accept that their personal data is flowing across international borders, being used for financial or some other gain. Arguably, and as this book has highlighted that

1050. *Ibid.*

with the opposing views taken by jurisdictions that a level of legal harmonisation is some years away.

In order for WTO-GATS rules to be effective, some scholars have called for the harmonisation of technical regulations, standards and rules that underpin the operation and application of technology. This proposition reinforces the overall argument of the book. However, this approach should be widened to include national laws, so as to achieve a level of internationalisation.

It is argued that this is an area where FTAs could play a role, along with reforms of national laws. Doing so would ensure that the same protections provided in one state are achieved in another state. It sets a stronger level of a minimum standard on individuals and entities involved in data flows. It will, in part, provide a better balance between data flows and the protection or security of that data.

Moreover, it was demonstrated how IAs do have an important role in securing data transfers. They help an organisation identify, manage and respond to risk. Yet, the approach taken by states is far from consistent. It further highlights the potential vulnerability of data transfers when some organisations are required to undertake comprehensive risk assessments. Yet other jurisdictions such as India and Indonesia, are two countries that do not require these assessments. It creates or adds to uncertainty in the legal framework, and data subjects may over time reject the very notion that their data can be transferred.

Finally, this chapter introduced IP addresses into the discussion of data flows. It demonstrated that while not being specifically defined by many jurisdictions' data laws, they have become increasingly important. They identify data subjects over the Internet. Such an address can be used to locate the device, and ultimately the data subject. While not often fully understood by non-technical people, it is this level of identification and intrusion that poses a high level of risk to data subjects and their personal data. This is because an IP address travels with them.

For instance, a citizen from Slovenia with the hypothetical IP address of 122.160.158.4 could be picked up at the Airport of Amsterdam, as soon as they log in and their computer or mobile phone connects with the free airport Wi-Fi. What happens after that is not fully understood by most data subjects. However, their personal location and identity have been confirmed, and other forms of personal data may be unwittingly extracted from their personal device. Therefore, the identifying information of the data subject, when data is transferred over national borders, through and by the data subject's device will expose this data to security risks. To conclude, this is an area of further research to determine whether the definition of personal data across national data laws appropriately addresses IP addresses. While there is a need for further information to be provided to the general public, this issue should not impact or dilute the overall proposal of this book to expand the digital economy.

CHAPTER 14

FinTech & TechFin

FinTech and TechFins, while not necessarily new they are somewhat a recent phenomenon. They are of growing importance to the digital economy. This chapter explores the growth in this sector of the economy and how data flows impact its expansion. It highlights how there is a need as part of the new digital economy and the need to open up data – to understand how data is managed across this sector. This chapter poses a number of questions that need to be reconciled. How are data flows to be regulated in and across this sector? To what extent do these sectors rely on personal data flows? Where does this data end up? How is it stored and where? Does it help to expand the digital economy and the Open Data concept? Are the OECD Principles still current for this new and emerging economic activity? In making the case for further research to be undertaken, the chapter will demonstrate how the OECD Principles must be retained and are current. It will argue that by doing so, more needs to be undertaken at the international level to harmonise data laws with FinTech law.

This chapter draws on the work undertaken by the EU in accordance with the GDPR and highlights how on the one hand there are competing laws, achieving different things. That is, the EU GDPR protects the use of personal data, while there is other legislation to regulate FinTech, which has been and continues to be in tension with the EU GDPR. This chapter reveals how a number of scholars have attempted to resolve this tension by calling for technology such as sandboxes and dashboards to be established. However, upon brief examination of these other proposals, without a higher level of legal harmonisation, in my view, this will continue to be a challenge.

In addition to the above, the chapter has demonstrated how the current FinTech legislation in Europe requires a level of reporting on transactions. The question arises: could a similar level of reporting be included for data flows to the Regulator? Problematic, is again, there are systems and functional arrangements-tools-mechanisms being developed that are in isolation of each other. While in part they are addressing separate issues, more needs to be done to take a whole sector approach. On that basis, this chapter raises more questions than provides solutions because of the status of the current FinTech-TechFin sector.

§14.01 INTRODUCTION

'FinTech', a contraction of 'financial technology', is a technology developed to improve financial activities and find solutions.[1051] It is an ever-growing part of the digital economy. Arner, Barberis and Buckley summarise FinTech as the marriage of financial services and information technology. They go on to say that the 'interlinkage of finance and technology has a long history and has evolved over three distinct eras, during which finance and technology have evolved together: first in the analogue context then with a process of digitalization of finance from the late twentieth century onwards'.[1052] While often considered a recent addition to the financial sector, the term itself has been around for some decades. Arner, Barberis and Buckley make the point that the term FinTech can be 'traced to the early 1990s and referred to Financial Services Technology Consortium, a project initiated by Citigroup. It facilitated technological developments for the financial sector. However, it is only since 2014 that the sector has attracted the focused attention of regulators, industry participants and consumers alike'.[1053] Thus, the term in the contemporary world has taken on a slightly different meaning that includes those entities entering the financial market offering different products and services. The authors are of the view that 'FinTech' today refers to 'a large and rapidly growing industry representing between US$12 billion and US$197 billion in investment as of 2014, depending on whether one considers start-ups (FinTech 3.0) only or the full spectrum of applications, including traditional financial institutions'.[1054]

In another example, Buckley and Webster assert that FinTech has been transforming the financial services landscape is First Access, 'a data analytics company that has used a combination of weather, market pricing and agricultural input data to develop unique credit scoring algorithms'.[1055] Buckley and Webster argue that these algorithms are specifically designed for borrowers in the agricultural sector of sub-Saharan Africa. Following a pilot study in Tanzania, microfinance organisation FINCA has partnered with First Access to provide uncollateralised loans across east Africa. The latter leverages its data analytics capabilities to form credit scores from local

1051. Douglas Arner, Jonas Barberis and Ross Buckley, *The Evolution of FinTech: A New Post-Crisis Paradigm?*, University of Hong Kong Faculty of Law Research Paper No. 2015/047, 2019, p. 1.
1052. *Ibid.*, p. 1.
1053. *Ibid.*, p. 3.
1054. *Ibid.*
1055. Ross Buckley and Sarah Webster, 'FinTech in Developing Countries: Charting New Customer Journeys' 44(105) (2016) Journal of Financial Transformation 18.

mobile phone usage and the existing client database.[1056] While not stated by the authors the significance of the capture, use and storage of this information is significant. It arguably includes personal data, and while it not be traded in the transaction, it is used in the transfer of other data to attribute a credit score. Therefore, it is the personal data that is intertwined with what might be otherwise innocuous transactions by the consumer. In other words, a simplistic view is that the consumer themselves input their financial data, along with their personal data and a credit score is provided. Both data sets go hand in hand and are rarely separated in order for the individual consumer to obtain their personalised credit score.

In another more recent example of the above, Julian Kangan reports that for 'consumers with no or poor credit, Tala, a platform accessible over the mobile phone, offers consumers in the developing world microloans by doing a deep data dig on their smartphones for their transaction history and seemingly unrelated things, such as what mobile games they play'.[1057] Tala seeks to give such consumers better options than local banks, unregulated lenders and other microfinance institutions. Kangan goes on to say that new technologies, like machine learning/AI, predictive behavioural analytics, and data-driven marketing, will take the guesswork and habit out of financial decisions. 'Learning' apps will not only learn the habits of users, of which the latter are often unaware, but will engage users in learning games to make their automatic, unconscious spending and saving decisions better.[1058] FinTech is also a keen adaptor of automated customer service technology, utilising chatbots and AI interfaces to assist customers with basic tasks and reduce staffing costs. FinTech is also being leveraged to fight fraud by monitoring payment history information in order to flag transactions that are outside the norm.[1059] While interwoven with cybersecurity and data within FinTech, the benefit of leveraging this data set is the ability to detect and trace fraudulent activity. Similar to nearly all other data inputs by consumers over the Internet, a level of personal data will be attached to that single or multiple inputs.

Constituted in this manner, AI adopted by and used within FinTech-TechFin comes with its own set of challenges that need to be reconciled. Recent work undertaken by David Mhlanga in 2020 reinforced the difficulties faced with AI in this evolving sector. Mhlanga is of the view that while 'AI is promising and doing a lot in fuelling digital financial inclusion, however, there are challenges associated with reaping the benefits from intelligent algorithms'.[1060] Of note, the challenges relate to

---

1056. *Ibid.*
1057. Julia Kagan, *Financial Technology – FinTech, Financial Technology & Automated Investing Financial Technology* (2021), pp. 5-7, https://www.cpaireland.ie/CPAIreland/media/Education-Training/Syllabus%20Articles/Financial-Technology---FintechDefinition.pdf.
1058. *Ibid.*, pp. 5-7.
1059. *Ibid.*
1060. David Mhlanga, 'Industry 4.0 in Finance: The Impact of Artificial Intelligence (AI) on Digital Financial Inclusion' (2020) International Journal of Financial Studies 10. Also *see*: Deloitte, *The Fourth Industrial Revolution Is Here – Are South African Executives Ready?* (2018a). Available online: https://www2.deloitte.com/za/en/pages/about-deloitte/articles/gx-preparing-tomorrow-workforce- for-the-fourth-industrial-revolution.html. Deloitte, *Challenges Artificial Intelligence in Financial Services – Deloitte Forward, Deloitte* (2018b).

data quality, and responsibility requirements to roll out AI technology.[1061] Data quality is a core principle of the OECD Guidelines as highlighted in Chapter 1. Without a high level of data quality, personal data that forms the wider data aggregated through and by AI technology, will dilute its protection and be vulnerable to misuse. Moreover, from a trade and economic perspective, the lack of high-quality data affects investment outcomes. Individuals and entities are likely to not be confident investing in a system that does not provide the level of certainty that has pervaded international trade over many decades. Mhlanga goes on to say that the use of intelligent machines represents a further challenge concerning liability. In his view, the questions which remain unanswered are who/what shall be responsible in case something goes wrong? Financial institutions are sometimes reluctant to give machines full autonomy since the behaviour of machines is not fully foreseeable.[1062] While, to date, governments around the world are working within the current regulatory framework to address where AI assists, it is far from settled. This is particularly the case in relation to the liability of the technology for when there is a breach, or in this case, significant amounts of money lost as a result of a flawed system. However, it is out of the scope of this chapter to reconcile all liability issues.

That said, it is argued personal data, today transcends both FinTech and TechFin. According to Zetzsche et al.:

> FinTechs build or acquire data sets over time (such as peer-to-peer lending platforms) and are frequently focused on data analysis (with algorithms integrating data from various sources), FinTechs are focused on finance first and the application of *Tech* to deliver improved *Fin*.[1063]

Zetzsche and others make the point that a FinTech is a financial intermediary while a TechFin is a data intermediary. In doing so, the authors make the point that TechFins rely on large-scale data sets and businesses developed in their primary course of business and then put them to use in financial services. They may do so by considering, or even providing, the front-end of financial services, i.e., the link between financial intermediary and client.[1064] When providing services, they may rely on de-individualised datasets, aggregating huge amounts of data in order to verify assumptions as to the client's solvency, payment behaviour, savings discipline, and other relevant factors.[1065] Viewed this way, this aggregation of large volumes of data will inevitably involve personal data. That in and of itself poses complex challenges as

---

Available online: https://www.deloitteforward.nl/en/artificial-intelligence/challenges-to-widespread- artificial-intelligence-in-financial-services/.

1061. *Ibid.*, p. 10. *See also* Willem Sundblad, *Data Is the Foundation for Artificial Intelligence and Machine Learning*, Forbes 2018. Available online: https://www.forbes.com/sites/willemsundbladeurope/2018/10/18/data-is-the-foundation- for-artificial-intelligence-and-machine-learning/#12324a7751b4.
1062. *Ibid.*, p. 10.
1063. Dirk A. Zetzsche, Ross P. Buckley, Douglas W. Arner and Janos N. Barberis, *From FinTech to TechFin: The Regulatory Challenges of Data-Driven Finance*, European Banking Institute, Working paper, No. 6. (2017), p. 12.
1064. *Ibid.*
1065. *Ibid.*

this type of data can be easily transferred across the national border daily. While it is acknowledged that financial institutions that originate from the traditional banking sector will already have systems and infrastructure in place and undertake these types of transfers through contractual arrangements. Zetzsche argues that TechFins, data accumulation and analytics are key, beginning with self-developed algorithms that look directly for data correlations, and later advancing to machine learning and AI. In work undertaken by Zetzsche, Buckley and others in 2017 made an important point about the aggregated use of data. It was stated that:

> TechFins should be held to similar standards to licensed entities to avoid discriminatory practices towards the public. Indeed, within the financial services industry, the law often protects certain values by disallowing discrimination based on certain factors, which we term protected factors. Yet the efficiency of these stipulations may be threatened by data analytics. For instance, if data analytics show a certain race or gender generally has a better credit score, that better score could derive from existing biases against other races or genders. There are also studies arguing that analytics-based booking systems discriminate on the basis of race or other protected factors. Algorithms can certainly discriminate wrongfully against certain groups of people. Combining this data lead to discrimination with automation decision that 'may simultaneously systematize and conceal discrimination. The more data analytics substitute for human judgement, the more important it will be to shield protected factors from abuse and enforce anti-discrimination laws, in order to avoid a new type of racial or other profiling which could result in denial of credit and services for certain demographics'.[1066]

This is problematic in sectors that are unregulated. In reconciling the differences in each sector, there are some that naturally fall with government regulation and certification. There are others that are not regulated. Significant too are the quantities of data that are being collected and used by these sectors, whether regulated or otherwise, which are unknown. It is the ability to use this personal data without ever meeting the individuals or individuals to whom the data belongs that issues such as discrimination can arise. Most noteworthy though is at the extreme spectrum of this proposition and the above put forward by Zetzsche is that over time, state actors or individuals or entities acting on behalf of the state, in countries who have more control over FinTech, TechFin, banking and financial sectors, could use this personal data pervasively.

On the one side, it can be used to deny people (individuals or groups of individuals) in nation states access to financial products unless it is undertaken according to their political outcome rather than economic outcome(s). On the other side, much of this type of activity has been regulated under national laws; however, they are highly fragmented. This important determination can be seen; for example, discrimination by the use of data in Australia is all but regulated to ensure there is fair treatment, based on economic grounds, and not race, religion, or ethnic background. However, in other countries, this could be significantly different over time. This will also have major implications as to how nation states enforce such activity. An ensuing

1066. *Ibid.*

question that arose from the work undertaken by Zetzsche, Buckley and others was who owns the data? That is, who owns the personal data? Who owns the property rights pertaining to the data points created by a person that results in a fully commercialised digital identity? Is there a right to provide access to one's digital identity to other service providers?

The above questions are correctly identified. However, in the new digital economy and the need to open up data, more needs to be done to understand how data is managed across this sector. First, how data flows and their regulations are to be regulated in and across this sector? Second, a further accentuating question is to what extent do these sectors rely on personal data flows? Where does this data end up? How is it stored and where? Does it help to expand the digital economy and the Open Data concept? While the balance between protection of data and privacy is of importance, can a balance be struck between the need for its protection and opening up the digital economy via FinTech-TechFin? Arguably, the sector has been growing significantly for more than a decade. It is the sector that is largely unregulated that is problematic. This is because, generally, it is an area that falls outside any current certification, licence or other regulatory requirements that other areas of the financial sector are required to uphold.

That said, FinTech is not banking that is otherwise traditionally understood as facilitating money transactions domestically and internationally. FinTech can be generally described as 'integrated digital platforms where they can remain obligatory passage points for other suppliers offering financial services to their clients'.[1067] It is the FinTech-TechFin sector that is somewhat different. FinTech-TechFin began with technology from the outset. The traditional banking sector did not and as a society and the economy have evolved, they have had to adopt the technological advances. Today, it is being adopted across markets worldwide – but not evenly.[1068] The adoption and arguably its regulation have many similarities with the regulation of data flows. It has emerged as a highly fragmented legal landscape, whereby there are either well-developed laws or a significant lack thereof.

A further problem is that some nation states are not as mature as others, or their citizens do not have access to the Internet in the same way as in other countries. The resulting effect is that some nation states will continue to be far behind in regulating this area of the law. Additionally, the size and reach of the FinTech sector which is not fully understood poses challenges to understanding the breadth and depth of personal data that is being transferred internationally. Nonetheless, Jon Frost is of the view that its 'adoption is being driven by an unmet demand for financial services. FinTech promises to deliver greater financial inclusion. In other economies, adoption can be

---

1067. Reijer Hendrikse, Michiel Van Meeteren and David Bassens, 'Strategic Coupling Between Finance, Technology and the State: Cultivating a FinTech Ecosystem for Incumbent Finance' (2019) EPA: Economy and Space 6, DOI: 10.1177/0308518X19887967.

1068. Jon Frost, *The Economic Forces Driving FinTech Adoption Across Countries*, BIS Working Papers No. 838, Monetary and Economic Department, Bank of International Settlements, (2020), p. 1.

related to the high cost of traditional finance, a supportive regulatory environment, and other macroeconomic factors'.[1069]

To put this into context, and while not surveying all jurisdictions examined throughout this book, for example, it is set to boost 'India's gross domestic product (GDP) by $950bn USD by 2025'.[1070] The extent of this new and evolving economic activity cannot be underestimated. It is set to drive the financial sector in more ways than one. Centrally, digital finance, which has been one of the direct beneficiaries of this new activity, 'has the potential to provide access to financial services for 1.6 billion people in emerging economies'.[1071] One study undertaken by McKinsey Group and reported in 2016, noted that this sector could increase the volume of loans extended to individuals and businesses by USD 2.1 trillion and allow governments to save USD 110 billion per year by reducing leakage in spending and tax revenue. They argue that the 'financial-services providers would benefit too, saving $400 billion annually in direct costs while sustainably increasing their balance sheets by as much as $4.2 trillion'.[1072] They further estimate that the widespread use of 'digital finance could boost annual GDP of all emerging economies by $3.7 trillion by 2025'.[1073] If realised, this would be a '6 percent increase versus a business-as-usual scenario'.[1074]

While this study was undertaken pre COVID-19, it predicted that 'two-thirds of the increase would come from raised productivity of financial and non-financial businesses and governments as a result of digital payments'.[1075] It noted that one-third would be from the additional investment that broader financial inclusion of people and micro-, small-, and medium-sized businesses would bring. The small remainder would come from time savings by individuals enabling more hours of work. This additional GDP could lead to the creation of up to 95 million jobs across all sectors.[1076]

Against this background, during COVID-19, there was an estimated '40 percent of consumers leverage a FinTech platform for daily financial activities, and more than 90 percent were satisfied with their experience'.[1077] That being the case, it is argued that this will only increase as more people experience online efficiencies. It is possibly generational, where people under the age of 30 who have grown up with technology,

1069. *Ibid.* p. 1.
1070. Derin Cag, *India's GDP Expected to Increase by $950bn due to FinTech*, 2021, https://fintechmagazine.com/financial-services-finserv/indias-gdp-expected-increase-dollar950bn-due-fintech, Also *see*, An Indian Economic Strategy to 2035, https://www.dfat.gov.au/sites/default/files/aic-ies-snapshot-financial-services.pdf.
1071. James Manyika, Marc Singer, Olivia White and Chris Berry, *Digital Finance for All: Powering Inclusive Growth in Emerging Economies*, McKinsey Group, 2016, https://www.mckinsey.com/~/media/mckinsey/featured%20insights/Employment%20and%20Growth/How%20digital%20finance%20could%20boost%20growth%20in%20emerging%20economies/MGI-Digital-Finance-For-All-Executive-summary-September-2016.ashx.
1072. *Ibid.*
1073. *Ibid.*
1074. *Ibid.*
1075. *Ibid.*
1076. *Ibid.*
1077. Rohit Bhapkar, Ido Segev, Chris Smith and Zac Townsend, *Disrupting the Disruptors: Business Building for Banks*, 2021, https://www.mckinsey.com/industries/financial-services/our-insights/disrupting-the-disruptors-business-building-for-banks.

are more likely to embrace the technology as opposed to those above 60. Yet, FinTech is also now included in the online payments sector. To put this into perspective, during COVID-19, Forbes reported that 'Stripe and Plaid nearly tripled their valuations in a year, reaching $95 and $13.4 billion, respectively.[1078] The entity, Marqeta, is preparing to go public at a valuation rumoured to be north of $10 billion, up from $4 billion a year ago'.[1079] The market and economic activity in FinTech are enormous and will continue to grow significantly. With that, the transfer of personal data will be vast and complex, bringing enormous benefits as well as challenges. This chapter examines the benefits that personal data transfers can offer the FinTech sector.

Essentially, this amounts to consumer activity. It is the consumer who engages in a financial activity over the Internet. In 2011, the G20 High-level Principles on Financial Consumer Protection addressed the issue of data privacy by establishing Principle 8 'Protection of Consumer Data and Privacy'. This Principle states:

> Consumers' financial and personal information should be protected through appropriate control and protection mechanisms. These mechanisms should define the purposes for which the data may be collected, processed, held, used and disclosed (especially to third parties). The mechanisms should also acknowledge the rights of consumers to be informed about data-sharing, to access data and to obtain the prompt correction and/or deletion of inaccurate, or unlawfully collected or processed data.[1080]

In 2022, a decade later, the above arguably reinforces the OECD Guidelines on Transborder flows and its principles which, in my view, are now more important than at any other time in history.[1081] Why? It is these Principles that underpin and develop current-day national data protection laws, as they have provided for a good level data protection. The Principles, go some way to developing a level of harmonisation for data flows, and its legal governance. While not perfect, they have gone a long way to changing attitudes and behaviours of government, the private sector and the community in terms of personal data transmitted via the Internet. They are needed and must be retained to ensure that the world has a robust set of Principles that also underscores the rule of law and rules-based systems.

Notwithstanding the above, according to Kangan, another area that is challenging regulators is that of cryptocurrencies. Kangan argues that the 'initial coin offerings (ICOs) are a new form of fundraising that allows start-ups to raise capital directly from lay investors. In most countries, they are unregulated and have become fertile ground

1078. *Ibid.*
1079. Jeff Kauflin, *The Future of Payments, FinTech 50 2021*, Forbes 2021, https://www.forbes.com/sites/jeffkauflin/2021/06/08/the-future-of-payments-fintech-50-2021/?sh=4af5be627585.
1080. Organisation for Economic Cooperation and Development, G20 High-Level Principles on Financial Consumer Protection, 2011, p. 7, https://www.oecd.org/daf/fin/financial-markets/48892010.pdf.
1081. OECD Guidelines on the Protection of Privacy and Transborder Flows of Personal Data 2013 edition, https://www.oecd.org/sti/ieconomy/oecdguidelinesontheprotectionofprivacyandtransborderflowsofpersonaldata.htm.

for scams and frauds'.[1082] The regulatory uncertainty surrounding ICOs has also allowed entrepreneurs to slip security tokens, disguised as utility tokens, past the SEC to avoid fees and compliance costs.[1083] Hence, given the diversity of offerings made available by financial technology, and the disparate industries it touches, it is difficult to formulate a single and comprehensive approach to these problems.[1084] For the most part, governments have used existing regulations and, in some cases, customised them to regulate FinTech.[1085] They have established FinTech sandboxes to evaluate the implications of technology in the sector. The passing of the General Data Protection Regulation, a framework for collecting and using personal data, in the EU is another attempt to limit the amount of personal data available to banks.[1086] However, it is not fully understood as to the extent to which the GDPR is effective in the area of personal data.

Nonetheless, it is expected that FinTech and TechFin will play a significant role in the IR4. As highlighted in Chapter 1, IR4 will rely on technology to drive the digital economy, given that financial institutions outside of FinTech have 'leveraged data to underwrite credit, authenticate customers, and flag potentially fraudulent transactions. The nature of that data – where it comes from, how it is generated and who provides it – has evolved rapidly'.[1087] All sorts of data, including personal data collected and collated from web apps, mobile devices, and social networking platforms are now leveraged in financial services and FinTech. Accordingly, innovators have leveraged these data sets, and others, to launch better credit, insurance, payments, and other financial services to customers.[1088] It has been further noted that this transition in technology has enabled data (is quantity and quality) for greater flows in personal data around the world. It allows companies to seamlessly issue payment credentials to their customers.[1089] The resulting effect is a level of open banking being established and growing.

Nonetheless, these technologies will adopt and embrace current unregulated areas of the economy such as FinTech and TechFin. In other words, it will be a game-changer for business and government projecting to grow over the next decade or more. Arguably, it is interlinked with the concept of Open Data, as outlined by the WEF in Chapter 1. Moreover, in 2016, the WEF published a book in 2016 titled 'The Fourth Industrial Revolution', whereby the author Klaus Schwab who also heads the WEF stated that a 'technological revolution is underway that is blurring the lines between

1082. Julia Kagan, *Financial Technology – FinTech, Financial Technology & Automated Investing Financial Technology* (2021), p. 9, https://www.cpaireland.ie/CPAIreland/media/Education-Training/Syllabus%20Articles/Financial-Technology---FintechDefinition.pdf.
1083. *Ibid.*, p. 9.
1084. *Ibid.*
1085. *Ibid.*
1086. *Ibid.*
1087. Roman Leal, *Data Flows and Money Flows Will Drive the Future of FinTech*, 2021, https://romanleal.medium.com/data-flows-and-money-flows-will-drive-the-future-of-fintech-5156658f2fa9.
1088. *Ibid.*
1089. *Ibid.*

the physical, digital and biological spheres'.[1090] It was further pointed out that 'technological changes are drastically altering how individuals, companies and governments operate, ultimately leading to a societal transformation similar to previous industrial revolutions'.[1091] On this basis, it is argued that there is still much work to be undertaken by regulators and the government to meet the challenges of cross-border data flows in the digital economy and that of IR4, as FinTechs expand. It will not be easy to resolve the challenges faced by an increasingly fragmented regulatory, policy and operational working environment. The next section examines recent work undertaken in the EU and how the GDPR interfaces with FinTech.

§14.02 FINTECH-TECHFIN AND DATA LAW

In 2021, a study was undertaken on how the GDPR has affected the privacy practices of FinTech firms.[1092] This section is limited in its analysis of the EU GDPR. A wider research study is required to better understand the competing areas of the laws amongst different jurisdictions. Noteworthy too is that this section may repeat some of the laws already discussed in the EU Chapter 3.

While the study did not investigate data flows, it did provide a level of insight into how data protection has been viewed by the FinTech industry. The study, while small, examined the content of 308 privacy statements of entities, respectively before and after the GDPR became binding.[1093] The findings by Dorfleitner, Hornuf and Kreppmeier questioned whether the GDPR has achieved its original goal – the protection of natural persons regarding the processing of personal data. The authors note that by law according to the GDPR, entities are not required to have a privacy statement. However, most that have an online presence do comply with Articles 13, 14 and 15.[1094] Apart from their own study, the authors also draw upon similar studies from the US. They highlight how in the US, whereby up to '4,078 privacy statements of US firms and find significant differences in accessibility, length, readability and quality between and within the same industries'.[1095] In the US study, it was determined that 'companies appear to use more legally secure privacy statements and are more likely to share user data with third parties. Furthermore, they noted that by analysing the readability of 216 privacy statements of the most popular websites in the UK and Ireland after the GDPR

1090. Elizabeth Schulze, *Everything You Need to KNOW about the Fourth Industrial Revolution*, 2019, the Davos Agenda, https://www.cnbc.com/2019/01/16/fourth-industrial-revolution-explained-davos-2019.html.
1091. *Ibid.*
1092. Gregor Dorfleitner, Lars Hornuf and Julia Kreppmeier, *Promise Not Fulfilled: FinTech, Data Privacy, and the GDPR*, Munich Society for the Promotion of Economic Research, 2021, pp. 1-2.
1093. *Ibid.*, pp. 1-2.
1094. *Ibid.*, pp. 2-3. General Data Protection Regulation 2016/1679, Article 13 Information to be provided where personal data are collected from the data subject, Article 14 Information to be provided where personal data have not been obtained from the data subject, OJ L 119, Article 15 Right of access by the data subject.
1095. *Ibid.*, pp. 2-3.

became binding, they concluded that privacy statements are hardly readable'.[1096] The ensuing question is what does this mean for cross-border data flows? Is there a need for these statements to include a level of information that also includes how that data would be used transitionally? The authors further make the point that 'privacy statements are the essential source of information about how companies put privacy into practice and process personal data'.[1097] It is the mention of how the personal data will be processed that is of importance to this book. A further accentuating question is whether data subjects are fully informed of how their data is processed, and how many other parties it could potentially be provided to? This is a significant gap in the knowledge.

In a 2017 study by Degeling et al. and reported by Dorfleitner, Hornuf and Kreppmeier examined five hundred websites across all EU Member States, gathering a sample of 6,579 privacy statements.[1098] The researchers found that the number of sites with privacy statements increased following the implementation of the GDPR.[1099] The authors also refer to another study of 6,278 privacy statements inside and outside the EU. They found that the GDPR was the main driver of textual adjustments, although many privacy statements are not yet fully compliant regarding disclosure and transparency.[1100] This lack of disclosure is problematic, as it prevents data subjects from knowing how much of their personal data is used and protected. This problem is exacerbated by the lack of transparency, which leads to a lack of trust in the legal framework. From 2022 onwards, not requiring such statements as a mandatory legal obligation may not be the best practice.

Conversely, it is argued that privacy statements are similar to consent authorisations. Simon Chesterman notes that today, most, if not all data subjects have a level of consent fatigue.[1101] So it is feasible to suggest that there would be a certain amount of privacy statement fatigue in the community. It is further argued that even people who are tech-savvy will generally click and move on without giving a second thought to what they have consented to, or what the privacy statement contains. This could be because people are in a rush to access the information they are seeking at the time. Furthermore, in some situations, the privacy statements might be either complex or cumbersome and, in some cases, very brief. Yet, it is difficult to gauge people's ability to understand such statements. In some cases, and while not fully examined in this chapter, the conditions and exemptions stipulated in the statements themselves make the statements all but useless. That is, there might be so many exemptions that the

1096. *Ibid.*
1097. *Ibid.*, p. 5.
1098. Gregor Dorfleitner, Lars Hornuf and Julia Kreppmeier, *Promise not Fulfilled: FinTech, Data Privacy, and the GDPR*, Munich Society for the Promotion of Economic Research, 2021, pp. 2-3. Martin Degeling, Christine Utz, Christopher Lentzsch, Henry Hosseini, Florian Schaub and Thorsten Holz, *We Value Your Privacy ... Now Take Some Cookies: Measuring the GDPR's Impact on Web Privacy*, in: 26th Annual Network and Distributed System Security Symposium, NDSS 2019, The Internet Society, San Diego (2019).
1099. *Ibid.*, pp. 2-3.
1100. *Ibid.*
1101. Simon Chesterman, *Privacy and Our Digital Selves*, https://simonchesterman.com/blog/2017/09/02/our-digital-selves/.

actual original statement is rendered ineffective. This is another area that warrants further research.

In reinforcing the above, the authors acknowledge that 'FinTechs appear to safeguard themselves with exact technical and legal termini and comprehensive statements instead of the user comprehension required by the GDPR.'[1102] Significant too was how the authors found that there was an 'increase in standardised policy language built on the literature of boilerplate after the GDPR became binding, reducing the informational content that users can draw from the texts'.[1103] On the one side, for Dorfleitner, Hornuf and Kreppmeier this approach contradicts the primary objectives of the GDPR. The resulting effect has been a reduced level of transparency. In conclusion, the study found that prior to the GDPR becoming binding on the broader community, FinTech had invoked a higher level of data practices as a result of investor demands. On the other side, they note that this has dropped away since the implementation of the GDPR. Arguably, striking the balance between the level of information provided to data subjects and an entity meeting its regulatory obligations is challenging. More problematic is where there is little to no actual legal obligation for organisations to provide a level of information to data subjects. Therefore, more work is needed to balance the need for information with that is regulation setting a minimum standard on the extent of information to be afforded to the public.

A further study undertaken by Karen Mills[1104] in relation to the interconnectedness of data law and the actual practice of using consumer data highlighted the extent to which personal data can be used. Mills states that a financial services entity in the UK provided information in relation to being able to predict human behaviour. The financial entity, 'had extensive information on a large share of the hotel's customer base, because many of those customers had used the bank's credit card to pay for their stay'.[1105] It was able to provide 'anonymized data and intelligence about the hotel's clientele'.[1106] The AI technology involved was able to determine how far clients had travelled to get to the holiday destination, food preferences and other social activities. In turn, from this valuable information, the hotel was able to target its marketing based on food dishes and social activities. This type of predictive tool can be beneficial for the overall economy and economic activity in local and rural areas. An ensuring question arises: while there was no breach of the GDPR, at the time when the UK was part of the EU, to what extent personal data is used to predict this activity and behaviour? From an economic perspective, it provides valuable information for a more targeted marketing

1102. Gregor Dorfleitner, Lars Hornuf and Julia Kreppmeier, *Promise Not Fulfilled: FinTech, Data Privacy, and the GDPR*, Munich Society for the Promotion of Economic Research, 2021, pp. 2-3. Martin Degeling, Christine Utz, Christopher Lentzsch, Henry Hosseini, Florian Schaub and Thorsten Holz*We Value Your Privacy ... Now Take Some Cookies: Measuring the GDPR's Impact on Web Privacy*, in: 26th Annual Network and Distributed System Security Symposium, NDSS 2019, The Internet Society, San Diego (2019).
1103. *Ibid.*, pp. 2-3.
1104. Karen Mills, *FinTech, Small Business & the American Dream: How Technology Is Transforming Lending and Shaping a New Era of Small Business Opportunity*, Palgrave McMillan (2018) p. 99.
1105. *Ibid.*, p. 99.
1106. *Ibid.*

approach to sell a good or service. However, this is nothing new as specific marketing has been used by businesses for decades to sell their products. Today, it is undertaken differently, with more accuracy, and access to people's personal data that was not available before. Multinational companies are using this data and information with significant success in advertising and marketing goods and services online. However, and as Mills points out, a major risk from this activity is the potential misuse of the data, from algorithm-driven decision making.[1107]

For all its benefits, AI will be challenging in terms of data. On the one side, it will assist in opening up FinTech and expanding the data-driven economy. On the other side, the protection of that data is at significant risk. Mills argues that:

economists have begun to explore the implications of AI on innovation. She notes AI has the potential to create significant advances across multiple industries, including FinTech. Entities that embrace and use this technology early will be the winners are 'are going to be those who have control over large amounts of unstructured data'.[1108] However, as Mills asserts, the risks to data from the use of AI are enormous. There is the potential for it to create large entities whereby competition is significantly disrupted or non-existent. In part, this already occurs with many of the largest multinational companies in the world controlling enormous quantities of personal data. To overcome the potential for monopolies to form in the FinTech sector, and more broadly the banking sector and the use of commercial data, which included personal data, Directive 2015/2366[1109] was established. This Directive while specifically related to personal data, Preamble 46 specifies:

> the minimum set of powers competent authorities should have when supervising the compliance of payment institutions, those powers are to be exercised while respecting fundamental rights, including the right to privacy. Without prejudice to the control of an independent authority (national data protection authority) and in accordance with the Charter of Fundamental Rights of the European Union, Member States should have in place adequate and effective safeguards where it is possible that the exercise of those powers could lead to abuse or arbitrariness amounting to serious interference with such rights, for instance, where appropriate, through the prior authorisation of the judicial authority of the Member State concerned.[1110]

However, and note that the above directive had been implemented before the GDPR, it went further to align personal data with that of payments data. It states in Preamble 89 that the 'provision of payment services by the payment services providers may entail processing of personal data'.[1111] It further required that the former Directive

1107. *Ibid.*, p. 101.
1108. *Ibid.*
1109. Directive (EU) 2015/2366 of the European Parliament and of the Council of 25 November 2015 on payment services in the internal market, amending Directives 2002/65/EC, 2009/110/EC and 2013/36/EU and Regulation (EU) No. 1093/2010, and repealing Directive 2007/64/EC (Text with EEA relevance), OJ L 337.
1110. *Ibid.*, Preamble 46.
1111. *Ibid.*

95/46/EC[1112] was to be complied with. This Directive has been superseded by the GDPR. Most noteworthy was the that 'data protection by design and data protection by default should be embedded in all data processing systems developed and used within the framework of this Directive'.[1113] The ensuing question is whether the reference to 'all data processing' systems includes those that include transnational data flows? In response, the answer would be in the affirmative - no. This is because Directive 2015/2366[1114] was specifically designed for payments within the single internal market of the EU. The point to be made from this law was the standardisation of how data is shared. It established a harmonised approach. While it has been easier for these activities to be achieved under the legal framework of the EU, it provides a solid baseline for other initiatives, including this to be established.

Even though, some authors such as Dorfleitner, Hornuf and Kreppmeier have questioned whether the GDPR is having the desired effect within and across the FinTech sector. It has been reported that the current framework of the GDPR provides an effective level of protection of personal data. This includes, but is not limited to:

> Assessing potential risks when processing payment data of EU citizens and keeping a record of such impact assessments. Be transparent towards individuals with respect to how their data is handled and shared with third parties, including with foreign governments. Data transfers to stringent legal mechanisms that require in-depth assessments and safeguards from companies.[1115]

In addition, and as highlighted earlier in the book, SCCs are another way of effectively managing the governance of data flows in FinTech, specifically when that data is destined for a third country. SCCs along with BCRs can also be used under these circumstances. Therefore, these tools can be used within all the jurisdictions examined in this book. It is argued that for FinTech-TechFin, these external tools outside the principal data laws can provide an adequate layer of governance. However, they need to be drafted with precision and by experts to ensure that the right balance is struck between protecting the data and allowing it to flow. The issue is that BCRs are generally non-binding instruments.

Definition of Personal Data

As highlighted in each of the country chapters throughout this book, the respective jurisdictions have defined personal data information differently. Therefore, it will be repeated in this section.

1112. Directive 95/46/EC of the European Parliament and of the Council of 24 October 1995 on the protection of individuals with regard to the processing of personal data and on the free movement of such data, OJ L 281.
1113. Directive (EU) 2015/2366 of the European Parliament and of the Council of 25 November 2015 on payment services in the internal market, amending Directives 2002/65/EC, 2009/110/EC and 2013/36/EU and Regulation (EU) No. 1093/2010, and repealing Directive 2007/64/EC (Text with EEA relevance), OJ L 337, Preamble 89.
1114. *Ibid.*
1115. General Data Protection Regulation 2016/1679, Article 13 Information to be provided where personal data are collected from the data subject, Article 14 Information to be provided where personal data have not been obtained from the data subject, OJ L 119.

Processing

To overcome any hurdles established by Directive 2015/2366 of the EDPB[1116] 2020, Guidelines were issued to clarify the intersection between this Directive and the GDPR. In particular, it was to clarify the processing of personal data by AISPs (account information service providers) and PISPs (payment initiation service providers). In a hypothetical scenario with the Guidelines stated:

> HappyPayments is a company that offers an online service consisting of the provision of information on one or more payment accounts through a mobile app in order to provide financial oversight (an Account Information Service). With this service the payment service user can see at a glance the balances and recent transactions in two or more payment accounts at different banks. It also offers, when a payment service user chooses to do so, a categorisation of spending and income according to different typologies (salary, leisure, energy, mortgage, etc.), thus helping the payment service user with financial planning. Within this app, HappyPayments also offers a service to initiate payments directly from the users designated payment account(s) (a Payment Initiation Service).[1117]

Viewed this way, the Guidelines provide a response to how the provisions of the EU GDPR respond. It is well understood that in accordance with the GDPR, controllers are provided with the legal basis in accordance with Article 6(1). Article 6(1) for the lawfulness of processing of personal data. It states:

> Processing shall be lawful only if and to the extent that at least one of the following applies: the data subject has given consent to the processing of his or her personal data for one or more specific purposes; processing is necessary for the performance of a contract to which the data subject is party or in order to take steps at the request of the data subject prior to entering into a contract; processing is necessary for compliance with a legal obligation to which the controller is subject; processing is necessary in order to protect the vital interests of the data subject or of another natural person; processing is necessary for the performance of a task carried out in the public interest or in the exercise of official authority vested in the controller; processing is necessary for the purposes of the legitimate interests pursued by the controller or by a third party, except where such interests are overridden by the interests or fundamental rights and freedoms of the data subject which require protection of personal data, in particular where the data subject is a child.[1118]

1116. Letter European Data Protection Board, https://edpb.europa.eu/sites/default/files/files/news/psd2_letter_en.pdf. Also *see* Guidelines 06/2020 on the interplay of the Second Payment Services Directive and the GDPR Version 2.0, 2020, p. 5, https://edpb.europa.eu/sites/default/files/files/file1/edpb_guidelines_202006_psd2_afterpublicconsultation_en.pdfhttps://edpb.europa.eu/sites/default/files/files/file1/edpb_guidelines_202006_psd2_afterpublicconsultation_en.pdf.
1117. *Ibid.*, p. 8.
1118. Regulation 2016/679 of the European Parliament and of the Council of 27 April 2016 on the protection of natural persons with regard to the processing of personal data and on the free movement of such data, and repealing Directive 95/46/EC (General Data Protection Regulation), OJ L 119/1, Article 6.

The point to note is that under the GDPR there is an obligation to appoint a controller.[1119] Thus, the controller has a high-level threshold of obligation to determine the level of legal basis for the processing of personal data. However, in some nation states, under the national data-privacy laws there is no obligation to appoint a controller. Walters, Trakman and Zeller note that under the current EU framework, there is a multilayered approach to require the appointment of (1) Data Controller, (2) Joint Controllers, (3) Processor, and (4) Data Protection Officer.[1120] The authors in their comparative examination of Australia, Japan, Singapore, India and Indonesia note that the countries take a very different position on the appointment and use of controllers. They note that Australia does not require the appointment of a controller.[1121] Furthermore, Australia does not distinguish between a data controller or a data processor. Data controllers are not appointed in India. Instead, to date, India uses Grievance Officers who have a limited role and are not accountable for extensive areas of privacy or data protection, unlike their European counterparts.[1122] Similarly in Indonesia under its current-day framework of 2022, there is no requirement for a controller to be appointed. Japan does not appoint controllers. Singapore only requires an organisation to designate a person to be responsible for the data protection laws. Singapore does not specify the title of the designated individual within an organisation.[1123] Likewise, under the FTC[1124] or the HIPPA[1125] in the US, there is no requirement for the establishment of a controller. Canada[1126] is in a similar situation to that of the US and Australia. Under the current legal frameworks of the above jurisdiction, the responsibility for the processing of personal data is highly fragmented. Some jurisdictions require that a controller be established. Most jurisdictions do not. A similar level of fragmentation exists with the definition of personal data information, consent, breach notification and storage limitation, amongst others.

Therefore, in continuing to use the EU GDPR as the benchmark, a core principle of the OECD Guidelines being expressed under Article 5 provides that the data can only be used for a specific purpose.[1127] Most noteworthy, 'controllers have to assess what is

1119. *Ibid.*, Articles 3, 24, 25, 26.
1120. Robert Walters, Leon Trakman and Bruno Zeller, *Data Protection Law: A Comparative Analysis of Asia-Pacific and European Approaches*, Springer (2019), pp. 271-272. Also *see* Robert Walters and Marko Novak, *Cyber Security, Artificial Intelligence, Data Protection & the Law*, 1st ed. (2021).
1121. *Ibid.*, pp. 271-272.
1122. *Ibid.*
1123. *Ibid.*
1124. Federal Trade Commission Act (15 U.S.C. §§41-58) https://uscode.house.gov/view. xhtml? req=granuleid%3AUSC-prelim-title15-chapter2-subchapter1&edition=prelim.
1125. *Ibid.*
1126. The Personal Information Protection and Electronic Documents Act 2013. Note that, in Canada, at the time of writing this book, the data legal framework was currently under review. Also, as of January 2022, data are regulated differently through and by separate legislation for the private and public sectors. The Privacy Act 1985 regulates the public sector.
1127. *Ibid.*, Article 5. Principles relating to processing of personal data (a) processed lawfully, fairly and in a transparent manner in relation to the data subject ('lawfulness, fairness and transparency'); (b) collected for specified, explicit and legitimate purposes and not further processed in a manner that is incompatible with those purposes; further processing for archiving purposes in the public interest, scientific or historical research purposes or

objectively necessary for the performance of the contract. Where controllers cannot demonstrate that the processing of the personal payment account data is objectively necessary for the provision of each of these services separately, Article 6(1)(b) of the GDPR is not a valid legal ground for processing. In these cases, the controller should consider another legal basis for processing'.[1128] As a further requirement for the processing of data, Article 6(4) GDPR determines the conditions for the processing of personal data for a purpose other than that for which the personal data have been collected.[1129]

More specifically, such further processing may take place, 'where it is based on a Union or Member State law, which constitutes a necessary and proportionate measure in a democratic society to safeguard the objectives referred to in Article 23(1), where the data subject has given their consent or where the processing for a purpose other than that for which the personal data were collected is compatible with the initial purpose'.[1130] On this basis, Articles 66(3)(g) and 67(2)(f) of the Directive 2015/2366 have to be taken into careful consideration.[1131] Furthermore, Article 66(3)(g) of the Directive 2015/2366 states that the PISP shall not use, access or store any data for purposes other than for the provision of the payment initiation service as explicitly requested by the payer. Article 67(2)(f) of the Directive 2015/2366 states that the AISP shall not use, access or store any data for purposes other than for performing the account information service explicitly requested by the payment service user, in accordance with data protection rules.[1132] Consequently:

> Article 66(3)(g) and Article 67(2)(f) of the Directive 2015/2366 considerably restrict the possibilities for processing for other purposes, meaning that the processing for another purpose is not allowed, unless the data subject has given consent pursuant to Article 6(1)(a) of the EU GDPR or the processing is laid down by Union law or Member State law to which the controller is subject, pursuant to Article 6 (4) of the EU GDPR. Where the processing for a purpose other than that for which the personal data have been collected is not based on the data subject's consent or on a Union or Member State law, the restrictions laid down in Article 66(3)(g) and Article 67(2)(f) of the PSD2 make clear that any other purpose is not compatible with the purpose for which the personal data are initially collected. The

statistical purposes shall, in accordance with Article 89(1), not be considered to be incompatible with the initial purposes ('purpose limitation'); Also *see* Guidelines 06/2020 on the interplay of the Second Payment Services Directive and the GDPR Version 2.0, 2020, p. 10, https://edpb.europa.eu/sites/default/files/files/file1/edpb_guidelines_202006_psd2_afterpublicconsultation_en.pdfhttps://edpb.europa.eu/sites/default/files/files/file1/edpb_guidelines_202006_psd2_afterpublicconsultation_en.pdf.

1128. *Ibid.*, Guidelines 06/2020, p. 10. Also *see*, Guidelines 2/2019 on the processing of personal data under Article 6(1)(b) GDPR in the context of the provision of online services to data subjects, https://edpb.europa.eu/sites/default/files/files/file1/edpb_guidelines-art_6-1-b-adopted_after_public_consultation_en.pdf, Having regard to Article 70(1)e of Regulation 2016/679/EU of the European Parliament and of the Council of 27 April 2016 on the protection of natural persons with regard to the processing of personal data and on the free movement of such data, and repealing Directive 95/46/EC.

1129. Guidelines 06/2020, p. 10.

1130. *Ibid.*, p. 10.

1131. *Ibid.*

1132. *Ibid.*

compatibility test of Article 6(4) EU GDPR cannot result in a legal basis for processing.[1133]

Viewed this way, Article 6(4) of the EU GDPR allows for further processing based on Union or Member State law. Guidelines 06/2020 go on to explain that 'all PISPs and AISPs are obliged entities under Article 3(2)(a) Directive 2015/849 of the European Parliament and of the Council of 20 May 2015 on the 'prevention of the use of the financial system for the purposes of money laundering or terrorist financing of the anti-money laundering directive. These obliged entities are therefore compelled to apply the customer due diligence measures as specified in the directive. The personal data processed in connection with a PSD2 service are, therefore, further processed based on at least one legal obligation resting on the service provider'.[1134] Therefore, under these circumstances alone there is an obligation on the controller, but more broadly on the service provider (the entity), allowing access and use of the platform to make the financial transaction.

Consent

The concept of concept has become synonymous with the processing of personal data. This section will only examine how the EU GDPR deals with consent related to FinTech. Consent, by and large, has been dealt with earlier in the book within each of the country chapters. The application of the concept is far from harmonised across the countries examined. It poses a number of challenges for data transfers in and across the FinTech sectors, particularly when that transfer involves the data going out to a third country, outside of the EU. Therefore, this section will repeat some of the laws and information in Chapter 3 EU law.

Against the backdrop of the above, consent serves as one of the six legal grounds for the lawfulness of processing of personal data.[1135] That is, in accordance with Article 4(11) GDPR defines consent to mean 'any freely given, specific, informed and unambiguous indication of the data subject's wishes by which he or she, by a statement or by a clear affirmative action, signifies agreement to the processing of personal data relating to him or her'.[1136] Centrally in accordance with Article 4(11), consent is (1) free, (2) specific, (3) informed, and (4) unambiguous. Formally and functionally, the concept itself provides a level of control for the data subject of their personal data used in transnational transfers. Conceptually, the concept is not difficult to understand. In other words, a data subject either provides consent or otherwise. However, in practice and based on Article 4(11), it can be onerous for an organisation or controller to manage consent. Arguably, it can also be complex for mainstream society to understand the operation of consent, and how it applies to their data transfers.

Therefore, 'consent can only be an appropriate lawful basis if a data subject is offered control and a genuine choice with regard to accepting or declining the terms

1133. *Ibid.*
1134. *Ibid.*, pp. 10-11.
1135. *Ibid.*, p. 13.
1136. *Ibid.* Regulation 2016/679, Article 4 (11).

offered or declining them without detriment'.[1137] Additionally, the GDPR also contains further safeguards under Article 7, which 'sets out that the data controller must be in a position to demonstrate that there had been valid consent at the time of processing'.[1138] Also, the request for consent must be presented in a manner which is clearly distinguishable from the other matters, in an intelligible and easily accessible form, using clear and plain language. Furthermore, the data subject must be informed of the right to withdraw consent at any time, in just as simple a way as it was to grant consent. Furthermore, and according to Article 9 GDPR, consent is one of the exceptions from the general prohibition for processing special categories of personal data. However, in such cases, the data subject's consent must be 'explicit', such as through an express statement.[1139] On this basis, an ensuring question arises: are there corresponding consent requirements required under Directive 2015/2366? If not, then arguably the EU GDPR would continue to operate unabated. However, if so, then what consent takes precedence?

In examining Directive 2015/2366, Article 64 requires explicit consent to be obtained for AISPs for the provision of the service. Article 64 states that Member States shall ensure that a payment transaction is considered to be authorised only if the payer has given consent to execute the payment transaction. A payment transaction may be authorised by the payer prior to or, if agreed between the payer and the payment service provider, after the execution of the payment transaction. Taking the concept further, it provides that consent to execute a payment transaction or a series of payment transactions shall be given in the form agreed between the payer and the payment service provider. Consent to execute a payment transaction may also be given via the payee or the payment initiation service provider.[1140] However, in the absence of consent, a payment transaction shall be considered to be unauthorised. This is an important point. Article 64 generally requires that consent be provided, and where it is not, then the transaction does not proceed. It is arguably, a safety mechanism for a FinTech company. In other words, where an individual has provided consent to the transaction, there can be no dispute as to who agreed to the transaction. It not only controls the subject to some extent but also imposes some responsibility for the transaction on the data subject, not on the platform developer/owner. Nevertheless, data subjects can withdraw their consent, although any withdrawal of consent is invalid after a payee has received payment for the transaction.[1141]

1137. *Ibid.*, Regulation 2016/679, Article 4 (11) and Guidelines 05/2020.
1138. *Ibid.*, p. 13.
1139. *Ibid.*
1140. Regulation 2016/679, Article 64.
1141. Directive 2015/2366, Article 80. Irrevocability of a payment order (1) Member States shall ensure that the payment service user shall not revoke a payment order once it has been received by the payer's payment service provider unless otherwise specified in this Article (2) Where the payment transaction is initiated by a payment initiation service provider or by or through the payee, the payer shall not revoke the payment order after giving consent to the payment initiation service provider to initiate the payment transaction or after giving consent to execute the payment transaction to the payee.

The formal and functional data-processing requirements in practice and in accordance with the EU GDPR are significant.[1142] They require the practitioner to understand and know what the definition of personal data is, and how consent operates. This arguably becomes increasingly more difficult when having to reconcile transactions that are cross-border into and out of third countries. Most noteworthy is the transaction out of the EU and into a third country such as Australia. Because of the extraterritorial approach of the GDPR, the Australian entity may need to abide by elements of EU law. While the law itself does not address this issue, because it only deals with the recipient of that data. The point here is that if the transaction is undertaken over a cloud-based technology, it could be transmitted over multiple international borders before the recipient obtains the payment and data stored on a cloud server that might be in Europe, Singapore, the US or China. This is another area of further research.

Nonetheless, care needs to be undertaken to look at the words of each provision-Articles, depending on the laws being examined. In other words, the EU will refer to articles, while under Australian and UK law, legislation is often referred to as provisions or sections. It requires specialist interpretative skills. For example, on analysing Article 94(2) of Directive 2015/2366, states 'payment service providers shall only access, process and retain personal data necessary for the provision of their payment services, with the explicit consent of the payment service user'.[1143] The critical word is consent, then explicit. When combined there is explicit consent. What does this mean? According to Guidelines 05/2020, 'explicit consent' is a contractual consent. That is, there must be a genuine contract in place between the parties for explicit consent to apply.

In addition to the above, there is processing data to a silent party and processing special categories of data. Adding another layer of complexity, a silent party and the data itself is 'personal data concerning a data subject who is not the user of a specific payment service provider, but whose personal data are processed by that specific payment service provider for the performance of a contract between the provider and the payment service user'.[1144] In accordance with Article 6(1)(f) of the GDPR, the processing of client party data can be undertaken provided that the legitimate interest of the controller is not 'overridden by the interests or fundamental rights and freedoms

1142. Guidelines 05/2020, p. 14.

1143. Directive 2015/2366, Article 94, Data protection Member States shall permit processing of personal data by payment systems and payment service providers when necessary to safeguard the prevention, investigation and detection of payment fraud. The provision of information to individuals about the processing of personal data and the processing of such personal data and any other processing of personal data for the purposes of this Directive shall be carried out in accordance with Directive 95/46/EC, the national rules which transpose Directive 95/46/EC and with Regulation (EC) No. 45/2001. Payment service providers shall only access, process and retain personal data necessary for the provision of their payment services, with the explicit consent of the payment service user.

1144. *Ibid.*, p. 16. That is, data subject A, makes use of the services of an AISP, and data subject B has made a series of payment transactions to the payment account of data subject A. In this case, data subject B is regarded as the 'silent party' and the personal data (such as the account number of data subject B and the amount of money that was involved in these transactions) relating to data subject B, is regarded as 'silent party data'.

of the data subject which require protection of personal data'.[1145] In this case, it is advised that a contract exists. These types of data that have been defined under the GDPR and other national laws do vary. Some states and the EU specifically identify racial, religious, ethnic and biometric data as requiring a higher level of control and protection. This data falls within Article 9(1) EU GDPR that prohibits the processing of 'personal data revealing racial or ethnic origin, political opinions, religious or philosophical beliefs, or trade union membership, and the processing of genetic data, biometric data for the purpose of uniquely identifying a natural person, data concerning health or data concerning a natural person's sex life or sexual orientation'.[1146] The otherwise referred to as special data under the GDPR needs to be read in accordance with sensitive payment data as described by Directive 2015/2366.

Sensitive payment data means data, including personalised security credentials which can be used to carry out fraud. For the activities of payment initiation service providers and account information service providers, the name of the account owner and the account number do not constitute sensitive payment data.[1147] To fully understand the kind and level of sensitive payment data being used, a Data Protection Impact Assessment will be required in accordance with Article 35 EU GDPR. In other words, a risk assessment is undertaken to determine what the data and the risk to that data will be in the payment system. At issue is whether such an assessment is mandatory or otherwise. Generally, they are not, and some jurisdictions promote an Impact Assessment, while many others do not.

In reconciling the above, the European Data Protection Board recommends that dashboards be used. In their view, a privacy dashboard is a single point from which data subjects can view 'privacy information' and manage their privacy preferences by allowing or preventing their data from being used in certain ways by the controller in question.[1148] Such a dashboard could allow for a data subject's explicit consent. It could also offer relevant information on the nature and amount of personal data that has been accessed. However, this does not overcome the fragmented legal approach that underpins the facilitation of personal data under FinTech. While, I am not advocating for greater controls to protect privacy, in my view, that balance has not been achieved. More work is needed to better understand and develop the relevant technology whether that is a dashboard or some other mechanism to ensure protection of personal data before, during and post-transaction transmission.

Whether society likes it or not FinTech-TechFin is here to stay. Apart from the urgent need to reconcile the above, it has demonstrated that having to consider other legislation outside of the main legislation for that sector becomes highly complex. It further demonstrates how, in only using the EU as an example, applying the same to other jurisdictions is going to be a significant challenge. For instance, and as highlighted in the data area, some nation states are yet to regulate it comprehensively. In other states, the regulation of FinTech is lacking or either absent altogether. Significant

1145. *Ibid.*, pp. 16-17.
1146. *Ibid.*, Regulation 2016/679, Article 9.
1147. Directive 2015/236, Article 4(32).
1148. Guidelines 05/2020, p. 24.

too is that today this sector increasingly relies on big data and cloud computing to transmit the transaction. Problematic is to understand whether and how the data is transmitted and the number of international borders the data transcends, before being received by the recipient.

On the one hand, new entities are entering the market and challenging traditional players such as the banking sector, by giving smaller loans that can be made available quickly and offering terms that assist the borrower to fund the loan. This type of activity acquires significant amounts of personal data, the implications of which are only beginning to be fully understood by governments and regulators. Nevertheless, and as this book promotes the need to open up data flows to expand national economies, in the example above, arguably, it is the rights-based approach that prevails over regulation, that is supporting this sector. Whether this will change, and the type of approach other states will take, is far from settled.

On the other hand, the benefits arising from the open banking framework provided two components. Mills believes that first, it allows customers and small businesses to their own their data.[1149] Second, the financial institution can also release that data seamlessly to be used by other entities. The resulting intent is to both protect data privacy and allow greater innovation in the use of data for the benefit of consumers and small businesses.[1150] This concept works well across the EU as they have a well-established legal framework that requires Member States to transpose EU law into national law. How this would work externally would be complex, yet, not insurmountable. A third and emerging indirect benefit arising from data in FinTech is its contribution to combating fraud and money-laundering activities. That is, 'safeguarding the international free flow of data is a powerful weapon in preventing the consequences of financial crime, which materially affects the wellbeing of businesses and consumers'.[1151] It has been reported that the scale, sophistication and complexity of fraud and other financial crimes are rising and are estimated to cost the global economy almost EUR 2 trillion annually. Data is viewed as being integral to addressing the ongoing financial criminal activity.[1152]

Viewed this way, the link back to the OECD Principles, and therefore, as repeated throughout the book, it is these principles that form the baseline for future legal harmonisation of not only privacy protection but also cross-border data flows. Emerging research shows the next generation of revolution will be built upon interactions these new technologies have along the data pathway, meshing together like virtual gears.[1153] That is the Internet of Things, blockchain and big data represent each

1149. Karen Mills, *FinTech, Small Business & the American Dream: How Technology Is Transforming Lending and Shaping a New Era of Small Business Opportunity*, Palgrave McMillan (2018) p. 144.
1150. *Ibid.*
1151. Digital Europe, *The Importance of International Data Flows in the European Financial Ecosystem*, 2021, https://www.digitaleurope.org/wp/wp-content/uploads/2021/05/DIGITALEUROPE_The-importance-of-international-data-flows-in-the-European-financial-ecosystem-002.pdf.
1152. *Ibid.*
1153. Geoffrey Gunn and Madeline Stanley, *Harnessing the Flow of Data: FinTech opportunities for ecosystem management*, International Institute for Sustainable Development, (2018), p. 3.

individual gear that, as Gunn and Stanley point out, become meshed together. Data is pivotal to this interconnectedness between the three layers of technology.

§14.03 CONCLUSION

FinTech and TechFin, while conceptually they are different things, both collect and use personal data. Prior to the emergence of this sector in the economy, it was largely left to banks and financial institutions to lend money. Today, this has been turned upside down with FinTech and TechFin. The traditional banks have for many years had a stable economic environment underpinned by a strong legal and institutional framework.

Some scholars have proposed the establishment of sandboxes to assist in regulating FinTech-TechFin.[1154] Buckley et al. are of the view that the advantages of sandboxes outweigh their negatives and include the potential for the regulator to issue informal advice and directions regarding regulatory compliance. Further, guidance on how to interpret requirements for a firm's specific test; waiver or modification of any 'unduly burdensome rule' for the purpose of the test; and 'no action' letters where individual guidance or waivers are not possible, provide an indication that disciplinary action will not be pursued for a finite duration if certain conditions are met (but do not offer any protection against liabilities to consumers).[1155]

However, they note that the data so far available does not justify the statement that regulatory sandboxes, on a stand-alone basis, are the most effective means to further FinTech innovation. Therefore, what is? Is it a combination of innovative technology and legal tools? Should this be realised, it will only further complicate and fragment the sector potentially diluting its very existence over the longer term. Yet, one of the major beneficiaries of this new sector is the ability of government, law enforcement and regulators to track and trace money transactions. It has the potential to significantly reduce financial crimes such as money laundering and fraud.

In a further response to the evolving nature of AI and the FinTech sector and its current fragmented regulatory landscape, the UK established an initiative of establishing a reporting framework for data. Mills asserts that the UK by creating the British Business Bank, which became responsible for gathering quarterly data from banks and online lenders on loan originations and loan stocks, including metrics on costs and defaults, to better track the availability of credit and the progress of market reforms.[1156] It focused particularly on the smaller FinTech lending market and on the FinTech marketplace in general. Further, the financial institutions were required to share commercial loan data in confidential formats with regulators and policymakers and

1154. Ross Buckley, Dougles Arner, Robin Veidt and Dirk Zetzsche, 'Building FinTech Ecosystems: Regulatory Sandboxes, Innovation Hubs and Beyond' (2020) 61(055) Washington University Journal of Law & Policy 83, https://openscholarship.wustl.edu/law_journal_law_policy/vol61/iss1/10.

1155. *Ibid.*, p. 83.

1156. Karen Mills, *FinTech, Small Business & the American Dream: How Technology Is Transforming Lending and Shaping a New Era of Small Business Opportunity*, Palgrave McMillan (2018) p. 139.

make this information available to competitors via credit agencies to improve credit assessments and oversight of potential discrimination. Mills makes the point that this effort appeared to be valuable for policymaking and monitoring of the market's recovery.[1157] This is an important point that cannot be disregarded or discarded. It provides a benchmark for the future management of personal data use in cross-border data flows.

It is argued that a similar reporting process should be established at a national level for all personal data that flows out of the country of origin. In making the case for this proposal, there is an urgent need for governments to oblige their regulators with the necessary powers to acquire this information. The benefit of doing so will, in my view, strike a better balance between the flow of and protecting that data.

Centrally, it will provide data subjects with a higher level of transparency, placing greater accountability on entities transferring data internationally. Furthermore, and while potentially viewed by some as a further regulatory burden, it reinforces all of the OECD Principles and expands on them through further law reform. If not achieved at a national level, which is the obvious place where this responsibility should lie, the next step would be to establish an international organisation that collects and monitors the use of the data. Doing so will also provide another layer of trust and confidence in the regulatory landscape. It will go some way to opening up data flows and provide further economic activity. It will further assist a country's national security apparatus by being able to track and know where its data is going and how it is potentially being used. Thus, the multilayered benefits of such a proposal far outweigh any further regulatory burden, compliance costs or resource costs.

Another response is to create dashboards that can manage privacy better and more efficiently, by providing access to the data information by the data subject. While this view is sound and good for privacy advocates, it has the potential to restrict data flows and therefore results in a limited expansion of this new and emerging sector in the digital economy.

This chapter has highlighted the difficulties within the EU alone when, on the one hand, there was a need for regulation for FinTech payments and transactions, while on the other hand, there was a need to reconcile the controls and protections within the GDPR. This has not been easy for the EU to reconcile the two. There has been the requirement to provide distinct definitions of sensitive data within FinTech legislation versus the need to follow the definition of personal data in the GDPR. It has been rather complex to reconcile whether the GDPR or the FinTech legislation prevails. On the one hand, it is well understood that the GDPR governs and controls personal data over the Internet, and it is rights-based. On the other hand, the FinTech Directive is economic-based, while balancing the need to uphold the fundamental right to data protection. However, in my view, what has emerged is a clash in the law. Determining what prevails is not readily and effectively understood.

Yet, in applying the EU GDPR to cross-border transfers of data, it is clear that there needs to be a controller appointed to understand the definition of personal data

1157. *Ibid.*

and the concept of consent. Furthermore, it became clear that in reconciling the obligations of the EU GDPR, it is my view that data no matter where and how it is regulated in other sectors within the EU legal framework, the EU GDPR will prevail. The ensuing question is why? This position is based on the fact that the appointment of controls is responsible for the collection use and more importantly the processing of the data. Therefore, there is a person with a clear level of responsibility.

Problematic though is that other nation states such as Australia, India, Indonesia and US, amongst others do not have the obligation for a controller to be appointed. They hold the organisation accountable as a whole. Therefore, this approach, somewhat, dilutes the overall accountability and possibly transparency of the law and data flows. It is argued that this is yet another example that the current national and supranational approach to regulating data flows is far from adequate and there is a need for harmonisation. However, having additional policy measures in place can also incentivise and promote this sector of the economy. A way forward is to reflect FinTech-TechFin in FTAs broadly and the governance of data flows.

In summary, data flows within FinTech-TechFin and other forms of online financial services will only grow. The highlighted complex legal landscape and lack thereof in some countries and regions of the world confirm that this is an area that is far from settled. It could take a decade or more for any legal convergence or harmonisation to occur. This is both in regulating the sector and its use of data flows. It is argued that more research is urgently needed to better understand the interface between data flows and their protection within this sector. More needs to be done to better understand how data flows with cloud and other infrastructure, so as to understand where regulation is needed, if at all. This chapter has further demonstrated that there is a need for an international framework to open up this new sector within the digital economy. Doing so will bring substantial benefits economically and socially to the world.

CHAPTER 15

Cross-Border Insolvency

The proposition that data flows would be part of cross-border insolvency or restructuring of an entity was unfathomable a decade ago. Today, when companies experience financial stress, they invariably have the choice to manage it in a number of ways. For instance, the individuals involved in a company experiencing financial stress may choose to either restructure their commercial enterprise or declare insolvency.

This chapter gives an overview of the ways that the COVID-19 pandemic has changed the economic and financial landscape for businesses around the world. It also examines the response to the financial stress that may have resulted in entities declaring insolvency or undertaking a restructure. While this chapter focuses on cross-border insolvency, it does not comprehensively discuss how jurisdictions have adopted or applied international law in this area. Rather, the chapter discusses what jurisdictions examined throughout this book have adopted the UNCITRAL Model Law on Cross-Border Insolvency.

Doing so, further highlights how this is another area of international commercial law that has not been fully embraced. It further demonstrates that some jurisdictions continue to exacerbate the problem of legal fragmentation by continually holding onto their sovereign choice for adopting internationally agreed frameworks. Centrally, the question is what and how does data have an impact on cross-border insolvency or restructure? A particular challenge is to first understand the nature of the business under financial stress. For example, the airline industry which has been particularly impacted by the COVID-19 pandemic has experienced high levels of financial stress. In other words, as the pandemic was declared the general response from governments around the world has been to close all international borders. The resulting effect had airlines grounded, and passenger travel all but stopped in some countries. The customer data that airlines have is enormous.

Thus, the ensuing question is what happened with that data when the entity has been placed into administration or declared insolvent? A further ensuring question is what amount of data, if any was subject to data flows, and what international border did that data cross? Under the law, these are difficult and complex answers to reconcile. Moreover, it is complex to understand the interconnectedness of technology that has facilitated data flows and storage. In further exploring this area of the law as it pertains to the international airline sector, a data subject could be located in Slovenia, Europe and make a transaction to purchase a flight with British Airways in the UK. Therefore, the data subject's personal information has travelled across international borders, but, how many? Where was this data stored and what local data laws apply?

Against *the backdrop of the above, this chapter diverges from the traditional discussion of the law. Significantly, it provides an overview of the core elements of data laws that insolvency and restructuring practitioners need to know and understand. When managing a company's insolvency or restructuring programme current and future customer personal data requires specific and careful management. It may require practitioners to know a number of different jurisdictional data laws. This, in and of itself will be not only challenging but also highly technical and complex. This is because, as this book demonstrates, the fragmented approach to data law and cross-border insolvency law, do not provide a clear and efficient pathway to minimise the financial impact on the company or the broader economy. Constituted in this manner, there appear to be more obstacles than solutions to data flows and data pertaining to international insolvency.*

However, this could not be further from the truth. In fact, this chapter highlights how recent case law from the UK, demonstrated how the court viewed and applied data law as part of a liquidation. While it was unclear that the matter was transnational, its importance cannot be underestimated regardless of the result. What it demonstrated was the extent of understanding of data laws needed to appropriately manage the liquidation when dealing with up to 50,000 or more data subjects' personal information.

§15.01 INTRODUCTION

The digital economy and data flows are raising more questions than providing solutions. However, as an evolving area of the law, data flows have not been addressed in cross-border insolvency or cross-border restructuring. This chapter examines the importance of the consideration of data that will be subject to cross-border insolvency restructure. Recently, in 2021, 'insolvency administrators must bear in mind the protection of the personal data of all parties taking part in insolvency proceedings. First, what personal data is regulated in the insolvency cloud? This touches on issues such as data anonymisation, the ability to access this data, data fragmentation, etc. Second, who is responsible for handling data in the insolvency cloud – debtor, creditors, insolvency administrators, insolvency courts or other data processors such as cloud providers?'.[1158] Another question that needs to be addressed is: what national data privacy rules apply, and what are the obligations of a data controller or processor in these circumstances?[1159] This also begs the question: what, if any, influence does cross-border insolvency and restructuring have on data flows or the protection of that data? How has this data been considered and managed through insolvency or restructuring?

It was estimated that in 2014 alone, '50% of companies survive less than five years, and around 200,000 firms go bankrupt in the EU each year. That equates to about 600 companies in Europe'[1160] experiencing significant financial stress, forcing them to declare insolvency, or undertake a restructure. Fast forward to 2020–2022 when the outbreak of COVID-19 saw governments around the world respond with various law reforms and financial packages.[1161] Yet, in another study by the OECD in 2021, they noted that the financial stress as a result of a decline in profit was substantial. It was estimated that 'between 40% and 50% of business-as-usual profits in our sample and will cause the value of equity to decline. Around 7-9% of otherwise viable companies would become distressed, i.e., the book value of their equity becomes negative'.[1162] However, the OECD notes that these 'percentages are heterogeneous across sectors and types of firms. Intangible-intensive sectors have been significantly impacted but positioned to bridge the crisis, while the Hospitality, Entertainment and Transport (airline industry) sectors are the most severely hit. Young, small and low productivity firms are predicted to suffer more compared to their

1158. Natalya Spuling-Kryvosheyenko, *Cross-Border Insolvencies in Southeast Asia: Regional Insolvency Framework for ASEAN*, Thesis, Tilburg University (2021), p. 153, https://pure.uvt.nl/ws/portalfiles/portal/47673358/Spuling_Cross_22_01_2021.pdf This chapter draws on the work undertaken by Leon Trakman and Robert Walters *Contemporary Issues in Finance and Insolvency Law*, Volumes 1 & 2, Routledge (2022 in print). *See also* Robert Walters, 'Insolvency and Data Protection' (2020) BULA, 11, 42-1, Wolters Kluwer. Organisation for Economic Development and Cooperation, Bankruptcy rates.

1159. *Ibid.*

1160. European Commission, Vice-President of the European Commission, EU Commissioner for Justice Today's Justice Council – A Council of Progress Justice Council press conference Luxembourg, 6 June 2014. *See also*, Leon Trakman and Robert Walters, *Contemporary Issues in Finance and Insolvency Law*, Volumes 1 & 2, Routledge (2022 in print). Robert Walters, 'Insolvency and Data Protection' (2020) BULA, 11, 42-1, Wolters Kluwer.

1161. Organisation for Economic Development and Cooperation, Bankruptcy rates fall during COVID-19, 2021, https://www.oecd.org/coronavirus/en/data-insights/bankruptcy-rates-fall-during-covid-19 Note, that the statistics will different from country to country. For example, in Australia the rate had declined in 2021, when compared to the United States which had increased.

1162. Lilas Demmou et al., *Insolvency and Debt Overhang Following the COVID-19 Outbreak: Assessment of Risks and Policy Responses*, OECD Economics Department Working Papers No. 1651, (2021), p. 8.

old, large and productive counterparts'.[1163] Thus, this accounts for start-up entities, and while there were no specific details on the impact or whether a decline existed in the digital economy, arguably there would have been some. Furthermore, in highlighting the level of financial stress that some entities have experienced, the OECD estimate that the 'book value of equity due to the COVID-19 shock would have immediate consequences on firms' leverage ratios, which increase relative to a business-as-usual scenario by between 6.7 and 8 percentage points. The decline in profits also impairs firms' ability to service their debt: between 30% and 36% of firms would not be profitable enough to cover their interest expenses'.[1164] The outcome of surviving financial stress would in part be attributed to the level of debt an entity is managing. Put another way, the ability of the entity to service the debt throughout the pandemic has been the key feature as to whether an insolvency or restructuring has occurred. Moreover, there have been no statistics on the number of entities that have been subject to cross-border financial stress that would result in a cross-border insolvency or restructuring.

A general response by the government(s) has been to minimise the number of businesses that would experience financial stress and declare insolvent. The International Monetary Fund notes that:

> The pandemic is hitting small and medium enterprises (SMEs) disproportionately hard. SMEs account for 99 percent of all firms, more than 60 percent of jobs, and more than 50 percent of sales in most economies. They account for an even larger share of jobs in services sectors that have been most affected by the COVID-19 outbreak and containment measures. For example, just before the onset of COVID-19, firms with fewer than 50 employees accounted for about two-thirds of jobs in food, accommodation services, and wholesale and retail trade, versus only one-third in manufacturing Rising insolvency risks among SMEs could take the center stage and become a persistent drag on the economic recovery. Insofar as sales remain depressed while costs cannot be cut accordingly, a growing share of SMEs could accumulate losses and become insolvent, destroying millions of jobs, weakening the recovery, and also strengthening the market power of large firms in advanced economies. Liquidity support cannot address insolvency risks.[1165]

The IMF has demonstrated that even more than two years into the pandemic, there is a lot of work for governments to consider to ensure that this sector alone does not fall victim to further financial stress. Additionally, the above does not equate to the larger multinational organisations that have fallen into financial stress. The airline industry has arguably borne a significant impact on their bottom line from governments closing borders; effectively, overnight the entire world airline industry came to

1163. *Ibid.*, p. 8.
1164. *Ibid.*, p. 8.
1165. Federico J. Díez et al., *Insolvency Prospects Among Small and Medium Enterprises in Advanced Economies: Assessment and Policy Options*, International Monetary Fund (2021), pp. 5-6.

a standstill. Major regional and international airlines[1166] experienced significant financial stress. These included but were not limited to Air Italia,[1167] Flybe,[1168] Virgin Australia,[1169] Avianca,[1170] Thai Airways,[1171] Virgin Atlantic[1172] and Philippine Airlines.[1173] The financial stress imposed on these airlines was rapid and unexpected. What this signifies is that any industry sector can be vulnerable to world events that may result in entities being forced to declare insolvency. Of equal importance is the way that these entities dealt with the large quantities of data that they received either domestically or transnationally. This is an issue that has yet to be resolved. The complex nature of this work alone would result in possibly a number of different countries' data laws having to be consulted to ensure the appropriate controls and protection mechanisms have been established. As financial stress has the potential to increase significantly from geopolitical, economic, environmental and human health shocks, the nature and extent of cross-border insolvency or restructuring could also expand. This will increase the need to understand data flows and their regulation. This chapter addresses the aforementioned questions and will examine those jurisdictions that have adopted the UNCITRAL Model Law on Cross-border Insolvency.

However, where was the starting point of insolvency? Can the law pertaining to insolvency be traced historically? Trakman and Walters note that the history of insolvency can be traced to before the Roman Empire.[1174] In those early times of commercial activity, a legal procedure was developed to regulate the relationship between creditors and insolvent debtors.[1175] Essentially, the regulatory system deemed that the life and property of an insolvent debtor were owed to his creditors.[1176] This

1166. Joe Cusmano, Key *Airlines That Entered Bankruptcy due to the Pandemic*, Travel Daily Media, November 2021, https://www.traveldailymedia.com/key-airlines-that-entered-bankruptcy-due-to-the-pandemic/.
1167. *Ibid.*, When Air Italy suspended operations on the 11 February 2020, it was one of the first carriers to do so.
1168. *Ibid.*, Flybe was one of the most noteworthy companies to go bankrupt as a result of the epidemic. It was one of the largest regional airlines in Europe, accounting for more than half of all domestic flights in the United Kingdom at its peak.
1169. *Ibid.*, Virgin Australia was another airline that suffered a significant loss as a result of the virus. Virgin Australia, along with its competitor Qantas, is one of the most well-known names in Australian aviation.
1170. *Ibid.*, Flights to and from the United States were suspended on 11 May 2020, when Avianca, the world's second-oldest airline, filed for Chapter 11 bankruptcy.
1171. *Ibid.*, A bankruptcy court has ordered Thai Airways, a 61-year-old airline, to restructure its operations under bankruptcy court supervision.
1172. *Ibid.*, Virgin Atlantic filed for Chapter 15 Bankruptcy on 4 August 2020. Even though the airline is no longer in the process of ceasing operations, it is still running on a regular schedule.
1173. *Ibid.*, Philippine Airlines, the country's flag carrier, has filed for Chapter 11 bankruptcy. Early this year, on 3 September 2021, the airline filed for Chapter 11 protection.
1174. Leon Trakman and Robert Walters, *Contemporary Issues in Finance and Insolvency Law*, Volumes 1 & 2, Routledge (2023).
1175. Karl Gratzer, *Default and Imprisonment for Debt in Sweden: From the Lost Chances of a Ruined Life to the Lost Capital of a Bankrupt Company* (2008) pp. 18-20. In Karl Gratzer and Dieter Stiefel, *History of Insolvency and Bankruptcy from an International Perspective*, Södertörns högskola (2008). Also in Leon Trakman and Robert Walters, *Contemporary Issues in Finance and Insolvency Law*, Volumes 1 & 2, Routledge (2023).
1176. *Ibid.*, pp. 18-19.

notion has not changed fundamentally. Today, insolvency is intended to ensure that creditors are able to recoup some or all of their costs. In 1834, a British parliamentary commission reported that imprisonment for debt existed in every country in Europe, except Portugal.[1177] Thus, in practice, an individual or entity applies for and obtains credit from another person or organisation (bank or financial institution). Upon application, both parties enter into contractual arrangements to ensure the debtor makes repayments on the monies borrowed. It is when the debtor defaults on the credit or otherwise referred to as loan arrangements.[1178]

Trakman and Walters make the point that in the next stage, when referring to Gratzer's study, creditors were given instant access to the debtor's property on the non-payment of that debt. Through the lex Poetelia, the debtor's failure to fulfil his duty to pay the debt became a criminal offence.[1179] However, the creditor's unlimited rights to the life, property and family of the debtor were restricted. Amongst other things, the lex Poetelia abolished the right to ill-treat, kill or sell the debtor and his family as slaves. The debtor was still forced to stay in the creditor's private prison in a kind of debtor's servitude, but he regained his freedom if the debt was settled. Only if the debtor was suspected of trying to escape, was the creditor allowed to put him in chains.[1180] A debtor who went into hiding could be subjected to a bankruptcy process in which the creditor received a letter of attorney from the receiver to dispose of the debtor's property (bona). As a result, the debtor also lost his civil rights. No consideration was taken of whether he had become insolvent by accident, or whether he was responsible for his insolvency. The sanctions on the debtor remained harsh. Even the temporary inability to pay a due debt led to the loss of both the debtor's property and liberty.[1181] Thus, the early development of the law of insolvency can best be described as brutal. The debtor was subject to horrendous treatment for not being able to service the creditor, even when that inability was due to circumstances beyond the debtor's control.

Following the collapse of the Roman Empire, Germanic law rose to the forefront, including in the regulation of debt.[1182] In further referring to Gratzer, Trakman and Walters note that 'according to old Germanic law, an insolvent debtor was subjected to just as severe a treatment as in old Rome. Default was in itself seen as a crime'.[1183] In the ensuing centuries, with the development of the embryonic nation state in the Sixteenth Centuries, the law regulating debt was primarily inward-looking, focusing on the responsibility of the debtor to creditors in the jurisdiction for failure to repay the debt. However, domestic law still needed to regulate the consequence of debtors

1177. *Ibid.*, p. 17.
1178. *Ibid.*, p. 15.
1179. *Ibid.*, p. 19.
1180. *Ibid.*, p. 20.
1181. *Ibid.*
1182. Karl Gratzer, *Default and Imprisonment for Debt in Sweden: From the Lost Chances of a Ruined Life to the Lost Capital of a Bankrupt Company* (2008),p. 21. In Karl Gratzer and Dieter Stiefel, *History of Insolvency and Bankruptcy from an International Perspective*, Södertörns högskola (2008). Also in Leon Trakman and Robert Walters, *Contemporary Issues in Finance and Insolvency Law*, Volumes 1 & 2, Routledge (2023).
1183. *Ibid.*

absconding by fleeing the jurisdiction. As a result, some of the first bankruptcy statutes, such as the Statute of Bankrupts of Henry VIII in 1542 in England and the French Insolvency Ordinances of the 1560s provided for such eventualities. The bankruptcy statute of Henry VIII sought to prevent debtors from leaving the jurisdiction, including by ensuring their physical containment by domestic courts.[1184] The French Ordinances took a slightly different route. It concentrated on finding the absconded debtor and bringing him back to the jurisdiction. Even today, many modern insolvency systems incorporate elements of these two styles of dealing with debtors leaving the jurisdiction.[1185] Thus, it can be seen that, throughout history, the underlying principles of insolvency have not changed, notably, in involving essentially two parties, a creditor and a debtor. What has changed is the number of creditors that are engaged in insolvency proceedings, the complexity of those proceedings, the involvement of creditors from multiple jurisdictions and the need to engage in transborder insolvency proceedings.

In addition to the above, Trakman and Walters note that from 1706, a regulation under the English law of bankruptcy provided that a bankrupt person could be released from liability for a debt contracted before the act of bankruptcy and could start anew. In contrast, an insolvent debtor was not given this option. He could not be discharged from his old debts but remained responsible for them for the rest of his life, including the likelihood of imprisonment.[1186] This distinction between 'the increase of economic activities and the emergence of new occupations, the definition of who was a trader and who was not became more and more controversial and the distinctions became increasingly blurred'.[1187] For Margrit Schulte Beerbuöhl, the process of bankruptcy was a rather simple procedure. It started with the denial of payment by the debtor. Any further proceeding rested with the creditor because a debtor could not declare himself bankrupt until 1825.[1188] The process for commencing legal proceedings rested with the creditor who was responsible for initiating proceedings with a petition to the Lord Chancellor in Chancery Lane for a commission of bankruptcy.

Fast forward to the contemporary period, and as Sefa Franken argues two theories have emerged from cross-border insolvency.[1189] For Franken what has emerged is the territorial and universal approach. Franken asserts that under a territorial approach to cross-border insolvency law:

> jurisdiction vests with the bankruptcy court of each state where a multinational firm has assets. Each state opening insolvency proceedings applies its own substantive insolvency law to the administration of the firm's assets located in its jurisdiction. It also applies its own distributive rules to the division of the proceeds

---

1184. *Ibid.*
1185. *Ibid.*
1186. Margrit Schulte Beerbuöhl, *The Risk of Bankruptcy among German Merchants in Eighteenth-century England*, 67. In Karl Gratzer and Dieter Stiefel, *History of Insolvency and Bankruptcy from an International Perspective*, Södertörns högskola (2008).
1187. *Ibid.*, 67.
1188. *Ibid.*
1189. Sefa Franken, 'Cross-Border Insolvency Law: A Comparative Institutional Analysis' (2014) 34(1) Oxford Journal of Legal Studies 102.

> of the assets located in its jurisdiction. Creditors have to file their claims in each state in which an insolvency proceeding is opened. As a result, they will be confronted with a myriad of diverging distributive rules and policies. This territorial approach guarantees that each state can apply its own distributive rules and policies to assets located within its jurisdiction.[1190]

On this basis and viewed this way, according to the universalist approach, jurisdiction vests with the bankruptcy court of the state where the centre of main interest of a multinational firm is located.[1191] Franken further argues that the court which has jurisdiction opens a single universal insolvency proceeding - referred to as the 'main' insolvency proceeding - with respect to a multinational firm. The insolvency law of the state opening the main proceeding applies to the administration of the firm's assets wherever located. Likewise, the distributive rules of the state opening the main proceeding apply to the distribution of the proceeds of the assets wherever located.[1192] Creditors have to file their claims only once with the main proceeding and they are confronted with a single set of distributive rules and policies. Therefore, and according to the universalist approach, states need to accept the application of foreign distributive rules and policies to assets located in their jurisdiction, if a court in a foreign state has opened the main insolvency proceeding.[1193] Furthermore, Franken notes that the 'fundamental difference between territorialism and the question of whether the law of the jurisdiction where the insolvency proceeding is opened governs the administration and distribution of the debtor's assets wherever located'.[1194] The next section discusses to what extent the jurisdictions compared in this book have or otherwise adopted the UNCITRAL Model Law on Cross-Border Insolvency.

§15.02 JURISDICTIONS WHICH HAVE ADOPTED THE UNCITRAL MODEL LAW ON CROSS-BORDER INSOLVENCY

This section confirms or otherwise what jurisdictions have adopted the UNCITRAL Model Law. First, the UNCITRAL Model Law on Cross-Border Insolvency was established in 1997 (Model Law). This section does not describe the provisions or articles of the Model Law. Moreover, the UNCITRAL Model Law recognises the growing need to respond to the changing global landscape surrounding:

> the increasing incidence of cross-border insolvencies reflects the continuing global expansion of trade and investment. However, national insolvency laws have by and large not kept pace with the trend, and they are often ill-equipped to deal with

1190. *Ibid.*, p. 102.
1191. *Ibid.*, p. 102. Also *see*, Gerard McCormack, 'Universalism in Insolvency Proceedings and the Common Law' (2012) 32(2) Oxford Journal of Legal Studies 325-347. Jonathan Howell, 'International Insolvency Law, The International Lawyer' (2008) 42(1) American Bar Association 113-151.
1192. *Ibid.*, p. 102.
1193. *Ibid.*, p. 102.
1194. *Ibid.*, pp. 102-103.

> cases of a cross-border nature. This frequently results in inadequate and inharmonious legal approaches, which hamper the rescue of financially troubled businesses, are not conducive to a fair and efficient administration of cross-border insolvencies, impede the protection of the assets of the insolvent debtor against dissipation, and hinder the maximisation of the value of those assets. Moreover, the absence of predictability in the handling of cross-border insolvency cases impedes capital flow and is a disincentive to cross-border investment.[1195]

Viewed this way, the history of the UN Model Law can be best described as being complex, but, in my view, one of the most important additions to transnational commercial law. It is an excellent example of legal harmonisation and the internationalisation of commercial law. On that basis alone, and as the digital economy becomes increasingly more commercial, providing significant economic benefits to the global community, cross-border insolvency can be used as an example. Nonetheless, in the Judicial Colloquium on Cross-border Insolvency in Canada on 22 March 1995, the Model Law responded to growing concerns by the UNCITRAL, national governments and the legal profession, about the perceived lack of transnational harmonisation on cross-border insolvency.[1196] The perceived problems were attributed to diverse and inconsistent legal approaches to cross-border insolvency arising from disparate laws across and within legal systems. The idealised response to such legal divergence was for a universal insolvency law to provide legitimate legal avenues to resolve financial obstacles arising from compounding debt that extended across national boundaries. In the absence of an international insolvency law that harmonises domestic law, regulation was left to the disparate domestic statutes and divergent judicial practices of states.

In the ensuing years following the implementation of the Model Law, nation states including the EU have embarked on its adoption. Trakman and Walters note that the EU has not fully implemented the UNCITRAL Model Law on Cross-Border Insolvency Regulation 2006 (CBIR). The insolvency law of the EU traces back to the 1995 European Convention on Insolvency Proceedings which was not fully adopted and never came into effect.[1197] It took another five years before the EU adopted preliminary legislation on a framework for insolvency. However, European states did enact insolvency laws before the formation of the EU. These laws were designed largely to liquidate company assets and distribute to creditors the proceeds of an insolvency based on the legal ranking of their claims.[1198] Their insolvency laws were primarily designed to punish a delinquent debtor, rather than aid in its rehabilitation or

1195. UNCITRAL Model Law on Cross-Border Insolvency with Guide to Enactment and Interpretation, (2013), pp. 20-21.

1196. United Nations General Assembly, Cross-border Insolvency, Report on UNCITRAL – INSOL Judicial Colloquium on Cross-border Insolvency, A/CN.9/413, March 1995. In Leon Trakman and Robert Walters, *Contemporary Issues in Finance and Insolvency Law*, Volumes 1 & 2, Routledge (2023).

1197. European Union Council, Convention on Insolvency, 1995, http://aei.pitt.edu/2840/1/2840.pdf. In Leon Trakman and Robert Walters, *Contemporary Issues in Finance and Insolvency Law*, Volumes 1 & 2, Routledge (2022 in print).

1198. *Ibid.*, Article 3. Paolo Manganelli, 'The Evolution of the Italian and U.S. Bankruptcy Systems – A Comparative Analysis' (2010) 5 Journal of Business and Technology 237-238. In Leon Trakman and Robert Walters, *Contemporary Issues in Finance and Insolvency Law*, Volumes 1 & 2, Routledge (2022 in print).

reorganisation:[1199] '[a]n entrepreneur who failed to succeed in business was considered as a social threat'.[1200] The problem was that these insolvency regulations were not consistently adopted across European states, nor effectively addressed on the formation of the EU. To remedy this lack of EU-wide insolvency law, the Council of the EU established its first insolvency law by Council Regulation No. 1346/2000. However, that law did not provide common rules to regulate European insolvency proceedings; rather, it focused on coordinating insolvency proceedings as they existed and continue to exist under the national laws of Member States.[1201]

When embarking on writing this book, the UK had not long vacated the EU. Thus, nothing had changed in the area of cross-border insolvency. They had not commenced with reforming their national cross-border insolvency laws. Trakman and Walters' note that the UK's adoption of the Model Law came into effect through the Cross-Border Insolvency Regulations 2006 (UKIR).[1202] The UK was one of only a handful of Member States that embraced the Model Law, along with Slovenia, Greece, Poland and Romania at that time.[1203] Regulations also gave effect to the EU Council Insolvency Regulation/2015/848 (Recast Regulation) being an update to Regulation 1346/2000.[1204] The Recast Regulation sought to ensure the efficient administration of insolvency proceedings involving an individual or business with business activities or financial interests in an EU state, other than the one in which that individual or business was usually based. The Recast Regulation also had direct application within each EU Member State (apart from Denmark which opted out), without the need for separate state enactments. Section 1 of the UKIR highlights the importance of the Model Law to the overall regulatory framework governing cross-border insolvency in the UK. The UKIR provides that, in accordance with Article 21, 'relief application' means an application for relief submitted to the UK court by a foreign representative under Article 21(1) or (2) of the Model Law. It also recognises that EU law is followed in any territorial proceedings that fall within Articles 3(2) and 3(4) of the EIR and within the definition of insolvency proceedings in Article 2(a) of the EIR. The UKIR also provides that the definitions adopted in the Model Law have the same meaning when they are used in the Schedule of the UKIR.

1199. *Ibid.*, p. 237.
1200. *Ibid.*, p. 238.
1201. Paolo Manganelli 'The Modernization of European Insolvency Law: An Ongoing Process' (2016) 11 Journal of Business and Technology 152-154. In Leon Trakman and Robert Walters, *Contemporary Issues in Finance and Insolvency Law*, Volumes 1 & 2, Routledge (2022 in print).
1202. Cross-Border Insolvency Regulations 2006, SI 2006/1030, United Kingdom. Insolvency Act 2000 s 14(1), provided the overall power for the Regulations to be established. The Insolvency Act 1986 also deals with the issue of cross-border insolvency and allows a court to take action to assist a foreign court in a designated country. *See* Part 1, in relation to the reference to EC.
1203. Status: UNCITRAL Model Law on Cross-Border Insolvency (1997), https://uncitral.un.org/en/texts/insolvency/modellaw/cross-border_insolvency/status.
1204. Council Regulation 1346/2000 of 29 May 2000 on Insolvency Proceedings 2000 O.J. (L 160) 1, Recast by Regulation (EU) 2015/848 of the European Parliament and of the Council of 20 May 2015 on insolvency proceedings, OJ L 141.

Australia adopted the UNCITRAL Model Law on Cross-Border Insolvency as an annex to Schedule 1 of its Cross-border Insolvency Act 2008 (Cth) (ACBI Act).[1205] Prior to that, Australia had, by and large, adopted the cross-border laws of the UK. Therefore, indirectly, and in part, it could be argued that Australia also had adopted elements of the EU insolvency framework. Australia's adoption of the UNCITRAL Model Law in its ACBI Act reflects its intention to facilitate cross-border trade and investment.[1206] Therefore, this will also extend to those entities that also experience financial stress in the digital economy. Australia's ACBI Act relates entirely to international and not domestic insolvency. It relies on UNCITRAL Model Law on Cross-border Insolvency,[1207] and it applies it to both corporate and personal insolvency. It does not apply to domestic insolvency matters.

Trakman and Walters make the point that cross-border insolvency law in Singapore, resides in 2020, the Insolvency, Restructuring and Dissolution Act (IRDA) was implemented. The IRDA is an omnibus legislation that consolidates Singapore's personal insolvency, corporate insolvency and debt restructuring laws into a single Act. The IRDA will replace the Bankruptcy Act and the corporate insolvency and restructuring provisions in the Companies Act. Part 11, section 251 of IRDA refers directly to the UNCITRAL Model Law. The Third Schedule in the IRDA is the starting point in understanding the application of the Model Law in Singapore. By replicating most of Article 1 of the Model Law, the IRDA extends its scope of application to where a foreign court or a foreign representative seeks assistance in Singapore in connection with a foreign proceeding. That assistance is sought in proceedings in a foreign State that are connected to the proceedings under Singapore insolvency law in which both proceedings are taking place concurrently with the same debtor.[1208] Such recognition of foreign insolvency proceedings or requests for assistance also arise where creditors or other interested persons in that foreign State have an interest in requesting the commencement of, or participating in, a proceeding under Singapore insolvency law. Trakman and Walters, in their examination of a number of national insolvency laws, note that in a similar way to that of Australia, Singapore has generally replicated the relevant Articles of the Model Law in the IRDA.

Japan, in a similar way, has only partly adopted the UNCITRAL Model Law. In other words, the Act on Recognition of and Assistance for Foreign Insolvency Proceedings (RAFIP) was enacted in Japan to enable the Tokyo District Court to recognise and provide assistance in respect of foreign insolvency proceedings in Japan.[1209] Canada is another country to have adopted the Model Law. Neil Hannan highlights how Canada

1205. Cross-border Insolvency Act 2008, Act No. 33.
1206. Gerard McCormack and Anil Hargovan, 'Australia and the International Insolvency Paradigm' (2015) 37(3) Sydney Law Review, 389. In Leon Trakman and Robert Walters, *Contemporary Issues in Finance and Insolvency Law*, Volumes 1 & 2, Routledge (2022 in print).
1207. Cross-border Insolvency Act 2008, Act No. 33, defines the Model Law to mean the Model Law on Cross-Border Insolvency of the United Nations Commission on International Trade Law, set out in the Annex to United Nations General Assembly Resolution A/RES/52/158 (1997).
1208. Leon Trakman and Robert Walters, *Contemporary Issues in Finance and Insolvency Law*, Volumes 1 & 2, Routledge (2022 in print).
1209. Yuri Ide, Atushi Nishitani, *Legal Framework of Cross-Border Insolvency in Japan – Ancillary Proceeding for Foreign Insolvency Proceedings*, Anderson, Mori, Tomotsune, (2017), p. 1.

has based its legislation on the Model Law by incorporating the spirit and enacted by An Act to Amend the Bankruptcy and Insolvency Act, the Companies' Creditors Arrangement Act, the Wage Earner Protection Program Act and Chapter 47 of the Statutes of Canada 2005, which inserted the same into Part IV of the purpose of the Model Law in their domestic legislation.[1210] The Model Law was CCAA in respect of large corporate insolvency, and restructuring and by inserting it into Part XIII of the BIA in respect of other insolvencies. Hannan's both pieces of legislation in which the provisions of the Model Law have been inserted were pre-existing, the language of the Model Law has been adapted so as to make it consistent with the terminology and definitions contained in that legislation. These definitions are not always consistent between the two pieces of legislation.

Neither India nor Indonesia has adopted the UNCITRAL Model Law on Cross-border Insolvency. For Indonesia, generally, bankruptcy is regulated in Law no. 37/2004 on Bankruptcy and Postponement of Debt Payment Obligations. However, Law 37/2014 does not yet regulate the mechanism or procedure for cross-border bankruptcy. Article 212 of Law 37/2004 provides for creditors who, after the pronouncement of the declaration of bankruptcy, take full or part of the bankruptcy assets which are located outside the territory of the Republic of Indonesia, which are granted to them with the right to precedence, are obliged to replace the bankruptcy assets with everything they get. Both states have the principle of territoriality. Finally, the US has also adopted the Model Law. Neil Hannan makes the point that the US enacted the Model Law by the:

> Bankruptcy Abuse Prevention and Consumer Protection Act which replaced section 304 of the Bankruptcy Code with Chap. 15 of that Code. Chapter 15 alters some of the language from the Model Law, to make it consistent with the existing provisions of the US Bankruptcy Code and does not contain its own exhaustive definition section, but cross-references its definition with other chapters within the Code. Chapter 15 also picks up a number of exclusions contained in other Chapters which are not present in the Model Law; these are discussed in Section 6.2. A knowledge of the concepts contained in the other chapters of the Code is necessary in order to understand the meanings of terms contained in Chapter 15. Section 103 stipulates that the general provisions in Chap. 1 of the Bankruptcy Code apply to Chapter 15 cases. In addition, the following sections apply to these cases: a) section 307 granting standing to the US Trustee to act in Chapter 15 cases; b) section 362(n) excepting from the automatic stay cases involving certain small business debtors; and c) sections 555-557 and 559-562, protecting broad rights under financial contracts from stay, avoidance or other limitation in any proceeding under the Bankruptcy Code.[1211]

The internationalisation of cross-border insolvency law has been further strengthened with a number of lower-level guidelines and principles being developed.

Japan is one of the first countries to enact legislation enabling recognition of and provision of assistance in foreign insolvency proceedings pursuant to the UNCITRAL Model Law on Cross-Border Insolvency.

1210. Neil Hannan, *Cross-Border Insolvency The Enactment and Interpretation of the UNCITRAL Model Law*, Springer (2017), p. 16.

1211. *Ibid.*, p. 20.

However, as this section has briefly demonstrated, there continue to be nation states that adopt the notion of universalism. The next section briefly discusses a small number of these instruments and their adopting data flows and the protection of data.

§15.03 PRINCIPLES AND GUIDELINES

This section highlights a selected few principles and guidelines that have been established at the international level to assist in the management of cross-border insolvency matters. It highlights that while there is a general understanding of privacy, more needs to be done in this area to reform the guidance information. Doing so will assist practitioners, individuals and entities to improve their understanding of data flows and their security protection at the beginning, during and post a cross-border insolvency or restructuring process.

In 2001, the World Bank Group released the Principles for Effective Insolvency and Creditors regimes (the Principles), which were later revised in 2011 and 2015.[1212] Worthy of note is that the Principles account for privacy. In other words, privacy concerns should be addressed through notice of the existence of such systems, a notice of when information from such systems is used to make adverse decisions, and access by data subjects to stored credit information with the ability to dispute and have corrected any inaccurate or incomplete information.[1213] An effective enforcement and supervision mechanism should be in place that is efficient, inexpensive, transparent, and consistent. This is reflected in most data protection and privacy laws today. However, they vary from nation state to nation state. B1.4 states that Privacy:

> Subjects of information in credit information systems should be made aware of the existence of such systems and be able to access information about themselves. In particular, they should be notified when information from such systems is used to make adverse decisions about them. They should be able to dispute inaccurate or incomplete information and mechanisms should exist to have such disputes investigated and have errors corrected.[1214]

Arguably, more needs to be done to this aspect of the regulatory framework. It is argued that data flows and their security and protection need to be reflected within these Principles. This will improve and accommodate data in the digital economy. In doing so, and in continuing the need for the internationalisation of data flows and data protection law(s), there is a need for a top-down and a bottom-up approach. That is, principles, Guidelines and Codes sit at the bottom of the regulatory framework, while conventions, treaties and national laws reside at the top.

1212. World Bank Group, Principles for Effective Insolvency and Creditor/Debtor Regimes, 2015, https://openknowledge.worldbank.org/bitstream/handle/10986/35506/Principles-for-Effective-Insolvency-and-Creditor-and-Debtor-Regimes.pdf?sequence = 1&isAllowed = y.

1213. *Ibid.*, p. 6. Risk Management and Informal Workout Systems – Credit information systems. A modern credit-based economy requires access to complete, accurate, and reliable information concerning borrowers' payment histories. This invariably constitutes personal data.

1214. *Ibid.*, p. 18.

In regard to the above, the UNCITRAL Legislative Guide on Insolvency Law also implies the importance of privacy today. It states:

> Some assets may be freely sold or exchanged in the course of the proceedings, while others may be subject to limitations that arise from contract or other law (a non-assignable government licence or a customer list that is subject to privacy restrictions) or involve mediating problems that can arise with respect to other rights in those assets. The inclusion of some intangible assets in the estate may give rise to conflicts with other laws, such as those restricting transferability or laws relating to privacy protection.[1215]

Similar to the Principles established by the World Bank, the UNCITRAL Guide on Insolvency should be amended to take into account data flows and their security throughout a cycle of data flows-protection. Most noteworthy, in part, the UNCITRAL Practice Guide on Cross-Border Insolvency Cooperation 2010 addresses the protection of data flows. It states:

> The Model Law envisages that communication as authorized would be subject to any mandatory rules applicable in an enacting State, such a person or body may be appointed by a court to facilitate such as rules restricting the communication of information for reasons, inter alia, of protection of privacy or confidentiality.[1216]

The above relates to the appointment of a person or body to act at the direction of the court in accordance with Article 27, paragraph (a). However, it is not clear whether this would extend to personal data held by an entity (party) involved in a cross-border insolvency. A strict reading suggests that privacy pertains only to the appointment or body that has been appointed by the court to undertake the insolvency. That said, the Guidelines appear to require further work. It is argued that similar to other principles and guidelines, they need to be amended to better reflect personal data and their transnational flows and security/protection in the new digital economy. This revision is necessary since many entities make up the digital economy, and these are prone to experiencing financial stress. Thus, the current international legal framework for insolvency and, to a lesser extent, restructuring, provides a baseline for those entities wanting to restructure or declare insolvency. Therefore, the ensuing question is what does an insolvency practitioner need to understand and be aware of in relation to data flows and the security of that data? Rather than restating the data laws that have already been compared, the next section considers those areas of the law of which practitioners (insolvency and restructuring) should know.

What Practitioners Need to Know

This section explains the important areas of data laws that an insolvency or restructuring practitioner will need to understand. It will predominantly draw on the EU GDPR

1215. United Nations Commission on International Trade Law (UNCITRAL), UNCITRAL Legislative Guide on Insolvency Law, 2005, p. 76, https://uncitral.un.org/sites/uncitral.un.org/files/media-documents/uncitral/en/05-80722_ebook.pdf.
1216. UNCITRAL Practice Guide on Cross-Border Insolvency Cooperation 2010, p. 19, https://uncitral.un.org/sites/uncitral.un.org/files/media-documents/uncitral/en/practice_guide_ebook_eng.pdf.

and industry guidelines. It will define key terms such as 'controller' and 'processor'. Practitioners will need to expand on the national and EU laws which will need to be consulted extensively. To begin with, the following terms need to be defined from the perspective of national or EU law. The most common terms include, but are not limited to:

- access;
- controller;
- data subject;
- disclosure;
- deletion;
- person;
- processor;
- personal;
- processing;
- personal data;[1217]
- storage limitation;
- international data flows; and
- supervising authority.

It must be noted, however, that the definition of the terms listed above will vary from jurisdiction to jurisdiction. Practitioners will need to understand the obligations to maintain records of the personal data being collected, and how it is used, processed and managed with limited exceptions to this rule along with mandatory reporting of data breaches.[1218] Additionally, data protection IAs are required where the collection and processing of data carry high risk, and contracts are required between joint controllers outlining their respective responsibilities.[1219]

Some national laws prescribe responsibilities for 'data controllers' (being those persons who are responsible for the purposes and means of the processing of personal information) and directly applies to 'data processors' (those who process personal data on behalf of the data controller).[1220] In corporate insolvency proceedings, the practitioner will need to know whether joint controllers have been operating or a single controller. Drawing on a recent judicial decision from the UK highlighted some of the core elements a practitioner must take into consideration. In *Southern Pacific Personal Loans Ltd,*[1221] whereby an application to the Court is made by the joint liquidators of Southern Pacific Personal Loans Limited (the company) under section 112(1) of the Insolvency Act 1986 for the determination of certain questions and consequential directions. The question for the Court was do the liquidators constitute controllers?

1217. Paul Smith, Róisín Liddy-Murphy, Data Protection Law for Insolvency Practitioners, Conyers, 2019, https://www.conyers.com/wp-content/uploads/2019/11/2019-11-CAY-Article-Data-Protection-Law-for-Insolvency-Practitioners.pdf.
1218. *Ibid.*
1219. *Ibid.*
1220. *Ibid.*
1221. *Southern Pacific Personal Loans Ltd [2013] EWHC 2485 (Ch).*

This case is an excellent demonstration of the additional complexities when having to deal with two very different areas of law. It highlights that the balance between commercial law and rights-based law is difficult to obtain. The ensuing case also highlights that regardless of whether there is insolvency, restructure or liquidation, practitioners will need to be across the governance of data, its flows, use and protection. Nonetheless, there is no respondent named in the application, but the Information Commissioner (the Commissioner) was notified of the application and provided with the application notice and supporting evidence. At the invitation of Roth J in a letter dated 9 July 2013 which drew attention to the potentially wide-reaching implications of any declaration the court might make, the Commissioner has appeared by counsel and made representations.[1222] The background to this matter is lengthy and is worthwhile to be understood, so as to understand the role that data had in this liquidation. The court noted that:

> The company is a member of the Lehman Brothers group of companies. It did not go into any insolvency process at the time of the collapse of the Lehman group in September 2008, when the principal operating companies in the UK were placed in administration. It entered creditors' voluntary liquidation on 4 September 2012 and the applicants were appointed joint liquidators. The company was incorporated in October 2000 and its business comprised the provision of personal loans to individual's resident in Great Britain, secured by way of second charge on their homes. It ceased making loans in about September 2007. It appears that all loans were provided through independent brokers who introduced borrowers to the company. Once loans were made, the company generally held the loans and supporting security on trust for various special purpose vehicles for inclusion in securitisation transactions. The special purpose vehicles were entitled to call for a transfer of the legal title to the loans and supporting security and did so in about August 2010. The company complied with those requirements and retained no further connection, legal or beneficial, with the transferred loans. The company continued to hold the legal title to loans and supporting security only in those cases where the loans had been redeemed prior to the date of the transfers (redeemed loans). From the start of its business, the company collected and retained data relating to its borrowers. The data included names and addresses, the amount of loans, the borrowers' repayment records and details of proceedings brought against them by third parties. The data clearly comprises or includes 'personal data' for the purposes of the Data Protection Act 1998 (the DPA). The company was a 'data controller' within the meaning of the DPA and was and remains registered as such. From 2006 the data in question was stored with a loan servicing company called Acenden Limited (Acenden), which is also a member of the Lehman group. Acenden continues to hold the data relating to the redeemed loans for the company. Acenden performed various servicing activities in respect of loans made by the company. They included dealing with customer enquiries, monitoring and collecting loan repayments, initiating legal action for loans in default, handling complaints, producing annual statements and quarterly arrears statements, retaining records of mortgage files and correspondence and processing data subject access requests (DSARs) made under the DPA. It was a 'data processor' for the purposes of the DPA and was and remains registered as such. Following the transfer of the live loans to the special purpose vehicles in 2010, the

1222. *Ibid.*, paragraph, 1.

> data with respect to those loans has ceased to be retained by or for the company. Acenden continues to hold data in respect of the redeemed loans. This comprises approximately 50,000 files, of which approximately 32,000 are held both electronically and in paper form and the remainder are held in paper form only.[1223]

Based on the above there are a number of areas that the practitioner would need to understand very well when dealing with data. What is not clear with whether this involved data being transferred outside of the UK. Nonetheless, it reinforced the points made earlier that know what constitutes personal data, its collection, storage, use, and the data subjects involved would be a complex exercise. This complexity is further heightened when dealing with large numbers such as 50,000 files and a third party being involved in the use of that data. Nevertheless, the Court went further detailing the extensive provisions of the data laws that were applicable in this case. These include:

> The relevant provisions of the DPA may be summarised as follows. Section 1 contains definitions. 'Data' extends to data held both in hardcopy and electronic form. 'Data controller' is defined to mean – *'a person who (either alone or jointly or in common with other persons) determines the purposes for which and the manner in which any personal data are, or are to be, processed'*. A 'data processor', in relation to personal data, means 'any person (other than an employee of the data controller) who processes the data on behalf of the data controller'. 'Processing' includes 'obtaining, recording or holding the information or data'. A *'data subject' is an individual who is the subject of personal data.* Furthermore, section 4(4) of the DPA provides that it is the duty of a data controller to comply with 'the data protection principles' in relation to all personal data for which he is the data controller. The data protection principles are set out in part 1 of schedule 1 to the DPA. They include that personal data must be processed fairly and lawfully, that it shall be obtained only for one or more specified and lawful purposes and not further processed in any manner incompatible with such purpose or purposes, that it shall be adequate, relevant and not excessive in relation to the purpose or purposes for which it is processed, and that it shall be accurate and, where necessary, kept up to date. Principles 5 and 6 are as follows: '5. *Personal data processed for any purpose or purposes shall not be kept for longer than is necessary for that purpose or those purposes. 6. Personal data shall be processed in accordance with the rights of data subjects under this Act.*'[1224]

Additionally, the Court went further stating:

> Section 7 sets out the rights of access that individuals enjoy as regards personal data held in respect of them, and provides:
>
> Subject to the following provisions of this section and to sections 8, 9 and 9A, an individual is entitled-
>
> (a) *to be informed by any data controller whether personal data of which that individual is the data subject are being processed by or on behalf of that controller,*
> (b) *if that is the case, to be given by the data controller a description of –*
> (i) *the personal data of which that individual is the data subject,*

1223. *Ibid.*, paragraph 4-8.
1224. *Ibid.*, paragraph 11-13.

(ii) *the purposes for which they are being or are to be processed, and*
(iii) *the recipients or classes of recipients to whom they are or may be disclosed,*
(c) *to have communicated to him in an intelligible form –*
(i) *the information constituting any personal data of which that individual is the data subject, and*
(ii) *any information available to the data controller as to the source of those data.*[1225]

Section 7(8) requires a data controller to comply with a request promptly and in any event within forty days or such other period as may be prescribed after receipt of the request. This requirement is enforceable by two means. First, the court may order compliance on an application made under section 7(9). Secondly, on the basis that a failure to comply with a DSAR would contravene paragraph 6 of the data protection principles, the Commissioner may serve the data controller with an enforcement notice under section 40, requiring the data controller to comply with the request. The exercise of these powers by the court and the Commissioner are in both cases discretionary. In addition, under section 13, an individual who suffers damage by reason of any contravention by a data controller of any requirement of the DPA is entitled to compensation from the data controller. Section 13(3) provides that it is a defence to any such claim to prove that the data controller had taken such care as in all the circumstances was reasonably required to comply with the relevant obligation.[1226]

Regardless of the outcome of this case, it demonstrated that the broad scope and reach of data laws need to be understood and managed according to the applicable laws. In this case, it was the Data Protection Laws of the UK before they exited the EU. Not only does the practitioner need to be across the key terms that were highlighted earlier but also needs to understand the extent of a data subject's rights and ensure those rights are practised throughout the administration process. The Court concluded in paragraph 51 that the liquidators were not to be declared as controllers for the purposes of the data laws, in relation to the data processed by the company with respect to the redeemed loans. The UK High court reaffirmed the above position in 2019.[1227] Even so, and while not determined as controllers, the administrators need to understand and confirm who the controllers are or would have been. Arguably, this is an evolving area of the law, and this section has only highlighted a single case.

§15.04 CONCLUSION

This chapter has confirmed that data flows and the security protection of data will have an important role in cross-border insolvency or restructuring. As the digital economy continues to expand and grow, there will inevitably be individuals and entities that will experience financial stress and declare insolvency or undertake a restructure. No matter what process is undertaken to manage the financial stress entity, the need to understand and know the obligations set out in the national data laws will be significantly important.

1225. *Ibid.*, paragraphs 13-14.
1226. *Ibid.*, paragraphs 13-14.
1227. *Green v. Group Ltd & Others [2019] EWHC 954 (Ch).*

Personal data, its protection, security and transnational flows are finding their way into nearly every area of economic activity. It is a significantly diverse, complex, cumbersome and technical area of the law and technology to understand. When coupled with other areas of the law such as transnational contract law or insolvency and restructuring law, that complexity is heightened significantly.

In answering the questions raised in this chapter, data flows and their security will be regulated by an insolvency cloud, whether domestically or internationally. A practitioner will need to know and confirm whether those data subjects who have requested such, had their personal data anonymised. This chapter also confirms that, while administrators may not assume the legal responsibility of a controller or processor in the administration of a company going through a liquidation process, they will need to understand the regulation of data, which often necessitates understanding laws established in different jurisdictions.

Moreover, the practitioner will need to distinguish between the personal data and its flows that have been used by the entity undergoing insolvency or a restructure, and the data of the entity being represented by a practitioner. Practitioners will need to be clear on their role and responsibilities in the management of the data, particularly where it involves personal data that is subject to a number of jurisdictional data laws. It is important for practitioners to understand who the regulator is and what needs to be reported to him/her. Again, this can vary from country to country.

Arguably, there will be a high-level threshold in some jurisdictions than in other jurisdictions to meet with the Regulator. That said, there will be nation states that have no data laws. In other nation states, where there is a lack of data laws there will likely be no specific regulator. In this small example, it is one of many areas where data laws and the obligations of the company, rights of the data subject and responsibilities of a regulator vary significantly.

This chapter has given some indication of the breadth and depth of the data laws that a court will need to examine when dealing with an insolvency, whether domestic or international. Therefore, it can be argued that this will only become even more complex if there continues to be an unwillingness to have data law internationalised.

It is essential that the appointment of an insolvency practitioner be managed with care. This appointment is important to the current and future digital economy, as practitioners will need to fully understand their powers and limitations, along with the extent of personal data the entity has been handling. They will need to understand not only the responsibilities, but they will also need to analyse comprehensively the extent of the data captured, used and stored by the entity undertaking an insolvency or restructuring.

While the above case confirmed that an administrator would not be a controller for the purposes of the respective data laws, problematic though is that other jurisdictions may rule differently. This will depend on the local data laws. While not closely examined in this book, some jurisdictional laws do not require a controller or processor to be designated by an organisation to assume responsibility for handling data laws. In conclusion, the fragmented regulatory approach may find its way into the judiciary and further complicate the way in which data flows and their use and storage are managed throughout the insolvency or restructuring process.

Chapter 16
Dispute Resolution

In following on from the previous Chapter, data flows, their protection, security, use and storage will be subject to transitional insolvency or restructuring. This examines the interface of data flows in relation to international commercial arbitration, along with cross-border insolvency. It will draw upon the practical implication of having to deal with and manage data in an arbitration that is also subject to insolvency. This chapter will draw on the recent work undertaken by the International Council for Commercial Arbitration and International Bar Association.

This chapter will discuss the separate but increasingly interconnectedness of transnational data flows, data protection, arbitration and cross-border insolvency. It will not compare or discuss whether each jurisdiction discussed in this book has adopted the international legal framework for commercial arbitration. Rather the chapter will examine the relevant legal and practical challenges that need to be considered in an international commercial arbitration when dealing with data flows, their protection, use and storage impact or otherwise are to be considered.

Centrally, there are three areas of laws when having to consider the issues of data as part of an insolvency, and then further in relation to arbitration. In the previous, it was evident the issues insolvency practitioners need to know and understand in relation to data laws. Noteworthy, there is no case law available that examines all three areas of law, arbitration data flows-protection and insolvency and a collective. On the one hand, this is because data flows in arbitration are a new area of the law. On the other hand, there are a number of countries that have not established data laws, let alone law that facilitates data flows internationally. In many respects, data flow(s), to date, has been silent in arbitration. However, that could be about to change. There may never be issues that arise and are contested in the courts are usually based on procedural aspects of an arbitration or a cross-border insolvency.

§16.01 INTRODUCTION

Since 2008, the world has experienced a Global Financial Crisis, continued conflict in the Middle East, a global pandemic in 2022 and significant conflict in Eastern Europe. In addition to these events, the world has experienced a significant shift in the economy. While the traditional sectors such as transport, manufacturing, health, agriculture, and mining amongst others still have a major foothold, they are slowly being replaced by the new technology-driven economy. As highlighted throughout the book, the outbreak of coronavirus had placed companies that undertake cross-border economic activity in the trade of goods and services to experience significant financial stress. This chapter will discuss the separate but increasingly interconnectedness of transnational data flows, data protection, arbitration and cross-border insolvency. It will not compare or discuss whether each jurisdiction discussed in this book has adopted the international legal framework for commercial arbitration. Rather the chapter will examine the relevant legal issues that need to be considered in an international commercial arbitration when dealing with a transnational insolvency matter, and how data flows, their protection, use and storage impact or otherwise are to be considered. Centrally, there are three areas of laws when having to consider the issues of data as part of an insolvency, and then further in relation to arbitration. In the previous Chapter 15, it was evident that the issues insolvency practitioners need to know and understand in relation to data laws. Unfortunately to date, there is no case law available that examines all three areas of law, arbitration data flow protection and insolvency and a collective. There may never be issues that arise and are contested in the courts are usually based on procedural aspects of an arbitration or a cross-border insolvency.

First, all three areas of the law, arbitration, data flows and insolvency are cross-border in nature. International commercial arbitration is often used to resolve complex commercial disputes between companies that are located in different nation states. Second, data flows enable the transfer and trade of data across international borders. Third, insolvency is dealing with a company engaged in data flows that have fallen into financial stress and is seeking to manage a way out of the debt. That said:

> insolvency and arbitration are two distinct proceedings governed by two different sets of procedural rules, each having its own unique purpose and underlying principles. For this reason, the relationship between insolvency and arbitration has been described as 'a conflict of extremes'. However, despite their distinct nature, the interaction between arbitration and cross-border insolvency seems feasible from the outset, as long as arbitrability and public policy matters are carefully addressed. Insolvency proceedings may entail a cross-border character, for instance, when the insolvent debtor possesses assets in more than one state or when the creditors are not located in the jurisdiction where the insolvency

> proceedings take place. The coordination of such cross-border insolvency proceedings is often a cause of discord. Traditionally, it is acknowledged that not all insolvency-related issues may be arbitrable. There are two types of insolvency issues, 'pure' or 'core', on the one hand, and 'non-pure' or 'non-core', on the other hand. The main difference between these two categories is that 'pure' or 'core' insolvency proceedings pertain to the bankruptcy court's central functions; for instance, the opening of the insolvency proceedings or the appointment of the estate's administrator. 'Pure' insolvency issues have been consistently considered non-arbitrable. Whereas non-core or non-pure insolvency-related issues are deemed arbitrable in principle, they may nonetheless create some concerns regarding public policy.[1228]

Viewed this way, it is well understood that where there is a contract between two parties that requires the transfer or sale of data, such a contrast involving transnational commercial trade in services is likely to contain a dispute resolution clause. That clause will either direct the parties to undertake mediation or arbitration when a contractual dispute arises. However, that will depend on how the dispute resolution clause of the contract has been drafted.

Against the backdrop of the above, one of the most prolific practitioners and writers on transnational arbitration Gary Born, and Wendy Miles are of the view that:

> one of the most significant global trends in arbitration has been its increasing popularity as the preferred means of resolving international commercial disputes, and the corresponding increase in the support of arbitration by courts in most states. Arbitration has been an enduringly popular choice for parties, in both state-to-state and commercial dispute resolution, since the beginning of recorded history. The attractions of arbitration have remained largely constant since antiquity: parties choose to arbitrate in order to avoid the expense, delays, and rigidities of litigation in state courts, as well as the peculiar uncertainties of international litigation (including jurisdictional, choice-of-law and enforcement disputes). Rather, they seek neutral, expert dispute resolution in a tribunal of their choosing and a single, centralized forum.[1229]

Redfern and Hunter reinforce Born and Miles' position arguing that 'arbitration is now the principal method of resolving international disputes involving states, individuals, and corporations'.[1230] Redfern and Hunter further point out how this reality has led the arbitral process to distance itself, where possible, from the risk of domestic judicial parochialism. Modern international arbitration has consequently achieved a

1228. Velislava Hristova, Andrés Eduardo and Alvarado Garzón, 'International Arbitration and Cross-Border Insolvency – Friends or Foes? Revisiting the Role of Arbitration in Resolving Cross-border Insolvency-Related Disputes' (December 2021) 12(4) Journal of International Dispute Settlement 693-711, https://doi.org/10.1093/jnlids/idab013.
1229. Gary Born, Wendy Miles, *Global Trends in International Arbitration*, 2015, https://biblioteca.cejamericas.org/bitstream/handle/2015/812/Global-Trends-in-International-Arbitration.pdf?sequence=1&isAllowed=y.
1230. Alan Redfern, Marcus Hunter, *International Arbitration*, 6th ed. Oxford university Press (2015) pp. 415-416.

considerable degree of independence from national courts.[1231] Therefore, in evaluating the importance and growth of arbitration, the international legal framework has been transformed over the last five decades. Born and Miles note:

> The current legal framework for international arbitration was initiated by the Geneva Protocol in 1923 and Geneva Convention in 1927 and culminated in the signing of the United Nations Convention on the Recognition and Enforcement of Foreign Arbitral Awards in 1958 ('New York Convention'), the promulgation of the UNCITRAL Arbitration Rules in 1976, the adoption of the UNCITRAL Model Law in 1985 and the enactment of 'modern' arbitration statutes in many developed jurisdictions from 1980 to the present day.[1232]

However, this chapter does not examine at length the provisions of the UNCITRAL Model Law.[1233] Nevertheless, centrally, Article V(2)(a) of the New York Convention, a court may refuse to recognise and enforce an arbitral award when it finds that 'the subject-matter is not capable of settlement by arbitration under the law of that country'.[1234] Histrova asserts that:

> given the lack of indications in the New York Convention to define what disputes are arbitrable, the contracting states decide this at their own discretion. During the last decades, there is a trend towards widening the list of issues that are arbitrable in many states. This might certainly respond to extrinsic policy considerations, but the arbitrability of insolvency-related disputes usually remains at the margin of the discussions.[1235]

The author goes on to discuss a case in 2011 from the UK and make reference to a Singapore case in 2015, and an Australian case in 2016. The next section draws on and expands on the points made by Hristova.

In 2011, in the case of *Fulham Football Club (1987) Ltd v. Richards,*[1236] the Court was required to consider elements of insolvency, specifically petitions. Fulham Football Club 1987 Limited appealed against an order dated 1 December 2010 made under section 9 of the Arbitration Act 1996. Under this order, the judge stayed a petition presented on 27 April 2010 under section 994 of the Companies Act 2006. The background to this case arose from a petition in relation to the conduct of the Premier League. The Court noted:

> The petition relates to the affairs of the Second Respondent, The Association Premier League Limited ('the FAPL'), which was incorporated in 1992 in order to

1231. Gary Born and Wendy Miles, *Global Trends in International Arbitration*, 2015, https://biblioteca.cejamericas.org/bitstream/handle/2015/812/Global-Trends-in-International-Arbitration.pdf?sequence = 1&isAllowed = y.
1232. *Ibid.*
1233. United Nations Commission on International Trade Law, Model Law on International Commercial Arbitration 1985 (With amendments as adopted in 2006).
1234. Velislava Hristova, Andrés Eduardo and Alvarado Garzón, 'International Arbitration and Cross-Border Insolvency – Friends or Foes? Revisiting the Role of Arbitration in Resolving Cross-border Insolvency-Related Disputes' (December 2021) 12(4) Journal of International Dispute Settlement 693-711, https://doi.org/10.1093/jnlids/idab013.
1235. *Ibid.*
1236. *Fulham Football Club (1987) Ltd v. Richards* [2011] EWCA Civ 855.

> give the Premier League the commercial independence to organise its own broadcast and sponsorship agreements. Under its memorandum of association, the FAPL is empowered to organise and manage the Premier League (under the jurisdiction of the Association ('the FA')) and, for these purposes, to make its own rules. Each of the 20 in the Premier League holds a share in the company. The allegations of unfair prejudice raised in the petition do not, however, relate to the conduct of the other members of the FAPL but rather to that of the First Respondent, Sir David who is its chairman. What is alleged is that Sir David acted as an unauthorised agent in breach of the FA Agents Regulations ('the Agents Regulations') when in July 2009 he was asked by the Chief Executive of Portsmouth City Limited ('Portsmouth') (Mr Peter Storrie) to approach the chairman of Tottenham Hotspur & Athletic Company Limited ('Tottenham') (Mr Daniel Levy) in order to facilitate the transfer to Tottenham of one of Portsmouth's players, Mr Peter Crouch. At the time Portsmouth was in severe financial difficulties and needed to raise £9 million in order to avoid winding-up proceedings threatened by HM Revenue & Customs. It is alleged that by 25th July had made an offer of £9 million to secure the registration of Mr Crouch which had been rejected but was prepared to increase its offer to £11 million. Mr Crouch had indicated his preference to play for Tottenham but Tottenham had made lower offers for the player which had also been rejected.[1237]

Patten LJ made the point that:

> Such disputes as are likely to occur in the conduct of the affairs of the Company (not the competition) are therefore likely to be limited and the same will apply to the scope for relief. Buy-out orders are not appropriate for the reasons I have mentioned and an order for the winding-up of the FAPL on just and equitable grounds under s. 122(1)(g) of the Insolvency Act 1986 ('the IA 1986') is similarly unrealistic as well as being highly undesirable in the interests of the member whose fortunes depend upon the income generated by the broadcasting of Premier League fixtures.[1238]

On the point of the prejudicial petition in accordance with section 994 of the Companies Act 2006, the subject matter was not arbitrable. Section 994 states that a 'member of a company may apply to the court by petition for an order under this Part on the ground that a) that the company's affairs are being or have been conducted in a manner that is unfairly prejudicial to the interests of members generally or of some part of its members (including at least himself), or b) that an actual or proposed act or omission of the company (including an act or omission on its behalf) is or would be so prejudicial'.[1239] While personal data or data flows did not form part of this matter, the entities involved and the shareholders all contain large quantities of personal data. Whether data flows could have been involved is uncertain. However, it is these matters that are decided on points of traditional areas of law that, invoke considerable challenge. Furthermore, when applying the public interest test, the Court stated the principle set out in section 1(b) of the Arbitration Act 1996 namely the parties should be free to agree on how their disputes are resolved, subject only to such safeguards as

1237. *Ibid.*, paragraphs 2-4.
1238. *Ibid.*, paragraph 48.
1239. *Ibid.*, paragraph 44.

are necessary for the public interest.[1240] To the extent therefore that public policy has a part to play it can only be as a safeguard necessary in the public interest. This is a demanding test and it is necessary in the public interest that agreements to refer to disputes about the internal management of a company should in general be prohibited; nor it is necessary to prohibit arbitration agreements to the extent that they, in particular, apply to disputes whether a company's affairs are being (or have been) conducted in a manner unfairly prejudicial to the interests of its members.[1241]

Four years later, in *Tomolugen Holdings Ltd*[1242] the Court had to reconcile a claim involving an insolvent company and whether it was arbitrable when the rights of the creditors are affected. The background to this case was that:

> The plaintiff in the Suit is Silica Investors Limited ('Silica Investors'), a minority shareholder which holds approximately 4.2% of the issued share capital of Auzminerals Resource Group Limited ('AMRG'), the eighth defendant in the Suit. AMRG is the company whose affairs Silica Investors alleges have been conducted in a manner that is oppressive or unfairly prejudicial towards it. AMRG is a listed Singapore company that develops, explores and exploits mines in Australia. Its wholly-owned subsidiary, Solar Silicon Resources Group Pte Ltd ('SSRG'), is also involved in mine development and exploration, and owns Australian mining licences and exploration permits. Silica Investors first acquired shares in AMRG from Lionsgate Holdings Pte Ltd ('Lionsgate'), the second defendant in the Suit. The share sale agreement between Silica Investors and Lionsgate ('the Share Sale Agreement') contains an arbitration clause. Lionsgate currently remains a shareholder of AMRG and holds approximately 9% of its issued share capital. Lionsgate is wholly owned by Tomolugen Holdings Limited ('Tomolugen Holdings'), the first defendant in the Suit. Tomolugen Holdings is the majority shareholder of AMRG and holds approximately 55% of its issued share capital directly. The third to seventh defendants in the Suit are shareholders and current or former directors of Lionsgate, AMRG or SSRG; together, they hold just over 3% of the issued share capital of AMRG.[1243]

The Court went further and highlighted how:

> Lionsgate made an application pursuant to s 6 of the IAA for a stay of the court proceedings against it in the Suit. Lionsgate said that a part of the dispute in the Suit fell within the scope of the arbitration clause in the Share Sale Agreement and the court proceedings against it in respect of that part of the dispute therefore had to be stayed in favour of arbitration; it further submitted that the remainder of the court proceedings against it should be stayed as well in the interests of appropriate case management pending the resolution of the arbitration. The other seven defendants named in the Suit (collectively, 'the remaining defendants') also filed stay applications that were contingent on the success of Lionsgate's application. They argued that if the court proceedings between Silica Investors and Lionsgate

1240. *Ibid.*, paragraphs 98-99.
1241. *Ibid.*
1242. *Tomolugen Holdings Ltd and another v. Silica Investors Ltd* [2015] SGCA 57 (Singapore Court of Appeals (Civil Appeals)).
1243. *Ibid.*, paragraphs 4-6.

> were stayed in favour of arbitration, then the rest of the court proceedings in the Suit should also be stayed pending the resolution of that arbitration.[1244]

In looking at the English judiciary, the Court argued that:

> In our judgment, the approach taken by the courts in England commends itself to us because it seeks to strike a balance between, on the one hand, upholding the agreement of the parties as to how their disputes are to be resolved and, on the other hand, recognising that there are jurisdictional limitations on the powers that are conferred on an arbitral tribunal. This has the effect of enhancing the procedural complexity of a dispute which is covered by an arbitration agreement where one or more of the reliefs sought is beyond the arbitral tribunal's powers to grant, and such complexity will be further exacerbated if, in addition, the dispute concerns other parties who are not party to the arbitration agreement in question. It is to this that we turn next; but we are satisfied that an arbitral tribunal's inability to grant certain reliefs which may be sought would not in itself render the subject matter of the dispute non-arbitrable.[1245]

Moreover, the Court highlighted how the arbitration of claims which arose upon insolvency would run contrary to the objectives of the insolvency regime stating:

> Many of the statutory provisions in the insolvency regime are in place to recoup for the benefit of the company's creditors losses caused by the misfeasance and/or malfeasance of its former management. This is especially true of the avoidance and wrongful trading provisions. This objective could be compromised if a company's pre-insolvency management had the ability to restrict the avenues by which the company's creditors could enforce the very statutory remedies which were meant to protect them against the company's management. It is not [an] unimportant consideration that some of these remedies may include claims against former management who would not be parties to any arbitration agreement. The need to avoid different findings by different adjudicators is another reason why a collective enforcement procedure is clearly in the wider public interest.[1246]

Again, and while there was no mention or consideration of data flows or data protection, the ensuring question is when there are more than one or two legal issues of a cross-border nature to resolve the court has a formidable task in navigating the respective laws. While it is acknowledged that it will depend on the issue at hand, the cases above involve individual shareholders, debtors and creditors, along with customers data that needs to be managed not only within the arbitration, but also, through the insolvency stage. It also highlighted those licences that were involved, contain possibly highly sensitive personal data that is commercial. This is because a license will generally be issued by a government and be held commercially. Thus, it has a government and commercial element. Therefore, it has become a formidable task as disputes continue to rise in relation to not only the commercial activities of companies, when they have a dispute over contractual arrangement pertaining to data transfers and trade. It will also arise where the entity experiences financial stress, undertakes an insolvency, and an element of that insolvency is contested through the court. A further

1244. *Ibid.*, paragraphs 7-9.
1245. *Ibid.*, paragraph 103.
1246. *Ibid.*, paragraph 77.

layer that may also present itself is the security of the data. In other words, as data continues to proliferate, there will be cybersecurity issues to be managed at arbitration and insolvency.

In overcoming these issues, it will fall to practitioners to ensure they establish well-thought-through contractual clauses, to minimise the potential for a dispute. However, it is noted that entities falling into financial stress and declaring insolvency are out of the control of any practitioner. They cannot control the behaviour of company representatives in the broader economy. For example, an arbitrator that is based in Australia has been appointed to an arbitration that is administered by the UK arbitration institution. This appointment has been supported by the appointment of two other arbitrators. Therefore, there is a panel of three arbitrators. The problem arises in a cross-border flow of data dispute that which neither of the arbitrators is familiar with the UK GDPR. Problematic too, is where the arbitration agreement is silent on what data laws to implement. The ensuing question is: is it the UK or is it Australian law? On the other hand, the management of such an issue will have more clarity where the arbitration agreement reflects data laws to be applied. For example, Australia. Even then there will be problems, depending on where the other two arbitrators who make up the three panellists come from. They may, for example, come from Singapore and the US. On this basis, those two arbitrators would need to understand the data laws of Australia. It may not necessarily conclude at this point. Centrally, data flows could involve data that is transferred between more than one state. The data may be transferred or traded across several international borders.

The prevailing view is that arbitration itself is not subject to PDP obligations.[1247] However, if only one participant of the arbitration is subject to PDP obligations, the arbitration may be impacted as a whole. Whether personal data processing falls within the relevant laws, material and jurisdictional scope will determine whether the PDP laws apply.[1248] Neva Cirkveni and Per Neuberger assert that:

> Modern personal data protection laws apply whenever personal data about a data subject is processed during the activities falling within the relevant personal data protection laws' jurisdictional scope. Personal data includes 'any information relating to an identified or identifiable natural person'. During typical arbitration proceedings, substantial portions of information are exchanged relating inter alia to the parties, their counsel, the tribunal and third parties. As such, they are likely to be seen as qualifying under the definition of 'personal data'. 'Data subjects' refers to the above-mentioned individuals who are identified or identifiable. Processing includes active and passive operations, thus encompassing using, disseminating, and deleting personal data as well as receiving, organising and storing personal data. The scope of application encompasses actions whenever personal data is processed in the context of the activities of an establishment of a controller or a processor in the EU and extraterritorially, such as when personal data is transferred outside the EU.[1249]

1247. *Ibid.*
1248. *Ibid.*
1249. *Ibid.*

Notwithstanding the above, the same would apply where there are arbitration proceedings in Canada or New Zealand, and there are data transfers outside of those countries of origin. It demonstrates that data laws do not necessarily pertain to the arbitration itself, but rather, the when the personal data is being collected, used, transferred or processed. Therefore, in an arbitration where these activities take place, arbitrators need to ensure they meet the obligations of the respective data laws of the country or countries they are dealing with.

In response to the above dichotomy, the International Council for Commercial Arbitration-International Bar Association (ICCA-IBA), in 2020, released a Roadmap to Data Protection in International Arbitration has been developed by the ICCA-IBA Task Force on Data Protection in International Arbitration to help arbitration professionals better understand the data protection and privacy obligations to which they may be subject in relation to international arbitration proceedings.[1250] At the time of writing this book, the Draft Roadmap was not available to be cited. However, Roadmap addresses the following issues, but is not limited to:

- the applicability of GDPR to arbitrations held outside the EU;
- GDPR in the context of NAFTA;
- the issue of videoconferencing, which has greatly increased in importance throughout the COVID-19 pandemic;
- 'third-party funders' and how they are taken into account;
- not meeting the obligations of the GDPR, especially as a shield for non-disclosure; and
- the potential of using non-compliance with PDP requirements as a path to annulment or refusal of recognition and enforcement of the arbitral award.[1251]

The forgoing developments in data flows will require another level of obligations to be carried out by arbitrators. Therefore, and as Cirkveni and Per Neuberger believe increasingly arbitrators will be qualified as data controllers, meaning that they will be responsible for compliance with PDP laws.[1252] Yet they note the importance that understanding the various definitions with the respective data laws will be just as important. In agreeing with the authors, they state, for example:

> based on the definition of 'data controller'; most arbitral participants are likely to be considered as such, including counsel, parties, and the institution. Data controllers can delegate data processing to data processors, who will be under their control and will require data processing agreements on terms prescribed by the applicable law. Thus, secretaries, transcribers, translators, and others are all likely to be considered data processors. There is the further issue of joint controllers who jointly determine the purposes and means of data processing. Joint controllership is broadly interpreted, but the joint controller's liability is

1250. *Ibid.*
1251. *Ibid.*, including references to the 'ICCA-NYC Bar-CPR Protocol on Cybersecurity in International Arbitration' (Cybersecurity Protocol) the IBA's Cybersecurity Guidelines and the ICC Guidance Note on Possible Measures Aimed at Mitigating the Effects of the COVID-19 Pandemic.
1252. *Ibid.*

limited to only the processing that the controller has determined, its purpose and means and not the overall processing.[1253]

On this basis, Cirkveni and Per Neuberger are of the view that the restrictions on personal data transfers between jurisdictions are an evident way in which PDP laws apply. The background of different arbitral participants will determine the application of different PDP regimes.[1254] More specifically, when related to data flows and data transfers or data trade, the authors argue that modern 'personal data protection laws restrict personal data transfers to third countries to ensure that legal obligations are not circumvented by the transfer of personal data to jurisdictions with lower standards of personal data protection'.[1255] In citing the EU GDPR allows third-country personal data transfers if one of the following occurs:

- the country has been deemed by the EU Commission to provide adequate PDP;
- one of the expressly listed safeguards is put into place;
- a derogation allowing transfers where necessary for the establishment, exercise or defence of legal claims; or
- a party's compelling legitimate interest.[1256]

They go onto say that it is these rules that apply to arbitral participants and not to the arbitration as a whole, thus mandating that every arbitral participant considers what personal data transfer restrictions apply to them. The PDP principles applicable in arbitration include fair and lawful processing, proportionality, data minimisation, purpose limitation, data subject rights, accuracy, data security, transparency and accountability.[1257]

To date, there is no case law that has to deal with all three issues of arbitration, insolvency and data flows, let along arbitration and data flows as two distinctive legal issues. The formal and functional dilemma highlights the increasing challenges the digital economy is going to face in relation to arbitration. On the other side, this will be further heightened, under the current international and national laws that do not specifically address data flows or data transfers outside of the country of origin. Some practitioners[1258] have cited that, today, there is a fundamental clash and tension between law of data and arbitration. Problematic too, is the increasing role of conducting arbitration online. The sector has had to rapidly adjust and understand the implication of videoconferencing and the data management issues that can arise. The point is, that currently this book has addressed the data transfer laws within the jurisdictions compared. In doing so, it has not covered all the relevant area of rights and other obligations that arise for the management and governance of data in an

1253. *Ibid.*
1254. *Ibid.*
1255. *Ibid.*
1256. *Ibid.*
1257. *Ibid.*
1258. Gary Born, *International Arbitration*, Kluwer Law International (2021), p. 2064. *See also*, Neva Cirkveni, Per Neuberger, *Clash of the Titans: GDPR and International Arbitration: A Look at the Future*, Oblin Rechtsanwalte (November 2021), https://oblin.at/publication/clash-of-the-titans-gdpr-and-international-arbitration-a-look-at-the-future/.

arbitration or insolvency proceeding. Therefore, for a practitioner to only focus of data flow and its ensuing provisions. There will need to be wider consideration of the laws, to ensure all protections, controls and obligations are implemented.

Undoubtedly, the obligations of arbitrators are increasing as the digital economy evolves and changes. These obligations are also being tested and strengthened, because it is only in recent times that data flows and data protection have had to be considered in commercial arbitration. There is a need for arbitrators to build their skills and capacity to ensure they address data law in preparation for, and throughout, an arbitration proceeding. This may well differ when arbitration is conducted online, as additional data related issues will arise and need to be managed. Significantly, there will be the need for the arbitration proceeding to identify the relevant data laws that will apply, within the arbitration agreement. A failure to do so, will be costly to the Parties, but also, it will require a lot more work to reconcile the differences between the laws, where there are cross-border transfers involved.

Nonetheless, this less, and at times, this may be unavoidable because of the nature of data flows and where and what country that have transcended. In addition to the above, and to add another dimension to the understanding of data flows within arbitration proceedings, any contracts, memorandums of understanding, BCR or some other agreement should be attached to the arbitration agreement to ensure the parties and, particularly the panel, are fully aware of a transfer-trade agreement. As a final point, apart from the general obligations, parties' rights should be ensured including the right to access; the right to disclosure; and the right to deletion. This is because the rights of data subjects in the EU, might, in some respects, be very different from those of data subjects in Australia, Canada, the US, Singapore, India, Japan or Indonesia.

§16.02 ONLINE ARBITRATION

The emerging area of international commercial arbitration is being undertaken online over the Internet. For the first time in history due to COVID-19,[1259] there had to be a rapid shift in the use and application of online services. Thus, increasingly online arbitrations can pose significant security issues to the Parties. Yet scholars have been writing about online arbitration and what it can offer and the challenges for more than decades.[1260] In other words, when an arbitration is done in person, it will be undertaken in an office environment that is closed off to the rest of the world. Therefore, there is a very high degree of security. However, when transferred to an online environment, the security not only of data but also the hearing can be easily compromised. This is further heightened depending on where the online hearing is

1259. Toni Deskoski, Vangel Dokovski and Ljuben Kocev, '(De) Localisation od Arbitration v. Offline Arbitration E-Arbitration in Time of Covid 19' (2021) Iustinianus Primus Law Review 1-12.

1260. Antonis Patrikos, 'The Role of Transnational Online Arbitration in Regulating Cross-Border e-Business- Part II' (2008) 24(2) Computer Law & Security Review 129-131. Also *see*, Karen Sewart and Joseph Matthews, 'Online Arbitration of Cross-border, Business to Consumer Disputes' (2002)56(1111) University Miami Law Review 1111 (2002).

undertaken. For instance, if undertaken over an unsecured Wi-Fi, the hearing is significantly more vulnerable to being compromised than it would be undertaken in the company office. Likewise, and as more people work from home, the level of security over the Internet is generally not as high as would a company (depending on the size) have. In further drawing on Cirkveni and Per Neuberger[1261] who point to some initial work that has been undertaken by international legal associations.

Nonetheless, a definition of ODR was proposed in the UNCITRAL Draft Procedural Rules on Online Dispute resolution for Cross-border Electronic Commerce Transactions 2013 Article 2(1) as follows:

> 'ODR' means online dispute resolution which is a mechanism for resolving disputes facilitated through the use of electronic communications and other information and communication technology.[1262]

While there are current issues related to conducting online arbitration, it is argued that many of the obstacles have been experienced by the judiciary over a longer period of time. Gary Born notes that while the examination of witnesses in general criminal and other trials by online technology is not new, parties have to agree to an online hearing for arbitration.[1263] However, to date, Born notes that there is a limited authority in relation to one party's objection to an online hearing, and request for an in-person hearing. What has emerged is a debate amongst leading scholars and practitioners in this field. Born goes further and argues that some commentators are of the view that remote hearings and remote examination of witnesses have a negative impact on arbitration, due to the inability of parties to adequately present their cases. Further Born notes that most if not all courts acknowledge the use of technology and the role it plays in the modern period. Put another way, 'resolving cross-border disputes concerning electronic transactions is inevitably more complicated than in a paper-based environment, because connecting factors such as the place of domicile, the place of business and the place of performance are difficult to determine in the online environment. The determination of Internet jurisdiction and applicable law has been greatly challenged when online contracting or transactions are executed in several places and it is difficult to ascertain the principal place of performance'.[1264]

Although it is beyond the scope of this chapter to examine every jurisdiction's judiciary response to the use of technology, an Australian example gives some idea of the advanced thinking and approach being undertaken. In Born's reference to the case

1261. Neva Cirkveni and Per Neuberger, *Clash of the Titans: GDPR and International Arbitration – A Look at the future*, Oblin Rechtsanwalte (November 2021), https://oblin.at/publication/clash-of-the-titans-gdpr-and-international-arbitration-a-look-at-the-future/.
1262. Faye Fangfei Wang, *Online Arbitration*, Informa Law from Routledge (2017), pp. 8-9. A/CN.9/WG.III/WP.133 – Online dispute resolution for cross- border electronic commerce transactions: draft procedural rules, United Nations Commission on International Trade Law, Working Group III (Online dispute resolution), Thirty-first session, New York, 9-13 February 2015.
1263. Gary Born, *International Arbitration*, Kluwer Law International (2021), p. 2064.
1264. Faye Fangfei Wang, *Online Arbitration*, Informa Law from Routledge (2017), pp. 8-9.

of *Capic,*[1265] the Australian Federal Court pointed to section 37M of the Federal Court of Australia Act 1976 which:

> provides that the overarching purpose of the civil practice and procedure provisions is to facilitate the just resolution of disputes according to law and as quickly, inexpensively and efficiently as possible. The requirement that proceedings be conducted according to law is inflexible but the exhortations to speed, thrift and efficiency are subject to the rider that this be achieved so far as possible.[1266]

The Court concluded that the current situation related to COVID-19 made it all but impossible for parties to physically attend the court hearing. The Court stated:

> The primary matter I take into account in the present situation is the health risk posed to practitioners, witnesses, court and transcript staff, and myself. There are two aspects to this risk; that of spreading the virus and that of contracting the virus. It is imperative that this Court's orders not result in a situation where these risks are increased. At the moment movement is restricted in New South Wales and Victoria by measures under State law: *Public Health (COVID-19 Restrictions on Gathering and Movement) Order 2020*(NSW) made 30 March 2020 ('NSW Order') and *Public Health (COVID-19 Restrictions on Gathering and Movement) Amendment Order 2020* (NSW) made 3 April 2020 under s 7 of the Public Health Act 2010 (NSW); *Stay at Home Directions (No 3)* (Vic) made 7 April 2020 ('Vic Direction') under s 199(2)(a) of the Public Health and Wellbeing Act 2008 (Vic). Failure to comply with those measures is an offence in both States. It is plain these must be observed and to the extent that there is any doubt about their application to persons engaged in litigation in federal jurisdiction, I direct the parties and the representatives at all times to comply with the relevant health and public order regulations.[1267]

Here, it is apparent that the Court has no option other than to either adjourn the matter until the end of the pandemic or proceed with an online process. Furthermore, the Court stated that under the COVID-19 restrictions:

> in practice, this means that practitioners must work from home if they can and may attend the office only if they cannot do their work from home. Although workplaces appear to be exempt, State governments advise in favour of (and otherwise enforce) a density quotient of one person per four square metres: New South Wales Order cl 8(1)(c); Victoria Direction cl 11(2).[1268]

Moreover, the Court did:

> not wish to see practitioners, witnesses or court staff working from their offices. On the other hand, it is apparent that public institutions such as the Court must do all they can to facilitate the continuation of the economy and essential services of government, including the administration of justice. The combination of those two considerations would suggest a mode of trial conducted over virtual platforms from participants' homes. Having regard to events overseas and the relatively early

---

1265. *Ibid.*, p. 2065, *Capic v. Ford Motor Company of Australia Limited* (Adjournment) [2020] FCA 486.
1266. *Ibid.*, paragraph 2.
1267. *Ibid.*, paragraph 3.
1268. *Ibid.*, paragraph 4.

> stages this country may be in, a precautionary approach to what may happen by June 2020 points in the same direction. The question then is whether s 37M and considerations of fairness to the parties mean that a virtual solution – which is the only viable solution – is not feasible and that the trial must be postponed.[1269]

Perram J concluded:

> Under ordinary circumstances, I would not remotely contemplate imposing such an unsatisfactory mode of a trial on a party against its will. But these are not ordinary circumstances and we have entered a period in which much that is around us is and is going to continue to be unsatisfactory. I think we must try our best to make this trial work. If it becomes unworkable then it can be adjourned, but we must at least try.[1270]

Given the above, and although jurisdictions will adopt different approaches to suit their local requirements, the Australian case demon the judiciary's shift in thinking. It paves the way for online hearings to be undertaken more readily. It ensures the court complies with the law and continues to implement a process that sees matters being resolved as quickly and efficiently as possible. This is a further demonstration that the court will adjust its approach because no one knows or can predict the end of the current day (2020-2022) pandemic. While not a direct response to the above case, outside national judiciaries, legal associations had already begun thinking about these matters when the pandemic emerged.

In practice, the International Council for Commercial Arbitration, New York City Bar Association, and International Institute for Conflict Prevention and Resolution – Cybersecurity Protocol and the Cybersecurity Guidelines have gone some way to addressing this issue.[1271] Fourteen principles have been established that include:

- Principle 1 establishes the basic approach of the Protocol, which is to provide a framework for the consideration of the security measures to be applied to the information processed during a particular arbitration matter.[1272]
- Principle 2 recognises it is important that all persons who have access to arbitration-related information apply reasonable information security measures in their general business activities ('baseline security').[1273]

1269. *Ibid.*, paragraphs 4 and 5.
1270. *Ibid.*, paragraph 25.
1271. ICCA and New York City Bar and International Institute for Conflict Prevention & Resolution, 'ICCA-NYC Bar-CPR Protocol on Cybersecurity in International Arbitration (2020 Edition)' (ICCA), *see* https://cdn.arbitration-icca.org/s3fs-public/document/media_document/icca-nyc_bar-cpr_cybersecurity_protocol_for_international_arbitration_-_electronic_version.pdf. *See also*, Regulation (EU) No. 524/2013 of the European Parliament and of the Council of 21 May 2013 on online dispute resolution for consumer disputes and amending Regulation (EC) No. 2006/2004 and Directive 2009/22/EC (Regulation on consumer ODR), OJ L 165, 18 June 2013, pp. 1-12. Model standards of Conduct for Mediators, by the American Arbitration Association (AAA), American Bar Association (ABA) and Association for Conflict Resolution (ACR), September 2005.
1272. *Ibid.*, p. 6.
1273. *Ibid.*, p. 10.

- Principle 3 recognises that many persons, other than the parties, tribunals, and institutions directly involved in an arbitration, may have access to arbitration-related information and that the security of such information may be undermined if reasonable information security measures are not applied by all such persons, each of whom could cause a security incident.[1274]
- Principle 4 recognises that the principles and other guidance in the Protocol may be subject to overriding legal or other binding obligations and that such obligations may determine or affect the information security measures that are adopted in the individual circumstances of the arbitration.[1275]
- Principle 5 recognises that there is no one-size-fits-all approach to information security in arbitration matters and that the application of the reasonableness standard in the Protocol is always subject to superseding legal and other obligations.[1276]
- Principle 6 sets out factors to be considered in determining what information security measures are reasonable in particular arbitration matters.[1277]
- Principle 7, upon determining what level of security is reasonable in consideration of the risk profile and addresses the broad categories of security measures that should be considered. These categories may be useful to consider in an individual arbitration, taking into account, and adapting as necessary to reflect, the risk assessment.[1278]
- Principle 8 recognises that certain information security measures, may be applied differently to different aspects of the arbitration.[1279]
- Principle 9 recognises the important role that parties and their legal representatives play in establishing information security measures.[1280]
- Principle 10 recognises that information security should be raised as early as practicable in the arbitration.[1281]
- Principle 11 recognises that the arbitral tribunal has the authority to determine the information security measures applicable to the arbitration and that, ordinarily, it should defer to any agreement of the parties.[1282]
- Principle 12 recognises that the procedures adopted at the outset of the arbitration may be modified as necessary.[1283]

1274. *Ibid.*, p. 12.
1275. *Ibid.*, p. 13.
1276. *Ibid.*, p. 16.
1277. *Ibid.*, p. 18.
1278. *Ibid.*, p. 20.
1279. *Ibid.*, p. 22. In some cases, it may be reasonable to tailor the information security measures applied to the arbitration to the risks present in different aspects of the arbitration, which may include: (a) information exchanges and transmission of arbitration-related information; (b) storage of arbitration-related information; (c) travel; (d) hearings and conferences; and/or (e) post-arbitration retention and destruction policies.
1280. *Ibid.*, p. 25.
1281. *Ibid.*, p. 26.
1282. *Ibid.*, p. 27.
1283. *Ibid.*, p. 29. Throughout the course of the proceeding, including updates as to: what qualifies as the nature of the information being processed; required procedures based on the specific

- Principle 13 clarifies the power of the arbitral tribunal to order costs or sanctions in the event of a breach of the information security measures adopted for an arbitration proceeding or the occurrence of an information security incident.[1284]
- Principle 14 clarifies that the Protocol is not intended to establish any liability or any liability standard for any purpose.[1285]

The ensuring question is why the above is important to this book and data flows? A further ensuring question is such a Protocol or a standard? Is it setting a level of standard by which arbitrators are to operate? In my view it is a combination of both that, as has been outlined above carefully thought through as this area of arbitration evolves. The Protocol has been promoted as a resource that enable arbitrators to comply with data laws such as the GDPR. That said, it only applies to this people that are members or operate under the rules of the International Bar Association. Problematic is that there are a number of arbitration institutions that may develop their own Protocols or Guidelines. That in and of itself will pose challenges to arbitrations, as they are likely not to talk to each other. Importantly, the above Protocol deals with a number of issues that arise within arbitration. On the one hand, it addresses data protection issues directly and data flows indirectly. This is achieved by the understanding that processing of data is a core issue of consideration pre, during and post an arbitration. Furthermore, it addresses at arm's length insolvency when having access to and management of financial records of a company. It also deals with intellectual property and confidentially agreement. While out of scope of this chapter, confidentiality in an arbitration is a significantly important concept that also creates tensions with the management and governance of data flows and data protection. Most noteworthy, is the costs that could be incurred by the Parties for a breach or information security measures could be large. While this, to date has not been fully tested, it is an area of note. Finally, it calls for risk to be managed appropriately. Risk includes security, technology, cybersecurity, data and information along with the full arbitral process. The new online process for arbitration will further evolve, change and be challenged. Arbitrators will need to ensure they have sound processes in place and importantly apply the data laws of the respective jurisdictions diligently. Failure to do so, is likely to result in significant costs to a Party or both Parties where those laws have been found to have been breached.

In addition to the above, the International Bar Association (IBA)[1286] has also released guidelines for the management of cybersecurity online. However, to date, these guidelines focus on law firms managing data and information to ensure that the

circumstances of the case as it develops; and changed circumstances, such as changes in applicable law, risks in the proceeding, institutional rules/requirements, or technological developments.

1284. *Ibid.*, p. 30.
1285. *Ibid.*, p. 30.
1286. International Bar Association, Cybersecurity Guidelines *By the IBA's Presidential Task Force on Cybersecurity*, 2018, https://www.ibanet.org/MediaHandler?id=2F9FA5D6-6E9D-413C-AF80-681BAFD300B0.

firm itself has adequate systems in place to secure the processing, storage and management of data, It states:

> Law firms hold large volumes of valuable personal and commercially sensitive information about their firms, employees, case information and clients. This makes law firms of all sizes a highly attractive target for cybercriminals. Breaches of data security can have devastating legal, financial and reputational consequences for a law firm's clients and business, as well as the law firm. As such, it is critical that firms have effective cybersecurity technologies and processes that focus on protecting the confidentiality, integrity and availability of sensitive data.[1287]

Noteworthy too, the IBA has also developed the Technology Resources for Arbitration Practitioners-Cybersecurity and data privacy, as a resource for managing information and files during an arbitration. It does not provide a comprehensive outline of how and what security should look like. A further problem and challenges and while this chapter has taken a broader view of the issues surrounding the technical aspects of managing arbitrations than the law of arbitration itself, it demonstrates that practically the approaches taken are widely diverse.

Nonetheless, UNCITRAL, in response to the increase in ODR and before the global pandemic, released the Technical Notes on Online Dispute Resolution 2017 that fosters the development of ODR and assists ODR administrators, ODR platforms, neutrals, and the parties to ODR proceedings. It reflects approaches to ODR systems that embody principles of impartiality, independence, efficiency, effectiveness, due process, fairness, accountability and transparency, and are intended for use in disputes arising from cross-border low-value sales or service contracts concluded using electronic communications.[1288] They do not promote any practice of ODR as best practice. It stops short of providing a comprehensive level of procedural rules for parties to follow in an online arbitration. Rather they are guidance notes on what parties need to take into consideration when undertaking an online arbitration. UNCITRAL could consider doing further work in this area of online arbitration. The next section briefly examines the enforcement of awards that have been concluded through an online arbitration process.

§16.03 ENFORCING ARBITRAL AWARDS

The enforcement of arbitral awards is a key feature of arbitration. In further drawing on the work of Cirkveni and Neuberger,[1289] make the case that there is a lack of guidance for an arbitration tribunal to deal with non-compliance with PDP and more broadly,

1287. International Bar Association, Technology Resources for Arbitration Practitioners-Cyber security and data privacy, https://www.ibanet.org/technology-resources-for-arbitration-cybersecurity.

1288. United Nations Commission on International Trade Law, Technical Notes on Online Dispute Resolution 2017, pp. 1.

1289. Neva Cirkveni, Per Neuberger, *Clash of the Titans: GDPR and International Arbitration: A Look at the future,* Oblin Rechtsanwalte (November 2021), https://oblin.at/publication/clash-of-the-titans-gdpr-and-international-arbitration-a-look-at-the-future/.

data flows and its processing. The authors note that the New York Convention currently has 168 contracting states,[1290] making it the primary legal basis for the recognition and enforcement of foreign awards in international commercial arbitration.

Of importance is Article V. It states the recognition and enforcement of the award may be refused, at the request of the party against whom it is invoked, only if that party furnishes to the competent authority where the recognition and enforcement are sought, proof that:

> (a) The parties to the agreement referred to in Article II were, under the law applicable to them, under some incapacity, or the said agreement is not valid under the law to which the parties have subjected it or, failing any indication thereon, under the law of the country where the award was made; or (b) The party against whom the award is invoked was not given proper notice of the appointment of the arbitrator or of the arbitration proceedings or was otherwise unable to present his case; or (c) The award deals with a difference not contemplated by or not falling within the terms of the submission to arbitration, or it contains decisions on matters beyond the scope of the submission to arbitration, provided that, if the decisions on matters submitted to arbitration can be separated from those not so submitted, that part of the award which contains decisions on matters submitted to arbitration may be recognised and enforced; or (d) The composition of the arbitral authority or the arbitral procedure was not in accordance with the agreement of the parties, or, failing such agreement, was not in accordance with the law of the country where the arbitration took place; or (e) The award has not yet become binding on the parties, or has been set aside or suspended by a competent authority of the country in which, or under the law of which, that award was made.[1291]

Further Article V 2 provides that the recognition and enforcement of an arbitral award may also be refused if the competent authority in the country where recognition and enforcement are sought finds that: (a) the subject matter of the difference is not capable of settlement by arbitration under the law of that country; or (b) the recognition or enforcement of the award would be contrary to the public policy of that country.[1292]

The New York Convention has arguably been a highly successful international legal instrument for the management of the enforcement of arbitral awards. It has stood the test of time, with nearly all nation states having signed up to the convention. Yet, Article V is central to limiting and refusing specific areas of where an arbitral award will be enforced. As highlighted by Cirkveni and Neuberger Article V 2(b) is significantly important where by the enforcement of an award can be refused in public policy grounds. In agreeing with the authors, it is the grounds of public policy in data flows and data protection that pose some of the most significant challenges in this area of the law.

Nonetheless, Cirkveni and Neuberger make an important distinction at international law on the setting aside of arbitral awards. They argue that the 'grounds on

1290. United Nations Convention on the Recognition and Enforcement of Foreign Arbitral Awards (New York, 10 June 1958), https://www.newyorkconvention.org/english.
1291. *Ibid.*, Article V.
1292. *Ibid.*

which an arbitral award may be set aside vary among different jurisdictions'.[1293] The UNCITRAL Model Law on International Commercial Arbitration,[1294] which has been widely adopted, sets out a list of grounds for annulment in Article 34(2). It states that Recourse to a court against an arbitral award may be made only by an application for setting aside in accordance with paragraphs (2) and (3) of this article.[1295] An arbitral award may be set aside by the court specified in Article 6 only if *a)* the party making the application furnishes proof that:

> (i) a party to the arbitration agreement referred to in Article 7 was under some incapacity; or the said agreement is not valid under the law to which the parties have subjected it or, failing any indication thereon, under the law of this State; or (ii) the party making the application was not given proper notice of the appointment of an arbitrator or of the arbitral proceedings or was otherwise unable to present his case; or (iii) the award deals with a dispute not contemplated by or not falling within the terms of the submission to arbitration, or contains decisions on matters beyond the scope of the submission to arbitration, provided that, if the decisions on matters submitted to arbitration can be separated from those not so submitted, only that part of the award which contains decisions on matters not submitted to arbitration may be set aside; or (iv) the composition of the arbitral tribunal or the arbitral procedure was not in accordance with the agreement of the parties, unless such agreement was in conflict with a provision of this Law from which the parties cannot derogate, or, failing such agreement, was not in accordance with this Law; or *(b)* the court finds that: (i) the subject-matter of the dispute is not capable of settlement by arbitration under the law of this State; or (ii) the award is in conflict with the public policy of this State.[1296]

Article 34(3) provides that an application for setting aside may not be made after three months have elapsed from the date on which the party making that application had received the award or, if a request had been made under Article 33, from the date on which that request had been disposed of by the arbitral tribunal. Further Article 34(4) provides that the court, when asked to set aside an award, may, where appropriate and so requested by a party, suspend the setting aside proceedings for a period of time determined by it in order to give the arbitral tribunal an opportunity to resume the arbitral proceedings or to take such other action as in the arbitral tribunal's opinion will eliminate the grounds for setting aside. Comparably, both the New York Convention and the UNCTIRAL Model Law are similar.

Article 34(2)(b)(ii) states that an arbitral award may be set aside by the court if the award is in conflict with the state's public policy.[1297] The ensuing question is how broad does public policy extend in relation to data flows or data protection.

1293. Neva Cirkveni and Per Neuberger, *Clash of the Titans: GDPR and International Arbitration: A Look at the future,* Oblin Rechtsanwalte (November 2021) https://oblin.at/publication/clash-of-the-titans-gdpr-and-international-arbitration-a-look-at-the-future/.
1294. UNCITRAL Model Law on International Commercial Arbitration, https://uncitral.un.org/sites/uncitral.un.org/files/media-documents/uncitral/en/06-54671_ebook.pdf.
1295. *Ibid.*
1296. *Ibid.*, Article 32.
1297. Neva Cirkveni and Per Neuberger, *Clash of the Titans: GDPR and International Arbitration: A Look at the future,* Oblin Rechtsanwalte (November 2021), https://oblin.at/publication/clash-of-the-titans-gdpr-and-international-arbitration-a-look-at-the-future/.

Cirkveni and Neuberger highlight what public policy is likely to constitute in referring to the case of *Eco Swiss*.[1298] This case was required to deal with questions raised by Benetton International NV ('Benetton') for stay of enforcement of an arbitration award ordering it to pay damages to Eco Swiss China Time Ltd ('Eco Swiss') for breach of a licensing agreement concluded with the latter, on the ground that the award in question was contrary to public policy. This contrary position was within the meaning of Article 1065(1)(e) of the Wetboek van Burgerlijke Rechtsvordering (hereinafter referred to as 'the Code of Civil Procedure') by virtue of the nullity of the licensing agreement under Article 85 of the Treaty.[1299] On 14 July 1995, Benetton applied to the Rechtbank for annulment of the PFA and the FAA on the ground, *inter alia*, that those arbitration awards were contrary to public policy by virtue of the nullity of the licensing agreement under Article 85 of the Treaty, although during the arbitration proceedings neither the parties nor the arbitrators had raised the point that the licensing agreement might be contrary to that provision.[1300] The Court noted that in judicial review of arbitration awards, Article 1064 of the Code of Civil Procedure provides:

> An action contesting (a) a final arbitration award, whether complete or partial, against which no appeal may be made to a higher arbitration tribunal or (b) a final arbitration award, whether complete or partial, made on appeal to a higher arbitration tribunal may be brought only by way of an application for annulment or a request in accordance with the provisions of this section.[1301]

In laying down the approach to be taken on public policy, the Court pointed to Article 1065 which provides that an annulment may be ordered only on one or more of the following grounds: (a) there is no valid arbitration agreement; (b) the arbitration tribunal has been constituted in breach of the applicable rules; (c) the arbitration tribunal has failed to comply with its terms of reference; (d) the award has not been signed or does not state the reasons on which it is based, contrary to the provisions of Article 1057; (e) the award or the manner in which it has been made is contrary to public policy or accepted principles of morality.[1302]

The Court also stated that:

> an arbitration award is contrary to public policy within the meaning of Article 1065(l)(e) of the Code of Civil Procedure only if its terms or enforcement conflict with a mandatory rule so fundamental that no restrictions of a procedural nature should prevent its application. It states that, in Netherlands law, the mere fact that, because of the terms or enforcement of an arbitration award, a prohibition laid down in competition law is not applied is not generally regarded as being contrary to public policy. If the court considers that an arbitration award is in fact contrary to Article 85 of the EC Treaty, must it, on that ground and notwithstanding the

---

1298. Case C-126/97, *Eco Swiss China Time Ltd v. Benetton International* NV Judgment of 1 June 1999, https://eur-lex.europa.eu/legal-content/EN/TXT/PDF/?uri=CELEX:61997CJ0126&from=EN.
1299. *Ibid.*, paragraph 1.
1300. *Ibid.*, paragraph 14.
1301. *Ibid.*, paragraph 6.
1302. *Ibid.*, paragraph 7.

> rules of Netherlands procedural law set out in paragraphs 4.2 and 4.4 above [according to which a party may claim annulment of an arbitration award only on a limited number of grounds, one ground being that an award is contrary to public policy, which generally does not cover the mere fact that through the terms or enforcement of an arbitration award no effect is given to a prohibition laid down by competition law], allow a claim for annulment of that award if the claim otherwise complies with statutory requirements?[1303]

In its analysis of public policy in regard to the New York Convention, the Court concluded that:

> the New York Convention of 10 June 1958 on the Recognition and Enforcement of Foreign Arbitral Awards, provides that recognition and enforcement of an arbitration award may be refused only on certain specific grounds, namely where the award does not fall within the terms of the submission to arbitration or goes beyond its scope, where the award is not binding on the parties or where recognition or enforcement of the award would be contrary to the public policy of the country where such recognition and enforcement are sought (Article V(l)(c) and (e) and 11(b) of the New York Convention). For the reasons, the provisions of Article 85 of the Treaty may be regarded as a matter of public policy within the meaning of the New York Convention.[1304]

On this basis, the Court ruled that:

> The answer to be given to the second question must therefore be that a national court to which application is made for annulment of an arbitration award must grant that application if it considers that the award in question is in fact contrary to Article 85 of the Treaty, where its domestic rules of procedure require it to grant an application for annulment founded on failure to observe national rules of public policy. A national court to which application is made for annulment of an arbitration award must grant that application if it considers that the award in question is in fact contrary to Article 85 of the EC Treaty (now Article 81 EC), where its domestic rules of procedure require it to grant an application for annulment founded on failure to observe national rules of public policy.[1305]

Arguably, the annulment of an arbitral award on public policy grounds is a broad concept that affords a court substantial discretion. While in this case, it does not specifically state whether data is included in public policy, it could constitute the same grounds. The ensuing proposition (noted by Cirkveni Neuberger) as to whether an arbitral award can be set aside or its enforcement be refused due to non-compliance with data laws will depend on the rules of a particular nation state's applicable data laws. Secondly, can the refusal of enforcement or the setting aside of an arbitral award take place on grounds of public policy? What can be determined is that data laws are placing increasing pressure on all sectors of the community to comply with the established rules, protections, controls and obligations. Arguably, this is an unsettled area of the law, requiring further research as data flows increase and data law develops. This is because data transfers will inevitably see data going from Australia to

1303. *Ibid.*, paragraphs 24 and 30.
1304. *Ibid.*, paragraphs 38 and 39.
1305. *Ibid.*, paragraph 49.

the UK that is subject to both commercial and national security policy. A high priority is to clarify whether the setting aside or the annulment of an award is the appropriate course of action for courts to take. Evidently, this is an area where arbitrators and tribunals will need to be vigilant.

§16.04 CONCLUSION

This chapter has diverged from a standard examination of arbitration as it relates to data flows and data protection. Rather than compare how the jurisdictions adopted the international law pertaining to international commercial arbitral or otherwise, it has analysed the practical elements of arbitration in the digital economy. It has demonstrated that the role of data flows in arbitration has not been fully examined. In part, this is because there have been no contested disputes regarding contractual obligations in relation to the transfer or trade in data. Some may view this as problematic. However, others will view this as an opportunity.

Significantly problematic is, as this book continues to reinforce, the fragmented approach to data laws. This also includes the regulation of data flows and data transfers. Those nation states such as India and India, are yet to establish specific data laws. The resulting effect has seen slow progress in implementing data laws. Their respective sectoral approaches to data law do not provide for data transfers internationally, in the same way as the other jurisdictions examined in this book. Therefore, this will continue to be problematic for arbitrators that will need to navigate the varied approach to the regulation of data flows. This chapter has also highlighted that data flows and their protection will likely be subject, at some stage, to both cross-border insolvency and arbitration. While it is understood these are very separate areas of international and national law, how to deal with data that is part of an insolvency arbitration is going to be challenging. It will require the tribunal to manage the data pre, during and post the arbitration, along with ensuring that the Parties to the insolvency have complied with the respective data laws.

The critical issue that has emerged from the lack of guidance afforded to the arbitral tribunal is the understanding of data flows and its lack of regulation. Additionally, the understand and knowledge of data protection and what both of these areas mean to an arbitration. More critically, it, by and large, hinges on the processing of personal data pre, during and post the tribunal. However, it can at a time go beyond the tribunal hearing itself, where there have been entities involved, for instance, in a contractual dispute regarding the performance of data flows, its protection, processing and data subjects' rights.

The lack of judicial decisions by the courts in this area of the law is not surprising. That is, at the time of writing this book, there was no actual case law that has dealt with data flows, other than those in the EU that were examined in this book. Moreover, there is no judicial decision that has decided upon a collection of matters such as data flows, arbitration and insolvency. Thus, the ensuing question is whether such a matter is likely to arise. In my view, never rule it out. As companies in the digital economy grow and expand, there only needs to be a different direction that governments around the world can take, which could result in financial stress for an entity.

Undoubtedly, in my view, the move to a more permanent online arbitration will bring its own challenges. On the other side, the opportunities to reduce costs to the parties are significant. It does not require the tribunal panel or parties to travel and be located in a third country. It can be more efficient in bringing the parties together, as there will be less time needed to arrange flights and accommodation, amongst other administrative matters. As highlighted above, the challenges of security could be an issue. In other words, where the arbitration is undertaken – at home or in an office. This is particularly important to the security of the arbitration procedure and the data issues that are part of the arbitration.

On this basis, the security issues can be two-fold. First is the compromising position that the entire arbitration could be subject to cyber incursions, exposing valuable commercial and personal information. This could not just apply to a single data subject. The large volumes of information could involve thousands of data subjects. Second is the exposure of data flows and where, how and why data has been transferred to another commercial or government entity. It could also significantly compromise public policy objectives of data laws.

However, this will vary from jurisdiction to jurisdiction because the laws vary significantly. The resulting effect will be higher costs. A further problem that may arise at the practical level is the traditional arbitrator having everyone in the same room and being able to identify and respond to the Parties and their representatives based on body language and their vocalisation of matters. To the traditional arbitrator, this could be problematic in managing an online arbitration. Although, it is argued that the younger generation that has grown up on technology may not have the same view or response.

Finally, the enforcement or setting aside of an arbitration award that has been based on public policy grounds has the potential to pose complex challenges to arbitration. As highlighted above, the notion of public policy in data flows and data protection will vary from jurisdiction to jurisdiction. It is another area that is not settled and requires further research. There are challenges facing data flows; however, these challenges are to be viewed as opportunities and Australia, the UK, the US, Singapore, India, Indonesia, Canada, Japan along with the EU have the opportunity to set the international rules by coming together and considering a joint project to ensure data flows and their regulation are consistent, coherent and above all internationalised. In conclusion, the standards, guidelines and protocols being developed by arbitration institutions have the potential to add a further layer of fragmentation to data flows in arbitration. While there is a minimalist approach, what is emerging is a continued varied approach.

CHAPTER 17

Data-Digital Diplomacy and Pathway Forward

This book has demonstrated how cross-border data flows have become important to the global economy and future international trade. Data flows are the movement of personal data whether on its own or coupled with other commercial data, that is information which is transferred across national borders. The book has further demonstrated how data needs to move freely in order for the full potential of the digital economy to be fully realised. It is this data that is critical to commerce and government that is reported to have significant benefits economically, socially, environmentally and to human health. However, data in the new digital economy does not come without its own challenges. The current regulatory landscape is highly fragmented. The book has highlighted that the current FTAs – Digital Agreements of the jurisdictions compared are significantly divergent. This is also the case for multilateral agreements, to be improved to account for data flows. More questions have been raised from this book than answered or even reconciled.

It has been argued that more research is required in specific areas. In making the case for the internationalisation of data flows and data protection law, an international convention or model law is urgently needed. This will allow like-minded states to establish the rules for data flows and their future regulation. There is a high level of urgency in the same way as Professor Simon Chesterman has called for an international institution for the governance of AI. There are a number of examples where international law has served commercial law well, such as transitional contract law and cross-border insolvency law. Dispute resolution and its gradual shift to being undertaken online is another area of growth.

In diverging from the law, this book has discussed the important role that data diplomacy will have for governments to engage with and develop deeper relationships as data flows become mainstream. Data diplomacy is not often considered to be an important part of the development of the law. It allows for nation states to identify and develop a level of harmonisation in the law. This chapter identifies some of the programmes and stakeholders that will become important in current and future data diplomacy programmes used by governments.

The book concludes by arguing for a stronger response to the development of international laws for data flows and the establishment of an international organisation for data. It further calls for the need for such an organisation to have oversight of all data transfers and trades, and the need for national governments and the proposed international organisation to establish a reporting process for data flows. Such an approach will provide greater trust, transparency and accountability in the governance and use of personal data in international trade.

§17.01 DATA DIPLOMACY

The book has demonstrated the increasing importance of cross-border data flows economically, socially, environmentally and to human health amongst others. Countries have exchanged data in areas of law enforcement, national security, banking and finance (public and private) for decades. However, the importance of data to the new digital economy has taken on a new role. In other words, the technologies that will be used to build the IR4 economy, including AI, the IoT and blockchain (technology), are exceptionally reliant on accessing and processing data particularly personal data. To realise the potential of such data-intensive technologies, or to fully harness the power and efficiency of cloud computing solutions for start-ups and SMEs (small- and medium-sized enterprises), data needs to be able to move seamlessly across international borders.[1306] The ability to move, store and process data across borders is foundational to the modern international data economy. As global growth relies increasingly on digital growth in the post-COVID-19 era, progressive cross-border flows of data are now a policy and legal issue for governments, regulators, business sectors and the broader community. What has developed is the need for data diplomacy. Arguably, today, 'diplomacy in the twenty-first century must grapple with both the potential and the limits of technology in foreign policy, and respond to the disruptions that it causes in international relations'.[1307]

Jacobson, Höne and Kurbalija in referring to big data, highlight the importance of data diplomacy to national government foreign programmes. They argue that in 'order to capture the benefits of big data, certain organisational considerations need to be kept

1306. This chapter calls upon the work understood by the government of Switzerland in the area of Digital – Data Diplomacy.

1307. Alec Ross, 'Digital Diplomacy and US Foreign Policy' (2011) The Hague Journal of Diplomacy 1.

in mind. In order to maintain flexibility while being able to feed big data insights into multiple areas of diplomacy, data sources provide insights across the full range of diplomatic functions'.[1308] In extending this beyond just government the authors argue that data diplomacy can also be developed on a more ad hoc basis, for example through partnerships with academia or the private sector, when in-house data analysis capacity is not available.

Notwithstanding the above, experts in the field are likely to ask what is data diplomacy and what does it mean for data and the digital economy. Data diplomacy is an effective policy tool that can be used by governments, the private sector and non-government organisations to come together and form deep partnerships, to build a high level of trust in the legal frameworks that underpin data flows. As highlighted earlier in the book, the concept of trust is a major policy driver to and for governments to create an environment of certainty for data flows and the digital economy. This section draws upon the work undertaken by the UK upon leaving the EU. In other words, since leaving the EU, the UK has been on a pathway to establishing new relationships with former commonwealth trade and investment partners.

The prevailing view has been that data diplomacy is a new programme that governments have either implemented or are considering implementing. However, this could not be further from the truth. With the advent of what is considered today as the simple telegraph message, in 1800, it has raised the status of data in the contemporary world. Notwithstanding the more recent approach to data governance, the reported reaction of Lord Palmerston, British Prime Minister and Foreign Secretary, on receiving the first telegraph message in the 1850s was: 'my god this is the end of diplomacy'.[1309] Since then diplomacy not only survived Palmerston's proclamation about the telegraph but has also embraced many activities undertaken by the government as the economy and society have evolved and changed. Similar occurred with the onset and use of the humble telephone, radio, television, and many subsequent communications technologies. In the contemporary world, diplomacy faces the challenge of digitalisation that falls within three main inquiry areas:

(1) changes in the political, social, and economic environment in which diplomacy is conducted (the nature and distribution of power, new types of conflicts, and the changing nature of sovereignty and interdependence in international relations;
(2) the emergence of new policy issues in foreign policy such as cybersecurity, privacy, data governance, e-commerce, and cybercrime; and

1308. Barbara Rosen Jacobson, Katharina E Höne and Jovan Kurbalija, *Data Diplomacy Updating Diplomacy to the Big Data Era,* DiploFoundation (2018), p. 65, https://www.diplomacy.edu/wp-content/uploads/2018/02/Data_Diplomacy_Report_2018-1.pdf. *See also,* Andy Boyd, Jane Gatewood, Stuart, Thorson and Timothy Dye, *Data Diplomacy*, United States National Library of Medicine, National Institute of Health, 2019, https://www.ncbi.nlm.nih.gov/pmc/articles/PMC6785044/.
1309. Digital Diplomacy, 2022, https://www.diplomacy.edu/topics/digital-diplomacy/.

(3) the use of digital tools in the practice of diplomacy such as social media, online conferencing, and big data analysis.[1310]

Viewed this way, data will play a pivotal role in transnational diplomacy. It builds trust and provides a pathway for the transfer of information, knowledge, skills and resources to combat security breaches for both government and the private sector. For instance, in 2021, the government of Switzerland released their first-ever Digital Foreign Policy Strategy (DFPS).[1311] Today other countries such as Australia and the UK have, in part, followed suit. In citing Australia and the UK's national Data strategies, there are not only many similarities but also differences to the DFPS.

Arguably, it may be the titles of the respective national data strategies that are the material difference. However, it is argued that following the Switzerland example makes it clear to the world that the 'digital economy and data' are, today, a foreign policy issue. The DFPS provides a key role in promoting digital governance, as a comparable policy for cybersecurity, and establishes high-level values for a free, open and secure digital space. Centrally, it notes that:

> with the ongoing shifts in global power, there has been a rise political fragmentation. The geopolitical renaissance is also evident in the digital space, creating the risk of networks decoupling between countries that are already integrated, thereby diluting the push for an open – global internet. Deglobalisation trends witnessed during the COVID-19 pandemic, have in addition encouraged regionalisation in the form of competing economic, developmental and social systems. While the liberal-democratic model continues to be successful, it is coming under increased pressure. Authoritarian trends and models that do not link development and prosperity with individual rights or with political and social pluralism are on the rise in many parts of the world. The misuse of digital technologies, for example, can be used to keep governments in power, is also increasing in several countries. In this polarised context, a European approach is gradually emerging in which the economic and social potential of digitalisation could be utilised while allowing individual rights to be protected to the greatest extent possible.[1312]

This shift globally has created an environment of uncertainty. It further undermines the current rules-based system and countries that do not agree with the current framework and want to change that order. If achieved, it will have a profound impact on data flows. It is likely to see nation states withdraw further and put further barriers to restrict the movement of data internationally. The DFPS reinforces the overall argument of this book. It takes the position that legal uncertainty will dilute data flows. It states:

> While regulation of the digital space is progressing in various countries and in some cases regionally, the international rules and standards for the digital space remain incomplete. While there are multilateral rules that were largely put in place

1310. *Ibid.*
1311. Switzerland Digital Foreign Policy Strategy 2021-2024, https://www.fdfa.admin.ch/dam/eda/en/documents/publications/SchweizerischeAussenpolitik/20201104-strategie-digitalaussenpolitik_EN.pdf.
1312. *Ibid.*, p. 6.

> before digitalisation and still in principle apply in the digital space, there is often uncertainty or disagreement regarding their concrete application, as they are frequently subject to interpretation with regard to specific facts. There are many parallel processes underway for which numerous actors have developed specific rules and standards. This means that there is an overlap between old and new instruments that vary in scope and in terms of the degree to which they are binding. This can result in legal uncertainty and discriminatory measures, stifling investment and innovation, and lead to ambiguities over who is responsible for what in the digital space.[1313]

Most noteworthy is how Switzerland is arguing that the principle-based approach currently in place at the multilateral level has been adopted inconsistently around the world. The incoherent approach to their interpretation has also resulted in some jurisdictions not fully embracing the idea of an international approach to data flows and the law. In addition, as demonstrated in this book, this incoherent approach has also resulted in rules, standards and legal mechanisms, not only being recognised inconsistently within data laws but also in some cases, they are not recognised at all. While the DFPS takes what appears to be a whole technology approach, it importantly includes the regulation of data. In relation to data more specifically, the DFPS takes the position that:

> Given that data is becoming a strategic resource, and thus a key commodity in the digital economy, it now occupies a pivotal role as data linkage can be used to produce faster and more precise forecasts. It therefore has the potential to change existing power structures. The increased concentration of data in the hands of a small number of countries or companies also gives rise to new political and economic dependencies. Having equal access to network infrastructures and network speed thus plays an important role in this (net neutrality).[1314]

Following a lengthy analysis, what Switzerland has identified, without calling for the internationalisation of data laws, is the need for a greater level of consistency in the adoption and administration of these laws. This is particularly important to the growing area of regulation for transnational data flows. Apart from using the other legal and policy tools that have been identified throughout this book, such as bilateral and multilateral trade agreements, along with national laws, Data Diplomacy is an emerging programme that can serve national governments. What is remarkable is that data used as a tool of diplomacy can advance a nation state's position in the national and international regulation of data. It can provide a pathway to the internationalisation of data laws, and seek to obtain a deep level of legal harmonisation. Data diplomacy can be used to establish long-term relationships between nation states. It can also be used to open up data flows and enhance and produce news skills, jobs and investment opportunities between countries. It can complement current cyber [security] diplomacy programmes. On this basis, the Switzerland model has identified four key areas that include:

1313. *Ibid.*, p. 7.
1314. *Ibid.*

(1) *Moderate legislation* – where possible, new rules should not be created, but rather existing rules should be applied to the digital space.
(2) *Capacity building* – in developing countries in the area of digital technologies and cybersecurity.
(3) *International* – placing Switzerland in a position to influence the international legal landscape.
(4) *Science* – whereby regulatory bodies and technology developers exchange information.[1315]

Against the backdrop of this Swiss DFPS, the ensuring question is what other benefits would such a programme provide to the broader economy. Apart from the above, the stark reality is that implemented correctly, a well-designed data diplomacy programme can create competition in the market. This alone brings with it many economic and social benefits. It will open up new and emerging avenues of trade in the digital economy. It can be argued that such a programme will assist in balancing the economic benefits of data flows, with the increasing need to protect that data. More importantly, it will establish an environment of awareness of the law, which in turn will result in governments and regulators having to enforce the law. In my view, one of the major issues that has emerged in countries that have only recently established data laws is the lack of institutional awareness and institutional capacity. Another area of policy that is not often discussed to complement the development and implementation of diplomacy programmes is gender. Some countries such as Australia,[1316] the UK[1317] and the EU[1318] have established strong policy initiatives to ensure there is no gender discrimination. It is out of the scope of this chapter to identify gender equality programmes of all jurisdictions compared in this book. Importantly, gender is important to data diplomacy and having the right balance can ensure there are significant outcomes with country-to-country engagement and implementation of programmes.

§17.02 FUTURE DATA DIPLOMACY

Embracing the idea of data diplomacy and a single diplomatic programme brings with it significant benefits. It will build significant country-to-country relationships. It can complement other technology diplomacy programmes. Such a programme will help stimulate and grow the digital economy and create pathways for nation states to fully

1315. *Ibid.*, p. 9.
1316. Australian Government, Department of Foreign Affairs, Gender Equality, https://www.dfat.gov.au/international-relations/themes/gender-equality.
1317. Government of United Kingdom, Gender equality at every stage: a roadmap for change, p. 2, https://assets.publishing.service.gov.uk/government/uploads/system/uploads/attachment_data/file/821889/GEO_GEEE_Strategy_Gender_Equality_Roadmap_Rev_1__1_.pdf, Reducing gender gaps in labour market participation, Science, Technology, Engineering and Maths (STEM) qualifications and wages, could increase the size of the UK economy by around 2% or GBP 55 billion by 2030.
1318. Council of Europe, Gender Equality, Gender Equality Strategy, https://www.coe.int/en/web/genderequality/home?desktop=true.

adopt the Open Data concept (*see* Chapter 1). It will enable the development of bilateral and multilateral coalitions, broaden their expansion on current long-term partnerships, work and operate across multiple countries, and further develop transnational data relations. Most significantly, it will help shape, influence and direct the international rules for data flows, data protection and indirectly cybersecurity. Moreover, to expand on and strengthen current diplomacy programmes led by national governments, four key areas have been identified. These include (1) capacity building, (2) research, (3) economic development, and (4) governance.

Table 17.1 outlines the core areas of Data Diplomacy that were identified in 2022, which can be expanded upon to suit the sovereign needs of the nation state.

Table 17.1 Digital-Data Diplomacy Considerations

Capacity Building

- Promote internationalisation and legal harmonisation of data flow laws, principles and rules. Develop international law in this area.
- Intergovernmental forums and interagency cooperation.
- Working with Regulators.
- Training.
- Transfer of skills and knowledge.
- Transfer of technology.
- Establishing harmonised values, rules, standards (e.g., International Standards Organisation) and the law.
- Standardisation of data collection, use and storage.
- Gender Equality and Balance.
- Assessing how human rights are to be addressed.
- Establishing an environment of resilience.
- Incident response.
- Workforce development.
- Infrastructure standardisation.
- Security and Cyber Hygiene.
- Economic-Sociocultural (policy, cultural, linguistics).
- Digital Trade.
- Digital Identity.
- Education.
- Communication.

Economic Development

It is well understood that the new digital economy will provide significant opportunities for national economies to expand and grow from the transnational flow of data. It will be important to engage with and bring along the private sector. Therefore, programmes should be established that can assess the economic benefit and drivers of data flows. This can be at a bilateral or multilateral level.

Research

Research into current and future policy mechanisms will be important for the future engagement of countries to develop and implement transnational data flows and adequacy arrangements. Research should include but is not limited to:

- Education (curriculum design, planning, staff selection and delivery amongst others).
- Technology (AI, quantum and new-emerging technologies).
- Partnerships between Universities and other education providers.
- Adult learning centres, particularly for rural areas.
- Understanding the level of knowledge of privacy and data protection over the Internet within the country.
- Other.

Source: Robert Walters-Leon Trakman.[1319]

However, data diplomacy has been questioned by some scholars, who see that it will face significant obstacles in the future. These obstacles have begun to emerge. For instance, governments are racing against time to effectively respond to the many security, political and cultural challenges caused by individuals, groups and state actors in cyberspace. It poses a significant threat to states' values, principles, rules of law, rules-based systems, sovereignty and the national interest.[1320] As a result not only has data sovereignty emerged but also cyber sovereignty.[1321] Thus, the problem is that when grouped together, both data and cyber sovereignty have seen nation states develop very different laws and policy responses to that of most of the world. In view of this development alone, data diplomacy in some regions of the world and countries may well be resisted at all costs. The ability for countries to engage with each other may not be achieved where there are such divergent views on what and how data and cybersecurity should be regulated. The resulting effect is that nation states are having to be constantly vigilant about cyber intrusions, and they will possibly be on a full-time war footing. That is, and while this chapter does not discuss cyberattacks, nation states are having to monitor intrusions around the clock.

Another view is that what has emerged is a form of public diplomacy whereby citizens exchange information and their personal details expressing their support or concerns about current government policy. This has been very evident throughout the global pandemic from 2020 to 2022. More recently, the conflict in Ukraine invoked a public backlash from citizens around the world as a result of information being shared online and on social media. Jane Wakefield recently wrote that the conflict in Ukraine

1319. Robert Walters and Leon Trakman *Cross Border Data Flows*, 2022, a report for the United Kingdom [unpublished].

1320. Mohammed Elkhaldi, *Digital Diplomacy and International Regulation of the Web*, p. 93, In Fatima Roumate, *Artificial Intelligence and Digital Diplomacy, Challenges and Opportunities*, Springer (2021). *See also*, Łukasz Antoni Król, 'Digital Foreign Policy: How Digital Tools Can Further Europe's Foreign Policy Goals' (2016) 15 European View 133-144, Doi 10.1007/s12290-016-0384-8.

1321. *Ibid.*

may accelerate the breakup of the Internet altogether.[1322] Wakefield notes that with the Ukraine government calling for Russia to be cut off from the Internet, and major social media providers pulling out of Russia, the longer-term effect will be a great divide on the Internet. Today there are already two, the West and China. This conflict in Eastern Europe could invoke a third. Wakefield goes further and refers to Professor Alan Woodward from the University of Surrey:

> Russia itself has been experimenting with a sovereign internet – dubbed Runet – for several years, albeit one that has been retrofitted to the existing internet rather than China's built-from-the-ground-up version.
>
> In 2019, the Russian government said it had successfully tested the system. At the time few understood the need for it, but now, in the context of the Ukraine invasion, it all 'makes a whole lot more sense'.[1323]

These developments challenge the very notion of digital-data diplomacy, but they should not be viewed as a complete obstacle. If nation states wish to take this path and move away from the majority, it is up to the majority to work even harder in this area of emerging diplomacy to ensure the international rules are developed and upheld by the majority vote. The security issues are not limited to only government; for some time, in 2008, it was highlighted 'business has as much to lose through disruption of the Internet or loss of private data, security solutions have been keeping just about one step ahead of the hackers, fraudsters and cyber-saboteurs'.[1324] On this basis, the concept of digital diplomacy 'can be framed as a new and revolutionary development, replacing the top-down, state-catered, processes of international relations with a more networked, civil society-focused diplomacy model'.[1325] It has also been described as a 'broad term that refers to the positive and negative impacts of digitalisation on diplomatic institutions. As such, the term "digital diplomacy" also refers to the overall impact ICTs (information and communication technologies) have had on the practice of diplomacy, ranging from the email to the smartphone and social networking sites'.[1326]

Olubukola Adesina, in referring to Lewis[1327] defines digital diplomacy as the use of digital tools of communication (social media) by diplomats to communicate with each other and with the general public. Olubukola argues that digital diplomacy by and large refers to diplomatic practices through digital and networked technologies,

---

1322. Jane Wakefield, *Russia-Ukraine: Is Internet on Verge of Break-up?* BBC News, 9 March 2022, *https://www.bbc.com/news/technology-60661987.*
1323. *Ibid.*
1324. Nicholas Westcott, *Digital Diplomacy: The Impact of the Internet on International Relations*, Formerly Chief Information Officer Foreign and Commonwealth Office, London Oxford Internet Institute, Research Report 16, (2008), p. 15.
1325. *M. Serdar* Erciş Enes Emre Başar, *New Communication Approaches in the Digitalized World*, Cambridge Scholars Publishing, (2020), pp. 249-251.
1326. Ilan Manor, *Are We There Yet: Have MFAs Realized the Potential of Digital Diplomacy*, Brill (2016) p. 3.
1327. Olubukola S. Adesina, 'Foreign Policy in an Era of Digital Diplomacy' (2017) 3(1) Cogent Social Sciences, DOI: 10.1080/23311886.2017.1297175 p. 3. Dev Lewis, *Digital diplomacy*. (2014) http://www. gatewayhouse.in/digital-diplomacy-2/.

including the Internet, mobile devices, and social media channels.[1328] Olubukola further argues that digital diplomacy is the use of the Internet and new Information Communications Technologies to help carry out diplomatic objectives.[1329] In referring to Hansen, outlines eight policy goals for digital diplomacy:

(1) Knowledge management.[1330]
(2) Public diplomacy.[1331]
(3) Information management.[1332]
(4) Consular communications and response.[1333]
(5) Disaster response.[1334]
(6) Internet freedom.[1335]
(7) External resources.[1336]
(8) Policy planning.[1337]

While scholars often make the distinction between digital diplomacy and data diplomacy, arguably, in part, they are inextricably linked. When coupled together, they form 'an important tool that enables direct communication and interaction between nation states to advance a nation's foreign policy'.[1338] They are a form of soft power and provide the opportunity to undertake capacity building and other programmes either in person or online.[1339] Erciş and Başar in referring to Brian Hocking and Jan

1328. Evan Potter, *Cyber-Diplomacy: Managing Foreign Policy in the Twenty-First Century*, Ontario: McGill-Queen's Press (2002). In Olubukola S. Adesina, 'Foreign Policy in an Era of Digital Diplomacy' (2017) 3(1) Cogent Social Sciences, DOI: 10.1080/23311886.2017.1297175 p. 3.
1329. Fergus Hanson, F *Baked in and wired: eDiplomacy@State*, Foreign Policy Paper Series No. 30, (2012). In Olubukola S. Adesina, 'Foreign Policy in an Era of Digital Diplomacy' (2017) 3(1) Cogent Social Sciences, DOI: 10.1080/23311886.2017.1297175 p. 3.
1330. *Ibid.*, p. 3. To harness departmental and whole of government knowledge, so that it is retained, shared and its use optimised in pursuit of national interests abroad.
1331. *Ibid.*, p. 3. To maintain contact with audiences as they migrate online and to harness new communications tools to listen to and target important audiences with key messages and to influence major online influencers.
1332. *Ibid.*, p. 3. To help aggregate the overwhelming flow of information and to use this to better inform policymaking and to help anticipate and respond to emerging social and political movements.
1333. *Ibid.*, p. 3. To create direct, personal communications channels with citizens travelling overseas, with manageable communications in crisis situations.
1334. *Ibid.*, p. 3. To harness the power of connective technologies in disaster response situations.
1335. *Ibid.*, p. 3. Creation of technologies to keep the Internet free and open. This has the related objectives of promoting freedom of speech and democracy as well as undermining authoritarian regimes.
1336. *Ibid.*, p. 3. Creating digital mechanisms to draw on and harness external expertise to advance national goals.
1337. *Ibid.*, p. 3. To allow for effective oversight, coordination and planning of international policy across government, in response to the internationalisation of the bureaucracy.
1338. M. Serdar Erciş Enes Emre Başar, *New Communication Approaches in the Digitalized World*, Cambridge Scholars Publishing, 2020, pp. 249-251.
1339. *Ibid.*

Melissen[1340] point out that digital diplomacy is often reduced to public diplomacy and has the following components:

> Changing the foreign policy agenda: depending on the speed issue, less control over events and the agenda is possible, and business processes and institutional structures can be adapted to network diplomacy in the digital age.
>
> Cyber agenda: digital diplomacy as a way to negotiate scenarios and problems: for example, internet freedom, internet governance, and cybersecurity.
>
> Information management: effectively managing information problems, including big data, and using resources to provide the best impact.
>
> Service provision: The use of digital resources in the conduct of consular affairs and crisis management.[1341]

Based on the above, personal data falls with all these areas identified by Hocking and Melissen. Given the developments in this area of international relations, Rhys Crilley asserts digital diplomacy has changed the way in which governments and international organisations seek to share and manage messages.[1342] Crilley further asserts that social media now enables the circumnavigation of the traditional routes for information dissemination through the media and to engage directly with consumers. This new era of diplomacy has been underpinned by the notion that as a function it maintains international order. Centrally, all international orders established in the modern period have been the result of conscious and diligent diplomatic efforts to restore international stability and cooperation after periods of systemic upheaval.[1343] This can be seen in the change in world politics over the past decade. It is an area of constant change and evolution. Hence, in a world where 'power and influence truly belong to the many, we must engage with more people in more places. People all around the world are clamouring to be heard. They are having important conversations rights now and they aren't waiting for us'.[1344] It is driven by complex and rather unpredictable factors, such as, military confrontations, technological developments and social learning the direction of change does not fall completely outside of human control. Diplomacy is particularly suitable for managing international change because at its core it represents a mode of understanding that privileges the plural character of human existence and treats as axiomatic the proposition that relations between groups are different from those within them.[1345]

1340. *Ibid.*, Brian Hocking, 'Rethinking the "New" Public Diplomacy'. In: Jan Melissen (ed.) *The New Public Diplomacy Soft Power in International Relations*, New York: Palgrave MacMillan (2005).
1341. *Ibid.*
1342. Rhys Crilley, Like and Share Forces Making Sense of Military Social Media Sites. In: Shepherd LJ and Hamilton C (eds) *Understanding Popular Culture and World Politics in the Digital Age*, Abingdon: Routledge (2016), pp. 51-67.
1343. Corneliu Bjola, Marcus Holmes, *Digital Diplomacy: Theory and Practice.* Routledge (2015), p. 3.
1344. Craig Hayden, 'Social Media at State: Power, Practice and Conceptual Limits for US Public Diplomacy?' (2012) 11(21) Global Media Journal American Edition 1-15.
1345. *Ibid.*

This is problematic for governments and regulators. It requires a more rapid response to societal issues. It can be argued that under such intense circumstances that policy is made on the run. Therefore, it will take skill and patience for governments and regulators today, to establish strong and deep relationships with other governments and regulators. Data diplomacy will have an important role to play on future diplomacy engagement.

§17.03 PATHWAY FORWARD

The book has demonstrated that cross-border data flows have become integral to international trade. The emergence of data in the area of international trade is not fully understood, in the same way as traditional international trade. In a time of economic, health, environmental and geopolitical tensions and shock, there has been a trend for de-globalisation in the traditional area of trade. However, data is not following this trend and is increasingly being globalised.

This book has demonstrated that the current approach to the regulation and law of data flows in the new digital economy is highly fragmented. The fragmentation is from the top-down and bottom-up. Chapter 1 showed that multiple international organisations are involved in setting the policy direction for data transfers and trade across international borders. However, it also demonstrated that these organisations do not appear to be collaborating and their approaches have little or no alignment.

Cross-border data flows, which are characteristic of the new online digital economy, are generally seen as a new regulatory and legal area. However, they can be traced back to the 1970s, from Europe, where they began their journey to other regions and countries across the globe. Since that early period, the rise in international and regional institution, along with national governments developing law in this area has grown significantly. On the other side, and while there has been substantial regulatory and legal growth, there remain gaps and tensions in the law and policy approach. These need to be addressed due to the many vested interests that national governments now have in trade law and, more specifically, data flows and the law. While some countries take the rights-based approach, others take a consumer-business approach, or a combination of rights and consumer-business protection. Yet other countries take a sovereign approach. What has emerged is a complex area where governments are trying to balance the needs of the digital economy, with the growing societal expectations that individuals' personal data will have a high level of protection when transmitted via the Internet. This approach further highlights the fragmentation of data law more generally, and the lack of alignment of nation states.

That said, another way of articulating the above is the four levels of fragmentation that currently exist. As highlighted in Chapter 1, the first institutional fragmentation is where there appears to be a lack of alignment. Second, the policy concepts being established do not necessarily talk to each other. Third, is the disconnection between binding and non-binding instruments. Fourth, nation states have by and large gone their own ways in the development of data laws, which has led to a highly complex and fragmented legal landscape. In drawing any salutary conclusion, we see today that there are possibly regional blocks of laws emerging. For instance, it is well understood that the EU is a strong regional block economically and its laws including the data laws underpin the protection of human rights while balancing those rights with the needs of the single market. Arguably, the EU legal framework has generally been used as a benchmark for a number of states in the development of their data laws, even though there is considerable divergence.

However, ASEAN as another regional block is also beginning to direct the law for its members however, they are not a supranational polity, Member States have not relinquished any sovereignty, and they act on consensus. It does not have a single market economy with a single currency. Whether such an approach can be maintained in an ever-increasing contested world remains to be seen. Another regional block that has begun to emerge but is not discussed in this book is the African Union. Without regional blocks or institutions involved, there are many similarities that have been developed at a national level between data flows and the law. Some states have had their respective laws in place for more than two decades, while other states are yet to develop laws in this area. In this book, India and Indonesia are the two states that stand out as not having specific data flows laws.

Notwithstanding the above, at the international level, the OECD Guidelines and Principles that were established in the early 1980s have been instrumental in setting the baseline of Principles for the development of national law for cross-border data flows. Yet, they are non-binding. Nation states can choose to adopt the Guidelines. They have arguably paved the way for data transfers to be an economic activity in their own right. Since then, the world economy has seen a significant shift and transformation from an industrial-based economy to a digital and online economy. The Internet today pervades nearly every aspect of personal life, particularly in developed countries. That is, the connectivity in developed countries is much higher than in developing countries. Thus, the question arises can the current international trading rules provide a level of direction for data flows in the digital economy? In response, Chapter 1 did make the case that, under current international trade law, data can fall within the WTO-GATS rules.

By adopting the WTO-GAT rules, those countries who are leading the way in implementing the 4th Industrial Revolution can do so with a high level of economic activity generated by data trade and transfers. One of the problems with the implementation of IR4 is balancing economic activity with privacy over the Internet. This will not be easy to achieve because the citizens of different countries and regions have different views and understanding of what data protection and privacy constitute. On the one hand, for some, privacy and protection of data are fundamental human rights, such as across the EU. On the other hand, in countries such as India, it is not widely understood, high fractured and localised. It is shaped by culture, linguistics and ethnicity. Significantly though, these localised approaches towards privacy and data protection could be overshadowed by the digital economy. Arguably, as technology continues to evolve and more and more of our daily lives are transferred to the Internet, countries may well be forced to put aside their response or approach to Internet privacy and data protection, in order for data flows and its economic benefits to be fully realised.

There are numerous technological advancements and changes in the economy making it difficult to maintain an effective oversight. Apart from the traditional areas of the economy that have transferred to online activity such as the purchase of goods and services, new economic sectors have begun. The FinTech sector is a very good example of where data flows and its security are vulnerable to economic, security and geopolitical shock. Coupled with IR4 in the FinTech sector, there is a lack of understanding of the extent of data flows. It is an unregulated area of the law and provides data subjects with new products of finance. This activity alone is creating significant data flows across international borders. Data flows within FinTech-TechFin and other forms of online financial services will only grow.

Problematic though is how governments around the world continue to grapple with how to regulate the FinTech sector. It is likely that government will view this in isolation from other areas of the economy such as data flows, and the resulting effect will be yet another area of fragmentation in transnational FinTech law.

Chapter 1 is one of the most important chapters of this book. It discussed and analysed at length the question of What is Data? Doing so, it demonstrated that data is far from settled. Models have emerged that categorise data into sectors and across nation states as being highly controlled or at the other end of the spectrum fully open. Even so, this is another area that is far from settled. A further accentuating question was whether Data can be defined as a good or a service? Based on the analysis provided, this is another area that is inconclusive. Depending on the economic activity and whether the data is subject to contractual obligations such as those within the CISG will determine whether the data is a good or a service. It will be on a case-by-case basis that data becomes a good or a service.

The book has undertaken a considerable analysis of up to forty-four trade and digital agreements, including relevant data ADs, of the jurisdictions compared. Of note are the recent DEPA and UK-Japan economic agreements. First, the DEPA was signed in an entirely online virtual signing ceremony by New Zealand, Chile and Singapore on Friday 12 June 2020 NZT and has entered into force for New Zealand and Singapore on 7 January 2021. It promotes the policy approach that countries participating in DEPA do develop national laws that protect personal data. However, it does not describe how that should be undertaken. It encourages participants to include the following principles in to their respective legal frameworks: (a) collection limitation; (b) data quality; (c) purpose specification; (d) use limitation; (e) security safeguards; (f) transparency; (g) individual participation; and (h) accountability.

Most notable, the DEPA is promoting a level of international harmonisation by and through the adoption of the OECD principles. IT further promotes compatibility and interoperability of legal frameworks. It is argued that providing for both at this early stage enables a level of agility in the development of legal frameworks so that participants can continue to operate, while their laws vary from other participants. It is an acknowledgement of the fragmented approach taken by nation states, in meeting their sovereign needs for protecting personal data. However, a new concept, Trustmarks, has been introduced within the DEPA that, has not been, to date, included in other trade agreements examined in this book. Trustmarks can be used to verify conformance with privacy standards. It has modules on e-invoicing and e-payments and has specified rules on non-discrimination for digital products. How effective these Trustmarks are in practice is yet to be fully understood. Further research is needed. Significant too are the participants in this Agreement; they do have diverging legal frameworks. An accentuating issue is a reference to the public policy objective. However, there is nothing in the Agreement that defines public policy and would arguably have a wide reach. Of further note is that there is no mention of data nationalisation or localisation. This, in my view, is one of the key elements being described in the reading of unjustifiable disguised discrimination or restrictions. Nation states today, in adopting data nationalism have by and large communicated those restrictions to the world. In my view, the DEPA is to date one of the most advanced agreements for the protection of personal data over the Internet and balancing those protections with cross-border data flows. Nonetheless, and while not comprehensive, the ensuing analysis further highlighted the inconsistent approach that has been taken by nation states at a national (bilateral and multilateral) level. This is an area, in my view, whereby, countries can begin to establish broader high-level rules for data flows and their security. The recent introduction of digital agreements has been a welcomed initiative. However, these alone do not go far enough to establish a harmonised approach to data flows and their regulation. They maintain the current approach to interoperability.

It has been argued that the concept of interoperability has served the current development of cross-border data flow technology and the emerging area of law well. It is further argued that in my view this is an area that requires further consideration, research and understanding in order to determine whether it is fit for purpose in the new digital economy. In making the case for further research on interoperability, the concept itself arose from the need for technology to talk with and align with each other. Centrally, technology developed by IBM needed to operate in with a level of compatibility with technology by Microsoft. The different systems and infrastructure posed challenges in aligning the transmission of data and its ability to flow across domestic and international borders. That said, the concept was by and large transferred across to the law and used as an easy option to ensure a level of comparable principles and concepts within the law. It has been used to attempt to create an environment of legal harmonisation. This, in part, has been achieved, but today it is argued that interoperability is creating more gaps and tension in the law. It is not legal harmonisation and is unlikely to ever achieve a deep level of legal convergence. A further central feature of interoperability is the different layers that have been formed. It features syntactic/technical interoperability refers to the possibility that systems can physically connect to each other and can exchange data, whereas semantic interoperability refers to the ability of systems to understand the meaning of the information exchanged (*see* Chapter 1). Rather than bringing together the different legal approaches and the application and administration of the law, it has allowed for the creation of more divergence than convergence. Thus, it is time for more research to be undertaken. Establishing an international approach and a convention or model law specifically for data flows would generally replace the concept and the problems of and from interoperability.

Making this transition to a more international approach with the OECD Principles being central to the development of any transnational law, will not be easy and will require skill to overcome the many different views taken by nation states. Data Adequacy is being used by the EU as a default to any internationalisation of data law(s). However, as highlighted in Chapter 1, this has come with its own problems. The current Adequacy approach relies on establishing similar protections. It, in part, creates gaps in the national laws when compared. A further accentuating problem has been that while some states have acceded to Convention 108, in theory, they do not need to obtain data adequacy from the EU. This again does not guarantee that there is a high level of legal harmonisation or protection in place for data. The focus is generally on the protection mechanisms for data subjects and the data. On that basis, this book has demonstrated the importance of cross-border data flows to the current and future economy and trade of the world, not just individual nation states. It has further demonstrated the expected growth in economic activity, if the policy and legal setting are right, will open up the small and medium business sectors. These sectors alone are in need of a much-needed policy boost, coming out of COVID-19 and its economic, social and health impacts.

An ensuing issue for governments and regulators to boost the economy through and by data transfers is by enabling this to occur. The debate and position by most governments has been to create a regulatory environment that instils trust and confidence in the market. Trust is a core element of all commercial law. Without it, there would be a significant lack of certainty. However, the next step for governments and regulators to enhance and strengthen the concept of trust is to go international (*see* Chapter 1). More needs to be done to ensure greater certainty in the data and digital economy, as this will create a higher level of investment and economic activity, and more job opportunities.

Problematic to the above is the approach taken by regulators to reconcile how data is regulated and then in turn enforced. The book comprehensively analysed the Regulators' decision of Cambridge Analytica. More questions were raised than answered from this analysis. An area that requires further clarification to ensure greater transparency, trust and accountability is how a data subject can be identified by the estimated thousand plus data points. It was unclear from the Regulators' investigation the extent to which a data subject can be identified by the many data points created by them, simply by undertaking activities over the Internet. It is, in my view, an urgent area of research and consideration that will provide significantly more trust in the Internet, systems and infrastructure that support both personal and commercial online activity.

Another example of the complex interwoven areas of technology and the law related to data flows and their security is emerging obstacles being established to restrict data flows. Data localisation is being used by states to protect their citizens. Yet, doing so automatically creates the situation where there is a further regulatory and technical burden an organisation is obligated to implement. Another obstacle is the area of tax, which is not often considered. It is a regulatory and direct impact on providers of online services. Problematic to imposing such a tax on digital activity involving data is the need to understand the life cycle of the transaction over the Internet. For example, where along the cycle of the transaction is it appropriate to impose the tax? More research is required to better understand the benefits and impacts on data flows from tax. The economic benefits to a nation state are by and large self-explanatory. A state imposes a tax to recover a level of revenue for a transaction.

Cybersecurity is increasingly part of securing data flows and their use. However, problematic is the view that cybersecurity and the law can impact and are contrary to WTO-GATS rules. That said, it is inevitable that there will be areas of law and rules that contradict each other. Cybersecurity cannot be totally discarded. People across society and organisations including the government expect a high level of security over the Internet, and therefore, the balance between security and flows of data is finely balanced. Will security measures ever get to a point of no cyber intrusions? The short response is no. Cybersecurity needs to be built into trade agreements to complement data flows.

In transcending other areas of the law, data flows will be subject to dispute resolution and cross-border insolvency. The book has demonstrated that there is a growing area of dispute resolution such as arbitration being undertaken online. This is posing challenges to the traditional notion of arbitration, with the practising rules and procedures still being developed. At a practice level, individuals and organisations will need to consider wider responses to other areas of the law that will influence the governance of data flows. With the increase in start-ups and in some cases their short lifespan, they are subject to cross-border activity and therefore open to cross-border insolvency. This is a complex area of law, yet, it is a good demonstration of where there is a level of internationalisation. There are many examples across international commercial law where it has been successful and can be used as an example to replicate data flows and data protection, which a number of scholars, including myself are urgently calling for.

Calling for an international organisation to be established for the governance of Data Flows is urgently needed in a time of increased international contestability. While aligned with data flows, Professor, Dr Simon Chesterman who has argued for an international AI Organisation to be established, this book is arguing similarly for the management data. Chesterman makes the case that:

> Effectively regulating artificial intelligence on a global scale will require countries to agree on a framework they can all stick to. Efforts to police research in nuclear technology could provide a good starting point. Earlier this year, the European Union proposed a draft regulation to protect the fundamental rights of its citizens from certain applications of artificial intelligence. In the USA last month, the Biden administration launched a taskforce seeking to spur AI innovation. On the same day, China adopted its new Data Security Law, asserting a stronger role for the state in controlling the data that fuels AI. These three approaches – rights, markets,

> sovereignty – highlight the competing priorities as governments grapple with how to reap the benefits of AI while minimising harm.[1346]

The challenge of Chesterman's proposal is no different to data. It requires nation states to come together and agreed to establish an international institution, and then work towards an agreeable framework with a set of rules and/or principles that can be used to underpin an international legal instrument. In the case of data, these principles have been well established as compared to AI. As this book has highlighted the importance that the OECD Principles have been significant to the regulation of data. Most nation states have based their current-day laws on the OECD Principles. In taking such a proposal to the next level, and as discussed in Chapter 1, Morgan Corley[1347] and others have suggested internationalising data law. In agreeing with Corley:

> creating this convention, the international community can create a mechanism whereby the free flow of data around the world can be facilitated. By doing so, technological innovation will be promoted, the freedom of information can be preserved, and transfers of data can be used to enhance the global economy, yielding increased prosperity instead of increased tensions amongst different nations around the world.[1348]

Viewed this way, developing the above is more important and urgent than at any other time since the development of data laws dating back to the 1980s. In other words, this book is not calling for the OECD Principles to be discarded. Rather, it is argued that they must be retained and form part of any internal legal instrument to govern data flows.

In responding to the questions raised in Chapter 1, the responses are solely a reflection of the author's views based on the research undertaken for this book, and two decades of experience in law and policy. The questions and subsequent responses will provoke more debate and discussion rather than resolve complex legal and policy questions. Yet, that is precisely what these questions and the responses are designed to achieve. If this research leads to other international, regional and national reviews to confirm whether law reform is required, this book, including these questions and responses, has achieved the author's overall research objective:

- *Can the current frameworks for data protection, data flows and data adequacy co-exist?*

  Response

  Yes. However, this is going to be complex and difficult to achieve. It will require regulators and governments to better understand the interconnectedness between data flows, the economic benefits thereof, and the fragmented approach taken by nation states. It will also require

1346. Simon Chesterman, *Beyond Asimov's Three Laws: The Case for an International AI Agency*, 2021, https://eandt.theiet.org/content/articles/2021/08/beyond-asimov-s-three-laws-the-case-for-an-international-ai-agency.
1347. Morgan Corley, 'The Need for an International Convention on Data Privacy: Taking a Cue from the CISG' (2016) 41 Brooklyn Journal International Law 779.
1348. *Ibid.*, p. 779.

a more comprehensive understanding of the technology, such as the infrastructure and systems, that support data flows, and data security. Cybersecurity is fundamental to the protection of data flows and data storage, particularly on the cloud.

- *Will data flows and the digital economy eventually require regulators to rethink the current legal landscape?*

  Response

  The issue relates to the policy concepts and principles that constitute the overall framework for data protection and data flows law which, at present, is incoherent. Currently, there are many competing international policy directions that create tensions and gaps because they are generally trying to include narrow, but important, elements of data regulation. An important point that this book has identified is the application of interoperability (*see* Chapter 1). This concept has been established by the technology sector to ensure that different systems developed by different companies can operate together. Data flow regulators take the same approach and apply it to the domain of law. While, arguably, this approach has been successful in the early stages of this area of the law, today and in future, it might not be capable of dealing with an evolving digital economy. Chapter 1 has demonstrated that interoperability has raised questions related to the shortcomings and tensions in the law.

- *How can privacy and data protection be secured over the Internet in the face of the trend to accept and promote open data?*

  Response

  This requires constant vigilance by regulators and governments. It requires constant reviews, evaluations, and risk management assessments. Improvement programmes should be scheduled to ensure that regulation is updated efficiently and effectively to keep pace with technology. Government and regulators need to work closely with the technology industry to ensure the highest possible protection is afforded to data and data privacy.

- *The current notion of the concept of interoperability has been developed for technology to co-exist, and the law has now been used to achieve a level of compatibility – is interoperability relevant for the law?*

  Response

  See above and Chapter 1. While there is a compelling argument that interoperability has been successful in enabling the current day legal framework to evolve and develop, it is argued that it is now increasing the fragmentation of the legal landscape. Although many nation states have adopted many of the principles and concepts of the EU data framework, they vary substantially in terms of practice. This inconsistency and incoherence have created a regulatory landscape within which there is no full cooperation between entities, as there are both proponents and opponents of interoperability. This book argues that it is time for a full review to be undertaken to confirm its applicability to the future legal regulation of data flows.

- *Legal harmonisation and convergence have been effective for the trade in goods and services – can they achieve the same effectiveness with data in the digital economy?*

  Response

  Yes. Significantly, this will require nation states to overcome their historical and current approach to privacy and data protection over the Internet. An agreed international convention or model law, while aspirational, can be achieved where there is the political will to do so. On the other hand, as geopolitical tensions continue to rise, this approach will be increasingly more difficult to achieve.

- *The concept of trust is a major policy outcome for some governments around the world in the area of data flows, can this ever be fully achieved?*

  Response

  Essentially, this will require an ongoing and concerted effort on behalf of the government, regulators, technology sector and industry. They need to collaborate to ensure that appropriate laws and policies are in place so as to engender a high level of community trust. This does not depend on the law alone; data diplomacy programmes will increasingly play a role in strengthening trust in the legal landscape. All of the aforementioned sectors will need to work together to ensure the community is educated and aware of the laws, and the rights and obligations of individuals.

- *Case law has identified areas of technology and the law – can we ever fully understand the extent to which a data subject can be identified online?*

  Response

  The technology sector needs to be transparent and inform the government, regulators and the entire community of the ways by which we can all be identified online via the Internet.

- *Data Diplomacy is emerging as an assistant to cyber diplomacy – how can this be transformed into a dedicated diplomacy programme?*

  Response

  Data diplomacy must become a separate programme within the government. This final chapter has demonstrated that some nation states have recently and successfully established specific data diplomacy programmes. While it is up to nation states to decide on such programmes, it is another tool that states can use to work with other like-minded states when establishing rules for data flows.

- *The current arrangements for data storage within the cloud are restricted to servers located in strategic locations around the world – how do law and policy experts need to understand and build their knowledge of this? This knowledge is largely retained by IT personnel.*

Response
Arguably, this has to be a priority. While not extensively discussed in this book, it has emerged as an area requiring research as a matter of urgency. It raises another question that needs to be resolved. For instance, when data flows from Australia to the UK via the cloud, what servers do that data pass through? Does it go from Australia via Singapore, to the US, to China, to Japan, then onto the EU, to its final stop in the UK? Along the way, can that data be syphoned off and be vulnerable to illegal use by state and non-state actors? Does the current data flow law address this issue? To date, there is not enough information available for regulators and governments to reconcile whether the current legal framework addresses the potential vulnerabilities of data and its transnational transfer via the cloud.

It is hoped that this book has raised a number of questions and encouraged further debate, research and thinking – all of which are needed in regard to data flows in the new and evolving digital economy. It argues for the relevance and retention of the OECD Principles (within the Guidelines on the Protection of Privacy and Transborder Flows of Personal Data) are significantly important to the future of data flows and the digital economy. In fact, the OECD Principles must be retained at all costs, and they should be constantly updated to ensure that data flows are underpinned by a strong and robust set of Principles for future technological developments. Essentially, is there a need for an international body to be established that deals with data flows and data protection? Such a body could bring together all the current international and regional bodies to develop a single approach towards data flows and more broadly its protection, globally. This could be an extension of the OECD, or of another body such as UNCITRAL.

In making the case for such a body to be established, data flows are viewed as an economic activity that brings economic benefits to all involved. It is this new economic activity, similar to the traditional trade in goods and services, that has seen the work undertaken by UNCITRAL as pivotal to facilitating greater global economic growth. There is a need to better understand the extent of data flows and the technology that determines how they operate. In addition to arguing the need for a global institution, this book emphasises the need to impose a regulatory obligation on organisations that undertake cross-border data transfers. Hence, there should be a reporting mechanism whereby all organisations transferring data internationally must be reported to the national regulatory body which, in turn, reports this to the international body.

The economic and social benefits of doing so, although not fully understood, would generate new areas of activity, and identify those areas where the digital economy could be improved. However, this would need a comprehensive research study. Finally, by examining WTO-GATS rules, this book has highlighted areas of future research that should be undertaken in the immediate future. Failure to do so will continue to exacerbate the fragmentation of the legal landscape for data flows. Furthermore, because the full potential of the digital economy is far from being realised, further work is required to strengthen the law, adopt an international approach and implement new programmes such as data diplomacy. This approach requires that the OECD Principles be retained because they will help to ensure greater accountability, transparency and accuracy in the data flow domain.

Index

D

L

M

N

O

P

R

www.ingramcontent.com/poc-product-compliance
Ingram Content Group UK Ltd.
Pitfield, Milton Keynes, MK11 3LW, UK
UKHW020231290926
15470UKWH00002B/485

9 789403 537252